Leading Iss...
in
South Africa...
Macroeconomics
Selected Readings

Leading Issues
in
South African
Macroeconomics
Selected Readings

PHILIP A. BLACK
Department of Economics, University of Stellenbosch

BRIAN E. DOLLERY
Department of Economics, University of New England

SOUTHERN
BOOK PUBLISHERS

ISBN 1 86812 179 8

First edition, first impression 1989

Southern Book Publishers (Pty) Ltd
P O Box 548, Bergvlei 2012
Johannesburg

Set in 10 on 12 pt Times Roman
by Book Productions, Pretoria

Printed and bound by Sigma Press, Pretoria

Contents

PREFACE vii

PART 1 ISSUES IN SOUTH AFRICAN MACROECONOMICS

1. Unemployment

1.1 Introduction 1
1.2 Unemployment in South Africa: A Survey of Research
    Norman Bromberger 4
1.3 The Question of Structural Unemployment in South Africa
    J. Gerson 27
1.4 Unemployment and Underemployment *P.A. Black* 42

2. Inflation

2.1 Introduction 47
2.2 Perspectives on Inflation in South Africa *P.J. Mohr* 50
2.3 The Causes of Inflation — and what can be done *Brian Kantor* 64
2.4 Industrial Concentration and Inflation in South Africa, 1972–1979
    F.C. v. N. Fourie 69
2.5 Structuralist and Sociological Views on the Inflation Problem
    W.N. Meyer 86

3. Cyclical Instability and the Phillips Trade-Off

3.1 Introduction 98
3.2 The Business Cycle and Public Policy *D.W. Goedhuys* 100
3.3 The Natural Rate Hypothesis: An Econometric Test for the South
    African Economy *E. Shostak* 112
3.4 The Phillips Trade-Off and Policy Implications for Developing
    Countries *P.A. Black* and *M.V. Leibbrandt* 120

PART 2 MACROECONOMIC POLICY IN SOUTH AFRICA

4. Monetary Policy

4.1 Introduction 132
4.2 An Overview of the South African Financial System *A.P. Faure* 134
4.3 Monetary Policy in South Africa: Main Findings *De Kock
    Commission* 144

4.4 Monetary Control as seen by the De Kock Commission:
An Assessment *G.L. de Wet* 172
4.5 The De Kock Commission Report: A Monetarist Perspective
B.S. Kantor 185
4.6 Monetary Policy: Its Scope and Limitations *J. Whittaker* 198
4.7 Monetarism and the South African Crisis *Duncan Innes* 209

5.   **Balance of Payments and Exchange Rate Policy**

5.1 Introduction 219
5.2 The Gold Price and the South African Economy *G.P.C. de Kock* 222
5.3 The Mechanics of the Financial Rand Market *A.B. Shuttleworth* 229
5.4 A Critical Assessment of the Equilibrium Approach to the Rate of
Exchange *P.D.F. Strydom* 234
5.5 Exchange Controls and Exchange Rate Policy in the South African
Economy *Brian Kahn* 245
5.6 Recent Exchange Rate Policy in South Africa: A Critique
J.J. Cloete 258
5.7 Economic Growth and Foreign Debt: The South African Case
G.P.C. de Kock 268

6.   **Fiscal Policy**

6.1 Introduction 279
6.2 Fiscal Policy in South Africa *P.J. Mohr* 281
6.3 The Short- and Long-run Consequences of the Government's Financing
Requirement *P.A. Black* and *J.H. Cooper* 293
6.4 The Behaviour of General Government Expenditure in South Africa
1948–1984 *J.A. Döckel* and *A.V. Seeber* 299
6.5 The Margo Commission Report *G.L. de Wet* 314

7.   **General Reflections on Macroeconomic Policy**

7.1 Introduction 319
7.2 Economic Policy and the Free Market System *G.P.C. de Kock* 322
7.3 The Choice Before Us: Economic Stabilisation or the Instability of
Free Markets *L.P. McCrystal* 327
7.4 Selective Intervention and the South African Economy *Philip Black*
and *Brian Dollery* 333
7.5 The Problem of 'Government Failure' in Mixed Economies
M.C. O'Dowd 338

Preface

This book is an integrated set of readings on macroeconomic problems and policies experienced in the South African economy. It is intended to complement standard macroeconomics texts by providing explicitly South African material on the major problems confronting the South African economy, as well as a variety of views on the efficacy of official policies directed at alleviating these problems.

Frustration with the rising prices of imported texts, delays experienced in obtaining books from abroad and occasional political difficulties in accessibility have led several South African economists to produce macroeconomics textbooks specifically designed for the local market. Two recent examples include *Macroeconomics* by Truu and Contogiannis and a South African adaptation of Dornbusch and Fisher's *Macroeconomics* by Mohr and Rogers. Both provide a lucid and broad coverage of the main issues in macroeconomic theory and policy with a distinctive South African flavour. Our experience at Rhodes University with both undergraduate and graduate students has led us to believe that the standard pedagogical treatment of macroeconomics can be substantially enhanced by the inclusion of supplementary readings drawn from the debates conducted by local economists concerning real-world diagnosis and macroeconomic policies in South Africa. Not only does this improve the students' understanding of the principles embodied in macroeconomic analysis; it also engenders an appreciation of the structures and functioning of the South African economy. It was thus felt that a carefully selected and logically coherent collection of readings would provide a highly instructive and convenient companion volume to the conventional macroeconomics textbook, especially in an undergraduate setting.

The text itself has been divided into two broad areas. Part One deals with the macroeconomic problems confronting the South African economy, and examines the familiar issues of unemployment, inflation, the Phillips curve, and some supply-side topics. Part 2 focuses on macroeconomic policy measures and explores monetary policy, exchange-rate policy, fiscal policy and overall economic policy. In those instances where it is appropriate, the empirical dimensions of the particular problem are outlined in order to give the student some idea of its magnitude. Each chapter begins with a brief introduction, placing the set of readings in a logical framework readily accessible to the student. The chapters include material on the relevant underlying institutional features, provide the official diagnosis and policy postures, and discuss the views of dissenting South African economists.

The material chosen has been carefully scrutinised in order to achieve expositional clarity and an appropriate degree of analytical rigour. Given the extensive range of works on macroeconomic aspects of the South African economy, it was necessary to be highly selective and this has meant that numerous papers had perforce to be excluded. This problem was particularly acute in the area of monetary policy, which has attracted much attention. Consequently, it is suggested that additional material is included for postgraduate courses. Although the readings are especially suited to students of intermediate macroeconomics, we have found that a shorter selection of the material has contributed to substantially improved introductory courses.

Part 1

Issues in South African Macroeconomics

1

Unemployment

1.1 INTRODUCTION

Unemployment refers to the stock of all those individuals who are not in
employment and who are either in the process of moving to a new job or who
are unable to find work at the prevailing real wage rate. An unemployed person
is thus someone who is actively searching for a job but unable to find one within
a specified time period. The *rate* of unemployment is defined as the number of
unemployed job-seekers divided by the total number of employed and unemployed persons. The unemployment rate is conventionally measured in
terms of particular registration procedures, or by means of representative
samples drawn from the economically active portion of the population on a
regular basis.

It should be noted that official estimates of unemployment do not usually
reveal the actual number of job-seekers, or the working conditions of
employed persons. They may, for example, exclude people who are working
on a part-time or temporary basis, or whose work is unrelated to their formal
qualifications and working experience. In developing nations in particular, the
official rate may exclude many potential job-seekers who eke out an existence
in the traditional agricultural sector and the urban informal sector. Nevertheless, official estimates of the unemployment rate do at least provide a
reasonably accurate indication of the state of the economy insofar as they tend
to vary inversely with cyclical fluctuations in economic activity.

Broadly speaking, economists distinguish between three types of unemployment, namely cyclical, structural and frictional unemployment. *Cyclical unemployment* arises from periodic downswings in the business cycle. Such
downturns may be initiated, for example, by autonomous decreases in consumption, investment, or exports, and reinforced by an attendant degree of
wage rigidity. Whilst the issue of wage rigidity has attracted a good deal of attention in the literature, it generally refers to the inability of wages to adjust in
a downward direction. When this occurs, any decrease in the demand for
labour must perforce give rise to an excess supply of labour, or cyclical unemployment.

It is possible to identify several reasons for the phenomenon of wage inflexibility. Firstly, in some sectors wage levels may be fixed, either by government

1

in the form of minimum wage legislation or by trade union monopoly power. Secondly, wage rigidity may result from the fact that workers are subject to a money illusion, insofar as they are unaware of changes in the prevailing price level in the economy. Thus, the supply of labour is based on an expected real wage which adjusts only slowly to changes in the actual price (and real wage) level. Since a cyclical decrease in actual prices will not affect expected real wages in the short term, labour may refuse to accept a drop in their nominal wage which will force firms to retrench some workers in order to maintain profitability. Thirdly, wage rigidity can also be explained in terms of the behaviour of firms. Many firms may be contractually obliged to keep wages and prices constant. Others might prefer not to employ workers below a certain minimum wage in order to prevent their turnover rate and the attendant costs associated with search and on-the-job training from rising. In all these cases an autonomous decrease in aggregate demand will give rise to the emergence of cyclical unemployment.

The second type of unemployment mentioned above is *structural unemployment*, which unlike cyclical unemployment is not sensitive to changes in aggregate demand. It refers to a situation in which the skill profile of unemployed persons does not match the skills demanded by employers, or where the unemployed find themselves in a different geographical location from where the job vacancies exist. Structural or 'mismatch' unemployment may result from changes in the composition of demand and supply, technological progress, and from various discriminatory practices in the labour market.

The third form of unemployment, namely *frictional unemployment*, can exist in a situation where there is no skill or locational mismatch. Frictional unemployment refers to an economically rational process of job search where people *voluntarily* remain unemployed while they seek out and weigh up suitable job vacancies. Frictional unemployment thus includes people in the process of searching for jobs which do exist but where complete information concerning these jobs is lacking.

Structural and frictional unemployment together constitute what economists term the natural rate of unemployment. The 'natural rate' may be defined as that rate of unemployment consistent with overall equilibrium in the labour market; in other words, the rate of unemployment to which the economy automatically gravitates in the long run. While there is much disagreement amongst economists over the size and composition of the natural rate, and about its responsiveness to changes in aggregate demand, it has become a focal point in recent debates on the efficacy of macroeconomic policy.

Chapter 1 contains three readings on the problem of unemployment. To begin with, Bromberger examines some of the conceptual and empirical difficulties inherent in defining and measuring the extent of unemployment in South Africa. He also presents a framework for analysing the determinants of the supply and demand for labour, and a tentative overview of policies which may assist in reducing unemployment. The next two papers in this chapter deal with the current debate over the nature of unemployment in South Africa. A central issue in this debate is the question of structural unemployment. Gerson disputes the existence of structural unemployment in South Africa on both theoretical and empirical grounds, while, in the final paper, Black presents some counter-arguments to explain the growing number of work seekers who have been unable to find wage employment in the modern sector of the economy.

1.2 UNEMPLOYMENT IN SOUTH AFRICA: A SURVEY OF RESEARCH

Norman Bromberger*

1. SOME CONCEPTUAL DIFFICULTIES ASSOCIATED WITH THE MEASUREMENT OF UNEMPLOYMENT IN SOUTH AFRICA

If there did not still exist in South Africa a (heavily modified) version of the traditional African subsistence economy, the problem of defining and measuring unemployment and underemployment would be rather easier than it is. In a fully capitalist economy potential wage- and salary-earners would either have jobs, or be looking for them and so be classified as unemployed; the self-employed in business, the professions or on the land would typically be fully occupied — if not, they must prefer not being so else they would take or seek employment. Admittedly there might still be problems having to do with whether some potential workers, e.g. housewives and some part-time workers, would not be looking for jobs if they were more readily or conveniently a-vailable — but one might judge this was not a central problem and was perhaps more one of diagnosis and measurement than of concept. However, South Africa is not a fully capitalist economy. In the Reserves or homelands it is still possible to produce part of one's subsistence by means other than performing wage-labour, and some access to land and pasture is also available to workers on White farms in some areas. Moreover, the practice of migratory labour and the legal restrictions on free movement between homelands and the rest of South Africa and on African ownership of land outside the homelands represent a structure in which individuals may make private choices involving 'labour-underutilisation' (in various forms) which would not be privately optional were the structures different. If it were easier to opt out of the one system fully into the other there might be less 'slippage' or 'waste' between them. It is worth emphasising in this context that in demographic terms the enclave represented by the homelands is large: roughly one half of the African population have *de jure* residence there. (Sadie estimates 44,8 per cent for 1960 and 52,6 per cent for 1970: Sadie, 1977 : 37.)

What are some of the problems of definition that arise when we try to apply concepts of unemployment and underemployment to this economy?

(a) Consider able-bodied African men in the homelands during a 'rest period' after a period of migrant labour in mines or towns. Perhaps they do some ploughing, or perhaps their contribution to agriculture is limited to some supervisory functions. Are they unemployed or not? Or are they preferring this pattern of intermittent work — given the set of options open to them and the

* Department of Economics, University of Natal, Pietermaritzburg. This is an abridged version of a paper which first appeared in *Social Dynamics*, Vol. 4, No. 1, 1978.

prevailing wage-rates attaching to various forms of employment — so that perhaps they might be classified (as by Sadie, 1977: 44–45) as in 'non-employment'? And if this distinction is made, a measurement problem arises because it is very difficult (without survey data) to determine how many men in the Reserves are unemployed and looking for jobs, and how many are merely non-employed and temporarily not interested in employment.

(b) What of women (housewives and others) in this context? Sadie refuses to try to define unemployment concepts for them in the Reserves. 'If "unemployment" is an operationally difficult concept among males, it becomes impossible among females' (Sadie, 1977: 48 n 20; also 38–39). There will often be no question of their going out to work in the capitalist economy outside of the homelands — but on the other hand it may well be that many of them would emerge as work-seekers if jobs were offered on any scale locally (as Smith, 1971: 2 reports has been the case for rural areas in some other countries). Since in the traditional system almost all women did some agricultural work, attempts have been made to classify them as agriculturalists. The 1970 Census, for instance, classified the homeland wives of household heads as 'housewives' (and so 'not economically active') whereas other females aged 16 or over were classified as 'peasant farmers' — and so 'economically active' and 'employed' (see Knight, 1977: 32). Is this satisfactory?

(c) This case of women in agriculture is one of a number where people have 'jobs' that only partially occupy them. Are they to be treated as employed or underemployed? Is there some point in trying to add them in with the fully unemployed — as contributing to the supply of surplus labour (or labour-time)? Or is this to be avoided (see Van der Merwe, 1976: 51; also 1977: Table 3)? Problems of definition may arise in relation to part-time workers in developed countries — but the phenomenon assumes larger importance in contexts where 'cooperant inputs' (e.g. land, material inputs, know-how) are deficient. These small family-farms may only partially occupy family labour and an environment of poverty gives rise to a range of jobs — such as porters, shoe-shine boys, hawkers, rickshaw-men — which may involve long hours of being available, only a small percentage of which really involve productive work.

It is clear enough that there are difficulties at the conceptual level. We must try to pull some threads together — not so as to legislate a set of definitions, but rather to provide a conceptual background against which it will be possible to set the often different definitions which have been used by the researchers whose work we are surveying.

1.1 Suppose for the moment that apart from unemployment (people wanting wage-employment and being unable to find it) the only labour-market problem is short hours. Then we might classify the economically active population as:
(a) employed: people who have jobs or work of normal duration, or voluntarily work part-time.
(b) underemployed: employed people who would like to work longer hours in

5

order to earn more, whether they actually seek a job with longer hours (visible) or not (invisible).

(c) unemployed: people who have no job or work but would like one whether they actually seek such a job (visible) or not (invisible).

1.2 It is possible to expand the classification — especially by expanding the cases to be included under the concept of underemployment, though unfortunately the categories then begin to overlap. We may say people are underemployed if the work they do is of low productivity (on a small, poorly watered, input-deficient family farm, say) or receives low earnings (a petty trader of some sort) — even though in both cases the hours formally 'at work' may be normal, or even very long. The low productivity and low earnings extensions to the underemployment concept may be collapsed in practice into a single low income extension. (See Bromberger, 1977: 2 for an example of the use of this extended concept by the ILO.) Note, however, that some of those now classified as underemployed are also employed (because they work normal hours). For this and other reasons there is strong resistance to this fully developed 'poverty approach' to un- and underemployment (see Bromberger, 1977: 5–6 for criticisms by F. Stewart and A.K. Sen, and references).

1.3 It becomes possible now to see how one might measure (a) employment, (b) underemployment, and (c) unemployment in terms of *full-time job equivalents* — and then reduce some combinations of them to single measures. Provided overlapping was removed, underemployed workers would each count for some fraction (x) of a full-time job equivalent — the fraction depending on the working hours or income or productivity norms defined as corresponding to those of a full-time job. Alternatively they would contribute the fraction $(1-x)$ to the unemployment total. Total unemployment would then be either the direct sum of unemployment and underemployment (in full-time job equivalents) or the difference between the labour force and total employment (measured as the employed plus the full-time job equivalent of the underemployed). Simkins (1978b: 7–8), as we shall see, has pioneered this method for application to the South African data. It — or a partial version of it — is also used by Knight (1977). But as we have also noted, others (Sadie, 1977; Van der Merwe, 1976) have held out against it.

1.4 It is probably worth making the point at this stage that how one defines and seeks to measure unemployment and related concepts will usually be influenced by what one is interested in or what problem one is concerned with. One may wish to know what surplus labour resources there are available for the expansion of the capitalist sector (see Knight, 1977: 31); or for the development of certain sectors of the homeland economies; or one's focus may be on problems of poverty throughout the country and on the contribution which the expansion of employment of various types might make to the alleviation of that poverty. In this last case one might well be more concerned (than in the others) to develop a single measure of labour underutilisation (un- *and* underemployment) to act as indicator of the success of employment-creation policies over time — though of course for intelligent policy-design one would probably also need considerable disaggregation by type of labour underutilisation.

2. SOME EMPIRICAL DIFFICULTIES INVOLVED IN THE MEASUREMENT OF UNEMPLOYMENT IN SOUTH AFRICA

My intention in this section is not to make an exhaustive survey of data difficulties which stand in the way of measuring unemployment in South Africa (however exactly it is to be defined). I hope rather to give a brief introduction to these difficulties so as (1) to make understandable the lack of firm and widely accepted estimates and (2) to point to the sources of the differences between various estimates that have been made.

2.1 How are reasonably reliable official unemployment statistics usually obtained? In general from two sources: first, from registration by the unemployed at employment exchanges (or similar institutions) in connection with the payment of unemployment benefits and the search for a job — as in the United Kingdom, for instance; secondly, from specially designed sample surveys — as in the United States of America. The second of these is likely to pick up some of the 'invisible' unemployment referred to in the previous section. In South Africa the first source is available for Whites, Coloureds and Asians and for some Africans — but it does not generate satisfactory statistics since large numbers of workers who qualify do not register and many do not qualify. The Theron Commission Report (1976: 84; see also paragraph 5.43) discusses Coloured unemployment and makes the point that 'the labour bureaux operate in such a way that those who are registered as unemployed are no indication of the unutilised labour potential among the Coloureds'. Van der Merwe (1977: 1–2) says of the registered unemployment figures for Africans that 'even their fluctuations hardly serve to indicate general trends'. The second possible source of unemployment statistics has, as we have seen, just begun to be available for Africans — now that the Current Population Survey is being conducted on a monthly basis; but of course it will tell us nothing directly about the past. One other possible source of direct information about unemployment, the Population Census, is unsatisfactory both because of its infrequency and because of a number of deficiencies attaching to the unemployment statistics collected. Knight (1977: 36–7) summarises these clearly. Loots (1977: 10–11) for instance quotes instructions to the census enumerators in 1970 which involved reporting as employed four classes of individuals who reported themselves as unemployed.

2.2 Given the absence of the normal sources we are thus pushed back on a more indirect method of trying to estimate unemployment currently and over time — if, that is, we want an overall economy-wide estimate. Basically it boils down to constructing a time series of figures for the labour force from population statistics and subtracting from it a constructed series for total employment — gathered and processed from a variety of sources. The difference between the two is the estimate of unemployment.

2.3 What are the data difficulties in estimating the labour force and employment time series? In the discussion that follows I rely on the outline provided by Loots (1977: 4–9). On the labour force side there are problems that arise in connection with:

(a) *Base year (i.e. census year) population totals and age/sex breakdowns:* the basic reason for this is that census underenumeration, on an unknown and probably varying scale, has taken place over the years. There are demographic techniques for making adjustments but at certain points guesses are unavoidable.

(b) *Population growth rates:* since we do not have direct measures of African vital statistics we must rely heavily on census figures for deriving their population growth rate and so the uncertainties of (a) are involved here too. Moreover, censuses are infrequent and as one moves away from a census year the possibility that the current population growth rate is diverging from the historic rate as determined between the last two censuses increases.

(c) *Labour force participation rates:* these rates (LFPRs) are used to calculate the labour force or economically active population from the population series. They tell us what percentage of each relevant age-sex category is working or wishes to work, i.e. is economically active. They are derived from population data and so the underenumeration problems of (a) are involved as are the inter-censal variation problems and uncertainties of (b). In addition there are problems about the interpretation of economically active (by respondents and enumerators and census designers) which raise questions about the census LFPRs: thus Sadie (1977: 40) elects to ignore the 70,8 per cent of African men in the 65–74 age group who classified themselves as economically active in 1970 when computing his male labour-force relevant for employment/unemployment estimates.

Not surprisingly, there are also difficulties with data in compiling figures for total employment — either directly or indirectly from figures of output and labour productivity.

(d) *Direct employment estimates:* for many sectors regular employment figures are available, but there are problems arising from the fact that there are alternative sources of such figures which conflict. Knight (1977: 32–5 and Table 2) illustrates one such conflict between figures for non-farm employment derived from Department of Statistics data and corresponding figures derived from the industrial classification of the economically active in the Population Censuses. A switch from reliance on the latter to the former source is fundamental to the major differences between the unemployment estimates in Simkins (1977 and 1978a). There are, in addition, three especially difficult cases of employment estimation which account for some of the differences between workers in the field. (1) There are no direct measures of *employment in homeland agriculture* apart from the dubious census classifications. What we need is a distribution of the economically active by hours worked per week throughout the year. We may get this with the CPS but we do not have anything like it at present. (2) *Casual labour on White farms* is measured in the Agricultural Censuses at a point in time each year. We have no regular figures for those who work at other times in the year — nor any direct evidence of hours worked. (3) There are a whole range of economic activities by which people earn a living or part of a living which fall quite outside the scope of the normal statistics-collecting net of official agencies — activities now commonly referred to as comprising *the informal sector*. By definition we have no explicit information about these types of employment at all.

(e) *Growth rates of output and labour productivity:* indirect methods of calculating employment rely on output and productivity figures — where they are available. They may be dubious (as in homeland agriculture) or may be missing for certain years — and have to be supplied by interpolation. Simkins (1978a) uses this latter method to great effect but inevitably the year-to-year series created are more smoothed than the 'true' (and unknown) series they estimate.

3. ECONOMY-WIDE ESTIMATES OF UNEMPLOYMENT IN SOUTH AFRICA

Now that we have some notion of the difficulties to be faced in defining unemployment and trying to measure it indirectly for the South African economy, I shall examine and try to summarise briefly the main features of the major estimates that have been made. In the process I shall make such comparisons as are possible, and try to identify both agreements and disagreements.

3.1 Perhaps a useful place to start is with the work of Professor J.L. Sadie (1977) — both because it reminds us of the lack of consensus on some issues and because it raises questions of method immediately. He is critical of some of the unemployment estimates we are about to review: '... most of the unemployed guestimates of formidable proportions bandied about appeared to have been pulled out of hats!'

The unemployment estimates he himself advances for 1975 and 1976 are confined to African males — as we saw before, he does not think it possible to 'operationalise' the term for females. The crucial feature of his approach is that it is tied to the 1970 Population Census self-classification — in which 119 000 African males 'described themselves as unemployed'. These unemployed constituted 16 per cent of the underemployed — a broader category which Sadie measures as that number of the available African manpower who do not have identified full-time wage-employment or belong to the 350 000 full-time workers assumed to be active in homeland 'peasant agriculture'. This group was 21 per cent of available manpower in 1970 and had increased to 25,5 per cent (or 1 036 000 men) by 1975. As a *minimum estimate* of unemployment in 1975 Sadie offers 16 per cent of these 1 036 000 underemployed males, i.e. 170 000. To obtain a *maximum estimate* he allows that the deterioration from 21 per cent to 25,5 per cent in the ratio of the underemployed to total manpower may be entirely due to an increase in the number of the unemployed; this involves 183 000 men in addition to the 119 000 unemployed in 1970, or a maximum estimate of 302 000 for 1975. Updating to mid-1976 raises this maximum to 338 000. So Sadie sets the range of male African unemployment for mid-1976 as 170 000 to 338 000 men, or 4 per cent – 8 per cent of available manpower.

There are two comments it seems worth making at this stage. The first is that Sadie's procedure seems fatally open to the objection that the unemployed were underenumerated at the census *by the enumerators*. Loots (1977: 10) reports that enumerators were instructed to classify a man living in a rural area and describing himself as unemployed or employed in agriculture; and to classify a man who indicated the occupation and industry of his last job but was unemployed, as employed in that industry. The statistical anchor of 119 000 in 1970 is thus no anchor at all. The second comment is that, as Sadie himself emphasises, his view of the labour market does involve the existence of a high rate of male underemployment. 'In the last resort it needs to be stressed that from the purely economic point of view an 8 per cent unemployment rate is not very significant when compared to an overall 21 per cent to 25 per cent underemployment' (Sadie, 1977: 48).

3.2 The work of P.J. van der Merwe (1976; 1977) is also tied to the 1970 Population Census figures on unemployment. However, he is interested in the first place in calculating annual *increases* in unemployment from 1970 to the end of 1976 and so is not so dependent on the unemployment *level* as recorded in the 1970 Census. He is also willing to work with data for females and he makes calculations for all racial groups (except the numerically small Indian group).

His method is a variant of the indirect one outlined in Section 2, viz. the calculation of annual increases of the labour force from which are subtracted annual increases in employment. The difference is the annual increase in unemployment. For Africans, Van der Merwe handles the material under three heads — all urban areas, White farms and the rural homelands; for the other groups these distinctions are not made. The various series of annual increases in unemployment are added cumulatively to the relevant 1970 Census totals for unemployment — thus creating a set of series for the unemployment levels in the various sectors. Two aggregate series can be constructed by suitable additon:

(1) the level of accumulated unemployment in all urban areas and White rural

areas (taking the 1970 Census total as the base-figure for the series); and
(2) the level of unemployment (in 1970) and the accumulated increase in underemployment in the homelands since 1970.

If the assumption is made that new entrants to the labour market in the homelands during the period 1970–1976 could not be absorbed within the traditional agricultural sector on an underemployed basis, then the 'increases in underemployment' of (2) become 'increases in unemployment' and it is possible to add (1) and (2) — as is done in Table 1 to derive what is for Van der Merwe a 'high' estimate of unemployment.

Table 1 UNEMPLOYMENT ESTIMATES, 1970–1976 (VAN DER MERWE) ALL RACES (THOUSANDS)

		(1)	(2)
1970	. . . .	269	301
1971	. . . .	323	456
1972	. . . .	442	669
1973	. . . .	482	740
1974	. . . .	529	854
1975	. . . .	602	979
1976	. . . .	746	1 142

Source: Loots (1977: Table 1).

Notes
1. Accumulated increase in unemployment in all urban areas and White rural areas (with 1970 Census unemployment as base).
2. Cumulative increases in underemployment in the homelands are added to (1) = 'high' estimate of unemployment.

The implications of Van der Merwe's work have been commented on by other researchers. Thus Loots (1977: 9), after noticing the problem about the precise *level* of unemployment in Van der Merwe's work nonetheless stresses that 'the trend of rising unemployment especially amongst blacks is undeniable and cannot be changed by any reasonable set of assumptions'. Simkins (1978a) draws attention to the startling fact that over the six years of Van der Merwe's study no less than 57 per cent of the increment in the African labour force had not been provided with employment. Similarly, in the case of the Coloured labour force 51 per cent of the increment over this period had joined the unemployed.

For *Africans* (both sexes) in mid-1976 Van der Merwe's range of unemployment estimates was 528 000 to 924 000, or 7,7 per cent to 13,5 per cent of the total African labour force.

11

3.3   The remaining three studies that we will look at, viz. those by Simkins, Loots and Knight, have all cut adrift from the 1970 census figures for unemployment. (In addition, Simkins cuts adrift from the census figures for employment and this change is responsible for a substantial worsening of the picture of unemployment between his second and his third set of estimates.) Not surprisingly, given the low rate of reported unemployment in the 1970 census, the levels of unemployment suggested by these three workers are in general in excess of those contained in the two studies we have looked at so far — though there are overlaps.

The first of these studies in the field, and the study which set the pace for most of what was to come, was produced by Simkins in mid-1976 (Simkins: 1976). He revised his work in March 1977 (Simkins: 1977) and then again later in that year for publication in 1978 (Simkins: 1978a). It is an illuminating study of how factual assumptions condition results in this field to work through the reasons why Simkins was led to change his estimates to the extent that he did. The first series ran from 8,9 per cent in 1961 to 20,0 per cent in 1976, the second raised the 1961 unemployment rate to 16,3 per cent and lowered the 1976 rate to 14,6 per cent. The third raised the initial rate still further to 19 per cent but put the terminal rate back to 21,4 per cent. Of course, the second of these had very different implications for the nature of the unemployment problem in South Africa from the other two. The basic reasons for the differences between the three series are

(1) a revision of the 1960 census figures for the number of economically active females in homeland agriculture (raising the figure considerably in line with the 1970 figures);

(2) the already mentioned dropping of reliance on census figures for employment — which in general lie above the inter-censal figures derived from other sources and which Simkins had used in his second study to correct the year-to-year figures in an upwards direction.

The major innovations of the Simkins work (which involved producing a single composite measure for unemployment and underemployment in the South African economy in line with the 'full-time job equivalent' method of section 1) were the methods used to measure employment in agriculture both in homelands and on White farms. Loots (as we shall see) demonstrates in great detail how alternative procedures under these heads can produce very different figures for the level of unemployment. In both cases Simkins uses an earnings criterion to deal with labour underutilisation. In the case of casual workers on White farms the total casual worker wage bill is divided by the average wage for regular farm workers to generate a series of casual employment measured in full-time job equivalents. In the case of homelands the value of agricultural production is divided by the Tomlinson Commission income norm to generate a series for employment in homeland agriculture.

There is an immense amount of finesse and detailed computation in this third set of estimates. The results obtained are reproduced in Table 2.

Table 2 UNEMPLOYMENT IN SOUTH AFRICA, 1960–1977 (SIMKINS) ALL RACES (THOUSANDS)

Date		Labour supply	Employment	Unemployment (No.)	Unemployment (%)
1960	....	6 769	5 533	1 236	18,3
1961	....	6 915	5 604	1 311	19,0
1962	....	7 066	5 691	1 375	19,5
1963	....	7 232	5 831	1 401	19,4
1964	....	7 404	6 026	1 378	18,6
1965	....	7 592	6 144	1 448	19,1
1966	....	7 785	6 396	1 389	17,8
1967	....	7 983	6 589	1 394	17,5
1968	....	8 187	6 542	1 645	20,1
1969	....	8 401	6 812	1 589	18,9
1970	....	8 614	6 856	1 758	20,4
1971	....	8 809	7 062	1 747	19,8
1972	....	9 066	7 175	1 891	20,9
1973	....	9 331	7 433	1 898	20,3
1974	....	9 576	7 586	1 990	20,8
1975	....	9 765	7 751	2 014	20,6
1976	....	9 997	7 858	2 139	21,4
1977	....	10 278	7 977	2 301	22,4

Source: Simkins (1978a: Table 20)

Whereas in the 1960s the unemployment rate, according to these calculations, fluctuated in the region of 19 per cent, the 1970s have seen it edging above 20 per cent and of course rising clearly in the last two years of recession. These figures imply both a very high level of unemployment (which goes back at least to 1960) and also a perverse trend over time — with the relatively fast national income growth of the 1960s failing to reduce unemployment in any sustained way. The absolute numbers involved are massive — rising from 1,24 million in 1960 to 2,30 million in 1977. However, care must be taken over the interpretation of these numbers. They do not mean that in 1977 2,30 million people had no jobs at all and were willing and eager to step into jobs in the metropolitan centres (say), but it does mean that *more than* that number of people had deficient employment in one of a number of senses.

3.4 Loots (1977) carried out the interesting exercise of showing how a whole range of Simkins-type estimates might be obtained (for the years 1970–1976) by varying the ways in which agricultural employment was treated. He produced four main estimates:
(a) a 'very high' estimate which used Simkins' assumptions (much homeland

underemployment and casual farm work equal on average to 25 per cent of a full-time job);

(b) a 'high' estimate which retained the casual farm work assumption but treated all workers in subsistence agriculture as employed 'albeit producing very little and earning poverty incomes';

(c) a 'median' estimate which likewise assumed no homelands unemployment and treated casual employment as equivalent to 50 per cent of full-time job opportunities;

(d) a 'low' estimate which repeated the no homelands unemployment assumption and assumed that 75 per cent of casual employment could be treated as full-time job opportunities.

For 1976 these different assumptions generate respectively the following unemployment rates: 18,6 per cent, 14,2 per cent, 11,8 per cent, 10,2 per cent. For each estimate over the period unemployment rises in absolute numbers and in percentage terms. Loots remains unconvinced that it is possible at this stage to determine the *true* level of unemployment — for data reasons and because of disagreements about what constitutes a job. However, he took the spread of estimates to establish

(1) that in 1977 South Africa probably had an unemployment rate of between 10–15 per cent of the labour force,

(2) that there were more than one million unemployed, and

(3) that there was a rising trend of unemployment.

3.5 The study which covers the longest time period is that of J.B. Knight (1977). Confining himself to the census years 1946, 1951, 1960 and 1970, Knight asks whether the trend is for the pool of unabsorbed, unskilled workers to diminish over time or to increase. In answering this question he defines two concepts, viz. *residual labour,* which is the difference between the country's labour force and the number in *wage* unemployment (i.e. employment excluding those in homeland agriculture), and *underemployment*, which is that part of residual labour after productive employment in homeland agriculture has been netted out from it. Since this productive employment is assumed not to have grown over time, an increase in residual labour involves an increase in underemployment — which is a category including both unemployment and underemployment as we have defined them earlier. A considerable interest attaches to Knight's work because of his permutation of a number of assumptions in the making of his estimates. While this blurs the results, it illuminates the structure of the investigation. A summary of his results is as follows:

(a) there has been a significant growth of residual labour in absolute numbers since 1951; however, the evidence is more ambiguous about what has happened to residual labour as a percentage of the labour force — on one estimate it has decreased slightly between 1946 and 1970 (he even allows for the possibility that numbers might have decreased in absolute terms between 1960 and 1970);

14

(b) there has been a significant growth in African underemployment since 1946 but it is again possible that it fell as a percentage of the labour force between 1960 and 1970 and there is considerable uncertainty about the actual level of underemployment.

3.6 All researchers agree on a rising trend in the 1970s; all who have abandoned the anchor of the 1970 census unemployment figures are willing to consider unemployment rates in excess of (and perhaps well in excess of) 10 per cent of the labour force, and the longer-run investigations of the past suggest that high levels of combined unemployment and underemployment are not new to the South African economy.

4. REASONS FOR UNEMPLOYMENT IN SOUTH AFRICA

We turn now to ask the question how it comes about that unemployment and underemployment exist on the scale that they do at present, why this scale has been increasing on trend throughout the 1970s and probably for a good deal longer than that, and why there seems little chance of its being reduced (this last fact follows from Simkins' finding (1978a: 41) that a growth rate of national income of 5,3 per cent would be required to stabilise the unemployment rate and of 6,7 per cent to stabilise the number of the unemployed).

Given the nature and the extent of the phenomenon to be explained we are going to have to advance more than purely cyclical factors (which have to do with the pattern of short-term fluctuations in the economy). Clearly the unemployment and the underemployment reported in Section 3 are the result of factors beyond the recession of 1975–1978 — though De Klerk (1978) reminds us that it is sometimes awkward to distinguish between cyclical and trend factors; today's recession may be the beginning of tomorrow's slower trend rate of growth. This point may have had a special relevance for South Africa in the late 1970s.

4.1 Voluntary or preferred unemployment

It seems to me necessary to look seriously at the possibility that some of the unemployment which researchers have measured in South Africa is not involuntary but (in some sense of the word) has been chosen by individuals as preferable for some of the time to the available work under going conditions at going rates (Sadie, 1977: 44–8). I do not agree with Maree (1978) that such a suggestion should be dismissed with contempt. It is worth pointing out at this stage that to accept such an explanation of some unemployment is not necessarily to approve the behaviour itself or the structures within which it is chosen. It may well be possible to change the behaviour in a number of ways — including the method of changing some of the structures within which such choices are privately optimal. And of course to say that some people make such choices is not to say that all do.

15

There is a distinction to be made between the view which says that many Blacks have a very different attitude to work from Whites (and will in general work as little as possible) and a view which, while it admits the possibility of differences in cultural attitudes to work, emphasises when explaining some Black work-choices the constraints operating on such choices and the peculiar nature of the options available. It is this latter view which I am suggesting is worth consideration. We need to consider the full list of the disutilities and opportunity costs of going out to work from the homelands (at least for some people at some times) and to set against these the very low remuneration available (at least historically) in agriculture and mining. It is worth remembering too the system of deferred payment operated by the mining industry which arranges income transfers across time and so finances *resting* after a period of work (or social system maintenance, or whatever else one wishes to call the practice). And of course it is correct to emphasise that influx controls increase the costs to the male worker and his family of going out to work. Furthermore, there are other administrative controls of a labour-allocation variety which might well impose undesirable costs on entering the labour market at a particular point in time. (Perhaps in a particular area only agricultural recruitment is allowed, for instance.)

There is a general theoretical argument, which may be relevant here, that the greater the rigidities or disjunctions in a social system, the greater the *slippages* and *frictions* which arise within it. Transactions and information costs will be higher, rational individuals will be less certain about preferred courses of action and will search longer and hesitate longer over making choices. This argument is moving somewhat away from the point at which I began (and is overlapping with material to be referred to in Section 4.5) but seems worth making at this point nevertheless.

It may help to clarify the extent to which this point is relevant if we consider the case of Coloured male workers. It appears that labour force participation rates among Coloured males have declined in all age groups from 20–24 upwards to 70–74 between 1960 and 1970. At the same time the participation rates for Coloured females rose in every age group from 20–24 to 50–55 (Theron Commission, 1976: Table 5.2). This raises the question whether, as a result of a number of labour market changes, increasing numbers of Coloured men have been (to put it crudely) living off their women. This is an interesting question in its own right but it is not clear that it is relevant for our studies of measured unemployment, because the reduced labour force participation rate revealed in the 1970 census will have been used by most researchers to reduce the size of the Coloured male labour force accordingly. Thus such men will feature as not economically active and not as unemployed. But if they return themselves as unemployed or unidentified the LFPRs are raised and measured unemployment (that may be voluntary) appears.

Evans (1976: 8–9) and Van der Vliet and Bromberger (1977: 123, 125, 221) record evidence of female casual workers on farms having as much work as they

16

want, or even reducing the amount of work that they choose to do — in Viljoenskroon during a time when male farm wages were rising strongly the number of female casual workers fell from 84 per cent of the permanent employees to 60 per cent over three years.

What is one to make of the fact that in 1975 and 1976, when according to our measurements unemployment and underemployment were rising, the gold mines in South Africa were recording the breaking of contracts by South African Black workers and a consequent shortage of labour? It appears to have taken one to two years of slackening demand for labour from the secondary and tertiary sectors before the gold mines in 1977 found that they had all the labour they wanted.

Satisfactory answers to problems raised under this head are not available, but I think it important to raise these questions about employment behaviour which are puzzling. They must not simply be dismissed.

Of course we know that the *bulk* of unemployment at least under our current conditions is involuntary. The problem remains to explain it. Unfortunately, to succeed would require a lot more detailed information about the unemployed than is currently available. This means that all we can do at present is to advance some explanatory hypotheses without being sure that we will be able to test them properly against the facts.

A simple initial framework often used to explain structural unemployment in less developed countries is to look at the determinants of the supply of labour and then of the demand for labour. On the supply side, we have unusually high rates of population growth and hence, in due course, of labour force growth. On the demand side, factors often pointed to are low rates of capital accumulation and imperfect factor substitutability, i.e. technology employed is such that it is not easy to modify techniques in the direction of increased labour-intensity if surplus labour exists. I suggest that we use this framework in a modified form to introduce the discussion about the South African case. (See Bromberger (1977) for a summary of Third World research of this type.)

4.2 Population and labour-force growth rate

Over the period that our unemployment studies deal with, these rates have risen — especially among the less-skilled, poorer elements of the population. Sadie (1977: 46) measures the rates of manpower growth as increasing in the following fashion: 2,2 per cent (1951–1960), 2,4 per cent (1960–1965), 2,6 per cent (1965–1970) and 3,1 per cent (1970–1975). It appears, moreover, that activity rates have been rising among women of all race groups during this period— we have already noticed it for the Coloured group. We know also that historically the South African economy has continually drawn upon foreign sources of labour of particular types (Black and White) in periods of expansion. We must remember that domestic growth rates of the labour force of the kind listed above were never experienced by the countries of the Northern Hemisphere which successfully developed in the nineteenth century. Labour-absorption at the rate we require would tax any growing economy.

4.3 Rates of capital accumulation

On the surface of it, it seems impossible to argue that low rates of capital accumulation are responsible for unemployment in South Africa. In the period 1956–1972 the real fixed capital stock of South Africa increased at an average annual rate of 5,7 per cent per annum, which was more than twice the rate at which the population increased (see De Jager, 1973 and Hindson, 1977). Moreover, each year South Africa is investing a very substantial portion of her available national resources. In the years 1970–1976 the ratio of Gross Domestic Fixed Investment to Gross Domestic Product (at market prices), was never less than 25 per cent and in 1975 and 1976 averaged 30 per cent (S.A. Reserve Bank Quarterly Bulletin, December 1977). It is difficult to conceive of a nation investing much more of available resources. It seems worth investigating then the nature of the investment taking place and of the technology embodied in it as a possible explanation of unemployment rather than the rate of investment itself.

4.4 Technology and technical influences on the growth of unemployment

There is a wide range of separate but related considerations which could be discussed under this head. The difficulty is to reduce them to coherence and to go beyond a mere rag-bag of hypotheses.

The kind of recent empirical experience which is sometimes advanced as indicative of technical influences working towards unemployment is

(a) the rise in the average capital-output ratio from 2,17 to 2,67 between mid-1971 and mid-1977, and

(b) the rise in the capital-labour ratio from R4 479 to R5 404 per worker in the same period (S.A. Reserve Bank, 1977: 10).

These suggest (although cyclical factors are relevant) capital deepening in the economy. I am not aware of really satisfactory studies of this phenomenon at present but there is no doubt that the subject deserves to be studied. (See Terreblanche, 1977 for an introductory discussion. Bell, 1978 is also relevant.)

Is the nature of technical change in general such that South Africa is now on too labour-saving a growth path? And if it is why is it so? There is a view which emphasises the fact that we import so much of our technology, in consequence of which it is a technology which suits economies where labour is not in surplus. There is another view which emphasises the fact that arguably the market signals influencing the choice of technology are distorted — roughly wages are too high and capital costs too low. There are a whole group of factors which bring this about. The complex of causes behind the industrial colour bar is one (see Maree, 1978); the political and social pressures behind rapid African wage increases in recent years is another (see Sadie, 1977; Terreblanche, 1977; Biggs, 1977; Bell, 1978; Simkins, 1978b); and then there is also the access of South Africa to the world capital market, and the set of investment allowances and subsidies which encourage capital intensity.

We can also argue that political factors of various kinds lean against labour absorption and encourage capital intensity. The ceilings of the employment of Blacks in some urban industries and the uncertainties of continued supply of Black labour to certain areas attach greater costs and uncertainties to the use of Black labour. Van der Merwe has referred to the activity of labour boards in farming areas in setting labour quotas and encouraging a reduction in Black farm employment.

Rosenberg (1976) has pointed to some socio-political factors lying behind mechanisation in the 19th century in Britain. It was imagined that greater mechanisation would reduce the vulnerability of employers to strike action by skilled workers who were then well organised. It seems to me not at all unlikely that there are a series of factors of this kind at work encouraging labour-saving technical change in this country. Machines are easier to manage than potentially hostile Black workers. In one case in the Western Cape, I heard a discussion of how, with his new combine harvester, a farmer would be able to reap the harvest helped only by his wife if it became necessary.

There is an argument which links technology to the particular mix of commodities produced in a country. Allegedly commodities produced for high income consumers will tend to be produced in more mechanised ways than others. This has been said to be of relevance to the South African case but there are some grounds for scepticism both in general (Cline, 1975: 375, 378–85, 395) and locally (see an initial investigation by Black, 1977).

To this basic scheme we add some sectoral disequilibria or imperfections or imbalances — which tend to throw up unemployment as a friction or adjustment to disequilibrium.

4.5 The urban-rural income gap, migration and the question of the 'underdevelopment' of homeland agriculture

There is by now a very standard argument which says that once a substantial gap exists between urban and rural incomes, it will be rational for rural dwellers to migrate to town and suffer unemployment for some period of time while they search for work so long as they expect on balance to do better by this move. Naturally, the larger the income gap the longer it will be rational for them to search unsuccessfully for such jobs, provided, of course, they are able to subsist in the meantime through the support of relatives or participation in so-called *informal sector* jobs in town. The normal argument supposes this form of unemployment to exist in towns. The South African system pens it back in the homelands where it must presumably be a less efficient search process since the information is more difficult to come by. It is almost certain that some of the evidence about Blacks turning down jobs in mining and agriculture while being unemployed can be explained by behaviour of this sort — given the historically large differential between wages in manufacturing and those in these sectors. Knight (1977: 42–7 and Figure 2) discusses this interpretation.

A school of writers has come to argue recently that the neglect and deterioration of homeland agriculture has been functional to the particular requirements of the capitalist mining economy in South Africa. If this is so (and it is not entirely proven) then the responsibility for the creation of the urban-rural disequilibrium we are discussing may be laid at the door of deep structural requirements of the economy (see De Klerk, 1978; Bell, 1977; and literature they cite).

There is a related but different argument that seems worth considering: What would the *level* of South Africa's labour absorptive capacity be if the 13 per cent of South Africa which is in the homelands had been developed and made productive?

4.6 A possible mismatch between education and employment opportunities

Blaug (1974) and others have shown that where there is considerable income inequality between white-collar jobs and others and where higher education is a passport to entry to those white-collar jobs, there is an inducement for individuals to invest in education and to suffer a period of unemployment at the beginning of their careers while waiting for a high-paying job to come along. This phenomenon may assume chronic and extraordinary proportions. Evidence, both of a general sort and of the survey variety which Simkins (1978c) summarises, suggests that *this is not yet a substantial determinant of unemployment in South Africa*. There are powerful arguments to suggest that it soon will be.

4.7 Other factors

It can be argued that inequality in income distribution which exists to a startling extent in South Africa (McGarth, 1978, provides some measures) operates to encourage unemployment via the factors listed in 4.4, 4.5, and 4.6. There is much more to be said under this heading but the discussion becomes too elaborate for the purposes of this survey.

Finally, there are two factors conditioning much of what has gone before, viz:

(a) a series of political policies connected with segregation and White control of the political system, and

(b) a set of international influences which work through South Africa's participation in the world trading and investment network (Erwin, 1977, raises some of the issues).

20

5. POLICIES TOWARDS UNEMPLOYMENT

Until recently there was little awareness that structural unemployment was a problem that South Africa had to face. In fact we were conscious of the relatively good labour-absorptive record of the South African economy (Hindson, 1977: 8–10). In consequence, thinking and research on the policies to cope with unemployment have tended to be confined to short-run measures — and even there probably less weight was attached to the goal of full employment (for all groups) than would have been the case had the unemployed had greater political power. There has been some recent discussion of policy options which might be useful in this country — though discussion is at a very preliminary stage and does not go much beyond the application of some Third World ideas. We shall note a few contributions by Terreblanche (1977a, b), Van der Merwe (1976) and others.

It might be of some use to summarise briefly the components of a typical policy package directed at this sort of problem in Third World countries. The package is described as aiming at the problem of urban unemployment but seeking to avoid the artificial creation of serious imbalances in economic opportunities between urban and rural areas. The five key elements in the package are:

(1) Creating an appropriate rural-urban balance by an *integrated development of the rural sector* with both directly productive and social investment aimed at raising incomes in the rural areas.
(2) The expansion of small-scale labour-intensive industries which may be promoted by measures to encourage the production of basic consumer goods.
(3) The elimination of factor-price distortions via the elimination of various capital subsidies and the restraint of the growth of urban wages.
(4) Choosing (and developing) appropriate labour-intensive technologies of production — including methods of building rural infrastructure.
(5) Modifying the direct linkage between education and employment, in order to reduce the phenomenon of educated unemployment.

What we need urgently is some thought about the applicability of this kind of package to our case. Is it what we need? If it is, is it feasible — given the political and economic power structures in this country? A stronger version of this package — though it overlaps with it — is the 'basic needs approach' to development advocated by the ILO and consistent with the current emphasis of the World Bank on income distribution as a high priority of development policy. Riddell (1977) has produced a discussion for Rhodesia/Zimbabwe in which he contrasts this approach with the strategy followed in recent decades (as formalised by Sadie) — a strategy similar in essentials to that of South Africa. Proper analysis of these questions has hardly begun. One would expect that the *relative size* of the 'modern' and 'traditional' sectors must influence the capacity of the former to absorb labour from the latter, but whether this is so or not, 'rural development' must become a more urgently considered policy in

South Africa than heretofore — and this must involve raising the question of how White agriculture can be made more labour-absorptive instead of actually shedding labour as it is at present.

There is one policy towards unemployment available in South Africa which *is* feasible and has been used in recent years — but which is controversial. I refer to 'the defensive strategy' of reducing employment of foreign labour and encouraging the substitution of South African-born workers in their place. This is to some degree advocated by Van der Merwe (1976) and has in fact been a policy that has been followed for some time (Clarke, 1978). The position adopted by Clarke and others is that this policy has dubious justification given that South Africa has historically contributed to creating (and benefited from) the dependence on her for employment of a number of the surrounding countries of Southern Africa. There is some similarity between this policy of displacing foreign Africans and the argument advanced by the Theron Commission that the policy of restricting the entry of Africans to the Western Cape should be tightened — since their entry was allegedly harming the employment prospects of the poorest 40 per cent of the Coloured population. (A summary of this position is presented in Terreblanche, 1977b: 95–98 — using a version of the infant-industry argument.) This issue is worth mentioning for a number of reasons — amongst others, because policy recommendations of this kind will continue to be advanced and 'group share' questions will continue to be raised.

6. NEED FOR FURTHER RESEARCH

If those who currently direct the South African system react rationally to the problem of long-term unemployment which has been emerging, and now needs to be carefully identified and measured, we can expect (and should encourage) research in a number of directions.

6.1 It seems justifiable to hope that as the monthly data from the Current Population Survey accumulate — in particular the precious information about the distribution of employment by hours worked per week — we shall be able to:
(a) measure underemployment more accurately and be able to distinguish it from unemployment,
(b) narrow down substantially the range in which the unemployment rate is thought to lie,
(c) form a clear impression of the size of the cyclical component in unemployment, and
(d) make more progress in establishing the main influences at work in creating long-term structural unemployment.

6.2 Time and again it will have been apparent in the course of this survey that we are seriously hampered in diagnosis and prescription by lack of detailed knowledge about the functioning of aspects of homeland economics. One understands that the concern of the mining houses with increasing South African recruitment has led them to subsidise some research in this area aimed at understanding better the decisions made by homeland residents. So far this work has not been published; one hopes it soon will be. Evidence of how much we need better information is provided by the excellent paper of Merle Lipton (1977) which sets out to question 'the myth that blacks are poor farmers' and casts doubt on some basic output and productivity statistics in Black agriculture in doing so. If she is right — or pointing in the right direction — the implications would be substantial. Certainly 'resting'-type behaviour would become more explicable — at least for some workers. But we need to know about the *distribution* of landlessness (see some average figures in Maree, 1977 and Simkins, 1978c – KwaZulu survey) and about the possibilities and determinants of agricultural development. Sadie (1977) has rejected the view that the migrant labour system, for instance, is an obstacle to agricultural development — whereas Westcott (1977: 150) sees it as one factor in a chain reaction of determinants. There is a very substantial research programme that needs to be tackled.

6.3 There is very little systematic information on the 'informal sector' in urban or rural areas in South Africa. However, information is beginning to come in and hopefully we shall have made progress with description, analysis and development of suitable policies before too long. We need to know more about the numbers of people involved and what the spread of incomes generated in the sector is like. The finding of Maree and Cornell (1978) for the Crossroads Squatter Settlement in Cape Town is of the greatest potential significance, viz. that up to (roughly) 10 per cent of economically active males were involved and earned average incomes equivalent to those earned by workers in the formal sector. A similar finding has apparently been made by Maasdorp for a similar social situation in Durban (though the details are not yet published). It is clear that these findings are not typical — but their existence is of interest for measurement and policy-making. Consistent with this view of the importance of the informal sector is the hypothesis of Nattrass (1977) that much of the transfer in the share of national income going to Blacks that took place during 1970–75 has been siphoned off as demanded to the informal sector.

6.4 Finally it is clear that we need to become more conscious of the processes of technological change that are taking place in the economy, and about the technological options available to us. This means a more detailed understanding of why, for instance, White agriculture has begun to shed labour in the 1970s (e.g. Van der Merwe, 1977, Tables 2 and 3) and why labour productivity has been increasing so rapidly in the mining of non-precious minerals in South Africa (Bromberger, 1978, outlines some of the statistical evidence). It will also mean encouragement of research and development in areas such as 'intermediate technology' and serious attention to the question of whether South Africa can, and ought, to be generating more of its own technology.

REFERENCES

Bell, R.T., 1977. 'Surplus labour and South African development'. Paper presented to Workshop on Unemployment and Labour Reallocation, Development Studies Research Group (DSRG), Department of Economics, University of Natal, Pietermaritzburg.
——— 1978. 'Capital intensity and employment in South African industry'. *South African Journal of Economics*, Vol. 46, No. 1, March, 48–61.
Biggs, F.P., 1977. *South African Wage and Interest Rate Ratios 1960–1975*. Special Report No. 2, Bureau for Economic Research, University of Stellenbosch.
Black, P.A., 1977. 'Income distribution and the composition of final demand in South Africa'. *South African Journal of Economics*, Vol. 45, No. 4, December, 394–407.
Blaug, M., 1974. *Education and the Employment Problem in Developing Countries*. ILO, Geneva.
Bromberger, N., 1977. 'Third World unemployment: some recent research'. Workshop on Unemployment and Labour Reallocation, Pietermaritzburg.
——— 1978. 'Mining in the South African Mining Industry: 1946–2000?' *SALDRU Working Paper No. 15*. University of Cape Town.
Clarke, D.G., 1978. 'Foreign African labour inflows to South Africa and "unemployment" in Southern Africa', pp. 51–82 in Charles Simkins and Duncan Clarke, *Structural Unemployment in Southern Africa*. Pietermaritzburg: Natal University Press. (Originally a paper to Workshop on Unemployment and Labour Reallocation.)
Cline, W.R., 1975. 'Distribution and development: a survey of literature'. *Journal of Development Economics* I, 359–400.
De Jager, B.L., 1973. 'The fixed capital stock and capital-output ratio of South Africa from 1946 to 1972'. *South African Reserve Bank Quarterly Bulletin* (June), 17–31.
De Klerk, M., 1978. 'Structural roots of unemployment', pp. 35–42 in C. Simkins and C. Desmond (eds.), *South African Unemployment: A Black Picture*. Pietermaritzburg and Johannesburg: DSRG and Agency for Industrial Mission.
Desmond, C., 1978. 'Limehill revisited: a case study of the longer-term effects of African resettlement'. *DSRG Working Paper No. 5*. University of Natal.
Erwin, A., 1977. 'Unemployment and "Marginalisation": a framework for the South African case'. Workshop on Unemployment and Labour Reallocation, Pietermaritzburg.
Evans, A.R., 1976. 'Farm labour in the Viljoenskroon district'. *SALDRU Farm Labour Conference Paper No. 41*. University of Cape Town.
Hindson, D.C., 1977. 'Conditions of labour supply and employment of African workers in urban based industries in South Africa, 1946–1975'. Workshop on Unemployment and Labour Reallocation, Pietermaritzburg.
Knight, J.B., 1977. 'Is South Africa running out of unskilled labour?' pp. 31–50 in F. Wilson. A. Kooy and D. Hendrie (eds.), *Farm Labour in South Africa*. Cape Town: David Philip. (Full version available as 'Labour supply in the South African economy'. *SALDRU Working Paper No. 7*. University of Cape Town.)
Lipton, Merle, 1977. 'South Africa: two agricultures?' pp. 72–85 in F. Wilson, A. Kooy and D. Hendrie (eds.), *Farm Labour in South Africa*. Cape Town: David Philip.
Loots, L.J., 1977. 'Alternative approaches to the estimation of unemployment'. Workshop on Unemployment and Labour Reallocation, Pietermaritzburg.
——— 1978. 'A profile of black unemployment in South Africa: two area surveys'. *SALDRU Working Paper No. 19*. University of Cape Town.
Maasdorp, G., 1978. 'Unemployment in South Africa and its implications', pp. 139–148 in L. Schlemmer and E. Webster (eds.), *Change, Reform and Economic Growth in South Africa*. Johannesburg: Ravan Press.

Maree, J., 1977. 'African urban and rural employment in Cape Town and Transkei'. Workshop on Unemployment and Labour Reallocation, Pietermaritzburg. (Fuller version available as, Janet Graaff and Johann Maree, 'Residential and migrant African workers in Cape Town'. *SALDRU Working Paper No. 12.* University of Cape Town.)

—— 1978. 'Unemployment and the labour market', pp. 26–31 in C. Simkins and C. Desmond (eds.), *South African Unemployment: A Black Picture.* Pietermaritzburg and Johannesburg: DSRG and Agency for Industrial Mission.

Maree, J. and J. Cornell, 1978. 'Sample survey of squatters in Crossroads, December 1977'. *SALDRU Working Paper No. 17.* University of Cape Town.

Market Research Africa, 1977. African Omnireef Unemployment Study (for *The Star*, Johannesburg).

McGrath, M., 1978. 'Income and material inequality in South Africa', pp. 149–172 in L. Schlemmer and E. Webster (eds.), *Change, Reform and Economic Growth in South Africa.* Johannesburg: Ravan Press.

Nattrass, J., 1977. 'The narrowing of wage differentials in South Africa'. *South African Journal of Economics*, Vol. 45, No. 4, December, 408–432.

Riddell, R., 1977. 'Which way Zimbabwe? Alternative development strategies for the future'. *South African Labour Bulletin*, Vol. 3, No. 5, May, 3–21.

Rosenberg, N., 1976. *Perspectives on Technology*, Cambridge: Cambridge University Press.

Sadie, J.L., 1977. 'RSA — Homelands Labour Relations'. *Journal for Studies in Economics and Econometrics,* No. 1, December, 35–56.

Schlemmer, L. and E. Webster (eds.), 1978. *Change, Reform and Economic Growth in South Africa.* Johannesburg: Ravan Press.

Simkins, C.E.W., 1976. 'Employment, unemployment and growth in South Africa'. *SALDRU Working Paper No. 4.* University of Cape Town.

—— 1977. 'Measuring and predicting unemployment in South Africa 1960–1977'. Workshop on Unemployment and Labour Reallocation. Pietermaritzburg.

—— 1978a. 'Measuring and predicting unemployment in South Africa 1960–1977', pp. 1–49 in Charles Simkins and Duncan Clarke, *Structural Unemployment in Southern Africa.* Pietermaritzburg: Natal University Press.

—— 1978b. 'Income distribution among settled urban African households in South Africa: 1970 and 1975'. *DSRG Working Paper No. 6.* University of Natal.

—— 1978c. 'African unemployment in urban and rural South Africa', p. 43 in C. Simkins and C. Desmond (eds.), *South African Unemployment: A Black Picture.* Pietermaritzburg and Johannesburg: DSRG and Agency for Industrial Mission.

Simkins, Charles and Duncan Clarke, 1978. *Structural Unemployment in Southern Africa.* Pietermaritzburg: Natal University Press.

Simkins, C. and C. Desmond (eds.), 1978. *South African Unemployment: A Black Picture.* Pietermaritzburg and Johannesburg: DSRG and Agency for Industrial Mission.

Smith, A.D., 1971. *Concepts of Labour Force Underutilisation.* Geneva: International Labour Office.

South African Reserve Bank, 1977. *Annual Economic Report.*

Terreblanche, S.J., 1977a. 'Die werkverskaffingsituasie en remediërende maatreëls vir die toekoms'. *Journal for Studies in Economics and Econometrics*, No. 1, December, 57–70.

—— 1977b. *Gemeenskapsarmoede.* Kaapstad: Tafelberg-Uitgewers.

Theron Commission (Kommissie van Ondersoek na Aangeleenthede rakende die Kleurlingbevolkingsgroep), 1976. *Report* RP 38/1976.

Van der Merwe, P.J., 1976. 'Black employment problems in South Africa'. *Bureau for Economic Policy and Analysis report No. 6.* University of Pretoria. (Also, *Financial and Trade Review* (December), 46–75.)

—— 1977. 'Unemployment Statistics'. Workshop on Unemployment and Labour Reallocation. Pietermaritzburg.

Van der Vliet, E. and N. Bromberger, 1977. 'Farm labour in the Albany district', pp. 121–130 and

221–2 in F. Wilson, A. Kooy and D. Hendrie (eds.), *Farm Labour in South Africa*. Cape Town: David Philip.

Westcott, G., 1977. 'Obstacles to agricultural development in the Transkei', pp. 139–153 in F. Wilson, A. Kooy and D. Hendrie (eds.) *op. cit.*

Wilson, F., A. Kooy and D. Hendrie (eds.), *Farm Labour in South Africa*. Cape Town: David Philip.

1.3 THE QUESTION OF STRUCTURAL UNEMPLOYMENT IN SOUTH AFRICA

J. Gerson*

Structure, I am afraid, is often a weaselword used to avoid commitment to a definite and clear thought.

Fritz Machlup[1]

Recent empirical studies have revealed alarmingly high estimates of unemployment among black workers in South Africa.[2] Furthermore, C.E.W. Simkins's research seems to indicate a secular increase in this trend over the past two decades.[3] These findings are frequently cited in support of the view that there exists in South Africa a high incidence of 'structural unemployment', which is largely unresponsive to the business cycle.[4] What is meant by 'structural unemployment' is not clear although it appears to suggest a failure of the market to clear, even in the long term.

In Section 1, the author attempts to argue to the contrary by invoking the 'Natural Rate Hypothesis' that the market always clears in the long term and that permanently high unemployment statistics are indicative of 'low labour force participation rates' rather than a failure of the market to clear. Section 2 criticises on a priori grounds notions of structural employment as developed by M. de Klerk, J. Maree, A. Erwin and others.[5] Section 3 presents some conclusions.

1. THE NATURAL RATE HYPOTHESIS: AN ANALYSIS OF UNEMPLOYMENT IN THE LONG RUN

Measured unemployment is always found to be greater than zero even in the upward phases of the business cycle. Long-term measured rates vary dramatically between countries and, less so, between (long) time periods. For 1969, Simkins's figure is 18,9 per cent.[6] In the United States it appears that the long-term rate has increased substantially and Gardiner Ackley has attempted to fix the current 'natural rate' at about 5,5 per cent.[7] The Current Population Survey[8] puts black unemployment for October 1977 at 9,4 per cent for males, 19,4 per cent for females, and 12,4 per cent combined. The 9,4 per cent for males probably contained a considerable cyclical component, so that the natural rate is somewhat lower at a figure not incomparable with that of the United States. Indeed the January 1979 estimates show male unemployment reduced to 6,1 per cent, which is comparable to current statistics in many Western countries. Black women bear the brunt of influx control measures; so,

* Formerly School of Economics, University of Cape Town. This paper was first published in *The South African Journal of Economics*, Vol. 49, No. 1, 1981.

naturally, their unemployment rate is much higher. None the less one should resist the temptation to explain any differences between countries by resorting to concepts such as 'structural unemployment', which appears to lack a solid theoretical foundation. Instead one ought to be mindful of the statistical hazards of measurement, the different procedures of compiling data between countries and the tendency of the natural rate to vary over time and space determined as it is by supply and demand. Furthermore, adjusting for cycles and cycles within cycles is problematical. On the question of measurement procedures, it may be added that had Simkins not used an income norm to estimate 'full-time job equivalents', his results would have been very different.

Three factors could be said to account for a positive long-run or 'natural' rate of unemployment, namely friction and search, voluntary unemployment* and institutionally induced unemployment. A change in any of these factors will cause the natural rate to change. The natural rate may be defined as that rate at which there exists no downward pressure on wages.[9]

Frictional and search unemployment[10]

In a world of scarce and costly information, there will be at any point of time an ever-changing pool of unemployed job-seekers in search of better-paid and more suitable jobs and employers in search of particular types of workers. Those engaged in search attempt to match the marginal costs and benefits of such activity. For the proper functioning of the market, search unemployment is both inevitable and useful.

Search theories have been attacked on a number of grounds, but all of these pertain to search as an explanation of cyclical unemployment and as an activity engaged in by workers who voluntarily quit their jobs. Search costs are generally accepted as *one* of the factors which make the natural unemployment rate greater than zero.[11] In South Africa, search involves more physical effort and time on the part of black job-seekers who are less able to make use of modern communication facilities (e.g. telephones) than, say, American workers. Furthermore, their geographical and vertical mobility is limited by a variety of labour market restrictions and the many urban dwellers who do not possess the required documents are deterred from seeking work through the normal channels.

'Pure' voluntary unemployment

Traditionally defined,[12] 'involuntary unemployment' arises from a failure of the labour markets (however segmented) to clear and the solution is *to reduce wages*. By market-clearing, one simply means that at the prevailing wage rate,

---

* The term 'voluntary' is problematical and will be clarified below.

the number of man-hours on offer are equal to the number demanded. More loosely one could say that all who wish to work at their 'normal' wage — which changes and is not easily known in a heterogeneous labour market — are able to find employment. 'Involuntary unemployment' and market-clearing can co-exist only in the case of the perfectly elastic labour supply curve which, as argued below, is implausible. There is a school of thought, however, which, contrary to the conventional neo-classical approach, views the market as always in equilibrium.[13] Notwithstanding their arguments, the conventional concept of market-clearing will continue to be employed in this paper.

Since the opposite of 'involuntary' is 'voluntary', all 'non-involuntary' forms of unemployment are then termed 'voluntary'. Semantic problems inevitably arise. It is tautologically true to say that *subject to the constraints* all economic decisions are voluntary. Yet if the constraints are severe enough, the choice to be exercised becomes trivial. To describe someone whose mobility is by law confined to a poverty-stricken area which has the capacity to generate very little economic activity, as 'voluntarily' unemployed is clearly offensive (even though it may be *technically* correct) simply because it seems to ignore the constraints imposed upon such a person. None the less, the formulation of a labour supply curve (which is critical to any analysis of unemployment) cannot be accomplished in the absence of a choice-theoretic framework; hence the retention of the term 'voluntary', however severe the constraints.

'Structuralists' implicitly make the convenient but implausible assumption of a Keynesian rectangular labour supply curve (see Fig. 3 below). The horizontal segment is determined by a subsistence wage and the vertical segment by the number of able-bodied adults in the population (i.e. the size of the potential labour force). These assumptions are more or less implicit in Simkins's work.[14] It would seem that firstly, the perfectly elastic segment of the labour supply curve is empirically implausible (see Fig. 2(a) and my criticism of Arthur Lewis's model below); secondly, the size of the potential labour force always exceeds a given point on the labour supply curve (except perhaps under conditions of total mobilisation during wartime) and that this relationship would hold even in the absence of man-made and informational constraints (hence the term 'pure' voluntary unemployment); and thirdly, all labour supply curves are on a priori grounds positively sloped in their lower regions. Above certain wage rates their sign becomes theoretically indeterminate.

The shape of the labour supply curve is of critical importance in the South African debate, in particular the supply function pertaining to migrant workers. The mining companies and white farmers apparently enjoy exclusive recruiting rights in certain parts of the black homelands. Work on the mines is regarded as dangerous and unpleasant, and on the farms it is considered both unpleasant and very poorly remunerated. It may be perfectly 'rational' and understandable, under these circumstances, for black males to engage in the minimum amount of wage-employment required to subsist. The tribal farms alone cannot in most places generate sufficient real income to maintain and reproduce the extended family. Subsistence is possible, however, if some of the members supplement such income with wage-income from the mines and the white farms. In Lesotho, where land resources are poorer, more resort must be made to wage-employment on the mines. This may explain the tendency of Basotho to become career miners as opposed to the temporary stints engaged in by mine workers from the Transkei which is richer in agricultural resources.

These conditions suggest that the aggregate labour supply curve is positively sloped. The argument rests on several grounds: firstly, the wage sector must compete for labour with the traditional sector. In this sense, the labour supply curve is not genuinely aggregative but is in fact a *relative* supply function pertaining to the wage sector only. Relative supply functions are always positively sloped and highly elastic. (Labour force participation rates are generally low in less developed countries because given the shape and elasticity of the relative labour supply curve, the wage sector is too underdeveloped and wages too low to attract many peasants off the land.) Secondly, the empirical findings of R. Lucas and L. Rapping[15] suggest that the aggregate supply curve of 'intermittent' workers (such as American women and teenagers) tends to be positively sloped. The same is likely to hold for South African migrant workers although it remains to be empirically tested. Lastly (although this proves nothing about the shape of the *aggregate* labour supply curve), the existence of a large pool of 'involuntary' unemployed male workers is not consistent with the dramatic increase in wages on the gold mines, which was motivated by a policy decision to increase the South African component of their labour force.[16]

Institutionally induced unemployment

Government policy can cause measured unemployment to increase. In South Africa the most relevant of these policies is the extraordinary set of occupational and geographical restrictions on the mobility of black labour, official and unofficial. The point that needs to be made, however, is that restrictions in one segment of the labour market will not in itself prevent other segments from clearing, despite the spillovers into the latter. This principle may be illustrated in a simple 3-sector diagram (Fig. 1).

The effect of restrictions on the supply of migrant labour to the urban sector (Fig. 1A) must be seen together with the spillover of labour into the other sectors (Figs. 1B and 1C). It is difficult to ascertain, however, whether scarce labour in the former sector is a cause or effect of the spillover.

A. *The Quota Effect:* Let us assume that the quota system is a cause of the spillover. Figure 1A illustrates the market for migrant labour in the urban sector. In the absence of influx control, the supply curve is $SdcS_f$ and the demand curve DD. With influx control, the supply curve becomes vertical at the level of the quota OQ_c. The controlled supply curve is kinked, SdS_c. In the absence of influx control, OQ workers (or man-hours) would be employed at wage rate

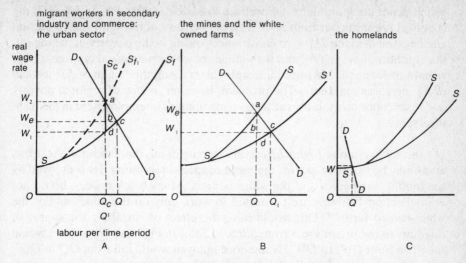

Figure 1 IMPACT OF INFLUX CONTROL ON THREE SEGMENTED
         MIGRANT LABOUR MARKETS

OW_e. With SdS_c in operation, the numbers employed fall to OQ_c. The dead-weight welfare loss is approximated by triangle acd. Under competitive conditions, the wage rate would rise to OW_2, compensating workers to a greater or lesser extent W_2abWe for their loss of welfare bcd. Under monopsonistic conditions, the wage rate could fall to OW_1, with the transfer $WebdW_1$ compensating employers for their loss of surplus abc. To establish a case for the monopsony view, one would have to construct a model based on a given method of recruiting. For example, if each firm went with a limited quota to a vast pool of labour (homelands) and offered the lowest wage necessary to fill the quota, the monopsony view would have some validity. We assume realistically that migrants are not permitted to change jobs during their contract in the urban areas. Thus competition for migrants still under contract is effectively ruled out. Given Section 10(I)(d) of the Black (Urban Areas) Consolidation Act and the Black Labour Regulations Act of 1953, the analysis is probably a fair approximation of the South African case, particularly in the Western Cape. The matter merits further elaboration but since it is of secondary importance to the wider issue, it will not be pursued here.

It may be mentioned that an indeterminate part of the rectangle W_2adW_1 may be used up in bribes ('rent-seeking'). In this case, influx control officials may be bribed by employers seeking larger quotas. Furthermore, the supply curve of illegal migrants will contain no vertical segment. The diagram, however, includes only legal migrants.

The restrictions on supply in Fig. 1A also cause a spillover effect into the other sectors. In Fig. 1B the supply curve shifts forward from SaS to $SdcS^1$, thereby lowering the wage rate from OW_e to OW_1. There is a welfare gain $abdc$

31

which is not comparable to the welfare loss *abdc* in Fig. 1A. In Fig. 1C, the supply curve shifts out from SS to SS^1, but because of its highly elastic section and because demand DD is so constrained, owing to the poverty of the region, the equilibrium wage OW and the number of workers engaged in wage-labour remain unchanged. Measured unemployment along the length of SS^1 instead of SS increases markedly. The problem, however, is one of regional poverty and restrictions on mobility rather than involuntary unemployment in the technical sense.

B. *Special Recruiting Rights Effect:* the scarcity of migrant labour in the urban areas may be, to some extent, the *result* of special recruiting rights enjoyed by the mining companies and the white farmers. Many black males who do not enjoy Section 10 rights are permitted to work only on the mines and/or the white-owned farms.* This would have the effect of curtailing the supply of migrants to the urban areas from $SdcS_f$ to SaS_{f1} in Fig. 1A. Wage rates would then rise from OW_e to OW_2. Numbers employed would fall from OQ to OQ^1. (which is only coincidentally the same as OQ_c).

The final outcome will be determined by the combined recruiting and quota effects. In the above diagram, for example, the special recruiting rights effect exactly outweighs the quota effect. In general, the matter remains an open empirical question.

2. OTHER NOTIONS OF STRUCTURAL UNEMPLOYMENT:
   ## A CRITIQUE

The previous three subsections attempted to establish that all manifestations of long-term unemployment can be adequately analysed within the framework of the Natural Rate Hypothesis. We now proceed to examine why notions of 'structural' or long-term 'involuntary' unemployment are, in the absence of artificial restrictions, inconsistent with maximising behaviour.

Various writers[17] have stressed the 'structural' nature of unemployment in South Africa. If by 'structural', they mean merely that labour markets are distorted by artificial restrictions, such as influx control, etc., then on this point there is no cause for disagreement. Such distortions have been analysed in the previous section by using simple supply and demand analysis.

However, proponents of the concept claim that structural unemployment is only partly accounted for by government restrictions. After all, in many developing countries where artificial restrictions on the mobility of labour are absent, measured unemployment is also high.

The concept of 'structural unemployment' draws its theoretical support from

---

* Institutional details are exceedingly difficult to obtain. Furthermore, one would like to know how easily these arrangements can be circumvented.

various different quarters. Firstly, there is the vaguely neo-classical approach found in some of the 'development economics' literature.[18]

There are basically two lines of argument here. The first, in the tradition of Arthur Lewis's dualistic models, rests on a labour supply function that is in part perfectly elastic. The demand curve intersects the horizontal segment of the supply curve (see Fig. 2A).

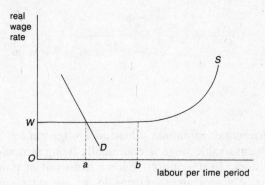

Figure 2A

According to the Pigovian definition of the term,[19] there exists 'involuntary unemployment', measured by the distance *ab* on the horizontal axis. Although a *perfectly* elastic supply curve is theoretically possible, it is empirically implausible. It implies that there is a unique wage rate at which all workers simultaneously leave. Each worker coincidentally has the same reserve price, the same utility function, the same asset-holding, the same degree of support from relatives. In the case of migrants, where transport costs have been used to argue the case for a horizontal supply curve, each worker must face the same transport cost and therefore each place of residence in the rural areas should be equidistant from the place of work concerned.

The second line of argument depends on a minimum subsistence wage (see Fig. 2B).

In Fig. 2B (p. 34) *W* constitutes the minimum subsistence wage. The excess supply of labour *ab* fails to depress wages below *W*. Why this is so is not clear. Structural or long-term involuntary unemployment is measured by the distance *ab*. The argument arouses one's scepticism on a number of counts. Firstly, the subsistence wage is exceedingly low and it is unlikely that wages in South Africa, although they are very low by Western standards, are anywhere near subsistence despite the notion of the Poverty Datum Line. In many other developing countries, wage rates are much lower. Secondly, there may exist a

33

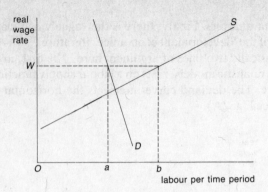

Figure 2B

sociologically determined minimum subsistence wage but one's sense of what constitutes a decent livable wage is continually being remoulded by feasible economic conditions. Furthermore, if some firms out of moral suasion pay higher than 'normal' wages but other firms do not, the extra supply of labour in the latter sector will simply depress wage rates there, that is, assuming that the 'enlightened' firms maximise profits subject to the higher than 'normal' wages (i.e. reduce employment, substitute capital, etc.). Either way, the labour markets will clear.

Other proponents of the notion of structural unemployment, especially those who apply it to South Africa, depart radically from neo-classical premises. The apparent 'structural' nature of long-run unemployment is attributed to certain alleged shortcomings of the market mechanism. These shortcomings are, in turn, related to (1) the apparently inappropriate choice of techniques and (2) deficient aggregate demand. These points will now be briefly dealt with.

The reliance on 'choice of technique' as a determinant of the aggregate level of employment commits the old and fundamental error of confusing partial with general equilibrium analysis and individual with aggregate phenomena. Whereas the individual firm, to a large extent, takes the prices of factors and commodities as given, its actions together with the actions of all other firms in the economy create new realities and new prices. In the long run, firms will choose the appropriate (i.e. the most profitable) technique (capital-labour mix) in accordance with their expectation of relative factor prices.

In the view of many structuralists, sophisticated machines that employ less labour per machine are responsible for putting people out of work. Sophisticated machinery is assumed to be more profitable and therefore more desirable from the firm's point of view but unemployment is alleged to be aggravated. Why the excess supply of labour should not lead to a change in relative factor prices and therefore in the profitability of the sophisticated machinery itself, is not adequately explained. None the less, structuralists are inclined to view a switch to labour-intensive techniques as, at least, a partial solution to the 'unemployment problem'.

Underlying the structuralists' view of the labour market is an implicit conception of the individual firm as having a fixed amount of capital and fixed factor coefficients. The firm's demand for labour is viewed not as a function of the wage rate but of the number and type of machines installed. This, combined with a labour supply function unrelated to real wages, produces a peculiar picture of the labour market, of which Fig. 3 is an extreme, perhaps caricatured, example.

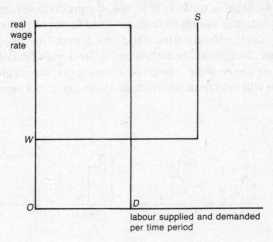

Figure 3

Unemployment in Fig. 3 is measured by the horizontal distance between the vertical segments of the two curves, and as can be seen, the imbalance cannot be resolved by changing the wage rate OW.

The nature of the labour supply function has already been dealt with in the previous subsections. It is now my purpose to demonstrate that the structuralists' view of the demand for labour is also fallacious and that an ordinary downward-sloping curve is appropriate. Hence, market-clearing is inevitable.

In an open economy such as that of South Africa, it is easy enough to argue the case. International markets are highly competitive and so, by cutting prices and hence costs marginally (i.e. including wages), South Africa could increase her exports and hence her output substantially, thereby increasing the local demand for labour (although, given a positively sloped labour supply curve, at these lower wage rates the extra labour demanded could be difficult to recruit). This analysis is consistent with the monetary approach to the balance of payments. None the less the author will, for the sake of argument, submit to more stringent assumptions and work within a closed-economy framework.

It is quite obvious that, in the short run, labour and capital are not perfectly substitutable. Once a certain technology has been installed, a firm may find it costly to change its techniques of production in response to a change in real wages. With fixed factor coefficients, this implies that the firm's demand for labour will remain relatively unaffected. However, when *new* decisions regarding appropriate techniques are made, the choice *will depend* on expected factor prices. Hence, in the long run, the demand for labour remains a function of the real wage rate.

It is sometimes argued, however, that even in the long run the range of alternative techniques is limited. A particular commodity may, for example, be produced in only two or three ways. In that case, the production function is discontinuous. Given extreme assumptions about fixed factor coefficients and a fixed level and composition of final output, the firm's demand for labour will be unresponsive to wage changes within certain limits. Its demand curve will therefore be kinked. *Even under these restrictive assumptions*, the aggregate demand curve for labour will tend to smooth out, as illustrated in the aggregate diagram in Fig. 4.

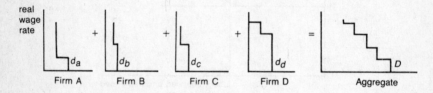

Figure 4

Real wages are measured vertically and the demand for labour horizontally. The 'severely' kinked demand curves (*d*) for each of the four firms A-D are summed to produce a much smoother aggregate demand curve (*D*). The greater the number of individual firms and alternative techniques of production, the smoother will be the aggregate curve. For good results, kinks in the individual demand curves must be randomly distributed in relation to real wages. However, most non-random distributions will still produce 'reasonable' results unless the kinks coincide uniquely.

Finally, the aim is to demonstrate that even under the most restrictive assumption, namely that there exists only one technique for the production of each good, the aggregate demand function for labour emerges as a conventional downward-sloping curve. We retain the assumption about fixed factor coefficients though we ultimately relax our assumption about a fixed level and composition of final output. In Fig. 5(a) we find that the firm has, *for a given level of output*, a totally inelastic demand curve for labour. We now assume that the wage (as a result of, say, population increase) falls from OW to OW_1. At the existing level of output, the wage reduction fails to induce the firm to hire additional labourers (or man-hours). However, the increase in the labour

36

supply pushes the production possibility frontier of the economy (in Fig. 5(b)) outwards and, more significantly, increases the *relative* profits of the labour-intensive industries. A re-allocation of resources away from capital-intensive towards labour-intensive sectors occurs and this is illustrated as a movement from *m* to *n* in Fig. 5(b). Compounding the effect of the overall increase in the level of aggregate output, the shift from *m* to *n* causes an additional increase in the demand for labour. Thus we see, as in Fig. 5(c), that the aggregate demand curve for labour is downward-sloping and that a fall in wages from OW to OW_1 increases the overall demand for labour from Oa to Ob.

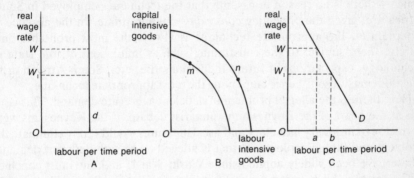

Figure 5

The purpose of these exercises is merely to show that, even under absurdly restrictive assumptions, the demand for labour is a negative function of real wages. Thus the labour market tends always to clear in the long run.

It may occur that technological innovation renders *certain kinds* of workers redundant. The workers concerned can, however, find employment in other sectors of the labour market, albeit at lower wages. Wassily Leontief,[20] for one, disagrees. He asks why, if displaced workers are assumed to find work in another segment of the labour market at *some* wage, did draft horses fail to find employment at some price when they were ousted by the motorcar. My reply rests on two points. Firstly, workers are far more substitutable for one another than horses are for cars, particularly in the long run. Admittedly, in the short run a redundant worker may lack the skills to compete effectively in many sectors of the labour market (although there is always the unskilled sector). However, with retraining — without underestimating the problems involved — he *can acquire* the requisite skills. A horse, however, cannot be trained to become a motorcar! If, by genetic mutation, we could breed a super-worker, ordinary workers might find themselves in serious trouble. Then only would the situation be comparable. My second point rests on the long-run complementarity between capital and labour. Although the introduction of new techniques may displace *some* workers in the short term, the accumulation of capital has the effect of raising the productivity of labour, not to mention the

37

employment opportunities afforded by the need to manufacture the equipment in the first place. Motorcars, however, do not raise the productivity of horses. Horses can be used neither to drive nor to manufacture them. In no reasonable way can they be regarded as complementary to one another.

From the above arguments we may deduce that the choice of technique, however 'inappropriate', has no significant long-term effect on the level of employment although it may substantially affect relative wages, profitability, growth, etc., thereby indirectly influencing the labour force participation rate. Furthermore — although this is of peripheral importance to the unemployment issue — there is no reason to assume that the techniques employed in South Africa are, given the prevailing *constraints*, inappropriate. In the absence of externalities, the appropriate technique is always the most profitable one. Surely, then, subject to the constraints, such as influx control, the state of technology, expectations of future industrial strife, etc., South African firms are profit maximisers, hence employing the most appropriate techniques.

Next there is the alleged problem of deficient aggregate demand. This issue lies at the heart of the Keynesian/monetarist debate. If the Keynesians were correct, expansionary monetary and fiscal measures would surely eliminate the problem and the unemployment that is alleged to go with deficient demand. These have been widely applied since World War II and one must conclude that since they have ended generally in higher inflation, the problem can be attributed to anything but deficient demand. Either way, Keynesian or monetarist, there is no serious argument in respect of structural unemployment. Deficient demand in the commodity market proves nothing about the workings of the labour market.

3. CONCLUSION

The term 'structural unemployment' is vague and imprecise and, as such, fails to meet the task at hand, which is to reconcile Simkins's findings of permanently high levels of measured unemployment with economic theory. Supply and demand analysis suggests that markets clear (at least in the long run) by means of adjustments in real prices (wages). If this is so (and all my arguments rest on this premise) then it appears that Simkins's findings are by and large measures *not* of 'involuntary' unemployment but of what E.S. Phelps and others term 'the natural rate' or alternatively, one minus the labour force participation rate. The natural rate is rather high in South Africa (even in terms of the estimates of the Current Population Survey) partly on account of influx control measures (particularly in the case of black women) and the complex system of labour bureaux, and partly on account of the higher costs of search in a less developed and highly bureaucratized economy. Furthermore, labour force participation in the wage sector is generally found to be low in less developed countries, particularly where the traditional and informal sectors provide alternative employment.

With regard to alternative and competing notions of structural unemployment this paper has endeavoured to show (in Section 2) that the hypothesis of 'technological unemployment' (i.e. long-term 'involuntary' unemployment arising from an inappropriate choice of production techniques) is entirely inconsistent with economic theory (at least, of the neo-classical type) unless exceedingly restrictive and implausible assumptions are made.

The general argument in this paper has essentially rested on three points, which are of critical importance in any analysis of unemployment: firstly, that the aggregate demand curve for labour is conventionally downward-sloping and is inversely related to real wages; secondly, that the aggregate labour supply curve is not *perfectly* elastic at any point and, in particular, is not a rectangular curve — though it does *not* have to be positively sloped throughout its length, and thirdly, that the labour market (like all other markets) is able to clear itself in the long run through adjustments in real wages.

Lastly, the author wishes to qualify this paper in two ways. Firstly, its purpose has been to reassert basic theoretical principles that ought to underpin any discussion of unemployment in South Africa or elsewhere. In doing so, the author has tended to overlook the institutional complexity of the South African labour market. In particular, the paper has neglected the possibility of 'speculative unemployment'* that is used by J.R. Harris and M.P. Todaro[21] to explain the phenomenon of persistent urban unemployment in developing countries where influx control measures are *not* in force. Their analysis may be especially relevant to the South African case on account of the peculiarities of the local system of labour bureaux. Secondly, the author wishes to emphasise that the analysis presented in this paper applies essentially to *long-term* unemployment. The short-term phenomenon, which primarily concerns cyclical fluctuations in the level of employment, is a different and far more complicated matter, in respect of which there is very little consensus even among relatively orthodox economists.[22]

---

* The term is the author's own and refers to the possibility that workers refuse work on offer in a low-wage sector because accepting such work may diminish their chance of eventually obtaining work in other sectors where wages are, for some or other reason, 'artificially' high.

NOTES

1 Machlup, F., *Essays in Economic Semantics*. Englewood Cliffs, N.J.: Prentice-Hall, 1963.
2 *Inter alia*, Simkins, C.E.W., 'Measuring and Predicting Unemployment in South Africa, 1960–1977' in Simkins, C.E.W. and Clarke, D.G. (eds), *Structural Unemployment in Southern Africa*. Durban: Natal University Press, 1978.
The *Current Population Survey*, Department of Statistics, October 1977 results in Statistical News Release, p. 27.
These and other important related work are summarised in: Bromberger, N., 'South African Unemployment: A Survey of Research', in Simkins, C.E.W. and Desmond, C. (eds), *Unemployment in South Africa: A Black Picture*. Agency for Industrial Mission and Development Studies Research Group, University of Natal, 1978.

3 Simkins, C.E.W., *op. cit.*, Table 20.
4 De Klerk, M., 'Structural Unemployment in South Africa', *South African Outlook*, March 1979. Maree, J., 'The Dimensions and Causes of Unemployment and Underemployment in South Africa', *South African Labour Bulletin*, Vol. 4, No. 4, July 1978.
   Erwin, A., 'An Essay on Structural Unemployment', *South African Labour Bulletin*, Vol. 4, No. 4, July 1978.
5 De Klerk, M., *op. cit.;* Erwin, A., *op. cit.*
6 Simkins, C.E.W., *op. cit.*, Table 20.
7 Grubel, H.G., 'What is Full Employment?' Unpublished paper, p. 2.
8 The *Current Population Survey, op. cit.*
9 Friedman, M., 'The Role of Monetary Policy', *American Economic Review*, Vol. 58, March 1968, No. 1, p. 8. (Presidential address delivered at 80th annual meeting of the American Economic Association, Washington D.C., 29 December 1967.)
10 Alchian, A., 'Information Costs, Pricing and Resource Unemployment', in Phelps, E.S. (ed.), *Microeconomic Foundations of Employment and Inflation Theory*. New York: W.W. Norton. 1970.
11 Gordon, R.J. 'Recent Developments in the Theory of Inflation and Unemployment', in Lundberg, E. (ed.), *Inflation Theory and Anti-inflation Policy*. London: Macmillan, 1976.
12 Pigou, A.C., *Unemployment*. New York: Holt & Co., 1914.
   Pigou, A.C., *The Theory of Unemployment*. London: Macmillan, 1933.
   Kahn, R., 'Unemployment as seen by the Keynesians', in Worswick, G.D.N. (ed.), *The Concept and Measurement of Involuntary Unemployment*. London: George Allen & Unwin, 1976.
13 Cheung, S.N.S., 'A Theory of Price Control', *Journal of Law and Economics*, Vol. 17(1), April 1974, pp. 54–56.
14 Simkins, C.E.W., *op. cit.*
15 Lucas, R.E. and Rapping, L.A., 'Real Wages, Employment and Inflation', *Journal of Political Economy*, Vol. 77, 1969, p. 721, footnote 1. They cite other works in this connection, among others Long, C.D., *The Labour Force under Changing Income and Employment*. Princeton, N.J.: Princeton University Press, 1958.
   Mincer, J., 'Labour Force Participation of Married Women', in Lewis, H.G. (ed.), *Aspects of Labour Economics*. Princeton, N.J.: Princeton University Press, 1962.
   Bowen, W.G. and Finegan, T.A., 'Labour Force Participation and Unemployment', in Ross, A.M. (ed.), *Employment Policy and the Labour Market*. Berkeley: University of California, 1965.
   Cain, G., *Married Women in the Labour Force: An Economic Analysis*. Chicago: University of Chicago Press, 1966.
16 *Employment Bureau of Africa,* Chamber of Mines, 1971–78. In 1971, the total black labour force on the mines numbered 386 000, of which the South African component (including Transkei, etc.) constituted 86 464 or 22,4 per cent. By 1977 these figures had increased respectively to 422 000 and 213 954 or 50,7 per cent.
17 De Klerk, M., *op. cit.;* Maree, J., *op cit.;* Erwin, A., *op cit.*
18 Fei, J.C.H. and Ranis, G., *Development of the Labour Surplus Economy, Theory and Policy*. Homewood, III: Richard D. Irwin, 1964.
   Lewis, W.A., 'Economic Development with Unlimited Supplies of Labour', *The Manchester School*, Vol. 22, No. 2, May 1954.
19 Pigou, A.C., *op. cit.*
20 Leontief, W., 'Issues of the Coming Years', *Economic Impact,* No. 24, 1978/4, pp. 75–76.
21 Harris, J.R. and Todaro, M.P., 'Migration, Unemployment and Development: A Two-Sector Analysis', *American Economic Review,* Vol. 60, 1970, pp. 126–42.
22 Among economists who argue that the labour market clears even in the short run and that all markets are in continuous equilibrium are K. Brunner and A.H. Meltzer.
   Brunner, K. and Meltzer, A.H., *Monetary Theory* (unpublished). Chapter 4, 'The Theory of

Employment and Unemployment'. Presented at the Konstanz Seminar, May 1978.
Among economists who argue to the contrary that labour markets fail to clear in the short run and that real wages are inflexible downwards in the short term (money wages being absolutely rigid downwards) are:

Gordon, R.J., *op. cit.;* Solow, R.M., 'On Theories of Unemployment', *American Economic Review,* Vol. 70, No. 1, March 1980. Presidential address delivered at the 92nd meeting of the American Economic Association, 29 December 1979.

1.4 UNEMPLOYMENT AND UNDEREMPLOYMENT

P.A. Black*

I

The problem of unemployment in South Africa has become a source of much debate amongst the academic fraternity in this country. There is little agreement over the actual size of the problem itself, or on the question of whether it is voluntary or involuntary, cyclical or structural or, indeed, whether it should be viewed as a matter of concern in the first place. A good deal of the discussion has been of a purely definitional and procedural nature, but recent contributions reflect a more fundamental difference of opinion about the speed with which markets adjust to changing demand and supply conditions.

In his analysis of unemployment in South Africa, Gerson (in this volume) adopts a strict neo-classical position claiming that 'the labour market tends always to clear in the long run'. He argues that 'surplus labour' and technological unemployment seldom exist at the aggregate level, and dismisses the 'efficiency wage' and 'labour turnover' hypotheses as mere *a priori* suggestions' (1982, p. 67). Even institutional restrictions need not create involuntary unemployment because workers can always find employment in markets where wages are completely flexible. Unemployment in South Africa is thus considered to be largely voluntary while the problem of 'regional poverty' is caused by institutional factors that are *external* to the market.

The market-clearing notion, on which much of Gerson's analysis depends, is largely a matter of faith: no one really knows the extent to which reservation wages might vary amongst individual workers, or whether the technical co-efficients of production and efficiency wages differ significantly between firms. Even if they did vary in practice, it would require something of a conjectural leap to conclude that the aggregate demand and supply schedules are therefore 'normally shaped'. At any rate, Gerson's argument tends to shift the focus of the debate away from what is arguably the most important feature of the labour market in South Africa, namely, the growing number of people who are *inadequately* employed.

In a recent article published in the *South African Journal of Economics*, Bell (1985, p. 29) argued that adjustments in the labour market can be 'exceedingly protracted' because of the need for extensive retraining and the inflexibility of real wages. The fact that a skilled person may choose not to accept an inferior job represents 'a real social problem' (p. 33), irrespective of whether he is deemed to be voluntarily unemployed or underemployed. As far as the demand for labour is concerned, Knight (1982) has given several reasons why (modern sector) wages may exceed the supply price of labour. These include

* Professor of Economics, University of Stellenbosch.

the 'efficiency wage' hypothesis (Leibenstein, 1957; Stiglitz, 1976), the 'labour turnover' argument (Stiglitz, 1974) and the fact that employers may be effectively compelled to raise wages above a socially acceptable minimum level. While such arguments do not preclude the possible existence of market-clearing wages in certain parts of the economy, such as the subsistent agricultural and informal sectors, they do suggest that many people in these sectors may be involuntarily *underemployed*.

II

It is generally known that the South African economy has been growing more slowly during the past fifteen years than at any time during the preceding two decades and that the supply of labour has grown more rapidly than demand over most of this period. It must therefore follow that a growing percentage of the labour force has been unable to secure wage employment in the modern sector of the economy. While some job-seekers would have become openly unemployed insofar as they could rely on charitable hand-outs from relatives, friends and the state, the vast majority have presumably had to eke out an existence in the traditional agricultural and urban informal sectors. It matters very little whether these people are considered to be unemployed in a voluntary or involuntary sense, or whether their marginal existence is blamed on cyclical downturns or frictional and structural constraints in the labour market. In a dynamic setting characterised by successive shocks to the system, it would be virtually impossible to distinguish between cyclical and structural unemployment, or to specify the relative importance of institutional and market-related forces in determining the size of frictional and structural unemployment.

The fact is that we are dealing with a problem of *growing* poverty which is a direct consequence of the inability of the modern sector to provide sufficient job opportunities for the rising number of work-seekers (Bell, 1985). In the absence of an adequate public support system, many have been forced to join the ranks of the 'working poor' where they usually end up working fewer hours for less pay than their counterparts in the formal sector. If these persons do not consider it worth while to search for formal job opportunities, they are bound to be excluded from the official estimates of unemployment. This fact alone does not, of course, imply that they are adequately employed, either in terms of the number of hours worked or in the sense of earning an income commensurate with their formal qualifications, experience and level of skill.

III

The above situation can be illustrated with the aid of Figure 1, where the labour market is divided into a formal (or 'primary') and informal (or 'secondary') sector. The formal-sector wage, w_f, is assumed to be at a minimum level being determined on the demand side for reasons relating to labour efficiency, customary procedures, moral suasion and the like, or on the supply side by government decree or union pressure. The supply of labour comprises OC labourers, each of whom wishes to work OG/OC hours to supply a total of OG hours. This exceeds the demand for labour in the formal sector which, at the prevailing wage rate, consists of OA labourers each working OE/OA $(= OG/OC)$ hours. The difference is AC labourers (or EG hours), of whom AB are assumed to be underemployed in the informal sector and BC are openly unemployed.

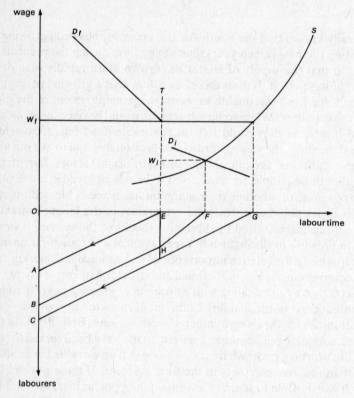

Figure 1

Capital formation in the informal sector — albeit on a limited scale only — creates a demand for labour, D_i, drawn with respect to the axis labelled TE in Figure 1. Its intersection with the supply schedule determines the informal wage rate, w_i, which is smaller than the average wage in the formal sector. At w_i a total of $AB = EH$ labourers each works for EF/EH hours which, in this example, are smaller than the average number of hours worked in the formal sector. People in the informal sector are therefore assumed to work fewer hours at a lower hourly wage rate than workers with similar skills in the formal sector.

44

Although the above analysis may be considered too aggregative to be of much use, it does at least suggest the possible existence of vast discrepancies in the conditions of work between the formal and informal sectors. From a dynamic perspective as well, it stands to reason that continuous increases in the supply relative to demand for formal labour will boost both the number of unemployed persons and the working poor in the informal sector.

IV

As far as the South African economy is concerned, Bell (1985) has recently revised Simkins's (1978; 1982) estimates and found that his (composite) unemployment rate rose from 16,2 per cent to 22,5 per cent during the period 1974–82. Likewise, Professor Sadie[1] estimates that the modern sector could only accommodate 7,9 million people or approximately 62 per cent of the total labour force in 1987. Of the remainder, some 1,9 million persons were considered to be openly unemployed and 2,9 million underemployed, representing approximately 15 per cent and 23 per cent of the labour force respectively. These figures are similar to the findings of several recent surveys conducted amongst unemployed persons (CSS, 1988) and people engaged in informal activities (Kirsten, 1988). While very little is known about working conditions in the informal sector, there is a strong suspicion that informal entrepreneurs earn a good deal less than people with similar skills in the formal sector (e.g. Du Plessis and Levin, 1986).

In the light of these findings, it would appear that there is an urgent need for further research into the nature of informal support systems and the working conditions of people outside the modern sector of the South African economy. Such efforts may well provide the necessary supportive evidence for what is already generally accepted, namely, that unemployment in South Africa — as conventionally defined — is merely the visible part of a much bigger problem.

NOTE

1 In private conversation.

REFERENCES

Bell, R.T., 1985. 'Issues in South African Unemployment', *South African Journal of Economics*, Vol. 53, No. 1.

Central Statistical Services (CSS), 1988. *Current Population Survey*, Statistical News Release, P 0344, Government Printer, September.

Du Plessis, A.P. and Levin, M., 1986. *The Informal Sector in Coloured Residential Areas in Port Elizabeth*, Research Report No. 5, Employment Research Unit, Vista University.

Gerson, J., 1982. 'Reply to Mr Knight', *South African Journal of Economics*, Vol. 50, No. 1.

Kirsten, M., 1988. 'n Kwalitatiewe en Kwantitatiewe Perspektief op die Informele Sektor, Mimeo, Department of Economics, University of Stellenbosch.

Knight, J.B., 1982. 'The Nature of Unemployment in South Africa', *South African Journal of Economics*, Vol. 50, No. 1.

Leibenstein, H., 1957. 'Underemployment in Backward Economies', *Journal of Political Economy,* Vol. 66.

Simkins, C.E.W., 1978. 'Measuring and Predicting Unemployment in South Africa, 1960–1977', in C.E.W. Simkins and D.G. Clarke, *Structural Unemployment in Southern Africa.* Pietermaritzburg: Natal University Press.

—— 1982. 'Structural Unemployment Revisited: A Revision and Updating of Earlier Estimates Incorporating New Data from the Current Population Survey and the 1980 Population Census'. Cape Town: South African Labour and Development Research Unit.

Stiglitz, J.E., 1974. 'Alternative Theories of Wage Determination and Unemployment in LDCs: The Labour Turnover Model', *Quarterly Journal of Economics*, Vol. 88, No. 2.

—— 1976. 'The Efficiency Wage Hypothesis, Surplus Labour and the Distribution of Labour in LDCs', *Oxford Economic Papers*, Vol. 28.

2

Inflation

2.1 INTRODUCTION

Inflation is customarily defined as a continual or persistent rise in the general level of prices. Thus, inflation refers to the rate of increase in the general price level, and not to a high level of prices *per se* or to changes in relative prices. Generally, inflation is measured in terms of price indexes such as the consumer price index and the producer price index, both of which are published in the South African Reserve Bank's *Quarterly Bulletin of Statistics*. Although the rate of increase in the level of prices, as measured in terms of an appropriate price index, is an acceptable estimate of inflation, to the economist inflation in strict terms refers to the persistent decrease in the quantity and quality of goods and services that can be purchased with a rand.

The table below provides some idea of the magnitude of the problem of inflation in South Africa since 1970, measured in terms of the consumer price index.

PERCENTAGE CHANGE IN CONSUMER PRICE INDEX 1970–1987

Year	%	Year	%
1970	4,2	1979	13,3
1971	6,1	1980	13,8
1972	6,5	1981	15,2
1973	9,6	1982	14,7
1974	11,6	1983	12,3
1975	13,4	1984	11,7
1976	11,1	1985	16,2
1977	11,3	1986	18,6
1978	10,9	1987	16,1

Source: South African Reserve Bank, *Quarterly Bulletin of Statistics*. Quarterly changes seasonally adjusted.

An examination of the data presented in the table shows clearly that since the early 1970s inflation in South Africa has shown a tendency to accelerate. Indeed, from 1974 onwards South Africans have experienced double-digit inflation of varying degrees of severity. This contrasts rather starkly with an annual inflation rate of 3,5 per cent in the 1950s and 2,7 per cent in the 1960s. Moreover, from about the middle of the seventies the nature of the rate of increase in the general price level appears to have changed. Specifically, the rate of inflation no longer seems to correlate with the level of economic activity: prices do not fall significantly during periods of recession nor rise during boom periods. This situation is referred to as the phenomenon of stagflation, or the co-existence of high rates of inflation together with low levels of economic growth, and the consequent underutilisation of productive capacity and high levels of unemployment.

The complex nature of inflation, both in South Africa and abroad, defies ready explanation. Economists do not agree on its causes, processes or consequences, and this disagreement has led to a proliferation of theories. One method of organising the large number of theories purporting to deal with inflation is to distinguish between inertial or core inflation, demand-pull inflation, and cost-push inflation.

A characteristic feature of inflation in modern times is its tendency to proceed at some historical rate. Consumers, firms and workers expect this inflation rate to continue at its present level, and consequently enter into contracts and other informal arrangements on the basis of this anticipated or core rate of inflation. As long as expectations of a given rate of inflation prevail, they can become self-fulfilling.

Whilst notions of an inertial or core rate of inflation can explain its persistence over time, they obviously cannot account for fluctuations in the inflation rate. In order to understand why the core rate of inflation changes through time, it is thus necessary to develop theories which can explain these changes.

Changes in the rate of inflation have traditionally been explained in terms of either demand-pull factors or cost-push factors. Demand-pull theories of inflation all rest on the same basic proposition: if aggregate demand exceeds aggregate supply, then the general level of prices in an economy will rise to accommodate this excess demand. Thus the cause of an increase in inflation resides in the demand side of the macroeconomy. Despite some disagreement on the nature of the equilibrating forces involved, Keynesians, monetarists and exponents of the rational expectations school are in general accord on demand-pull induced inflation. However, since inflationary episodes in the real world often occur in the absence of high levels of aggregate demand, it is clear that demand-pull theories of inflation do not provide a comprehensive explanation of inflation.

Cost-push theories of inflation attempt to account for persistent increases in the general level of prices which occur in periods when resources are underemployed; that is, when costs rather than demand factors push up prices. Cost-push or non-monetary theories of inflation all assume a degree of monopoly power in one or more of the major markets of the macroeconomy. Thus one line of reasoning sees trade unions as causing wage-push inflation where real

48

wages increase faster than productivity growth. Similarly, high degrees of economic concentration in the business sector are claimed to result in profit-push inflation. The interplay of monopoly power in labour and output markets is often viewed as the primary cause of wage–price spirals and, consequently, of changes in the core rate of inflation.

Although the traditional distinction between demand-pull and cost-push factors may be helpful in identifying the root causes of inflation, in practice and in theory the distinction often becomes blurred. Cost-push inflation cannot be divorced from the demand side of the economy, and indeed depends for its continued existence on accommodating increases in the money supply. Likewise, demand-pull inflation cannot exist unless accompanied by induced increases in the costs of production.

In the first of the four readings in this chapter, Philip Mohr identifies the main approaches to the analysis of the problem of inflation, places them in a South African context, and indicates the policy implications of each approach. In so doing, he stresses the need for an eclectic approach to inflation which incorporates elements drawn from various theoretical perspectives. In the second reading Brian Kantor presents a monetarist explanation of the inflationary process in South Africa. According to the monetarist school, inflation is essentially a monetary phenomenon brought about by expansionary monetary and fiscal policies. The solution to the problem thus lies in a concerted effort to curb the growth of the money supply, and to maintain it at a rate consistent with the growth of productivity in the economy.

By way of contrast, Fourie investigates the relationship between market power in output markets and the rate of inflation in South Africa; that is, whether firms in economically concentrated or monopolised industries can induce inflationary pressures through profit-push behaviour, or what economists term the administered price hypothesis. Likewise, the final paper in this chapter by Meyer views the question of inflation in a rather broader light by examining both the structuralist and sociological approaches. In essence, the structuralist approach views inflation in developing countries as being caused by the rapid promotion of economic growth in the face of severe structural constraints, which include an inelastic supply of food, continuing shortages of foreign exchange, and government budget constraints. Sociological theories, on the other hand, focus *inter alia* on the institutional underpinnings of inflation, the impact of rising expectations in a world of relative scarcity, and the politically induced behaviour of interest groups in society.

2.2 PERSPECTIVES ON INFLATION IN SOUTH AFRICA
P.J. Mohr*

Inflation has undoubtedly become one of the most contested areas in macro-economics in recent decades: a plethora of theoretical approaches have been advanced in an effort to explain this complex phenomenon. Moreover, the debate surrounding the origins and impact of inflation has vital implications for the conduct of macroeconomic policy in South Africa — a country which has experienced high and rising rates of inflation since the early 1970s.

This paper attempts to place the debate on inflation in perspective by examining four major views and their implications for macroeconomic policy prescription. Section 1 sets out the conventional monetarist view on inflation, while the Keynesian distinction between demand-pull and cost-push inflation is dealt with in Section 2. Section 3 investigates the structuralist conception of inflation and, in the final section, emphasis falls on the modern conflict approach. Throughout the paper explicit attention is paid to the phenomenon of inflation in the South African economy in order to highlight the relevance of the four main approaches to local experience.

1. MONEY AND INFLATION: THE MONETARIST APPROACH

Monetarists assert that inflation is a monetary phenomenon, in the sense that sustained high rates of monetary growth *cause* high inflation, and that low rates of monetary growth will eventually produce low inflation. In other words, they contend that high rates of inflation cannot be sustained without persistently high rates of money growth. This view is based on the quantity theory of money, which, in turn, is based on the Equation or (more precisely) the Equality of Exchange. We now explain how the monetarists argue their case.

We begin with the *income velocity of money, V,* which represents the number of times the nominal money stock is turned over per year in financing the annual flow of income. Thus, if the nominal national income PY during a particular year is R100 billion and the nominal money stock M averages R20 billion, then the income velocity of money V is $100 \div 20 = 5$. We therefore write:

$$V = \frac{PY}{M} \tag{1}$$

Note that we are now interested in *nominal (or money) variables* and that we therefore consider the nominal value of national income PY, which is the

---

* Professor of Economics, University of South Africa. This paper is a revised version of part of Chapter 8 in Mohr and Rogers (1987).

product of the price level P and the real national income Y, and not only the latter.

Identity (1), the definition of V, can be rewritten as:

$$MV = PY \tag{2}$$

Identity (2) is often presented as the *quantity equation*, which links the product of the price level and the level of the real output to the money supply. It is, however, only an identity. To transform it into an equation, and into a theory of the price level, three assumptions are made: first, that the income velocity of money V is fixed (or at least stable); second, that the level of real output or income Y is also fixed, at the full-employment level; and third, that the nominal money stock M is exogenously determined by the monetary authorities. Together these assumptions imply that the price level P is determined by M. We thus have:

$$\overrightarrow{MV} = PY \tag{3}$$

where the arrow denotes the direction of causality.

According to equation (3), which represents the *quantity theory of money*, the price level is proportional to the nominal money stock. This is, in effect, simply another way of stating the *neutrality of money*. In other words, the quantity theory of money is based on the notion of a *vertical aggregate supply curve*, at the full-employment level of income.

Equation (3) represents a theory of the *price level*. To transform it into a theory of *inflation*, the rates of change in the variables in Identity (2) have to be considered. As an approximation we can write:

$$\frac{\triangle M}{M} + \frac{\triangle V}{V} = \frac{\triangle P}{P} + \frac{\triangle Y}{Y} \tag{4}$$

which states that the rate of change in the nominal money stock plus the rate of change in the income velocity of money equals the sum of the rate of change in the price level (the inflation rate) and the rate of change in real output (the real growth rate). Assuming that the income velocity of money is stable, that the growth rate of real output is determined by *real* variables such as the availability and productivity of the different factors of production, and that money growth is determined by the monetary authorities (and is therefore exogenous), we have a theory which states that the rate of growth in the nominal money stock ($\triangle M/M$) determines the rate of inflation ($\triangle P/P$), with $\triangle P/P = \triangle M/M - \triangle Y/Y$. Thus, if the growth rate of real output is 3 per cent per annum and the nominal money supply is increasing at 20 per cent per annum, the inflation rate will be approximately 17 per cent per annum. Conversely, with a 3 per cent annual real growth rate, price stability will only be achieved if the nominal money stock is also increasing at 3 per cent per annum. We therefore still have a theory of *neutral money*, the only difference being that we are now dealing with the *rates of change* instead of the levels of the relevant variables. Diagrammatically this is tantamount to a vertical long-run Phillips curve.

Although it could be argued that this brief outline is an over-simplification of the monetarists' viewpoint, it nevertheless captures the essence of their argument, on which they base their case for a low and constant rate of increase in the nominal money stock. In South Africa this type of explanation of inflation has been propounded, among others, by Kantor (1983) and the De Kock Commission (1985).

How useful is this approach to the diagnosis of inflation and its concomitant implications for anti-inflation policy? To answer this question we have to assess the assumptions on which the theory is based.

As far as the income velocity of money is concerned, the De Kock Commission (1985: 166–168) found that it had fluctuated substantially in South Africa between 1976 and 1984. These fluctuations were ascribed to the nature of the instruments of monetary policy, and in particular to the application of direct controls on interest rates and bank credit during the seventies and the subsequent switch to indirect, market-related instruments during the eighties. Similar fluctuations in the income velocity of money have also been observed in other countries.

How do monetarists respond to these observed fluctuations? According to Milton Friedman (1968a), many

> ... have recognised that changes in the willingness of the community to hold money can occur for a variety of reasons and can introduce disparities between changes in the quantity of money per unit of output and changes in prices. What quantity theorists have held in common is the belief that these qualifications are of secondary importance for substantial changes in either prices or the quantity of money, so that the one will not in effect occur without the other.

In other words, Friedman concedes that factors other than increases in the nominal money stock can affect prices, but nevertheless argues that these other factors are of secondary importance.

As far as the level and growth of real output are concerned, it is well known that the South African economy has been suffering from severe unemployment in recent years and that the duration and amplitude of economic fluctuations have also increased since the early 1970s. It seems fruitless, therefore, to assume either that the economy is operating at full employment, or that there is some stable long-run growth rate determined by real variables.

Much more important, however, is the question whether the nominal money stock is exogenously determined by the monetary authorities, as we have been assuming thus far in this paper. We shall discuss this issue at greater length later on, when considering the structuralist approach to inflation. For the present we simply note that the simplifying assumption which is vital to the monetarist viewpoint can lead to inappropriate diagnoses of real world problems, since the nominal money stock may (in part at least) be endogenous, rather than exogenous.

Another aspect of the monetarist viewpoint which has been questioned is the concept of the *neutrality of money*, i.e. the notion that changes in the stock of money do not affect real variables such as real output and employment. While monetarists are in effect saying that 'money does not matter', others argue that nominal (monetary) variables, such as interest rates and exchange rates, have significant effects on real variables (see Rogers, 1986). We shall, however, not go into the details of this important debate. At this stage, it is sufficient to note that the monetarist approach to inflation is based primarily on the observed correlation between changes in the nominal money stock and changes in the price level, along with a particular belief in the inherent stability of the private market economy.[1]

2. DEMAND-PULL VS. COST-PUSH: THE KEYNESIAN APPROACH

A second popular approach to the diagnosis of inflation is based on the distinction between demand-pull inflation and cost-push inflation. This distinction can be illustrated by using either the aggregate demand and supply (*AD-AS*) model or the Phillips curve.

In terms of the *AD-AS* model an upward (rightward) shift of the *AD* curve and/or an upward (leftward) shift of the *AS* curve will result in an increase in the price level (which is often implicitly assumed to represent the inflation rate). If the price increase is the result of a shift of the *AD* curve, it is labelled demand-pull. If, on the other hand, the initial cause was an upward shift of the *AS* curve, it is termed cost-push. These two cases are illustrated in Figures 1a and 1b. Note the difference in the impact on the level of real output. Demand-pull is accompanied by an increase in the level of real output, whereas cost-push results in a drop in real output. One can see, therefore, why the cost-push explanation of inflation became so popular during the 1970s. During the sixties

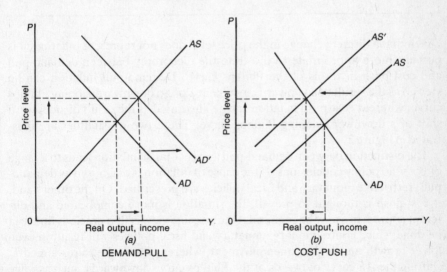

Figure 1 DEMAND-PULL AND COST-PUSH IN THE *AD-AS* MODEL

South Africa and most of the industrialised market economies experienced high economic growth and relatively low inflation. Inflation was thus attributed to the high (and increasing) levels of aggregate demand, i.e. to demand-pull. In the seventies, however, inflation increased (and remained high) while economic growth declined. Many economists attributed this stagflation to cost-push influences.

The major factors which can cause shifts in the *AD* and *AS* curves are summarised in Table 1. Note, in particular, that changes in the stock of money are also accommodated in this framework. However, whereas monetarists focus almost exclusively on the nominal money stock in their explanation of inflation, an exogenous change in the quantity of money is but one of a range of factors which can cause price level changes in the Keynesian framework.

Table 1 CAUSES OF DEMAND-PULL AND COST-PUSH

Demand-pull factors (i.e. those factors which cause an upward shift of the *AD* curve, or an upward movement along a downward-sloping Phillips curve)		Cost-push factors (i.e. those factors which cause an upward shift of the *AS* curve, or of the Phillips curve)
Exogenous increases in:		Increases in:
the nominal money stock	(M)	the nominal wage rate
government spending	(G)	profit margins
investment spending	(I)	import prices
consumption spending	(C)	
export demand	(X)	Declining productivity

Given that a discrete change in the price level does not represent inflation, it is perhaps more appropriate to illustrate the dichotomy between demand-pull and cost-push in terms of the Phillips curve. Demand-pull inflation can be viewed as the result of an upward movement along a downward-sloping Phillips curve, whereas cost-push inflation can be illustrated as the result of an upward shift of a downward-sloping Phillips curve. These two possibilities are illustrated in Figure 2.

The distinction between demand-pull and cost-push inflation leads to a range of possible policy conclusions. If the cause of inflation is diagnosed as demand-pull, restrictive monetary and fiscal policies are prescribed. On the other hand, if cost-push is thought to prevail, the situation is more complicated and different approaches may be required. One possible view is that precious little can be done, since contractionary monetary and fiscal policies will result in even lower growth and higher unemployment, whereas direct measures aimed at shifting the *AS* curve outwards or the Phillips curve downwards, such as wage and price controls (or incomes policies), will cause a serious misallocation of

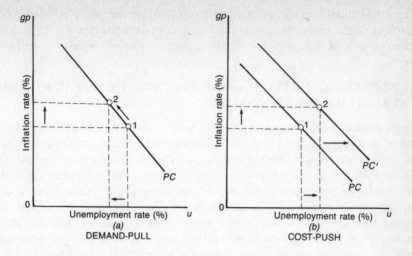

Figure 2 DEMAND-PULL AND COST-PUSH IN THE PHILLIPS CURVE

resources that will hamper the growth of real output and employment. Some proponents of the cost-push explanation even give up the fight formally, merely advocating widespread indexation as a method to make it easier to live with inflation. A second, contrasting, view is that the problem is so serious that blunt measures, such as a wage-price freeze, should be implemented. As to the possible effects of such measures on the allocation of resources, it is argued that the latter is already distorted by a whole range of factors (including inflation) and that it is therefore no use arguing as if the prevailing allocation of resources is desirable or efficient. A third possible view is that of the supply-siders, who advocate tax cuts and other measures aimed at shifting the *AS* curve to the right (or the Phillips curve to the left).

Although still very popular in discussions on economic policy, the demand-pull vs. cost-push distinction has come in for strong criticism (cf. Laidler & Parkin, 1975; Addison & Burton, 1980; Mohr, 1981). First, it has been argued that what appears to be cost-push is always a delayed response to prior increases in aggregate demand, hence cost-push is merely an illusion. This type of argument was particularly popular in the sixties, but lost most of its appeal with the onset of stagflation in the seventies. A second, more contemporary, argument is that cost-push cannot be an independent cause of inflation, since it has to be validated or accommodated by the monetary authorities (by allowing an increase in the money supply). Finally, it has been argued that inflation is a *process* and that, although it is sometimes useful to distinguish between cost-push and demand-pull factors in an attempt to pinpoint the initiating or aggravating factors in a particular inflationary episode, the dichotomy between demand-pull and cost-push is of no further use in the analysis of the process (once it has taken root) or, even more importantly, in the formulation of policy measures that are aimed at reversing this process. This last type of criticism has given rise to a third approach to the diagnosis of inflation, which we shall now discuss.

3. UNDERLYING, INITIATING AND PROPAGATING FACTORS: THE STRUCTURALIST APPROACH

This approach to the analysis of inflation involves the distinction between three interrelated sets of factors in the inflationary process: first, the *underlying factors*, which are responsible for the economy's inflationary bias; second, the *initiating factors*, which trigger or intensify a particular inflationary episode; and third, the *propagating factors*, which transmit the original impulse(s) through the economy over time and, in so doing, generate or sustain the process of rising prices (see Mohr, 1981). This approach is labelled structuralist, since the distinction between the three sets of factors was borrowed from the so-called structuralist approach to inflation developed in Latin America during the latter half of the 1950s.

According to the structuralist approach inflation is the combined result of the three interrelated sets of factors. Thus, even if there is a strong inflationary bias, specific initiating factors are still required to set the inflation process in motion. Moreover, the propagating factors are required to sustain the process, once it has taken root.

Some of the most important underlying, initiating and propagating factors are summarised in Table 2. Space does not permit us to explain all these factors, although in the next few paragraphs we attempt to give some indication of their nature and influence.

As far as the underlying factors are concerned, it has to be recognised that a wide range of *non-economic factors* (e.g. social, political and historical) have to be taken into account in any meaningful analysis of inflation. As Fred Hirsch (1978: 263) has stated: 'Economic factors, and they alone, can explain how inflation happens, but economic factors alone cannot explain why.' Many economists, including the monetarists and other free marketeers, reject this notion. In terms of their particular set of ideas or beliefs it is simply heretical to argue in these terms. 'But,' to quote Sadie (1980: 281), 'for the economist to disregard the socio-political environment of his Economics would be indicative of a lack of perspicacity.'

To understand inflation one also has to take cognisance of the processes whereby prices and wages are determined. In other words, the structures of the goods market and the labour market have to be examined.

In the South African *goods market*, for example, many prices in the private as well as public sectors are administered, usually on a cost-plus basis. In fact, some prices are even implicitly linked to some or other price index (usually the CPI). The upshot of this is that prices seldom fall. In fact, even the rate of increase of certain prices also seems to have acquired a downward rigidity.

Table 2 UNDERLYING, INITIATING AND PROPAGATING FACTORS IN THE INFLATION PROCESS

Underlying factors

The traditions, values and norms of society
The degree of conflict between different groups in society
The political strength and bargaining power of trade unions and other employee organisations
The degree of competition in the goods market
The extent of administered pricing
The extent of formal or informal indexation
The official commitment to full-employment policies
The ability and scope of the monetary authorities to control the money supply
The size of the public sector
The openness of the economy
The exchange rate regime

Initiating factors

Demand-pull, due to autonomous increases in C, I, G or X and/or exogenous increases in the money supply
Cost-push, due to exogenous increases in wages, profits or import prices
Other price increases, e.g. those due to increases in indirect taxes, drought, etc.

Propagating factors

Endogenous increases in the money supply (e.g. as a result of accommodation by the monetary authorities)
The various wage–price, price–wage, wage–wage and price–price interrelationships in the economy
Inflationary expectations
The interaction between domestic prices, the balance of payments and the exchange rate

---

Similarly, various features of the *labour market* have also contributed to the inflationary bias of the economy. It is widely recognised that the labour market does not conform to the textbook model of demand and supply. In South Africa, for example, approximately one-third of all the employees in the non-agricultural sectors are employed in the public sector. Their wages are governed by various social, political and economic considerations and therefore do not necessarily reflect the forces of supply and demand. The growth and influence of the trade union movement, the political strength and protected position of certain groups of workers, the increased tendency to link wages to increases in the CPI, etc., must also be taken into account.

57

Against this type of background, specific price and/or cost increases are required to initiate or aggravate a particular inflationary episode. The immediate causes of such increases, i.e. the *initiating factors*, can be classified into three broad categories: cost-push factors, demand-pull factors and 'other' price increases. The first two categories include the same factors as those listed in Table 1. The distinction between cost-push and demand-pull is therefore retained, albeit in a much narrower context. The residual category of 'other' price increases includes those price increases which cannot be regarded as 'inflationary' but which nevertheless act as initiating factors in the inflation process. A good example was the introduction of the general sales tax (GST) in South Africa in July 1978. This was reflected in an increase in the CPI (as were the subsequent increases in the rate of GST) and therefore had the same secondary effects on prices and wages as any of the other possible initiating factors.

These secondary effects are the result of the *propagating factors*, which transmit the original impulse(s) through the economy and over time, thereby generating or sustaining an inflation *process*. They are the most important factors in this process and therefore merit special attention.

Once prices and/or costs have risen in certain sectors of the economy, these increases are transmitted to the rest of the economy via the *various interrelationships that exist between prices, wages and profits*. These so-called price–wage, price–price, wage–price and wage–wage spirals have their origin in the structure of the goods market and the labour market, i.e. in the underlying factors. For instance, the fact that many prices are administered on a cost-plus basis virtually ensures that cost increases are automatically passed on, while the rigidity of the wage structure results in wage increases in certain sectors of the economy (e.g. mining or the civil service) having ripple effects in other sectors through efforts to maintain wage differentials. These processes are, of course, facilitated by the existence of indexation, as well as by inflationary expectations (once inflation has taken root).

Another element of the transmission mechanism is to be found in the interaction between domestic price increases, the balance of payments and the exchange rate. The following sequence of events serves as an illustration: if any of the domestic initiating factors cause price increases in the domestic economy, this could, through a process of substitution, lead to an increased demand for imports and/or a decreased demand for exports at the current exchange rate. Under a floating exchange rate regime, the resultant deterioration in the balance of payments could result in a vicious circle of exchange rate depreciation and domestic inflation.

This brings us to arguably the most important (and most controversial) of the propagating factors — the increase in the supply of money. Inflation is indeed 'always and everywhere a monetary phenomenon', as the monetarists claim. But this is merely a tautology. By definition inflation cannot occur in a moneyless economy. More precisely, a sustained increase in the supply of money (the product of the quantity of money and its velocity of circulation) is a necessary condition for inflation, in the same sense that water is a necessary condition for drowning (see Solow, 1976). But the fact that inflation is a monetary phenomenon does not imply that excessive monetary expansion is its sole or even principal cause. Even Milton Friedman (1966: 30) has recognised this: 'Emphasis on the key role of the quantity of money leaves open the question of what produced the changes in the quantity of money.' He adds, however, that '… if an analysis of inflation is to deal not only with the change in the quantity of money but with what brought it about, it will be a very pluralistic theory'. Herein lies the fundamental difference between the monetarist approach outlined at the beginning of this section and the structuralist approach currently under discussion. The monetarists assume that the quantity of money is exogenously determined by the monetary authorities. This assumption is one of the cornerstones of their theory of inflation, which they subsequently 'verify' empirically on the basis of the observed correlation between changes in the price level and changes in the quantity of money.

Structuralists, on the other hand, contend that the causes of the increase in the money supply have to be investigated (i.e. they opt for the 'pluralistic' approach), and that correlations are meaningless, unless they are supported by a plausible theory of causation.

The important question, therefore, is whether the money stock is an exogenous variable (controlled by the monetary authorities) or whether it also has a significant endogenous component, either in the sense of being credit-driven and demand-determined (Moore and Smit, 1986) or in the sense of being the result of accommodation by the monetary authorities. Policy-makers *accommodate* or *validate* inflation when they allow the money stock to increase in order to prevent the unemployment that could result if the money stock is held constant in the wake of cost and price increases. Such increases in the money stock are therefore symptoms (or consequences) of inflation, rather than 'causes'.

The question of whether (or to what extent) the money supply is exogenous or endogenous cannot be dealt with adequately in this paper.[2] However, the only point which needs to be emphasised in the context of our present discussion is that the structuralists recognise the important role of money in the inflation process (as a possible initiating factor as well as a necessary propagating factor), but that their view of how a modern money economy operates differs fundamentally from that of the monetarists.

The general *policy implication* of the structuralist approach is that inflation can only be combated effectively by way of a broad, coordinated anti-inflation strategy aimed at all three sets of factors in the inflationary process. In particular, neither restrictive monetary and fiscal policies nor an extensive system of wage and price controls, the two extreme policy recommendations emanating from the distinction between demand-pull and cost-push inflation, can offer any meaningful or lasting solution to the inflation experienced in South Africa in the 1980s (see Mohr, 1981).

4. THE CONFLICT APPROACH

Few economists deny that the structuralist approach provides a useful description of the inflation process. Some argue, however, that it is too broad (or too eclectic) and that it therefore does not provide an adequate *explanation* of inflation. A fourth approach to inflation, the conflict approach, abstracts from the details of the inflation process, but focuses on what are regarded to be the fundamental causes of inflation.

According to the conflict approach inflation is a symptom of a fundamental disharmony in society which results in a continuous imbalance between the rate of growth in the real national income and the rate of growth of the total effective claims on this income. Tobin (1983: 7) has summarised this view as follows:

> There is no consensus on the division of the pie. Neither the mechanisms of the competitive market nor the political process work with sufficient authority to reconcile the several economic interests to the rewards they receive for economic activity, or inactivity. The constituent economic and social groups claim collectively more 'pie' than there actually can be. Moreover, each group has the economic or political bargaining power to raise its money income. As the rival interest groups strive in turn to gain larger shares of the pie by claiming higher money incomes, inflation is the outcome.

We now explain the salient features of this approach with the aid of a simple, comparative static model.

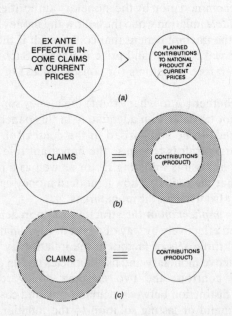

Figure 3 A SIMPLIFIED VIEW OF THE CONFLICT APPROACH

The different interest groups in society (e.g. the government, labour and the owners of capital) each possess a certain degree of economic and/or political power, which governs their effective claims on the national income. Each group also contributes to the national product (or income). There is, however, no economic and/or political mechanism which guarantees *ex ante* equilibrium between the total effective claims and the contributions at the existing price level. On the contrary, in present-day South Africa there is a chronic imbalance, in the sense that the sum of the effective income claims (at current prices) always exceeds the sum of the contributions (at current prices). This is illustrated in Figure 3a.

Since there is no reason why contributions should increase in response to such an *ex ante* imbalance, there are only two possible equilibrating forces *(ex post):* an increase in net imports (to supplement the domestic contributions) and/or an increase in price. Any increase in net imports will, however, have to be financed through an equivalent increase in the net inflow of capital, or decrease in foreign reserves (or a combination of the two). In South Africa this possible equilibrating mechanism was still available prior to 1976 when a net inflow of capital was the rule rather than the exception, but it disappeared during the latter half of the seventies. In fact, since 1985 South Africa's large foreign debt commitment has implied that a smaller portion of the domestically produced pie has been available for distribution among the domestic interest groups. The only remaining equilibrating mechanism at the aggregate level is an increase in the price level. This can be viewed either as an increase in the nominal value of the national product (to equate the nominal income with the claims on that income) or as a decrease in the real value of the effective income claims (to equate the real claims with real value of the product). These two possibilities, which amount to exactly the same thing, are illustrated in Figure 3b and 3c respectively. In other words, inflation can be seen as the symptom of a lack of effective economic and/or political mechanisms to achieve a prior *(ex ante)* reconciliation of the conflicting claims on the national income.

If we want to explain South Africa's inflation record since the early 1970s in terms of this approach, then we have to consider the rate of growth in the effective income claims relative to the growth of the real national income. As far as the latter is concerned, we now know (with the benefit of hindsight) that real growth was much lower during the 1970s than during the 1960s, and that it declined even further during the 1980s. Since the early seventies there has therefore been less scope for a non-inflationary growth in effective income claims than there was during the sixties. Even with an unchanged growth in effective income claims one could therefore have expected a higher inflation rate during the seventies than during the sixties. Moreover, a number of significant developments served to increase the growth of effective income claims. These include: increases in the claim of the government sector; significant increases in the effective claims of certain groups of employees (supported by factors such as the newly perceived 'social responsibility' on the part of employers, strike activity, an increased ability to pay in the mining industry, increased political power, certain manpower shortages and inflationary expectations); high profit claims (even in the face of declining demand); and increased foreign claims on the South African national product (such as those of the oil-producing countries). More fundamentally, basic conflicts in South African society (between labour and capital, between the various races, between the haves and the have-nots) as well as changes in lifestyles (Sadie, 1980: 283) have been exacerbated by increases and shifts in economic and political power, and the resulting increase in effective income claims (without a concomitant increase in contributions) can be considered as the root cause of the high inflation in South Africa since 1973.

The policy implications of this approach are somewhat disconcerting (especially for those who view inflation as a serious problem). The only real remedy for inflation lies in the creation of an effective mechanism to achieve an *ex ante* reconciliation of the competing claims on the national income. This points to the need for some form of anti-inflationary incomes policy, i.e. a voluntary or compulsory arrangement that limits the effective income claims of the various interest groups. In this respect the experience of Western economies suggests that there are three fundamental prerequisites for an effective incomes policy: mature political institutions, a certain national unity and a sense of national economic crisis. If any or all of these are absent, the real choice (in terms of the conflict approach) lies between inappropriate anti-inflation policies (such as monetary contraction) and continued high inflation. Finally, therefore, the acceptance of high inflation may even turn out to be the best available alternative.

NOTES

1　Wiles (1973: 395) has described this attitude as follows: 'The correlation holds, so to hell with explanation.'
2　In South Africa this issue was recently brought to the fore by the publication of the *Final report of the Commission of Inquiry into the Monetary System and Monetary Policy in South Africa* (De Kock Commission, 1985). The Commission's monetarist-type views were criticised in the March 1986 issue of *The South African Journal of Economics*.

REFERENCES

Addison, J.T. and Burton, J., 1980. 'The Demise of "Demand-Pull" and "Cost-Push" in Inflation Theory'. *Banca Nazionale del Lavoro Quarterly Review*, No. 133, June.
De Kock Commission, 1985. *Final Report of the Commission of Inquiry into the Monetary System and Monetary Policy in South Africa*. R/P 70/1984. Pretoria: Government Printer.
Friedman, M., 1966. 'What Price Guideposts?' In *Guidelines: Informal Controls and the Market Place*, edited by G.P. Schultz and R.Z. Aliber. Chicago: Chicago University Press.
—— 1968. 'Money: The Quantity Theory', in *The International Encyclopaedia of the Social Sciences*, Vol. X.
Hirsch, F., 1978. 'The Ideological Underlay of Inflation', in *The Political Economy of Inflation*, edited by F. Hirsch and J.H. Goldthorpe. London: Martin Robertson.

Kantor, B., 1983. 'The Decade of Inflation — A Perspective on Recent Monetary Development in South Africa. Inaugural lecture. University of Cape Town, 22 June.

Laider, D.E.W. and Parkin, J.M., 1975. 'Inflation — A Survey'. *Economic Journal*, Vol. 85, No. 340, March.

Mohr, P.J., 1981. 'A Possible Framework for Analysing the Inflationary Process'. In *Economic Development Programme for the Republic of South Africa 1978–1987*. Pretoria: Government Printer.

Mohr, P.J. and Rogers, C., 1987. *Macroeconomics*. Johannesburg: Lexicon.

Moore, B.J. and Smit, B.W., 1986. 'Wages, Money and Inflation', *South African Journal of Economics*, Vol. 54, No. 1, March.

Rogers, C., 1986. 'The Theory of Monetary Policy Reconsidered', *Studies in Economics and Econometrics*, No. 25, August.

Sadie, J.L., 1980. *Labour Demand and Supply*. Stellenbosch: Kosmo.

Solow, R.M., 1976. 'Learning the Lessons of Inflation'. *Economic Impact*, No. 15.

Tobin, J., 1983. 'Inflation: Monetary and Structural Causes and Cures'. In *Inflation Through the Ages*, edited by N. Schumkler and E. Marcus, New York: Brooklyn College Press.

Wiles, P.J.D., 1973. 'Cost-Push Inflation and the State of Economic Theory', *Economic Journal*, Vol. 83, No. 331, June.

2.3 THE CAUSES OF INFLATION — AND WHAT CAN BE DONE

Brian Kantor*

There has been nothing unusual about recent inflation in South Africa. The increases in consumer prices were an entirely predictable and unavoidable response to the increase in import and export prices that follows a major devaluation. Indeed, the devaluation worked in a classically effective way. It reduced the volume of domestic spending and imports, and increased the volume of exports, just as a devaluation is supposed to do. The criticism one can make is that the reduction in demand was, if anything, too severe and more, rather than less, monetary accommodation was called for.

The devaluation of the rand, against the currencies of our trading partners which began in 1984, accelerated after we crossed the Rubicon in July 1985, and continued through most of 1986. The volatile performance of the trade-weighted foreign exchange value of the rand is illustrated in Fig. 1. Had the rand held its gains of early 1986, the inflation would have been substantially lower by the end of the year. Unfortunately, we had to suffer a further substantial devaluation in mid-year. The rand is now back to where it was in early 1986 and the benefits of this recovery for the inflation rate are still to be seen.

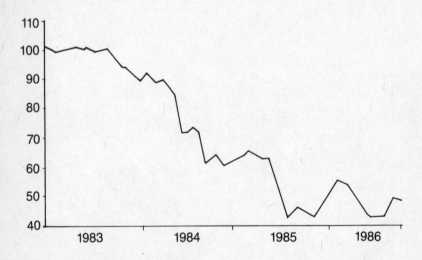

Figure 1 RAND EFFECTIVE EXCHANGE RATE (trade weighted)

* Director, School of Economics, University of Cape Town. This paper was first published in *Business Day*, 13 February 1987.

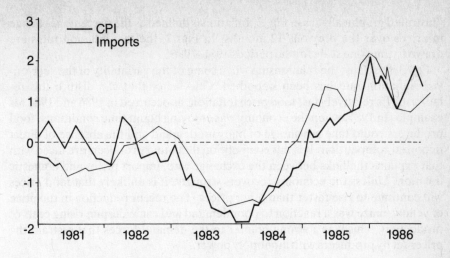

Figure 2 CPI AND IMPORT PRICE INFLATION (normalised)

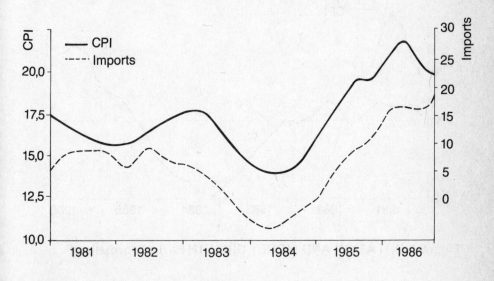

Figure 3 CPI AND IMPORT PRICE INFLATION (smoothed)

The devaluation has caused the prices of imported goods to rise rapidly and almost continuously between mid-1984 and November 1986, the latest month for which import price statistics are available. Imported price declines were recorded in only three months — April 1985, and May and June 1986. There are very strong links between import and consumer price inflation and this is best

65

illustrated graphically, as in Fig. 2. Inflation is defined as the percentage change in prices over the previous 12 months. In Fig. 2, the two inflation rates are drawn to the same scale for the periods 1981–1986.

Fig. 3 illustrates the relationship when some of the variability of the year-on-year inflation rate has been smoothed. One factor that can disturb this relationship is relatively fast food price inflation, as occurred in 1986 and 1981 for example. In 1981, when the economy was enjoying boom time conditions, food producers could take advantage of buoyant demand and the absence of direct imported competition. It is this competition that other producers are faced with that explains the links between the exchange rate, import prices and domestic inflation. Unless the economy recovers strongly, it is unlikely that food prices will continue to rise faster than other prices. The recent reduction in the price of yellow maize was a reaction to poor demand and came despite rising costs of production. This was a strong pointer to the demand forces that restrain the prices set by producers with monopoly power.

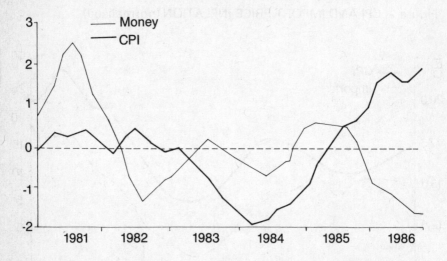

Figure 4 INFLATION AND MONEY GROWTH (% p.a.) normalised

Inflation in 1986 also had nothing to do with excess issues of money and the demand associated with monetary growth. The money supply grew much more slowly than prices, as is illustrated in Figs. 4 and 5, and helped restrain price increases — if anything, too much so. The relationship between money growth and inflation generally in SA is not a close one, as may be seen in Fig. 4. The relationship between money growth and spending is much closer.

The increase in prices in 1986 served to depress greatly the demands for goods and services and wages grew significantly more slowly than prices, so depressing real disposable incomes.

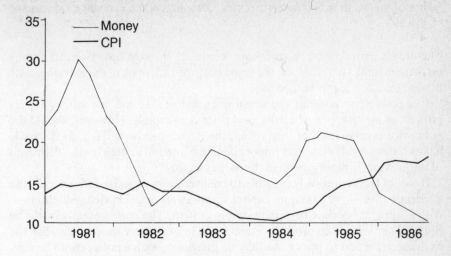

Figure 5 INFLATION AND MONEY GROWTH (% p.a.) smoothed

The devaluation of 1985 and 1986 acted on prices in the same way as would a substantial increase in sales taxes. The intended effect of higher prices — the result of a devaluation or a tax increase — is to reduce the value of goods and services consumed. Capital resources previously made available for use in South Africa were being withdrawn on a large scale. The demand for foreign exchange to satisfy capital withdrawals led to the devaluation which, in turn, brought higher prices, lower disposable incomes and depressed levels of domestic demand. Lower demands and higher prices for imports and exports — coupled with wages and salaries rising much more slowly than inflation — meant more profitable production for exporting and import replacing and more freely available supplies of export and import replacement goods. The growing surplus of exports over imports provided the foreign exchange to meet demands for capital withdrawals. The monetary authorities, as indicated by relatively slow growth in the money supply (see Fig. 5) seemed unable or unwilling to offset the depressing effect of higher prices on domestic demands. They naturally welcomed the export surpluses with which to repay foreign debts. Unfortunately, the decline in real consumption power and the shift to exports did not occur without less employment and much excess capacity.

The outlook for inflation in 1987 and beyond will be determined approximately as before by the performance of the rand against other currencies and world inflation. There are three major forces at work that influence the foreign exchange value of the rand. They are:

• political shocks and their effects on capital withdrawals;
• changes in the terms of trade, particularly in the price of gold; and
• money supply growth, which, by affecting the demand for goods and so for

67

imports and, in turn, trade surpluses, also affects the exchange rate and so prices.

The monetary influence on prices works mainly through the effects of money on demand and, therefore, on the trade balance and, in turn, the exchange rate in what may be a highly lagged way.

It is possible to have an appreciating exchange rate and fast money supply growth, as may happen when the gold price rises rapidly. However, should the gold price reverse itself or stop rising, the exchange rate will fall, as the trade balance deteriorates because import demands remain at high levels, the result of the previously rapid growth in the money supply.

It would be theoretically possible to counter every negative influence on the exchange rate — for example, capital withdrawals or gold price reductions — with a sufficient decline in money supply growth. The money supply might be reduced sufficiently to produce a decline in imports necessary to stabilise the exchange rate and so prices. As may be imagined, such a policy could be very severe indeed, should either foreign capital be withdrawn on a large scale or the gold price fall dramatically as occurred over recent years. Such a policy of maintaining price stability at all costs is surely not to be recommended. Exchange rate flexibility, and all it implies for higher prices, can help the economy adjust to adverse circumstances more easily.

The money supply should best be made to grow highly predictably at a rate consistent with low inflation over the long run. That is to say, the money supply growth rates should not decline when the economy is under stress or accelerate when the economy is booming. It is the failure of money supply policies to remain neutral in the face of real shocks to the economy, either favourable or unfavourable, that has made inflation and recessions unnecessarily difficult to control in South Africa.

Should the economy continue to recover, and confidence with it, money supply growth rates will be pushed upwards. Unless the growth in the money supply is then limited, the exchange rate sooner or later will again come under downward pressure, irrespective of the gold price factor or the confidence factor.

It is in the nature of the South African economy, subject as it is to shocks in the form of gold price changes and political developments, to have to put up with more variable inflation rates than those of more diversified and politically stable countries. What is completely avoidable is the additional instability caused by highly variable money supply growth rates. If the money supply growth rates were stabilised, the authorities would be doing as much as they could do to help stabilise the economy.

Any attempts to interfere further with the necessary adjustments of prices to any of the real or monetary forces at work would be highly counterproductive. The monetary causes of inflation can be treated and the real factors causing prices to rise are best understood for what they are, and tolerated accordingly.

2.4 INDUSTRIAL CONCENTRATION AND INFLATION IN SOUTH AFRICA 1972–1979

Frederick C. v. N. Fourie*

In the search for the cause of South Africa's inflation problem, and also for an appropriate solution, a new candidate has appeared. This is the so-called *non-competitive structure* of the South African economy, sometimes also called the question of 'administered prices'. This is being mentioned in publications and speeches more and more often. The purpose of this paper is to make a contribution to this debate and to see whether the popularity of this view is based on the quality of supporting theoretical arguments and empirical evidence.

In the first part the basic lines of the standard argument are set out, and in parts 2 and 3 the micro- and macroeconomic theoretical aspects are looked at critically. Part 4 contains some of the empirical results that shed light on the question, and part 5 contains conclusions drawn with regard to both the basic arguments and the related policy recommendations.

1. AN EXPOSITION OF THE STANDARD ARGUMENTS

The history of the theory of so-called administered inflation dates back to about 1957 (or even to the 1930s), when Gardiner Means in the USA maintained that the main source of inflation (in the USA) since 1955 had been the upward movement of so-called administered prices. Since then the theory has appeared in various forms (Scherer, 1980, ch. 13). In South Africa it is mostly found in two forms (De Wet, 1982a and 1982b, and Mohr, 1981).

In its simplest form the basic argument is that the non-competitive structure of the South African economy is the real cause of inflation because prices in such a structure are 'administered' and are therefore not a true reflection of so-called 'impersonal market forces'. More specifically, the accusation is that producers in non-competitive sectors have discretion over their prices (in contrast to those in competitive sectors) and that consequently they are able to increase their prices continuously in order to increase or maintain profit rates. The point at issue, therefore, is price increases — independent of, for example, cost increases (i.e. exogenous price increases). In this way they create inflation either directly or indirectly, the latter when their higher prices imply cost pressure for other producers. In addition, the point is sometimes made that the consumer does not have many alternatives; the inelasticity of demand facilitates price increases.

* Professor of Economics, University of the Orange Free State. This paper was read at the Conference of the Economic Society of South Africa, Johannesburg, September 1983, and is an extension of a paper read at the Conference of Economists and Business Economists, Port Elizabeth, November 1987.

Related to this is the more general argument that a non-competitive structure leads to prices that are rigid, especially downwards, and which create a so-called inflationary bias in the economy — 'prices can only go up' — in contrast to a competitive market where market forces can cause prices to move in any direction.

The second argument is that the market power of monopolistic or oligopolistic producers, and their discretion over their prices, enable them summarily to pass on cost increases to the buyer. In this argument, administered prices are therefore not seen so much as an original cause, but as a propagating factor. One specific form of this argument refers to the price-formation process in non-competitive markets, where producers do not strive for maximum profit, but for 'satisfactory' profit. In these circumstances, relieved of the discipline of the market, producers follow a cost-plus price policy; that is, price is set equal to average cost plus a margin that ensures 'satisfactory' profit. When costs increase for some reason or other, prices are increased accordingly without the producer absorbing any part of the cost increase (De Wet, 1982a and 1982b, pp. 6–7).

To substantiate these and related arguments in the South African context, reference is usually made to the non-competitive structure of the various sectors of the economy, giving as empirical evidence the high degree of concentration in the manufacturing sector. The existence of government-administered prices, as well as a wide range of government rules and regulations, is also mentioned at times.

Given these arguments and empirical data, one obvious recommendation for combating inflation in South Africa is for so-called *structural policy measures*. These measures are to be directed at establishing a competitive economic structure, one in which there will be room once again for impersonal market forces to determine prices.

2. A MICROECONOMIC EVALUATION OF THE ARGUMENT

1. Introductory remarks

First, a remark about the term 'administered prices'. Although the literature is fairly ambiguous about the exact meaning of this term, it would probably not be wrong to assume that those who use it refer to prices that are fixed at the discretion of the firm. This is contrasted with (perfectly) competitive markets where prices are said to be determined by 'impersonal market forces', by the 'market', with the firm as price taker.

This dichotomy is misleading, on the one hand because the imperfect competitor, e.g. an oligopolist, must in fact take the reactions of his competitors of his price decisions into account — his discretion is not absolute. On the other hand, the price of the smallest and most perfect competitor is still determined by the decision of the entrepreneur — he has complete freedom (discretion) to determine any price for his product (and face the consequences). Furthermore, even the smallest firm has discretion over its price in the sense that a relatively small increase will not cause its sales to drop to zero. Moreover, each firm is, in a spatial context, a monopolist, i.e. within a certain geographical area. At most, higher prices result in a decline in sales, which means that he too has a descending demand curve. The term administered prices therefore does not have a specific meaning, except of course in the case of prices fixed by administrative proclamation by the authorities. Perhaps it would be a good idea to reserve the term for the latter phenomenon.

Second, a remark on the statement that administered prices are the cause of inflation 'because they are not a true reflection of impersonal market forces'. Does this statement tacitly assume that a free-market economy is inherently or by nature free from inflation, that the operation of blind market forces in a (perfectly) competitive market is a guarantee against inflation? This is a question that everyone should ask himself, especially when a pro-competitive policy is suggested as a solution for inflation. As such, this question enters the field of ideological dispute between the main strains of thought in economics, which may produce interesting and possibly predictable answers, but perhaps also unexpected bed-fellows. Let us leave it at that.

A third remark concerns the phenomenon of permanent inflation and statements that 'in practice prices never drop' and 'prices only rise'. Is that not inflationary bias in the economy?

In this respect a great deal of clarity can be obtained with the concept of *real prices*. It may sound strange, but given a situation of established inflation, the relevant phenomenon may not be absolute decreases in price but decreases relative to the long-run rate of increase (the 'trend') — that is, decreases in real prices. If one looks at price indices for industrial sectors and product groups against this background, decreases in real prices are quite common, also in so-called non-competitive markets. One should therefore become accustomed to thinking within the framework of a 'moving train' — similar to the way we have been thinking of upswings and downswings relative to the long-run growth rate of GNP.

2. Profit-push inflation

When one looks more specifically at the accusation of profit-push inflation — that producers in a non-competitive market are able to use discretion over their prices constantly to increase their prices for the sake of higher profits — the critical insights here are firstly the distinction between high prices and rising prices, and secondly the existence of an optimum price. Although certain viewpoints deny it, there is probably a reasonable amount of consensus, based on both practice and theory, that market power leads to (potentially) high profits and prices. But *high* prices are not *rising* prices, whereas inflation, by definition, is a continuous increase in average price levels. This is probably the most common misunderstanding in this debate, but perhaps also the most important distinction.

Coupled to this is the question of an *optimum price*; that is, is there a price such that any higher or lower price would be harmful to the firm in some way? Note that this question is relevant irrespective of the goals of the firm — maximum profit, satisfactory profit, maximum sales or maximum revenue or maximum satisfaction for the manager (subject to a satisfactory return for shareholders and to the threat of entry into the market by new competitors) — and irrespective of the way in which such a price is established — by one-man decision (monopolist), 'the market' (perfect competition), oligopolistic interdependence or oligopolistic co-operation, etc.

In all cases one would think that such an optimum price does exist. If one wished to ascribe inflation over a certain period, e.g. the past decade, to 'administered' or profit-push inflation, one would have to explain (a) why the relevant firms previously were satisfied to be below their optimum price, and (b) why they decided more or less simultaneously to increase their prices to the optimum. If one wished to ascribe inflation generally to exogenous price increases by imperfect competitors, one would have to be able to explain why such firms do not reach the optimum at some stage and remain there, i.e. keep the (high) price without further price increases.

Continually increasing 'administered' prices can obviously occur if there is continuously increasing non-competitiveness, i.e. increasing or new formation of monopolies or oligopolies. If one uses concentration as a measure of non-competitiveness, that would require increasing concentration. The problem with this is that concentration is no recent phenomenon, whereas serious inflation is — why did concentration not cause inflation much earlier? Furthermore, it would appear that concentration changes very slowly, if at all. In South Africa concentration figures are unfortunately only available for one year (Du Plessis, 1977 and 1978), but trends in other Western countries indicate a levelling off (Scherer, 1980, ch. 3). In spite of a few sensational amalgamations and takeovers — which are often diversified in nature and therefore do not increase concentration in a single-product market — it is highly doubtful that concentration could have increased sufficiently since 1972 to provide a meaningful explanation for inflation. (It is to be hoped that the Central Statistical Service will start calculating such measures on a regular basis and make the results available, since it is, after all, an empirical question.)

On the whole, one can deduce from this argument that profit pressure alone could probably not be the cause of inflation. It can only cause temporary price increases, not continued increases. However, the latter could result from profit-push price increases if they are propagated in some way or other, e.g. by inflationary expectations. In addition, any supply inflation must be accommodated by the demand side to create fixed inflation. The problem with profit pressure, specifically as initiating factor, is once again that concentration levels probably did not increase dramatically recently. (Compare the increase in the oil price by the OPEC cartel in the 1970s, which is already a classic example of how profit-pressure price increases can be an initiating factor. At the same time, however, it is also an illustration that such price increases sooner or later reach a ceiling.)

3. The passing-on of cost increases

The second important argument is about the trouble-free passing-on of cost increases by firms with price discretion, which would make non-competitiveness a propagating factor. The relevant question here is, of course: how are cost increases accommodated in so-called *competitive* markets? Are they *not* propagated? Are they propagated *differently* from increases in non-competitive markets with 'administered prices'? Do cost increases not serve as motivation for price increases by competitive firms?

The first point one should keep in mind is that the probably supra-normal profit levels of so-called non-competitive firms at least enable them to absorb cost increases, whereas firms in competitive markets would probably be unable to do so. For a given market demand (curve) and a given cost increase one would therefore expect a relatively larger price increase in a competitive market. An ordinary (static) theoretical comparison of the reactions of a perfectly competitive market and a monopoly to an upward shift in the marginal cost curve indeed shows a *smaller* price increase by the monopolist (under profit maximisation).[1] Therefore it can be misleading to imply that firms in competitive markets do not pass on cost increases to the buyer. They probably have no choice other than to pass it on, which means that the extent of cost-motivated price increases in competitive markets is probably at least the same as in a comparable non-competitive market, if not larger (i.e. for a general cost increase for all the firms in the industry).

Consequently it is not at all clear why the cost–price relationship in non-competitive markets should be a greater so-called propagating factor in the inflation process than in competitive markets. Why should the cost–price spiral be limited to non-competitive markets?

One should also keep in mind that a firm in an oligopolistic market cannot, as compensation for cost increases, increase its price without a decline in its market share if its oligopolistic competitors do not do the same. (If one assumes implicit or explicit co-operation between the firms, this limitation is, of course, ruled out.)

This matter does not become less puzzling when one considers the cost-plus argument — the idea that 'non-competitive' producers, relieved of the discipline of the market, set price equal to average cost plus 'satisfactory' profit. That would make it seem obvious that cost increases are simply passed on in the form of higher prices. Without going into the details of this 'theory' or the misunderstandings that are often contained in it — e.g. that it is different from long-run profit maximisation, namely a striving for only 'satisfactory' profit (cf.

73

Koutsoyiannis, 1979, ch. 12 and Scherer, 1980, pp. 184–190) — the most basic question that this view must answer is: what about the observation that this kind of price formation is generally applied in both non-competitive and competitive markets, by large as well as small firms? (Koutsoyiannis, 1979, p. 277; Scherer, 1980, pp. 184–190). As such, this practice therefore does not imply different reactions to cost increases at all.

In one respect competitive and non-competitive firms do differ here, and that is in the *extent* of the profit margin. That is because the reactions of competitors and the threat of new entry into the market usually influence the margin of price above cost. But as before, it merely determines the level of prices, not the rate of increase.

Taking all aspects into account, it is therefore not clear why cost increases are simply passed on as price increases in non-competitive markets only, or why the price-formation process in non-competitive markets propagates inflation to a greater degree than that in competitive markets. And, please note, the point here is not that so-called non-competitive firms are not guilty of propagating inflation — the point is that they are probably not more guilty of it than competitive firms.

A single remark on the role of the elasticity of demand. In the accusation against non-competitive firms it is often stated that they can always increase their prices 'because the consumer does not have many alternatives'. The question simply is: is there any reason to think that inelasticity of demand is more common in non-competitive markets? What is the actual situation?

As far as rigid prices are concerned, it is generally accepted in the literature on imperfect competition that non-competitive market conditions, e.g. an oligopoly, lead to rigid prices — amongst other things as a result of interdependency (cf. Scherer, 1980, pp. 164–68). The theory of the kinked demand curve is but one (rather unsatisfactory) attempt at explaining this phenomenon. This 'phenomenon', however, is that such prices are rigid both downwards and upwards, even more so in the latter case. (This holds true for both demand and cost changes.)

As far as demand changes are concerned, it would appear that oligopolistic prices move counter-cyclically, i.e. in times of demand increase or demand inflation they increase relatively less than competitive market prices, which in effect *restrains* the inflation process. (On the other hand they also decrease less, or their rate of increase declines more slowly than that of competitive market prices. This has implications for the success of traditional macroeconomic demand policy especially. See par. 3.2 on p. 76.)

To summarise: microeconomic arguments have been presented to the effect that 'administered' prices alone cannot cause continued price increases, and that it is unlikely that such prices played even an initiating role in the inflation in South Africa; secondly that there is no reason to believe that 'administered' prices propagate inflation more than 'market-determined' prices.

3. MACROECONOMIC EVALUATION

Before considering empirical evidence on this matter, it would be useful to look at the argument of 'administered' inflation within a macroeconomic theoretical framework. Indeed, this subject is interesting precisely because it forces one to break through the traditional boundary between micro- and macroeconomic affairs and essentially to integrate or at least reconcile them.

1. Non-competitiveness and aggregate supply

Although the Phillips curve was declared defunct many years ago, after various onslaughts by the facts of the 1970s and by the monetarists, modern macroeconomic theory claims that it has found an explanation for Phillips's empirical observations and also for the failure of the curve in the previous decade. It is in the framework of aggregate demand and aggregate supply, where the Phillips curve can be seen to be (a) a short-run supply curve which (b) can create a trade-off for demand policy in the short run, but (c) can shift about for various reasons (e.g. as a result of changes in price or inflation expectations, changes in input prices, a change in productivity or the labour force, etc.).

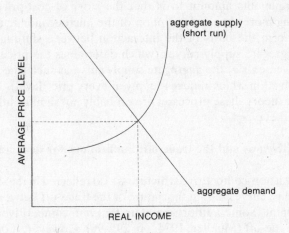

Figure 1

Within this framework average price levels therefore are determined by the interaction of aggregate demand and supply. Demand policy (monetary and fiscal) shifts the demand curve to the left or the right along the supply curve (the trade-off). Steady inflation is caused by both demand and supply when both move continuously, and at the same rate, outwards and inwards respectively (i.e. upwards on the graph).[2]

How do 'administered' prices and non-competitiveness fit into this framework? The relatively higher prices and decreased output that will probably occur in non-competitive sectors shift the supply curve to the left. When the non-competitiveness adversely affects the prices of inputs, it increases the cost structure of the economy and also shifts the supply curve to the left. Both cases therefore result in an increased average price level. And inflation? No, inflation — a sustained increase in the price level — requires a (graphically) continuously rising supply curve, not a (graphically) high supply curve — and the latter is absolutely all that is caused by non-competitiveness. Once the 'administered' prices reach their optimum levels, the supply curve is not shifted further, i.e. the profit-pressure affects the average price level only once or temporarily. (Continuous new monopoly formation can cause the process to be repeated continuously; however, that would require continuously increasing concentration, as explained earlier.)

In terms of the Phillips curve (with inflation, and not the price level, on the vertical axis) the above explanation implies that the curve moves up (graphically) only while administered prices rise to their optimum levels (if they are not there yet). Thereafter the curve moves back to its original position. Therefore administered prices alone cannot explain the permanent upward movements of the Phillips curve during the past decade (cf. Mueller, 1974).

As far as the propagation of cost increases is concerned, what the above microeconomic arguments amount to is that the story of cost-price spirals is probably nothing more than a description of the microeconomic adjustment processes that form the basis of the interaction between shifting aggregate demand and aggregate supply curves (which determines the price level) and the upward movements of the aggregate supply curve as such (the increase in the cost of production which reduces supply at every price level). In terms of macroeconomic theory these processes are probably not significantly different for different market types.

2. Non-competitiveness and the trade-off: implications for demand policy

The existence of a non-competitive structure is also reflected in the shape of the supply and Phillips curves, i.e. in the nature of the trade-off between inflation and unemployment. Some authors maintain that non-competitiveness establishes a worse trade-off (Mueller, 1974, pp. 295–96). However, if one looks at the phenomenon of rigid prices in non-competitive markets, the matter no longer seems so simple. As mentioned above, it would appear that the rigidity of such prices, for example, could result in oligopolistic prices reacting sluggishly to changes in demand — they increase relatively less than competitive prices when demand increases and decrease relatively less when demand decreases. In terms of the aggregate supply and Phillips curves this implies a flatter curve, so that a given change in unemployment (or real national income) is accompanied by a relatively smaller increase in the inflation rate. For expansions in aggregate demand (i.e. in times of demand inflation) it is therefore a better trade-off, because a smaller price is paid for the prosperity. Consequently, one could say that the non-competitive structure of the South African economy has, in theory, probably alleviated the inflationary impact of the demand expansion of the past decades.

On the other hand, the trade-off is worse for contractions in aggregate demand, which makes it more painful to fight inflation with recessions — a high price is paid in terms of unemployment. This is perhaps the most important implication that non-competitiveness may have with respect to the inflation problem, namely not as initiating or propagating factor, but as a factor that hampers anti-inflationary demand policy in the short run. It can therefore make it that much more difficult to wrest inflation from the system with monetary or fiscal policy.

However, it remains a double-edged sword, because more competitiveness makes any demand-led expansion considerably more painful, as the danger of demand inflation is increased. Therefore the question must be handled carefully. Whether a flatter Phillips curve is better or worse depends, in the end, on our priorities in terms of these two situations (expansion vs. contraction of aggregate demand).

To return to the debate on the causes of inflation: arguments from both micro- and macroeconomic analysis indicate that it is improbable that non-competitiveness and 'administered' prices either initiate or propagate inflation more than 'market-determined' prices in South Africa.

These arguments may be wrong, but before we declare non-competitiveness the great inflation scapegoat and prescribe competition policy as remedy, these arguments and conclusions will have to be accommodated or refuted. One should keep in mind that the obvious can sometimes be wrong — and in economics it often is.

4. EMPIRICAL RESULTS OF CONCENTRATION AND INFLATION IN SOUTH AFRICA

1. The hypotheses

In order to test empirically the two basic arguments of the theory of administered inflation, we must formulate them as testable hypotheses. The argument that administered prices are a cause or an initiating factor implies that prices rise more quickly in non-competitive markets than in so-called competitive markets. That is the first testable hypothesis. The argument that administered prices are a propagating factor implies (a) that similar cost increases result in relatively faster price increases in non-competitive markets, which amounts to the same as the first hypothesis, and (b) that cost increases lead to different reactions in the two classes of markets, i.e. cost variables should have higher coefficients for non-competitive industries. The latter is the second testable hypothesis.

2. The data

The data for this investigation pertain only to the manufacturing sector in South Africa. The sources of the data are the *Census of Manufacturing*, the *Bulletin of Statistics*, the *Report on Prices, Statistical Newsletters* and the *Du Plessis concentration figures* (Du Plessis, 1977 and 1978).

During the initial investigation the period was 1972–1976. It has now been extended to 1976–1979, with certain data up to 1982. (The concentration figures are available for 1972 only.)

The data include production price indices, revenue data and cost indices (calculated from 'Principal Statistics' in the *Census of Manufacturing*), indices of physical volume of production (P. 16.1), closing stocks of own manufactures (from the Census) and concentration figures (as a measure of non-competitiveness).

All the data are on main group basis (3-digit level) only, because only a few are available on 5-digit level. The number of usable data points are $n = 25$.

3. Concentration and price increases

The first relationship we would like to test is basically that between levels of concentration (K) and changes in the production price index (P). The standard procedure in the literature on the subject is to use the multiple regression technique.

I. *1972–1976*

Graphically no obvious relationship can be observed. If the data are divided into groups according to level of concentration, the price indices (1976-index with 1972 as base year) are as follows:

For two groups:	$0<K<20$	$20<K<100$	
	178,76	167,88	
	$(n = 11)$	$(n = 14)$	

For three groups:	$0<K<25$	$25<K<50$	$50<K<100$
	176,54	177,67	159,09
	$(n = 12)$	$(n = 7)$	$(n = 6)$

It appears that concentrated industries had lower rates of price increase. This is confirmed by the simple correlation coefficient between concentration and the price index, namely $r_{K;P} = 0,423$.

A simple regression of P on K gives the following:
$$P = 183,935 - 0,347K \tag{1}$$
$$\quad (29,85) \quad (2,24)$$
$$\bar{R}^2 = 14,33$$

(Figures in parentheses are t statistics.)

At this elementary level of investigation we therefore get a clear and (at $\alpha = 0,05$) a significant *negative* relationship between concentration and the rate of price increase. These results therefore indicate exactly the opposite of the administered inflation hypothesis.

II. *1976–1979*

The 1979 indices (with 1976 as base year) are as follows:

For two groups:	$0<K<20$	$20<K<100$	
	144,32	138,17	

For three groups:	$0<K<25$	$25<K<50$	$50<K<100$
	142,72	139,70	138,57

Correlation coefficient $r_{K;P} = 0,130$

Simple regression: $P = 93,073 - 0,151\,K$
  $(17,473)(-0,901)$
 $\bar{R}^2 = 0$

Autocorrelation was eliminated (retaining the first observation according to the Kadiyala method) (Koutsoyiannis, 1979, p. 219).

A negative coefficient for K is therefore also obtained for 1976–1979, but it has a very low level of statistical significance.

III. *1972–1979*

For the entire period one gets the following result:

$P = 266,59 - 0,671K$
  $(15,635)\,(-1,567)$
$\bar{R}^2 = 0,06$

This negative coefficient is significant at a significance level of $\alpha = \pm 0,07$ (one-sided test).

4. Concentration, prices and cost push

The first hypothesis is about exogenous price increases and concentration. It requires one to eliminate the effect of cost and demand changes to determine the actual effect of concentration as such. Initially only cost is considered — which also gives us the opportunity of evaluating the second hypothesis — and demand is added later.

Consider the second hypothesis, which is about the passing-on of cost increases into price increases. Consider the index for changes in unit costs[3] and compare it to the price index for the unconcentrated and concentrated groups respectively:

I. *1972–1976*

	$0<K<20$	$20<K<100$
ATC-index	182,77	203,32
P-index	178,76	167,88

Prices in the unconcentrated group therefore rose at approximately the same rate as unit costs, whereas prices in the more concentrated group increased significantly less than unit costs — the latter group apparently absorbed about 17 per cent of the cost increase and the former group only about 2 per cent. On the face of it these data seem to contradict the hypothesis. This information in fact agrees with the (counter-)arguments of Section 2, namely that non-competitive sectors probably pass on a smaller proportion of cost increases into prices than the so-called competitive sectors.

Multiple regression analysis confirms this result to some extent. The special use of a dummy variable makes it possible to allow for different reactions by the two groups to changes to unit costs, as it leads to different coefficients. For this purpose we define $ATC^* = ATC$ x DUMMY (with the value of the latter equal to 1 for $K<20$ and 0 for $K>20$) and use ATC^* as variable in the regression. (This method is therefore not equivalent to the conventional use of dummy variables, i.e. where the dummy itself is used as variable (Maddala, 1977, ch. 9.2).)

$$P = 153,316 - 0,187K + 10,991\,ATC + 5,097\,ATC^*$$
$$\quad\; (6,90) \quad\;\; (0,80) \quad\;\; (1,32) \quad\quad\;\;\; (0,867)$$
$$\overline{R}^2 = 14,59$$

The coefficient of ATC is relevant for the concentrated group and that of ATC^* indicates the difference between the coefficients of the two groups with respect to ATC. It therefore implies the following coefficients with respect to changes in unit costs:

$0<K<20$	$20<K<100$
16,088	10,991

(= 10,991 + 5,097)

A larger percentage of cost changes is therefore reflected in prices in the unconcentrated group. The difference between the coefficients has a very low significance level, however, and one should not attach too much importance to it.

As far as the first hypothesis is concerned, we see that the coefficient of concentration is still negative, but it now has a very low statistical significance level. When cost is kept constant, concentration apparently did not have a significant effect on prices (in 1972–76).

II. *1976–1979*

	$0 < K < 20$	$20 < K < 100$
ATC-index	130,90	128,40
P-index	144,32	138,17

In both groups prices rose more than unit cost and the gap is larger for the less concentrated group. (Also see Section 4.5.)

Multiple regression:

$$P = 35{,}079 - 0{,}039K + 56{,}169ATC + 3{,}762ATC^*$$
$$\quad (3{,}720) \ (0{,}204) \quad (3{,}955) \qquad (0{,}585)$$

$\bar{R}^2 = 49{,}33$

(Autocorrelation eliminated)

The unconcentrated group therefore shows slightly (but not significantly) more sensitivity with respect to cost changes.[4] The coefficient of concentration is still negative, but not significantly so, i.e. no statistically reliable relationship can be observed.

5. The role of demand factors

Thoroughness requires that the role of changes in demand (D) should also be involved in this investigation, otherwise we cannot really distinguish exogenous price increases and cost reactions. Demand is a rather problematic variable as no direct data are available. Some researchers use the quantity of output (Q) as a measure of demand (cf. Weiss, 1966; Ripley and Segal, 1973; Weston and Lustgarten, 1974), but the big objection against this is that this quantity is determined by both demand and supply. Therefore Q cannot represent demand (D).

A possible solution is to regard the behaviour of stock (relative to output) as a measure of demand conditions (cf. Wilder, 1977). An increase in the index of the stock/output ratio indicates a weakening demand, and vice versa.[5] (Normally one would therefore expect a negative sign for D.) Different reactions to demand changes can also be incorporated. The equations obtained in this way are:

Period	Const.	K	D	D^*	ATC	ATC*	$\bar{R}^2$
72–76	153,066	–0,186	0,003	–	10,920	5,143	
	(6,24)	(0,75)	(0,03)	–	(1,23)	(0,82)	10,3
72–76	173,860	–0,267	0,058	–0,688	0,439	34,470	
	(7,07)	(1,15)	(0,53)	(2,14)	(0,05)	(2,32)	23,98

Period	Const.	K	D	D*	ATC	ATC*	$\bar{R}^2$
76–79	75,73	–0,418	0,021	–0,461	27,544	38,265	
	(4,43)	(0,163)	(0,179)	(1,90)	(1,48)	(2,13)	41,45

(Autocorrelation eliminated with the Kadiyala method)

The inclusion of demand (D), especially with allowance for different reactions to demand changes by the two groups, influences the estimates considerably. The last two equations also give the most complete picture of the estimated effect of concentration, demand and cost changes on changes in the production price index.

The effect of concentration on the rate of price increase remains negative, although it has low significance for 1972–1976 and almost no significance for 1976–1979. The data therefore indicate no significant (or at most a slightly significant negative) relationship between concentration (as a measure of the extent of non-competitiveness) and the rate of price increase (with cost and demand factors taken into account).

As far as the passing on of cost increases is concerned, the two groups do not differ significantly if only demand (D) is included. However, when different demand reactions are allowed, the unconcentrated group in both periods is significantly more sensitive with respect to cost, i.e. a significantly larger percentage of cost increases is passed on in price increases than for the concentrated group (35 per cent as against 0,4 per cent and 66 per cent as against 28 per cent for the two periods respectively). It is also interesting that both groups displayed greater sensitivity with respect to cost increases in the more recent period.

As far as reactions to demand changes are concerned, the concentrated group shows very little or no price reaction to it, whereas the unconcentrated group is significantly more sensitive to demand changes.

The low sensitivity of the concentrated group with respect to both cost and demand changes confirms the phenomenon of rigid prices in non-competitive markets (cf. the theory of the kinked demand curve). This apparently applies to both decreases and increases in demand, because in 1972–1976 this group experienced a net increase in demand, and in 1976–1979 a decrease. Therefore the concentrated group's prices apparently do react counter-cyclically with respect to demand.

6. Some qualifications

Before drawing final conclusions we must attach certain qualifications to these results. Briefly, they are the following:
1.   The study does not take the effect of different degrees of foreign compe-

tition on local prices into account. This is an omission that will have to be rectified.[6]

2. There are many objections to the use of concentration as a measure of non-competitiveness and/or market power. Unfortunately, nothing else is available at present and it is quite widely used for this purpose — but then with circumspection. However, one should always keep in mind that low concentration figures do not necessarily imply competitiveness, especially when one considers the often ignored spatial context of market power. In the latter context it is to be doubted whether any firm could be anything but an 'imperfect' competitor.

3. The data are much too aggregated to draw conclusions with much confidence. Not enough micro-information is reflected in the data. However, the problem is that data on a subgroup (5-digit) level are incomplete at present. One can only hope that the situation will improve in future.

4. The choice of $K = 20$ as discrimination point for dividing the two groups is arbitrary, and, in this case, based on the need for sufficient data points in each group, as well as on the coefficient of determination $\bar{R}^2$. Experiments with other discriminating points, however, consistently produced negative coefficients for concentration which were even larger in absolute terms.

5. The data do not distinguish between relative price increases and general price increases.

6. Changes in quality are ignored. As non-price competition, and therefore, *inter alia*, quality competition, is relatively more common in non-competitive markets, one could expect that the price index effectively overestimates price increases in these markets.

7. This study refers to the periods 1972–1976 and 1976–1979 only.

5. CONCLUSIONS

1. The inflation process

The empirical evidence which we have considered shows the same result throughout.

In more concentrated markets price increases occur either more slowly or at most (and more probably) just as fast as in unconcentrated markets. The groups probably contribute equally to the inflation process (if cost and demand are kept constant).

Secondly, in the concentrated group cost increases are passed on into higher prices to a lesser extent (or at most to the same extent) than in unconcentrated markets. Neither of the two hypotheses resulting from the theory of so-called administered prices is supported by the data. The process of price formation in concentrated sectors does not appear in any sense to have a relatively greater role with respect to inflation (in the relevant periods).

As far as the propagation of cost increases is concerned, I wish to state once again, emphatically, that the above results do not in any way 'prove' that firms in non-competitive markets are *not guilty* of passing on cost increases. A more defensible conclusion is that they are, if anything, only *less guilty* than, and perhaps *equally guilty* as firms in so-called competitive markets. No one is absolved by the results.

2. Policy implications

As far as anti-inflationary policy, especially demand policy, is concerned, it would appear that prices in concentrated markets are less sensitive to demand changes and therefore to demand policy. Such a policy could therefore be hampered by the rigid-price phenomenon in these markets. On the other hand, as mentioned before, it is a double-edged sword which can relieve inflation arising from excess demand.

In the case of structural anti-inflation policy the results question the ability of competition policy and deconcentration *as such* to solve inflation. The freer operation of more competitive markets apparently presents no automatic bulwark against the inflation process and may even aggravate the inflation problem (although it could make contractionary demand policy more effective).

Lastly, a word of warning, which I address to myself as well. The arguments I have raised are of a general nature, but the data are for 1972–1979 specifically. Strictly speaking the conclusions are therefore valid for that period only. Time and further research will show what happened after that. However, economists are rather too inclined to draw final and 'generally valid' conclusions on the basis of such research, as if we are dealing with fixed, eternal and law-like relationships. If we do not remain humble in our conclusions, we could find our reputations blemished when new facts emerge later.[7]

For 1972–1979, however, the empirical results, as well as the arguments raised, remain something that must be taken into account by everyone who wants to put the blame for inflation on so-called administered prices. This is especially important when policy recommendations have to be made, because it may be mistaken to think that competition policy and the decrease of concentration — however desirable it may be from other considerations — will solve inflation without further ado.

NOTES

1

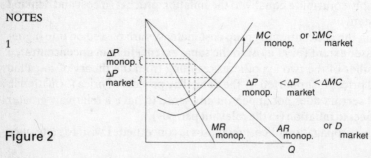

Figure 2

84

2 This set of curves could, of course, also be constructed with the inflation rate on the vertical axis. Then steady inflation is reflected in stationary demand and supply curves. This supply curve then corresponds to the Phillips curve in its modern form.

3 Unit cost $= \dfrac{\text{total cost}}{Q}$

   where $Q=$ index of physical production.
   Total cost $=$ gross output $-$ net profit, from Table 2.1 of the *Manufacturing Census*.

4 In investigations such as these it has become customary also to take the various components of cost into account, as firms possibly do not react to average *total* cost, but to specific kinds of cost. We therefore consider average labour cost *(ALC)*, materials cost *(AMC)* and overhead cost *(AOC)*, and for each observation each component is weighted with its average share in total cost. A dummy variable is used as above. (These data are only available for 1972–76 at present.)

$$P = \quad 146,730 - 0,192K + 0,063ALC + 0,295ALC^* - 0,149AMC + 0,295AMC^* + 1,103AOC - 1,55AOC^*$$
$$\quad (6,48) \quad\; (0,85) \quad\;\; (0,24) \quad\quad (0,496) \quad\;\; (0,16) \quad\quad (1,61) \quad\quad\quad\; (2,53) \quad\quad (1,26)$$
$$\bar{R}^2 = 23,89$$

   Concentration is negative again, but also still insignificant.

5 Closing stocks from Table 11.1, *Manufacturing Census*
   Output $=$ index of physical production (Q)

$$d = \frac{\text{closing stocks}}{(\text{output})} \; \% \text{ and } \; D = \frac{d76}{d72 \,\text{etc.}}$$

6 My thanks to Mr E. Calitz for this remark.

7 For the United States Leonard Weiss obtained negative, positive and no correlation between concentration and inflation for three different periods (cf. Weiss, 1966).

REFERENCES

De Wet, G.L., 1982a. 'Inflasie in Suid-Afrika: Oorsake en Moontlike Teenmaatreëls'. Chairman's address, Pretoria branch of the Economic Society of S.A., 1 March 1982.
—— 1982b. 'Faktore anders dan die Geldvoorraad wat Inflasie veroorsaak'. Paper, Conference of Economists and Business Economists, Port Elizabeth, November 1982.
Du Plessis, P.G., 1977. 'Concentration of Economic Power in the South African Manufacturing Industry'. D.Comm. thesis, University of Stellenbosch.
—— 1978. 'Concentration of Economic Power in the South African Manufacturing Industry', *South African Journal of Economics*, September.
Koutsoyiannis, A., 1979. *Modern Microeconomics* (2nd Edition). London: Macmillan.
Maddala, G.S., 1977. *Econometrics*. New York: McGraw-Hill.
Mohr, P.J., 1981. *'n Moontlike raamwerk vir die ontleding van die inflasieproses*. Appendix to the Economic Development Programme, Revised Edition for 1981–1987, Office of the Prime Minister, Pretoria.
Mueller, W.F., 1974. 'Industrial Concentration: An Important Inflationary Force?', in Goldschmid, H.J., Mann, H.M., Weston, J.F. (eds.), *Industrial Concentration: The New Learning*. Boston: Little Brown.
Ripley, F.C. and Segal, L., 1973. 'Price Determination in 395 Manufacturing Industries', *Review of Economics and Statistics*, August.
Scherer, F.M., 1980. *Industrial market structure and economic performance* (2nd edition). Chicago: Rand McNally.
Weiss, L.W., 1966. 'Business Pricing Policies and Inflation Reconsidered', *Journal of Political Economy*, April.
Weston, J.F. and Lustgarten, S., 1974. 'Concentration and Wage-Price Change', in Goldschmid, H., *et al.*, *op. cit.*
Wilder, R.P. *et al.*, 1977. 'The Price Equation: A Cross-Sectional Approach', *American Economic Review*, September.

2.5 STRUCTURALIST AND SOCIOLOGICAL VIEWS ON THE INFLATION PROBLEM

W.N. Meyer*

1. INTRODUCTION

Inflation, defined as a sustained rise in the price level, is a problem which has stimulated a great deal of debate on its causes and possible solution. Since the sixteenth century, when the French political philosopher Jean Bodin attributed contemporary inflationary pressure in Europe to the abundance of monetary metals imported from the Spanish colonies in South America, the money supply became an important factor in the analysis of inflation (Clough and Trap, 1975, p. 143). Bodin was the first to express the fundamental principles of the quantity theory of money, the basic tenet of which was that changes in the price level are determined by changes in the quantity of money in circulation. Today, Keynesian orthodoxy and monetarism are the major competing theories in analysing conditions in both the developed and the developing countries. But both theories essentially evolved in the context of the industrialised economies and have not adequately dealt with the peculiar historical and institutional circumstances of Third World countries. Thus, both theories have been rejected as superficial by scholars in Latin America — the continent of the oldest sovereign states among developing countries. There, an indigenous school of thought emerged emphasising structural factors in economic analysis.

The structuralist approach has by no means been confined to the Latin American scholars. In the 1970s there has emerged in the United Kingdom a cohesive structuralist approach to the study of inflation. This approach, which has been called the European Structuralist School (Canavese, 1982, p. 524), stresses the impact on inflation of a structural imbalance between the private sector and the public sector. Other recent developments include the Scandinavian models which combine elements of structural inflation with international transmissions of inflation to small open economies, i.e. price-takers in the world market.

Non-economic explanations of inflation have become strong alternatives to purely economic ones. It has been recognised lately that, although economic variables provide the mechanism for inflation, the fundamental problems in the economic system are generated by sociological and political factors.

In what follows an attempt has been made to delineate these theories of inflation with the purpose of highlighting their strengths and weaknesses and to

* Professor of Economics, University of the North. This paper was first published in *Studies in Economics and Econometrics*, No. 19, March 1984.

consider their relevance to the South African situation, the latter, however, in a very superficial manner.[1]

2. THE SCANDINAVIAN MODEL

The Scandinavian model (Aukrust, 1977) divides the economy into the sheltered (S) sector which produces non-tradable goods and the exposed (E) sector which produces tradable goods. Since the E sector is linked with the world economy the rate of inflation in this sector ($\dot{P}_E$) equals the world rate ($\dot{P}_W$). With given income distribution in E, the increase in money wages is determined by $\dot{P}_W$ and the rate of labour productivity in E. The firms in the E sector are price-takers. Productivity is higher in E than it is in S.

The firms in S add a constant profit mark-up to the labour cost. Owing to a productivity gap and a uniform wage increase for both sectors, cost-push inflation in the S sector ($\dot{P}_S$) is the difference between the percentage change in money wages and the rate of change of labour productivity in S. Overall domestic inflation then is the weighted average of $\dot{P}_S$ and $\dot{P}_E$ where the respective shares of E and S in total output are the weights.

Accordingly, the underlying assumptions of the Scandinavian structural inflation model are: (1) the profitability of the E industries is a major factor in determining the wage level in the E sector. Wages and profits are determined in such a way that when there is a rise in prices or productivity in E, the increase in income will be shared between profits and wages. And there is a tendency in the adjustment mechanism to maintain a 'normal' relation between profits and wages; (2) the wage level in the S sector is determined by the wage level in the E sector; (3) productivity is higher in the E sector than the S sector, and (4) the wage level and the productivity of the S sector determine the product price in this sector.

A major implication of the model is the burden placed on the E sector in holding down cost-push trends. In a situation of rising world prices, to oppose wage claims in the E sector would imply rising profits. Thus the fights against wage inflation will be influenced by the variance between actual profit levels and the socially acceptable levels which can be determined for each country as 'normal' profits.

The determination of wages in the S sector by trends in the E sector appears to be a bold assumption for labour markets in developing countries. The inequalities in the wage structures of many developing countries are not in accordance with this model's assumption of uniform wages. However, in South Africa, wage trends in the more productive exposed sectors have an unquestionable influence on the wages of the sheltered sector. Hence, the possibility of wages rising faster than productivity in the sheltered industries is strong. Since this deviation between wages and productivity is the essense of inflationary pressure in this sector, and not uniform wages *per se*, the Scandinavian model cannot be rejected simply on account of inequalities of wages.

3. STRUCTURALIST MODELS

Structuralism may be viewed as a conglomerate analytical framework, diverse in methodological, intellectual and ideological inclinations (Seers, 1962, pp. 192–5). It seeks to examine the structure of the factors that hamper economic growth and other socio-economic goals. These factors could include the following: structure of income, demand, output, industry, imports, administration, politics, society, etc. In Western countries, structuralist models were developed by Baumol (1967) and Streeten (1962), among others, to deal with isolated cases. However, in the 1970s there was a sustained interest among British analysts in the impact of labour structure on inflation (Bacon and Eltis, 1975, p. 269). This interest has resulted in a distinct approach to inflation, that of the so-called European School, which will be examined in Section 3.2. It will emerge that the models worked out by Latin American structuralists during the 1960s and models developed recently by European structuralists describe similar inflationary processes.

3.1 The Latin American Structuralist School

In 1962 Seers (p. 193) observed '... the (Latin American) School could acquire in the 1960s an international interest comparable to that of Keynesian economics during the slump ridden decade of the 1930s'. In retrospect, Seers appears to have been rather optimistic. What was the basis of that optimism about 'these theories forming an original and stimulating contribution to the field of economic growth' (Seers, p. 192–3)?

The basic concern of the Latin American structuralists is with economic growth, while inflation tends to be treated as a side issue. This is in sharp contrast with the approach in Western Europe, where 'high inflation rates have caused a re-ordering of policy targets, with both Labour and Conservative governments prepared to accept high levels of unemployment in order to reduce inflationary pressures ... Where present governments seem determined, come what may, to reduce inflation via a monetarist route, which will, they hope, destroy inflationary forces and inflationary expectations through the creation of high levels of unemployment' (Brown, 1980, p. 4). Inflation is in this view clearly an evil, even more destructive to society than unemployment.

The particular emphasis by the Latin American economists against the background of rampant inflation in most of their countries underscores not only their deep interest in economic growth, but also the structuralist view that inflation is inevitable in a growing economy burdened with structural maladjustments. In South America the customary Keynesian–monetarist controversy gave way to a structuralist–monetarist debate on inflation. While all the various economic and institutional factors hampering growth are considered by structuralists like Furtado (1970), the fundamental elements in the structuralist framework appear to be those connected with production and with internal and external trade. Structuralists make a sharp distinction between developed and less developed countries in inflationary behaviour and policies. While all economies can have structural imbalances, the adjustment process is very difficult in developing countries because of supply rigidities, various bottlenecks and the lack of integration among the sectors of the economy.

Thus, in a growing economy, the growth of real income and economic potential increase demand in some sectors, while bottlenecks prevent a corresponding increase in the supply of goods. Under such circumstances, prices in the sector where demand has risen will rise. A typical example is that of the demand for food rising as urban incomes rise faster than agricultural output, which is burdened with relatively poor technological and institutional rigidities. The resulting pressure on food prices sets off price increases in other sectors too, and a price spiral or price–wage spiral can thus be generated.

An important structuralist proposition is that development is a consequence of structural change. Thus, any restriction on credit, for instance, to fight inflation may result in economic stagnation by paralysing certain businesses and raising money costs of others. Indeed, the restrictive monetary policies prescribed by the IMF and followed by Chile, Argentina and Brazil in the 1950s and 1960s to fight inflation are seen by Furtado as the basic causes of recessions without relative price stability in those countries. The tacit assumptions underlying IMF policy recommendations (on which IMF assistance depends) is that if financial order is established, exports will benefit, private foreign capital will be attracted and growth will occur spontaneously. Thus, Furtado appears very sceptical about IMF policies, to say the least.

In terms of external trade, the failure of export earnings to keep abreast of the growth in other sectors of the economy could create balance of payments difficulties if demand for imports rises with incomes. Prices of imported goods will tend to rise, either directly through the cost of living index, or through higher costs of capital inputs. The import price increase may cause a price–wage spiral. This is a real problem for countries whose export earnings may decline not because of a decline in real exports, but because of reduced world market prices. The long-range price forecasts for developing countries' exports, dominated by raw materials, are pessimistic mainly because of a declining trend in world demand. This trend is a result of technological change which not only reduces input levels of materials, but also facilitates the substitution of synthetics for natural raw materials. This rather pessimistic view is generally associated with Raul Prebisch (1963).

To sum up, low agricultural sector productivity and balance of payments difficulties are the main elements in the Latin American structuralist analysis. Growing industrialisation and increasing urbanisation produce a change in the amount and structure of food and raw materials demanded. Low agricultural sector productivity does not allow for quick response of supply to new demand. Relative prices of agricultural goods tend to rise. If industrial prices are inflexible downwards because of an oligopolistic market structure, money prices of agricultural goods must rise. 'Propagation elements' then further transmit such structural inflationary pressure: rises in wages take place because of the rising costs of living and thus rises in costs of production in the industrial sector are induced; such rises in costs imply a higher money price for industrial goods if profit margins are to be kept constant and so a new adjustment of relative prices is needed, beginning once again the process just described. The whole process assumes the existence of a passive money supply that assures equilibrium in money markets: an increasing money supply validates higher prices. Balance of payments disequilibrium appears because industrialisation requires new and increasing expenditure on imports relative to income derived from exports. A low rate of growth of foreign demand for primary goods contributes to a deterioration of the terms of trade. Without autonomous compensating capital movements, disequilibrium-correcting policies are needed: rate of exchange devaluations and/or import quotas are adopted. Both measures result in changes in the relative prices of imported goods. Structural inflationary pressure appears and 'propagation elements' amplify it through the economic system.

It can be said therefore that Latin American countries have many similarities with other developing countries, but there are differences in historical circumstances and institutional factors. The fundamental challenge to an economic analyst using this school's basic analytical framework is a clear understanding of the socio-economic system under study.

3.2 The European Structuralist School

European structuralism studies those fluctuations related to wages that grow at the same rate in every sector of the economy in spite of differing sectoral rates of growth of labour productivity. It will be clear from what follows that European structuralists restrict their analytical work to changes stemming from supply shifts, while Latin American structuralists considered both demand and supply shifts causing relative prices to change.

In this manner, in the 1970s, Johnston (1975, pp. 288–308) and Bacon and Eltis (1975, pp. 269–95) have developed models focusing on the impact of structural shifts in employment from the private to the public sector on the price level. The essence of these models is to examine the effect of structural changes in labour supply on the relative growth of money expenditure and marketed output. The models postulate a public sector that provides (free) services to the population, and a private sector that produces goods and services for the market. Any employment bias in favour of the public sector will tend to raise money expenditure faster than the marketed output. This excess demand results in pressures on prices. In an open economy, a relative increase in public employment can also lead to a greater growth in imports than exports and thus create balance of payments difficulties. These labour-orientated models assume that the growth in the share of public sector employment is reflected in larger government deficits, which, in turn, produce an excess demand in the economy. The excess demand is absorbed by changes in the price level. Even in the absence of a budget deficit, a relative increase in government employment generates some potential for inflationary pressures. If government employment share is increased by raising taxes, the effect is that workers suffer a reduction in real consumption. If, consequently, workers demand higher wages to prevent a fall in real private consumption, then there is the possibility of a wage–price spiral. Alternatively, demands for higher wages may lead to higher unemployment. Mainly through these reactions to tax increases, prices are likely to rise.

Another problem of increased taxation is the adverse effect on investment in the long run. As Bacon and Eltis have pointed out, '... the larger the ratio of employment in the public sector, the smaller will be the aggregate amount of market sector output ... and this means that market sector investment will be less' (p. 287). Thus, whatever the static effects of fiscal policies may be, they will be complicated in the long run by a diminishing productive capacity of marketed goods, relative to what the capacity would otherwise have been.

When increased government employment is financed by a budget deficit, the induced excess demand can be directly related to the size of the deficit, unless the deficit financing methods affect the real sector. Possible sources of deviation include the crowding-out effects of bond financing on the private sector and the probable effects of money creation on the real sector. In particular, if monetary policy is accompanied by credit expansion for the private firms, then the production of marketed goods will be stimulated by the share of the deficit financed by money creation. The basic argument here is that if monetary policy affects the availability of commercial credit, then its impact is not confined to its effects on aggregate demand, but also extends to the supply side.

When government expenditure is associated with the improvement of social and economic infrastructure, it has some effect on the production of marketed goods. Since government investment in infrastructure has a long gestation period, its effect on output will only be felt in the long run. The effect on consumption demand, however, is immediate. Hence the long-run inflationary effects of the relative increase in public sector employment will be reduced by the impact of the public sector on the productivity of the private sector. But in the short run the inflationary impact of expansionary fiscal policy is not mitigated by current government investment in infrastructure. It is noted, however, that current productivity changes in the private sector will tend to reduce the inflationary impact of increased government spending.

In summary one can say that labour productivity grows at a different rate in each economic sector. Usually productivity grows faster in goods producing sectors than in those supplying services. Services have a low price elasticity and a high income elasticity (Canavese, p. 524). A uniform rate of growth of money wages in both sectors leads to a sustained cost pressure in the supply of services. If prices are set through a fixed profit margin markup policy on the rising wage costs, relative prices of services go up and the downward inflexibility of money wages and prices leads to inflation. The uniform rate of growth of money wages in both sectors may be explained either by a 'fairness' principle applied by unions or even by the operation of a competitive labour market as was pointed out by Frisch (1977, pp. 1289–1317).

4. SOCIOLOGICAL THEORIES OF INFLATION

After World War II, social stimulation of income claims gave rise to what came to be called 'income inflation' (as opposed to demand inflation) (Duesenberry, 1950, pp. 144–9). The essence of income inflation is that at full employment, different groups tend to raise or maintain their real incomes by raising their monetary share. In the absence of improvements in real output, any claims for higher monetary shares by labour, firms or landlords will simply create inflationary pressure. The inflationary pressure ceases once the powerless group has been sufficiently impoverished by rising prices to confer real gains on the powerful group. This approach to inflation is very relevant to those developing countries characterised by small increases in output, but very high consumption aspirations.

It is clear that the non-economic explanations of inflation have become strong alternatives to purely economic explanations in some policy decision centres (Hirsch and Goldthorpe, 1978, p. 3). Traditional economic explanations of inflation rely entirely on economic variables and ignore the socio-political and other variables which interact with, and reinforce, the economic variables. Thus, sociological and political theories of inflation are seen as complementing rather than competing with economic theories. Economic variables provide the mechanism for inflation, but fundamental problems in the economic system are generated by social and political factors (Panić, p. 138).

It is no coincidence that high rates of inflation are accompanied by high levels of social instability. Thus governments desire and are determined to curb demand and slow down the economy in order to reduce the rate of inflation. Hence the interaction of the economy with the process of government or organised society (the polity) comes about in the regulation of social interests. Economic action is directed at securing material goals. If there were an 'unchecked pursuit of scarce resources by boundless private interests, the inevitable conflicts would threaten civil order' (Crouch, p. 218). The polity's role is to maintain order that is conducive of free economic activity. The polity prevents any threat to social order through a variety of institutions backed by its 'monopolising in a central institution (the state) the control of the means of violence' (Crouch, p. 218).

Control of social action is also aided by international checks such as individual normative restraints that are acquired through socialisation, i.e. routine contact with the society to which the individual belongs. By incorporating society's normative ideas into the legal and other state institutions, the state has become the central normative institution in modern societies. In a competitive economy, this is as far as the polity can go in controlling human behaviour. Otherwise, the regulation of economic action is left to the price mechanism, the 'invisible hand' that allocates resources in market economies.

In practice, the regulatory roles of the polity and the price mechanism are not mutually exclusive. Moreover, institutional factors tend to interfere with the ability of the price mechanism to regulate economic action. In this regard, special attention is paid to the capacity for organisation among social groups and institutions.

It can be observed that once interest groups become organised they acquire a capacity for strategy, and are no longer easily amenable to all forms of regulation. An important example is the organisation of financial markets. 'Agencies like the IMF have acquired a capacity for strategy which produce results different from the normal effects of a mass of creditors simply pursuing their own self-interest within an atomistic market' (Crouch, p. 221). Another example is the power of organised labour to achieve their interests through political action if the market fails them. It needs to be remembered, however, that workers' capacity to organise is partly dependent on the level of employment. At any rate, 'increasingly frequent interventions by the polity have been needed in order to maintain the capitalist economy itself' (Crouch, p. 222). The polity intervenes to take care of the activity itself or to fashion it so that it conforms to the working of the market system.

As workers have acquired a capacity for gaining higher wages and better working conditions without a corresponding change in economic organisation, an irreconcilable conflict is generated between workers' interests and those of the profit earners. The conflict can be diffused by an increase in economic growth. But in the short run, 'only one thing prevents ... irreconcilable conflict within the economy; the fact that wages are fixed in money rather than real terms. In other words, inflation may result, and, ironically, begin as a means whereby conflicts are contained' (Crouch, p. 228).

However, in the long run frustration and discontent may appear and begin to grow. The reason for this is that during the early phases of rapid economic growth people may tolerate the existence of or even an increase in inequality, but as Hirschman (p. 545) has argued, 'this tolerance is like a credit that falls due at a certain date. It is extended in the expectation that eventually the disparities will narrow. If this does not occur, there is bound to be trouble and, perhaps, disaster.' Economic growth raises claims on resources which simply cannot be met from the world's existing productive capacity or indeed any productive capacity likely to be created in the foreseeable future. The irony is that we create economic development to reduce scarcity and unsatisfied wants; but at the same time the very process of economic development creates new wants, hopes and aspirations which cannot be fulfilled due to resource constraints. In the end there are more unsatisfied wants after development than before, because wants are increasingly the result of development rather than the causes.

'The locus of instability is the divergence between what is possible for the individual and what is possible for all individuals' (Hirsch, 1977, p. 67). Inflation, therefore, can be seen as a symptom of, as well as a safety valve for, socio-economic inequalities.

Panić (in Hirsch and Goldthorpe, ch. 6) has extended this thesis of a competitive ethos creating an aspiration gap with economic, social and political consequences to explain the international transmission of inflation. An empirical study of OECD countries leads him to conclude that reductions of income inequalities within countries, and higher levels of per capita social expenditure, tend to lessen inflationary pressures. He fears that the international aspirations gap between one nation and another, which is reflected in worldwide inflation, is already very bad. Any widening of the gap will accelerate long-term inflationary tendencies and the underlying socio-economic conflicts to a level where they could assume a much more disruptive and destructive form (Panić, p. 154).

If Panić paints a gloomy picture for international economic relations, the future is not any brighter for internal conflicts in major capitalist countries. According to Goldthorpe: '... over recent decades the generally rising rate of inflation reflects a situation in which conflict between social groups and strata has become more intense and also to some extent *more equally matched*, with these two tendencies interacting in a mutually reinforcing way. Less advantaged groups and strata have tended to become more free of various constraints on their actions in pursuit of what they see as their interest; hence, they have become more likely to punch their weight – to press their claims closer to the limits of the power they actually possess; and in turn then, they have become more effective in their conflicts with other parties, gaining in this way not only advantages but also a stronger position from which to fight for further claims' (Goldthorpe, p. 196). In the case of Britain, Goldthorpe identifies three interrelated factors which have induced a rising trend in social conflict, viz. (1) the decay of the status order; (2) the realisation of citizenship; (3) the emergence of a 'mature' working class. We now examine these factors separately.

Most sociologists would accept the importance of a distinction between 'class' and 'status'. The former pertains to differences in social advantage and power which have a material base. Status, on the other hand, pertains to social advantage and power resting not on a material, but a symbolic and a moral basis. Thus status inequalities have a normative basis which is lacking in class inequalities, which are 'from any moral standpoint largely arbitrary' (Goldthorpe, p. 198). Though analytically distinct, 'class' and 'status' are hardly distinguishable in practice because of easy convertibility of the various forms of social advantage and power. The traditional status system is incompatible with the social implications of capitalism. Hence, the development of a capitalist economy has led to declining status order, and ascending class order, as the market economy has become the major stratifying force, i.e. the major determinant of the distribution of social advantage and power.

Citizenship refers to the acquisition of civil, political and social rights by all citizens. Citizenship is an egalitarian phenomenon. Hence, it can be argued that the development of citizenship may form a basis for greater social harmony by legitimising class inequalities as the outcome of meritocratic achievement. On the other hand, citizenship is in inevitable conflict with the capitalist class system. 'While the possibility is created of legitimation in terms of meritocracy, the threat also arises that with the realization of citizenship, the contrast between the principled equality of rights that it bestows and the unprincipled inequalities thrown up by the market will be highlighted, and that the latter will thus be increasingly called into question' (Goldthorpe, p. 202).

Thus, civil rights which are indispensable to a competitive market economy also gave rise to full political citizenship which, in turn, formed the base for independent trade unions which have significantly distorted the market mechanism.

The maturity of the working class as defined by Goldthorpe deviates from the Marxist case of a working class ready to overthrow the capitalist system. The mature working class, then, is not one that is revolutionary in the Marxist sense, but one that remains only imperfectly accommodated by the capitalist system. It realises the inability of the market system to maximise workers' benefits without concerted industrial and political action by them. Thus, although not revolutionary, the working class possesses not only the capacity to engage in a distributional conflict, but also the potential for action that can create economic dislocation and civil disturbance. All three factors which have tended to encourage conflict in Britain can be found in most developing countries too. With the spread of capitalism, traditional norms have come under strong pressure from capitalist values. Before World War II, much of Africa and Asia were under colonial rule. The colonial system imposed strong restrictions on the economic, political and civil rights of the subjects. Thus, the gradual collapse of imperial powers and their hold over Africa and Asia which set in after World War II caused dramatic developments in 'citizenship' in the newly independent states. In the case of South Africa, where this process of attainment of independence for several new Black states is still in progress, this came with an equally dramatic buildup in socio-economic, if not also racial, tension.

If there is one thing trade unions know, it is that workers' interests cannot be left to the generosity of the market system. In this respect, most workers, in South Africa too, do meet the 'maturity' criteria of Goldthorpe.

When the current inflation is seen as a result of distributional conflict and the idea of a mature working class is a crucial element in the inflationary situation, the problem facing government is not only that of coping with inflation, but also, and more fundamentally, with the conflict that lies behind it. Thus, when preservation of the legitimacy of the government is the major concern of the polity, the government will have rational aversion to economic policies with the risk of a powerful challenge. Hence, government policy that encourages inflation or does nothing to stop it may be perfectly rational.

The question of legitimacy leads us to the ability of the government to prevent inflation. Whether in pursuit of electoral votes or legitimacy, the polity faces certain choices. For instance, wage settlements have been a major source of inflation, but the fear of a large-scale strike renders a government impotent to stop inflation. If it were not for the threat of a strike, strict monetary policy could be combined with an incomes policy to stabilise prices. Such difficult choices tend to limit the ability of the government to deal with inflation. Thus, in anti-inflation policies, what is economically rational may not necessarily be politically rational. To the extent to which inflation tends to diffuse socio-economic conflicts, moderate inflationary policies can conform with the best short-term political strategy. But the long-term policy must deal with the underlying social conflicts. If social conflict is inherent in the market economy, as argued by sociologists, then inflation appears a permanent feature of capitalist economies.

The sociologists' view of the market system is seen by Goldthorpe as the fundamental difference between sociologists and economists. The latter generally tend to view the market system as having an inherent propensity toward stability. Thus, according to the economist there are no inherent inflationary tendencies in the market economy; according to the monetarists inflation is a result of external interference in the market system, notably generated by unsound monetary policies or the monopoly power of unions. Even according to the cost-push theorists, who explain inflation partially in terms of the functioning of the economy, inflation is not linked to the form of the economy, but merely to its performance.

5. CONCLUSION

Inflation has traditionally been seen as an economic problem — indeed, as an essentially monetary problem — and has been studied by economists. These studies themselves have shown that inflation of the kind now endemic in the capitalist world is more than an economic problem. The great value of the theories reviewed here is that they have attempted to go beyond the recognition that inflation is a 'monetary disease' and have sought to identify the forces that lie behind excessive injections of money into the economic system. The examination of the theories presented in this article has made it clear that inflation is not just a technical economic problem, but is rather itself a 'solution', of sorts, to more fundamental problems of a socio-political character. It follows, therefore, that if a solution to the problem of inflation is to be found, it cannot be, as monetarist analysis would often imply, in economic policy alone. The key to the control of inflation and to the more successful regulation of organised interests in general must lie in a continuation of institutional development leading to the more effective political integration of these interests. What is needed, over and above economic technique, is political creativity.

NOTE

1 For an analysis more specific to the South African situation, emphasising the Structuralist approach, see P.J. Mohr, 'A Possible Framework for Analysing the Inflationary Process', in: *Ninth Economic Development Programme for the RSA, 1978–1987, Revised Edition for 1981–1987,* Pretoria, 1981.

REFERENCES

Aukrust, O., 1977. 'Inflation in the Open Economy: A Norwegian Model', in: L.B. Krause and W. Salant (eds.), *World Wide Inflation*. Washington D.C.: Brookings Institute.

Bacon, R.W. and Eltis, W.A., 1975. 'The Implications for Inflation, Employment and Growth of a fall in the share of output that is marketed', *Oxford Bulletin of Economics and Statistics*, November.

Baumol, W.J., 1967. 'Macroeconomics of Unbalanced Growth: the Anatomy of Urban Crises', *American Economic Review*, Vol. 57, No. 3.

Brown, C.D., 1980. *The Welfare Effects of Inflation – The British Case*. SUERF-Series, No. 29A.

Canavese, A.J., 1982. 'The Structuralist Explanation of the Theory of Inflation', *World Development*, Vol. 10, No. 7.

Clough, S.B. and Trap, R.T., 1975. *European Economic History*. London: McGraw-Hill.

Crouch, C., 1978. 'Inflation and the Political Organization of Economic Interests', in: Hirsch and Goldthorpe, Chapter 9.

Duesenberry, J.S., 1950. 'The Mechanics of Inflation', *Review of Economics and Statistics,* May.

Frisch, H., 1977. 'Inflation Theory 1963–1976: a Second Generation Survey', *Journal of Economic Literature*, Vol. 15, No. 4.

Furtado, C., 1970. *Economic Development of Latin America*. Cambridge: Cambridge University Press.

Goldthorpe, J.H., 1978. 'The Current Inflation: Towards a Sociological Account', in: Hirsch and Goldthorpe, Chapter 8.

Hirsch, F., 1977. *Social Limits to Growth*. London: Routledge.

Hirsch, F. and Goldthorpe, J.H. (eds.), 1978. *The Political Economy of Inflation*. London: Martin Robertson.

Hirschman, A., 1973. 'The Changing Tolerance for Income Inequality in the Course of Economic Development', *Quarterly Journal of Economics*, November.

Johnston, J., 1975. 'A Macro Model of Inflation', *Economic Journal*, June.

Panić, M., 1978. 'The Origin of Increasing Inflationary Tendencies in Contemporary Society', in: Hirsch and Goldthorpe, Chapter 6.

Prebisch, R., 1963. 'Development Problems of the Peripheral Countries and the Terms of Trade', in: *Towards a Dynamic Development Policy for Latin America*. New York: UN-ECLA.

Seers, D., 1962. 'A Theory of Inflation and Growth in Underdeveloped Economies based on the Experience of Latin America', *Oxford Economic Papers*, June.

Streeten, P., 1969. 'Wages, Prices and Productivity', in: Ball, R.J.S. and Doyle, P. (eds.), *Inflation*. Harmondsworth: Penguin Books.

3

Cyclical Instability and the Phillips Trade-Off

3.1 INTRODUCTION

One of the characteristic features of a modern, market-orientated economy is that it tends to oscillate over time between periods of economic upswing and recession. While the size and duration of these fluctuations have been extensively researched in the literature, there is little agreement amongst economists over the chief sources of instability in the modern economy. Indeed, it is probably fair to say that the recent literature on macroeconomics has been dominated by questions relating to the stability of private spending and the relevant policy implications.

Keynesian economists maintain that free market economies are inherently unstable because private consumers and producers do not have the information necessary to anticipate and act upon exogenous disturbances in a world of uncertainty. Such disturbances may push the economy into a state of perpetual disequilibrium, thus necessitating an activist policy to return it to its equilibrium path. Monetarists, on the other hand, argue that the private economy is basically stable if allowed to operate in a free and unfettered environment. The relative stability of private spending stems from the permanent income hypothesis, according to which private consumption expenditure is assumed to be a function of long-run or permanent income, rather than short-run fluctuations in current income. The chief source of instability is the government itself whose interventionist policies precipitate a temporary deviation from the natural level of real output. Thus, monetarists advocate adherence to a money-supply rule whereby the supply of money is allowed to increase at a rate commensurate with the growth of productivity in the economy.

The perennial debate between monetarists and Keynesians also features prominently in the literature on the Phillips curve. Keynesians argue that demand disturbances will see to it that the economy fluctuates along successive short-run Phillips curves, never quite reaching long-run stability, unless the government adopts an appropriate policy to counteract the erratic behaviour of private investors and consumers. In juxtaposition, monetarists believe that there is a natural tendency for the economy to gravitate toward its long-run equilibrium, and that any attempt to reduce unemployment below its natural rate will meet with only temporary success. Thus in the long run, the trade-off between inflation and employment will disappear completely, leaving the economy in a worse position than before.

The above debate is, in the final analysis, an empirical matter which depends on the nature of peoples' expectations about the future. While monetarists and Keynesians tend to disagree over the speed with which expectations are adjusted to past rates of inflation, supporters of the rational expectations school believe that people are able to fully anticipate the consequences of government policy and incorporate them into their current wage and price contracts. The Phillips curve thus becomes vertical even in the short run, so that monetary and fiscal policy will have no effect on the real level of output and employment.

In the first reading of this chapter, Goedhuys examines the nature of economic fluctuations and offers various explanations for the existence and duration of business cycles in the South African economy. Although it is not possible to eradicate economic fluctuations in a market economy altogether, he suggests that monetary rather than fiscal policy should be used to mitigate the effects of business cycles. The second reading, by Shostak, attempts an econometric test of the natural rate hypothesis for South Africa, and finds that there is no trade-off between unemployment and inflation in the long run. His analysis does, however, enable him to reject both the strong and weak versions of the rational expectations hypothesis. In the final contribution, Black and Leibbrandt discuss the nature of the Phillips trade-off in underdeveloped economies, and spell out the relevant implications for macroeconomic policy.

3.2 THE BUSINESS CYCLE AND PUBLIC POLICY

D.W. Goedhuys*

It is argued in this paper that the business cycle is ineradicable from the market economy and that fiscal policy can at best avoid amplifying it. Monetary policy, working through the actual or opportunity cost of spending, is rather better suited to exert a stabilising influence.

ECONOMIC FLUCTUATIONS

Fluctuations in economic activity are of many kinds. Some are short and sudden, others are like a long swell extending over decades. Some are clearly seasonal and, finally, there are the recurring upswings and downswings over periods longer than a year (business cycles) which have received the most systematic discussion. The fluctuations of a roughly cyclical nature are an attribute of the market economy, in which most of the decisions to produce and consume are made by independent parties producing for and buying in a market. The centrally planned economies are not immune to fluctuating fortunes either. Foreign trade, harvest results, discontinuities in leadership, restatement of priorities and experimentation with new techniques also tend to produce ups and downs in economic performance. In the economic systems with which we are more familiar and where economic activity depends for the most part on individual initiative, the longer-than-seasonal fluctuations appear to be self-generating and inherent in the mechanics of the economic process itself.

The individual decisions to invest and produce are made with an eye on a future which is uncertain. Each decision-maker is only imperfectly aware of the plans of his competitors and customers, and even if his estimate of the total market for his product is correct, he may overestimate the share of it that he can capture. The carrying out of all the production and purchasing plans together, aided by an elastic supply of credit, may result in rapid economic advance when new opportunities are perceived and exploited and markets expand. In time, however, some of the investment in production and marketing turns out to have been a malinvestment, in size or type or timing. The commitment of resources may have been too large or resulted in the production of goods and services different from those the market eventually demanded. The allocation of resources to such avenues of production is then abruptly cut back. Supply activities based on them must contract and, like falling dominoes, other businesses are hurt in turn. Plans still on the drawing board are scaled down or abandoned. Credit contracts in response to reduced demand or greater risk and

* Advisor, S.A. Reserve Bank. This paper is based on a paper read at the Biennial Conference of the Economic Society of South Africa, Johannesburg, 19–20 September 1983; first published in *The South African Journal of Economics*, Vol. 52, No. 2, 1984.

thus purchasing power vanishes. Markets at first correctly sized up begin to shrink and the whole economy turns down. The upturn must await the detection of new opportunities, some of them created by the very surpluses and misalignments inherited from the preceding depression.

This brief sketch is purely descriptive and allows many different 'causes' to be introduced in explanation of the turning points of the cycle. On the dynamic process lying *between* these points there is fairly wide agreement, perhaps because the interaction of business activity during expansion and contraction is so readily observable, but on the cause or causes of the turnaround many contending theories have been advanced. Which of these is adopted by policymakers is obviously important to the choice, scope and success of stabilisation policy.

THE QUEST FOR STABILITY

The waste of idle resources and the losses sustained during the downswing, and the strains and shortages of the upswing, at one time accepted as inevitable, began to appear less so when with the evolution of our economic system there rose to prominence one source of spending on goods and labour that was directed by motives other than profitable production for a market. That source is, of course, the public sector, whose inexorable growth during the past half-century has reached a level where in some ostensibly market economies it commands more than half the national product. What was more natural, then, than that the vast revenue-raising and spending powers of the public sector should be enlisted in the effort to moderate the swings in the total performance of the total economy? Considerable effort and ingenuity have been expended over several decades in order to adapt not only the amounts of revenue and spending, but also their sources, procedures and direction, as well as the nature of the activities undertaken, to the exigencies of a contra-cyclical, or stabilising, policy. Social objectives merged with economic ones in idealistic policies of 'economic engineering'. The wave of inflation this produced has left most capitalist economies stranded in the shoals of idle capacity and high unemployment, from which it seems only a new wave of inflation can lift them again.

This unfortunate outcome, however, has hardly dimmed the hopes of economic regulators, who are unlikely to be discouraged by results as long as reputations can be made by inventing new ways of tinkering with the market system. Therefore it remains necessary to go on analysing cyclical economic performance until either a workable, non-inflationary stabiliser is discovered, or the attempt is generally agreed to be futile. Let us first cast a glance at the facts of the cycle as they relate to this country.

SOME FEATURES OF THE SOUTH AFRICAN BUSINESS CYCLE

The South African business cycle is well documented, particularly since 1945.[1]

Since that time, eleven upswings of an average duration of 24 months and ten downswings of an average duration of 15 months have been measured. These averages conceal wide variation; the observed upswings lasted between 12 and 43 months and the downswings between 6 and 39 months. Only two upswings and three downswings were of the same duration. The ten full cycles varied from 22 to 62 months in length.

The distinguishing features of the eleven upswings are most often improved export earnings and a higher gold output or price, or both, but also include good crops, investment booms, devaluations, the Korean War and the closure of the Suez Canal. Most of these, it will be noted, are events of external origin and not generated by the dynamics of the South African economy itself. They could be said to be generated by the world economy as a whole, but that would amount to taking an extremely broad and untested view of causation in history. The downturns are similarly marked by weaker export performance and falling farm and mining revenues, though rather more often than the upswings by internal events, including bottlenecks and skills shortages, reduced investment activity and political disturbances.

It is not easy to fit a general theory of the cause of the business cycle to this pell-mell of events and policies so unevenly spaced in time.

CAN A CAUSE BE IDENTIFIED AS A BASIS FOR STABILISATION POLICY?

The bewildering variety of explanations of the business cycle (Haberler, 1964 and Estey, 1956, among others, present good overviews) do agree on the point that *cumulative* processes operate in the course of the expansion and the contraction. This is widely ascribed to (1) the interdependence of business activity, (2) the elasticity of credit, in both directions, and (3) the unequal responsiveness of individual prices of demand, causing a progressive widening or narrowing of profit margins. The downturn is commonly attributed to self-limiting forces, but for an explanation of the upturn almost any kind of event is pressed into service.

An understandable impatience for the advent of some such miraculous reviver lies behind the demands for government intervention heard in depression times, but less so during booms. In the absence of uniformly operative factors conducive to a revival, the intervention is almost bound to be misdirected or, at best, achieves good results for the wrong reasons and for a limited time only. An example of the latter is the deployment of public-sector activities in the United States in the 1930s to overcome the lack of private investment opportunities in a supposedly 'mature' capitalist economy. The stimulus this did provide may have been due, not to the uneconomic projects themselves, but simply to the injection of supplies of money and credit which a mistaken monetary policy had earlier withdrawn during the preceding 'Great Contraction', as M. Friedman has aptly renamed the Great Depression.

The dead weight of public-sector institutions, enterprises, redistribution programmes and development corporations, started for plausible reasons and never dismantled, from then on subsisted as an incubus on the private-enterprise sector, smothering business opportunities that would have been profitable but for high taxation, tariffs, levies, prohibitions and social security charges. The practice of deficit financing, so easily assumed in the depression, tends to persist during the upswing because proper funding of the swollen public sector and transfer obligations proves costlier than expected in a tight capital market, and a permanent inflationary bias to the economy thus turns out to be the legacy of a faulty analysis.

The downturn of the Western economies since 1974 and the inflationary risk of stimulation by government, or even of any revival in economies burdened by a large public sector, has left many despondent about anti-cyclical policies. It has also rekindled interest in a theory that implies the futility of fundamental stabilisation efforts, because the cycle that really matters is much longer than the span of any practicable official intervention. This cycle, named after Nikolai Kondratieff, extends over two generations. It has been statistically confirmed for price trends, but hardly for volume trends (Van Ewijk, 1982, and Cleary and Hobbs, 1983). Therefore, some attribute to the Kondratieff cycle a purely monetary character (Dupriez, 1976), but many other explanations have been grafted onto this phenomenon, among them Schumpeter's well-known innovation cycle (Schumpeter, 1939) and Rostow's (1978) emphasis on food production and migration. Others have dismissed the Kondratieff cycle as a statistical illusion; long swings emerge in any time series that spans business cycles of varying amplitudes (Citibank, 1978). Kondratieff himself took an agnostic line as to causes and regarded the causative factors adduced by others as essentially symptoms of the 'rhythm of the long wave' (Kondratieff, 1926). The vast amount of research on the subject offers no help to the designer of stabilisation policies seeking to attack some or other root cause.

The Marxist economists, who are among the most acute analysts of the capitalist economy, see as the essential feature of the business cycle that during the upswing the accumulation of capital proceeds faster than the growth of population, so that wages rise and surplus value diminishes. In the ensuing downswing wages decline while the capital stock is progressively 'devalorised' until the *rate* of profit is restored to a level where new investment and production are once more attractive. Attempts to moderate the fluctuations run counter to the dynamic of capitalism and can only hasten its collapse. Government measures to cushion a cyclical decline are particularly destructive. Sustaining consumer spending by unemployment benefits and other transfers increases the public debt and retards the decline in real wages required for improved profits. The bailing out of large, insolvent companies (and, one could add, Third World countries) prevents the pruning and devalorisation of capital, and thereby also the necessary recovery of the rate of profit. The next upturn must then be so much weaker and plagued from the start by the inflationary

103

expansion of credit employed earlier for 'stabilisation' (Mandel, 1980). The Marxist analysis, then, while assigning a clear cause to the cycle, at the same time dismisses stabilisation policies as counterproductive.

A STOCHASTIC VIEW

Another approach to the business cycle, as a possible basis for stabilisation policy, begins by recognising that a system propelled by millions of individual decisions and events exhibits certain intriguing properties akin to those of a smoothed series of random numbers. Statisticians know the Slutzky-Yule effect, which is that an irregular periodic function appears when a set of random numbers is smoothed with a moving average (Slutzky, 1937). The view that this is the origin of the business cycle has been criticised (Rostow, 1979) on the ground that the basic economic data, and not only the smoothed series, reveal major and concurrent reversals in direction in the course of time, but this criticism overlooks the possibility that the basic data themselves partake of the nature of a smoothed series. To see this, one has only to realise that successive economic or other events impinge upon each other just as the data points in a moving average jointly determine the value of the averaged entries in the series. Every decision or event is induced or led up to by others and in turn influences subsequent decisions and events; the past helps to shape the present, and coming events cast their shadows ahead. The after-effects of one event mesh with the advent of the next and this imparts a measure of serial correlation to otherwise random sequences. 'The moving finger writes,' says the Persian bard Omar Khayyam, and what that finger writes, I suggest, is a moving average.

If there is anything in this view, it would explain, on the basis of the Slutzky-Yule effect of moving averages, why the dispersal of initiatives and innovations of the market economy, together with other random occurrences, produces a periodic function in output series. This seems also intuitively probable: successive economic events either reinforce or neutralise one another, even if only remotely, and since it is a priori unlikely that they should always do either the one or the other persistently, the concatenation of events engenders a fluctuating series. Nor can the fluctuations be expected to be strictly regular in frequency and amplitude, and experience shows they are not. The swings and the turning points of the business cycle are unpredictable.

The search for one identifiable causative factor of the business cycle would appear to be a vain one; or put another way, the business cycle is 'caused' by the selfsame activity it consists of. This has the important implication for stabilisation policy that it cannot hope to address any central cause of business fluctuations, but must confine itself, like the elusive cure for the common cold, to alleviating symptoms. Upswings and downswings cannot be prevented, but one may, perhaps, try to moderate them once in progress.

MANAGING THE PUBLIC SECTOR FOR ECONOMIC STABILITY?

The subject of public-sector activity and its financing as a force for stability is so broad that only the more immediately relevant aspects of it can be indicated in this paper.

As a generalisation to start with, it seems fair to say that policy-makers have become more modest about government efforts to regulate the working of the economy. The Keynesians promised high employment, but delivered high inflation, and the attempt to tackle the latter problem has produced more unemployment than the decades-long experiment set out to remedy when it began. The instruments used towards macro-stabilisation turned out to have serious directional or structural effects, notably the inordinate growth of the public sector and the decline, in Western economies, of labour-intensive industries. Regulatory interference has diverted or stifled particular business activities without enabling the economy to cope any better with stagnation and inflation. Possibly arising from a need to rationalise the unhappy experience, the theory of rational expectations has been propounded, according to which government is powerless to influence the course of the real economy, because of anticipatory pricing behaviour by transactors. For example, if the markets expect that government spending to revive the economy will entail monetary expansion, prices will rise, while output expands hardly at all.

Even if the means employed are not without merit in particular circumstances, there remains the risk of mistaken diagnosis. De Kock (1975) warns of a tendency by the authorities to mistake the cyclical nature of the downswing for a structural problem: 'There is then a danger that the authorities might be persuaded to place excessive emphasis on the need to stimulate economic growth through such long-term measures as increased direct government participation in the economic process and indiscriminate protection of domestic industries. If this is done, the economy can be stimulated in the short term by measures which can have harmful effects on long-term economic growth by, for example, bringing about malinvestment of scarce resources and inflationary excesses in general' (p. 10).

The financing and timing of public sector expenditure, as distinct from the nature of the public works undertaken, may offer opportunities for stabilising behaviour. Let us look briefly, therefore, at public investment, tax policy, transfer payments, public debt management and the State Budget in the South African context.

Public investment

That public investment spending as a means of ironing out economic fluctuations is subject to several limitations has been well argued by Browne (1965), on the grounds of divided control as between central government, public corporations and local authorities; the difficulty of postponing urgent infrastructural (and strategic) projects; and the long lead and construction times of important works, which it would also be uneconomic to stop or interrupt when the general economy has meanwhile entered the cyclical upswing. This pro-cyclical outturn may unfortunately be repeated in the downswing, as it was in the 1982/3 and 1983/4 fiscal years, when several road construction works were stopped and funds for municipal housing-in-progress were curtailed, for lack of current revenue and because additional borrowing could lead to an undesired hardening of interest rates in the capital market. The public corporations are equally liable to pro-cyclical spending when straining to meet rising demand in the upswing phase, while during the depression future peak demand cannot be reliably forecast as to timing and size. What the public corporations and self-financing State enterprises could do, but have thus far not done, is so to arrange the funding of capital works as between revenue and borrowing that the business cycle is at least not aggravated. Greater recourse to loan financing during the downswing and to revenue financing in the upswing could be helpful.

Revenue

On the revenue side of fiscal policy, the progressive scale of personal income tax is an automatic stabiliser of disposable income as taxable income rises and falls with the cycle. Inflation, however, has removed most of this effect. Our scale of tax rates has not been adjusted for inflation, with the result that a newly qualified professional man today starts his working life at the top marginal rate and from then on all incremental earnings are taxed at a flat rate. Company tax, of course, has always been at a flat rate. The indirect taxes (customs tariffs, excise duties and the sales tax) can be varied at any time of the fiscal year. The sales tax particularly could be used for stabilisation by absorbing or releasing purchasing power, provided the revenue gained from a sales tax increase is not spent (which is unlikely to be the case) and a decrease is not matched by a cut in government spending.[2] The tax incentives to invest in plant and equipment (the initial, investment and depreciation allowances) tend to aggravate the cyclical nature of investment. Inoperative at nil profits, the incentives become progressively more valuable as profits rise, thus stimulating investment activity in the later stages of the upswing.

Transfer payments

The amount of transfer payments by the State to persons and businesses is difficult to estimate from the public accounts. It would include subsidies for production and investment, capital and revenue grants, unemployment and disability compensation, pensions, welfare contributions and relief payments, and the total cannot be much less than 20 per cent of all government expenditure. In some countries, social security payments alone account for half of total government spending. The stabilising effect of this on the economy depends on how the transfers are financed. Tending to be higher in the depression when revenue is down, the resultant borrowing from banks and institutional investors underpins consumer spending, which is favourable, provided the debt issues do not keep interest rates unduly high. In the upswing phase of the business cycle, however, the established 'customer base' of public hand-outs prevents the required scaling down of transfers, with the well-known results of inflationary pressure and a swollen public sector.

Public debt management

The phenomenal rise of the public debt in most countries during recent decades, right through prosperity and depression, has made the art of public debt management of great importance to economic management in general. The size, composition, maturity distribution, ownership and issue procedures of public-sector debt have come to dominate capital markets, interest rates and the outlook for inflation. Expected in the 1930s to become a valuable instrument of anti-cyclical demand management, the practice of occasional deficit financing has in most countries degenerated into one of perennial deficits. The policy issue today is no longer whether or not a deficit-before-borrowing should be incurred, but how, given the deficit, the growing public debt is to be structured, placed and managed.

The inflationary risk of placing public debt in the banking sector, and particularly with the central bank, is naturally greater as the annual borrowing requirement grows larger, so that it must be a constant policy objective, overriding intermittent stabilisation aims, to prevent public sector debt issues from overstraining the capital market and from spilling over into the money market. Also unfavourable for stabilising policies is the increasing complexity of public debt management owing to the separate policies as to revenue and debt financing followed by the public corporations, state enterprises, local authorities and public development and housing entities. Even if these policies could be properly co-ordinated overall, any attempt to bend them to a contra-cyclical pattern in the aggregate is hardly practical.

For the central government itself, the Stabilisation Account (a Treasury account with the Reserve Bank, established in 1961) represents a formal policy option of alternately absorbing excess monetary demand by overborrowing and releasing purchasing power when business conditions call for it. Under pressure of events, the authorities have not always succeeded in operating the Account in this manner. It has at times been drawn on to finance strategic imports for stockpiling, leaving it empty when a positive balance was needed for domestic spending. Nor has the Treasury always been able to refrain from drawing down the Account when aggregate demand in the economy was clearly excessive. The exigencies of public finance in the world as it is make it well-nigh impossible to adhere strictly to a policy of periodically sterilising funds and later spending them again, in phase with business upswings and downswings.

The State Budget

In conformity with the above trends in public finance, the annual budget of the central government has assumed a different significance. No longer is one of its main aims the influencing of private sector spending by deliberately planning for surplus, balance or deficit, but rather to set out government spending priorities, its taxation proposals and the estimated deficit that results. The demand management aspect has largely shifted to the overall amount of government expenditure and the degree of monetary expansion that different methods of financing the deficit may entail. This implies a correspondingly greater responsibility to be assumed by the monetary authorities, which of course include the Treasury.

It is the *total* financial transfer to the public sector, both as tax payments and as loan subscriptions, that measures public sector demands on the nation's financial resources and through that on real resources. Taxation *as well as* borrowing requires to be financed. One symptom of this is the greater borrowing need of companies when high taxation erodes their resources for financing from internally generated funds. Since credit is infinitely expansible, only an appropriately high level of interest rates (as regards the private sector) and policy restraint on spending (as regards the public sector) can avoid an inflationary overexpansion of credit. The reason why borrowing from banks is to be regarded as a perilous course for public finance is that bank credit can expand very rapidly as the cash needs of the banks are underwritten by the central bank. Yet increased taxation and long-term borrowing are also capable of expanding the total amount of credit outstanding if the private sector is not dissuaded by high interest rates from attempting to maintain its share of aggregate spending by drawing on sources of credit. 'Conservative' financing, i.e. from tax and long-term borrowing, may still upset monetary equilibrium; it all depends on the general level of interest rates in the economy.[3]

MONETARY POLICY

Reasons were given earlier for believing that no particular causes of the business cycle can be identified for purposes of fundamental stabilisation of the economy. An even course of the economic process can also be upset by many other disturbances that do have a specific origin, such as war or drought or civil disobedience, which demand their own policy responses. It probably remains true to say that purely economic stabilising action in the face of such events, as well as cyclical movements, can do little more than alleviate the symptoms on as broad a front as possible. It follows that the means employed ought to be at once very general, pervasive and non-discriminatory as to point of impact. Given the limited possibilities of anti-cyclical fiscal policy, it is to monetary policy that we must look for such attempts at economic stabilisation as may be practicable.

The domain of monetary policy is the influencing of aggregate demand by means of the rate of interest, which impinges on all spending decisions. The rate of interest has this broad effect because interest charges are incurred when spending out of credit facilities and potential interest earnings are foregone when spending credit balances owned ('money') on goods and services instead of financial assets.

The second favourable attribute of monetary policy in this context is the immediate and finely graduated response the central bank, unlike the fiscal authorities, can make to changing conditions. Of course, the indices to which it responds may be misleading and are certainly incomplete, and a transmission lag between interest rate changes and spending behaviour, conditioned by expectations, must be reckoned with. The oligopolistic features of our economy, hedged in by licences, permits, regulations, preferential credit and the tentacles of centralised control, further retard the spending response to changes in the cost of credit. The response is also distorted by the rules of taxation as to depreciation, stock valuation, capital gains, differences in gearing, the deduction of interest charges and the different tax regimes applying to particular types of business (Feldstein, 1982).

The record of our monetary policy as an instrument for stabilisation reveals past weaknesses in handling the very large fluctuations in the external accounts to which this country is subject, and in the regulation of credit whenever too little use was made of the interest weapon and resort was had instead to administrative allocation, often on a preferential basis to the public sector. The net effect on aggregate spending tended to be procyclical, because the need for public services rises during the upswing phase; because the private sector finds new, uncontrolled sources of credit when prospects for production and sales are good and the prevailing rates of interest are low; and because the central bank creates new credit (expands its balance sheet) if it builds up the foreign reserves from net export proceeds and capital inflow, rather than allowing the currency to appreciate in the foreign exchange market or facilitating a capital outflow, or both.

The Reserve Bank has since late 1980 progressively adopted market-orientated methods of regulating money and credit that imply the acceptance of flexible and realistic rates of interest as a means of influencing the flow of spending towards greater stability of the general price level. This will clearly not suffice to stabilise output as well, dependent as it is on productivity, export markets and much else, but the policy can at least help to prevent output swings generated by excessive credit expansion and contraction, allowance being made for the credit demands of innovation and business growth.

In the management of the total amount of credit outstanding, which sustains the flow of spending, bank credit is of particular significance for two reasons. Its cost is a benchmark for the many competing types of credit; secondly, it is capable of very rapid expansion, as mentioned above. In view of the recent change of policy by the Reserve Bank — from the liquid-assets method of controlling bank credit to a cash reserve control — it may be appropriate to conclude with a brief explanation of the way this is expected to work.

Cash reserve control

The clearing banks frequently need to borrow from the Reserve Bank, either through the intermediation of the discount houses or directly, when drawing banknotes for public circulation; when settling net payments from the private sector to the Treasury; when settling payments for bonds and bills sold by the Reserve Bank in the market; and when topping up the compulsory cash reserve calculated as a fixed percentage of their deposit liabilities. Even if there were no reserve requirements, the other three processes could create a borrowing need, though more intermittently. A proportional reserve requirement produces the desired continual bias towards recourse to the central bank, as the deposit liabilities of the clearing banks expand steadily.

The lending rate which the central bank charges, as the main element of its discount policy, is normally set higher than the market rate of interest in order to hold the latter at a level that will prevent an overexpansion of credit.[4] Recourse to central bank credit can, of course, also take the form of sales of financial assets to it at appropriately high yield rates. By means of varying the margin of its lending rate over comparable market rates the central bank can initiate, reinforce or counter movements in the general level of interest rates and so influence the flow of spending towards a more stable performance of the economy than it might otherwise achieve. Around this bare essence of central banking, the other components of discount policy, as well as the open market operations, exchange market intervention and public debt management are to be ranged in support.

It might be objected that the interest cost of complying with a fractional reserve requirement cannot have much effect on the total cost of funding by the clearing banks and, consequently, on their lending rates, but that would be to forget that lending and investing decisions are made by individual banks and not by the banks as a group. When an individual bank makes a loan it must *reckon* with having to settle the *full* amount through the clearing, though at the end of the day the projected cash loss may be compensated by an opposite clearing payment. To ensure that this does happen, the bank will raise an opposite clearing entry by attracting new deposits or drawing on the money market. In case of an overall shortage, rates will tend to rise up to the point where 'the market goes into the Bank'. Thus changes in the central bank's lending rate have a marked impact on the deposit and lending rates of the clearing banks and all other market rates of interest.

The limits to stabilisation by means of monetary policy will be apparent from the preceding discussion, but given the nature of our economy, monetary management may well achieve rather more and with less distortion than the interventionist policies of the past.

NOTES

1 See: Smit and Van der Walt, 1970, 1973 and 1982, and the bibliography of earlier work in De Kock, 1975.
2 If there is additional expenditure to be financed anyway, an increase in sales tax will normally be preferable to the use of bank credit.
3 Increases in the Exchequer Deposit, whether from tax or loan receipts, have been observed to stimulate bank credit to the private sector, presumably to make good the latter's loss of liquidity to the Treasury.
4 This would very probably occur if the market rate of interest should fall below the current rate of price increase.

REFERENCES

Browne, G.W.G., 1965. 'Investment in the public sector of South Africa', *South African Journal of Economics*, December.
Citibank, 1978. Monthly Newsletter, January.
Cleary, M.N. and G.D. Hobbs, 1983. 'The fifty-year cycle: a look at the empirical evidence', in: Freeman, C., *Long Waves in the World Economy*. London: Butterworth.
De Kock, G., 1975. 'The business cycle in South Africa — recent tendencies', *South African Journal of Economics*, March.
Dupriez, L.H., 1976. *La monnaie dans l'économie*. Louvain.
Estey, J.A., 1956. *Business Cycles — Their Nature, Causes and Control*. Englewood Cliffs: Prentice-Hall.
Feldstein, M., 1982. *The Fiscal Framework of Monetary Policy*. Working paper 966, National Bureau of Economic Research. Cambridge (Mass.).
Haberler, G., 1964. *Prosperity and Depression* (5th ed.) London: Allen & Unwin.
Kondratieff, N.D., 1935. 'The long waves in economic life', *Review of Economic Studies*, November. (First published in German, 1926.)
Mandel, E., 1980. *The Second Slump — A Marxist Analysis of Recession in the Seventies*. London: Verso Editions.
Rostow, W.W., 1978. *The World Economy: History and Prospect*. New York: Macmillan.
—— 1979. The long waves in economic life. (Letter to the editor.) Lloyds Bank Review, April.
Schumpeter, J.A., 1939. *Business Cycles: A Theoretical, Historical and Statistical Analysis of the Capitalist Process* (2 vols). New York: McGraw-Hill.
Slutzky, E., 1937. 'The summation of random causes as the source of cyclical processes, *Econometrica*, 19, p. 105.
Smit, D.J. and B.E. van der Walt, 1970. 'Business cycles in South Africa during the period 1946–1968', S.A. Reserve Bank, *Quarterly Bulletin*, September.
—— 1973. 'Business cycles in South Africa during the period 1968–1972', S.A. Reserve Bank, *Quarterly Bulletin*, June.
—— 1982. 'Growth trends and business cycles in the South African economy 1972–1981', S.A. Reserve Bank, *Quarterly Bulletin*, June.
Van Ewijk, C., 1982. 'A spectral analysis of the Kondratieff cycle', *Kyklos*, 1982(3).

3.3 THE NATURAL RATE HYPOTHESIS: AN ECONOMETRIC TEST FOR THE SOUTH AFRICAN ECONOMY

E. Shostak*

The contemporary phenomenon of inflation accompanied by stagnant economic growth has unsettled the established neo-Keynesian belief that inflation is a remedy for unemployment. In his presidential address delivered at the eighteenth annual meeting of the American Economic Association, Milton Friedman[1] argued that expected inflation cannot affect real economic activity. The only scope for macropolicy in influencing unemployment lies in the short term; it cannot influence the long-term rate of unemployment. In the long run, according to Milton Friedman, inflation will be fully anticipated and therefore nobody will allow the real wage to be affected. This implies the following: expected inflation will be fully reflected in actual wage settlements, and the rate of increase in money wages will be fully reflected in price inflation. This in turn implies that the long-term Phillips curve is vertical. According to this reasoning the rate of unemployment cannot depart in the long run from its natural rate, which is the rate which corresponds to full employment.

It is clear from Friedman's argument that he does not deny the existence of the short-term Phillips curve relationships. Recently, however, the relatively new Rational Expectations movement in economics has questioned the existence of the short-term Phillips curve.

The object of this paper is to evaluate the Rational Expectations proposition within the framework of the South African economy. The first part of the paper sets out the natural rate hypothesis, which is followed by a brief description of the rational expectations theory. The second part of the paper will present an empirical evaluation of the rational expectations hypothesis, while as a corollary the natural rate hypothesis will be confirmed.

THE NATURAL RATE HYPOTHESIS: FORMULATION

Let us assume that the inflationary process can be presented as

$$P = \beta p^e - \propto (u - \bar{u}) \tag{1}$$

where P is the actual inflation rate, p^e *the expected inflation rate,* u the unemployment rate, and $\bar{u}$ the natural unemployment rate; β is a parameter which tells us by how much an increase in the expected inflation rate causes the actual inflation rate to rise, holding the unemployment rate constant. Assuming that

* Formerly Economist, Econometrix. This paper was first published in *The South African Journal of Economics*, Vol. 49, No. 1, 1981.

in the long run actual inflation equals expected inflation, i.e. $P = P^e$, we can derive that

$$u = \bar{u} - \frac{1 - \beta}{\propto} P \tag{2}$$

These equations imply that there is no long-run trade-off between inflation and unemployment when $\beta = 1$. If $\beta < 1$, then there is a negatively sloped long-run Phillips curve, which implies that higher inflation is associated with lower unemployment even in the long run. If we assume that $\beta = 1$ then equation (1) can be rewritten as

$$P - P^e = - \propto (u - \bar{u}) \tag{3}$$

In terms of expression (3) it follows that to maintain the unemployment rate u below its natural rate $\bar{u}$, the actual inflation rate P has to be higher than the expected inflation rate P^e. This implies that individuals must permanently expect less inflation than actually occurs which in turn implies that people can be 'fooled' all the time, which is unlikely according to rational expectations economics.

THE RATIONAL EXPECTATIONS APPROACH

The proposition that people's expectations are formed rationally was proposed in the seminal article on rational expectations by J. Muth.[2] He maintains that rational economic agents must have expectations that are unbiased estimates of the actual stochastic economic process being anticipated. If the expectations were to differ from the mean of the true process, then the expectation would be systematically in error. The rational agent would observe this fact, and the expectations would be corrected appropriately. Thus, any errors in expectations must be random with mean zero. This implies that rational expectations will yield predictions of future events which differ from the corresponding eventual outcome only by errors, which are themselves independent of the variables used to generate the predictions. Accordingly, people not only observe or know in advance the values of economic variables, but also draw on the basis of these known values, inferences which are identical with the inferences of the process actually generating the outcome in question. According to the rational expectations propositions the Phillips curve relation exists as a result of expectational errors. Since the rational expectations hypothesis regards the likelihood of such errors as minimal, this hypothesis implies that, even in the short run, we cannot have a trade-off between inflation and unemployment. The rational expectations hypothesis also maintains that the behaviour of the economy is invariant with respect to pre-announced monetary policy measures since, essentially, only surprises produce a real response.

Because rational expectations postulate competition in all markets, this essentially means that market disequilibria are immediately eliminated by appropriate price and wage adjustments. This assumption means a direct adjustment of the expected rate of inflation to changes in the actual rate of inflation, resulting in a continuous macroeconomic equilibrium. Within this extreme rational expectations postulate, the public reasons in terms of relative prices instead of absolute prices.[3] This means that market participants are not guided in their economic decision-making process by nominal but rather by real developments in economic variables, that is, they are not susceptible to the phenomenon of money illusion.

According to the rational expectations theory, monetary policy aimed at stabilising the economy will be impotent, because the outcome of policy measures will be fully anticipated by the public. Since the private sector makes provision for anticipated changes, government policy will be influential only if the government's information is superior to that of the public, which is impossible by the very definition of the rational expectations postulate.

Since it is unrealistic to assume that economic agents possess all the necessary information, the weak rational expectations approach maintains that people are rational even under conditions of limited information, as long as this information is used optimally. According to this approach, when the authorities do have superior information monetary policy can be effective. For example,[4] government's superior information about its own actions can have systematic output effects during transition periods, in which the public gradually learns the nature of the policy. The weak rational expectations approach maintains that even if a deceptive policy is feasible, there is still a question about its desirability, since in the situation where the policy-maker lacks superior information about the economy, a systematic policy deception will move output away from its full current information position, which is the more optimal one.

Since the rational expectations theory is not explicit as to how the economic agent acquires all his information, and optimises it to make predictions which only have uncorrelated errors,[5] it has aroused strong reaction, and in this respect S. Fisher[6] points out that 'it is absurd to assume individuals can make the necessary calculations since most economists still cannot do so'.

F. Modigliani[7] made the following comment on the rational expectations theory in his presidential address to the American Economic Association: '... if it (the rational expectations) were valid, deviations of unemployment from the natural rate would be small and transitory in which case the General Theory would not have been written and neither would this paper'.

THE NATURAL RATE HYPOTHESIS TEST

The general form of the Phillips curve in (1) can be presented as

$$U_t = \beta_1(P_t - E_{t-1}P_t) + \beta_2 E_{t-1}P_t + \lambda U_{t-1} + \xi_t \tag{4}$$

where ξ_t is a random term, U_t is unemployment rate, P_t the rate of inflation at time t, and $E_{t-1}P_t$ the rate of inflation expected by the public at time $t-1$ to prevail at time t. According to the rational expectation hypothesis only unexpected inflation, that is $(P_t - E_{t-1} P_t)$, affects unemployment. An increase in $E_{t-1}P_t$ by itself would leave unemployment unaffected. Therefore, the natural unemployment rate hypothesis asserts that $\beta_2 = 0$. Of course, if there is a Phillips curve, then $\beta_1 < 0$, indicating that unexpected inflation causes unemployment to decrease.

The principal idea of the rational expectations approach is to base expectations on a model which explains the inflationary process, and is expected to reproduce it 'correctly'.[8]

The method adopted in this study was to evaluate the natural rate hypothesis under different forecasting models of inflation. In the first part of the empirical test we will assume that the inflationary process is well modelled by the following expression:

$$P_t = \lambda_0 P_{t-1} + \sum_{i=0}^{n} w_i M_{t-i} + \xi_t \tag{5}$$

where P is the first difference of the log (CPI), CPI the consumer price index, λ_0, w_i, are parameters, and M is the first difference of the log (M2), where M2 is the broad definition of the money stock, and ξ_2 an unpredictable residual with mean zero. According to the rational expectations postulate, the economic agent will use expression (5) to forecast the inflation and would set

$$E_{t-1} P_t = \lambda_0 P_{t-1} + \sum_{i=0}^{n} w_i M_{t-i} \tag{6}$$

In the second part of the empirical test we shall assume that the inflationary process is well modelled by the following autoregressive scheme:

$$P_t = \sum_{i=1}^{m} v_i P_{t-i} + U_t \tag{7}$$

where U_t is an unpredictable residual with zero mean. The forecast of the inflation according to (7) will be

$$E_{t-1} P_t = \sum_{i=1}^{m} v_i P_{t-i} \tag{8}$$

The test of the natural rate hypothesis within the framework of rational expectations involves two steps, firstly an estimate of (5) or (7) for the actual inflationary process, then an application of the values of $E_{t-1}P_t$ implied from either (6) or (8) and estimate

$$U_t = \beta_1(P_t - E_{t-1}P_t) + \beta_2 E_{t-1}P_t + \lambda U_{t-1} + \xi_t \tag{9}$$

where U_t is the first difference of the log of the unemployment level.

In order to evaluate the rational expectations postulate (which claims that even in the short run there cannot be a trade-off between inflation and unemployment, coupled with the assertion that should such a trade-off exist, it will disappear with improved information) we shall apply an increasing data sample and assume that an increase in the data sample is associated with an increase in the information.

The present study employs quarterly figures over the period 67(IV) to the 78(II), i.e. 43 observations. The data used in this research are seasonally adjusted and transformed into logarithmic form. The overall sample is partitioned into six parts, where the second part is larger in size than the first part, the third part is larger than the second, etc. For each part of the overall sample, estimates of the parameters β_1 and β_2 within the framework of different expectational models will be performed. If the rational expectations postulate is valid, we would expect to obtain statistically insignificant values for β_1, which should tend to approach zero as the sample size increases. Should the parameter estimate for β_2 be insignificant, the natural rate hypothesis would be supported.

Test 1

Using the specification in (5) for the estimate of the inflationary process the following regression was obtained:

$$E_{t-1}P_t = 0,767753\,P_{t-1} + \sum_{i=0}^{5} w_i M_{t-i} \tag{10}$$

$$(7,245)$$
$$R^2 = 0,6433 \qquad D\text{-}W = 2,36$$
$$(t\text{-value in brackets})$$

Quarters	w	t-value
0	0,01487	2,154
1	0,02478	2,154
2	0,02974	2,154
3	0,02974	2,154
4	0,02478	2,154
5	0,01487	2,154

In the estimation procedure it was postulated that the monetary impact on the inflation rate is a gradual one, and can be approximated by a bell-type distribution. Under this postulate we have used a second degree polynomial with zero restriction on the beginning and the end of the monetary impact. The estimates of the parameters obtained are all significantly different from zero at the 95 per cent confidence level. The R^2 of 0,6433 can be considered high since the data are in the first difference form.

116

Using the regression in (10) the inflationary expectation values were calculated which in turn were used as an input in the evaluation of the natural rate hypothesis according to the model in (9). Table 1 summarises the outcome of this estimate.

The evaluation of the result which is summarised in Table 1 will be done with the aid of the statistical t-test. The larger the t-statistic the greater our confidence in the value of the estimated parameters.

Though the sign of the β_1 estimates supports the existence of the short-run Phillips curve, the t-value of β_1 estimate is below the accepted range. Despite this fact, according to the results in Table 1, the t-value tends to increase with the rise in the sample size. This rise in the t-value tends to reject the rational expectations postulate: the β_1 tends to zero as the sample size increases. This rejection can be strengthened by the fact that because of multicollinearity the estimated standard errors will tend to be large, implying low t-values. The results obtained with respect to β_2 support the natural rate hypothesis, i.e. that there is no trade-off in the long run between inflation and unemployment.

Table 1 NATURAL RATE HYPOTHESIS TEST WITHIN THE FRAMEWORK OF EXPECTATIONS MODEL (5)

Period	β_1	β_2	λ	R^2	D-W
67 (IV) – 72 (II)	–1,13215	–0,70977	0,690	0,435	1,923
t-value	0,556	0,827	3,847		
67 (IV) – 74 (II)	–2,7629	–0,684	0,588	0,344	2,19
t-value	1,373	0,871	3,3		
67 (IV) – 75 (II)	–3,073	0,182	0,624	0,369	2,01
t-value	1,635	0,293	4,01		
67 (IV) – 76 (II)	–2,553	0,323	0,617	0,353	1,922
t-value	1,382	0,593	4,12		
67 (IV) – 77 (II)	–2,993	0,661	0,776	0,561	2,02
t-value	1,622	1,275	6,49		
67 (IV) – 78 (II)	–3,3899	0,5484	0,735	0,5379	1,9385
t-value	1,841	1,094	6,532		

Test 2

Using the specification in (7) to estimate the inflationary process, the following regression was obtained:

$$E_{t-1} P_t = \sum_{i=0}^{5} v_i P_{t-1-i} \tag{11}$$

$$R^2 = 0,6852 \qquad D\text{-}W = 1,8460$$

117

Quarters	v	t-value
0	0,4183	3,521
1	0,1983	3,821
2	0,07011	1,013
3	0,03384	0,48
4	0,08945	1,596
5	0,2369	1,965

The weights in (11) were estimated with the aid of the second degree polynomial without any restriction. Using the regression in (11) inflationary expectations were calculated, which in turn were used in the evaluation of the natural rate hypothesis. The results of this analysis are summarised in Table 2.

Table 2 THE NATURAL RATE HYPOTHESIS TEST UNDER THE
AUTOREGRESSIVE INFLATIONARY PROCESS MODEL

Period	β_1	β_2	λ	R^2	D-W
67 (IV) – 72 (II)	−2,452	−0,343	0,674	0,45	1,95
t-value	1,126	0,364	3,95		
67 (IV) – 74 (II)	−4,151	−0,263	0,558	0,385	2,22
t-value	1,965	0,316	3,50		
67 (IV) – 75 (II)	−4,152	0,54	0,552	0,40	2,01
t-value	2,055	0,82	3,73		
67 (IV) – 76 (II)	−3,702	0,4778	0,5368	0,39	1,93
t-value	1,961	0,885	3,73		
67 (IV) – 77 (II)	−4,176	0,8219	0,663	0,589	2,01
t-value	2,242	1,608	5,80		
67 (IV) – 78 (II)	−3,987	0,5725	0,637	0,555	1,87
t-value	2,198	1,17	5,8		

In terms of these results we may confidently reject the rational expectations postulate that the Phillips curve will vanish with an increase in information. Out of six sub-periods five have yielded a t-value for β_1 in excess of the accepted range. The relative stability of the parameter β_1 is indicative that the unemployment/inflation trade-off can be maintained persistently in the short run. With regard to the β_2 parameter the test supports the natural rate hypothesis.

SUMMARY

The econometric test conducted has indicated that there is no trade-off between unemployment and inflation in the long run. This supports the natural rate hypothesis that unemployment cannot deviate from its natural level or the equilibrium level, in the long run.

As opposed to the extreme rational expectations postulate, claiming that even in the short run the likelihood of obtaining a Phillips curve relation is minimal, the econometric test has indicated that such a relation is indeed sustainable in the short run. The econometric test has also rejected the weak rational expectations approach, which asserts that with the increase in the availability of information, the Phillips curve relation will tend to vanish. The rejection of the weak rational expectations hypothesis was obtained within the framework of two different inflationary expectation models. In the first test it was assumed that the economic agent uses changes in the money stock as an indicator for forecasting the future rate of inflation, while in the second test it was postulated that the economic agent uses past inflation in order to forecast future inflation. The evaluation of the weak hypothesis was performed with the aid of the rising sample size method, which served as a proxy for the increase in the availability of information. The results of the test obtained reject the rational expectations proposition even under the strong assumption that the economic agent behaves according to monetarist rules. Since this postulate can hardly be regarded as realistic, as long as economists themselves are in disagreement on this issue, it is more realistic to assume that the economic agent uses information on past inflation in order to forecast future inflation. Within the framework of this expectational model the econometric test conducted strongly rejects the rational expectations proposition.

NOTES

1 Friedman, M., 'The Role of Monetary Policy', *The American Economic Review*, March 1968.
2 Muth, J.F., 'Rational Expectations, and the Theory of Price Movements', *Econometrica*, Vol. 29, July 1961.
3 Sijben, J.J., *Rational Expectations and Monetary Policy*. Leyden: Sijthoff and Noordhoff, 1980.
4 Barro, R., 'Rational Expectations and the Role of Monetary Policy', *Journal of Monetary Economics*, Vol. 2, January 1976, pp. 1–32.
5 Friedman, B., 'Optimal Expectations and the Extreme Information Assumptions of Rational Expectations Macromodels', *Journal of Monetary Economics*, Vol. 5, January 1979.
6 Fisher, S., 'Recent Developments in Monetary Theory', *The American Economic Review*, May 1975.
7 Modigliani, F., 'The Monetarist Controversy, or Should We Forsake Stabilisation Policies?', *The American Economic Review*, March 1977.
8 Sargent, T.J., 'Rational Expectations and the Theory of Economic Policy. Part II: Arguments and Evidence', Research Department, Federal Reserve Bank of Minneapolis, June 1976.

3.4 THE PHILLIPS TRADE-OFF AND POLICY IMPLICATIONS FOR DEVELOPING COUNTRIES

P.A. Black and M.V. Leibbrandt*

It is widely believed that industrial development in many developing countries is constrained by a common set of structural rigidities.[1] This paper will incorporate a few of these structural factors into a standard Phillips curve analysis in order to derive a Phillips relation which is considered to be appropriate to a developing country. The result should prove useful in highlighting some of the macroeconomic policy dilemmas facing policy-makers in these countries.

Our analysis will be developed in stages. Section 1 considers the original contributions in the field and briefly comments on their relevance to developing countries. Section 2 introduces expectations into the Phillips model which, in Section 3, is extended to allow for the dependence of developing countries on imported intermediate and capital inputs. The final section sets out the relevant policy implications.

1. THE RELATIONSHIP BETWEEN THE RATE OF CHANGE OF WAGES AND THE UNEMPLOYMENT RATE

In his seminal article, Phillips (1958) conducted an empirical investigation into the relationship between the rate of change of nominal wages ($\dot{W}$) and the unemployment rate (U) in the United Kingdom over the period 1861–1957. His results indicated a negative relationship between $\dot{W}$ and U, as represented in Figure 1. Clearly, U^* is the level of unemployment associated with stable wages ($\dot{W} = 0$). In the Phillips study, U^* was found to be approximately 5,5 per cent.

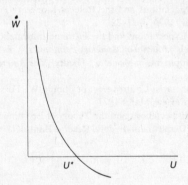

Figure 1

* Department of Economics, University of Stellenbosch and Department of Economics and Economic History, Rhodes University, respectively. The financial assistance of the HSRC is gratefully acknowledged.

Lipsey (1960) was the first to provide a theoretical explanation of the Phillips curve in terms of simple labour market dynamics.[2] For Lipsey, U^* represented equilibrium in the labour market. Any point to the left of U^* therefore represented an excess demand for labour and a situation in which wages would rise, i.e. $\dot{W} > 0$. Conversely, any point to the right of U^* represented an excess supply of labour and a situation in which wages would fall, or $\dot{W} < 0$. Lipsey explained the fact that the labour market could be in equilibrium at a positive unemployment rate (U^*) in the following way:

> When demand is equal to supply ... there will be jobs available for all who wish to work at the going wage rate. This is *not* equivalent to saying that there will be no one unemployed, but rather that the number of unemployed will be matched by an equal number of unfilled vacancies (p. 14).

Therefore, for Lipsey, U^* reflected the presence of frictional unemployment in the economy. Even in the industrialised countries this interpretation of U^* has proved controversial. Tobin (1972) pointed out that, even if vacancies are matched by the number of unemployed, there is no guarantee that the *skill requirements* of the vacant jobs will be matched by the stock of skills embodied in the unemployed. Indeed, Tobin postulated job mismatch as an important cause of unemployment. Clearly, within such an analysis, U^* represents a group of workers who are structurally unemployed as well as any frictionally unemployed, and should not be seen as the unemployment rate consistent with equilibrium (or full employment) in the labour market.[3]

There are several important implications arising from the above analysis. The argument that U^* embodies structural as well as frictional elements assumes even greater significance in a developing country context.[5] The long-term rate of economic growth in many developing countries has been insufficient to ensure a demand for labour of adequate magnitude to meet the growing supply of labour. In addition, the long-term pattern of economic growth has tended to stifle the capacity of the economy for labour absorption because of the adoption of relatively capital-intensive production techniques and the persistence of seasonal labour-demand patterns in agriculture. In a typical developing country U^* can be expected to equal at least 15 per cent rather than the 5,5 per cent suggested by Phillips and Lipsey. Likewise, given the long-term decline in economic growth rates world-wide, U^* has been increasing in most developing countries over the last twenty years.[5] In terms of Figure 1, this suggests that the Phillips curve has been shifting to the right.

Another important implication for developing countries has to do with the nature of the trade-off between unemployment and wage inflation. The Phillips curve of Figure 1 can be represented by the following equation:

$$\dot{W} = w \ (U^* - U) \tag{1}$$

where w represents the slope of the Phillips curve, or the responsiveness of $\dot{W}$ to any divergence of U from U^*. It seems reasonable to postulate a high w for

121

developing countries, since most of them would appear to be constrained by a severe shortage of skilled industrial workers.[6] More specifically, if in the process of industrial expansion U is less than U^*, this implies an excess demand for skilled industrial labour rather than for all labour. This labour is already employed and therefore has to be attracted by significantly higher wage offers.[7]

2. FROM MONEY WAGES TO REAL WAGES: THE ROLE OF EXPECTED INFLATION

Thus far we have followed Lipsey in explaining the relationship between the rate of change of *nominal wages* and the unemployment rate, using conventional labour market analysis. But there is a problem here, as Hines (1972, p. 160) makes clear:

> (T)he neoclassical theory which is usually taken to be the basis of such equations specifies relationships in *real wages* (our emphasis).

Although both Phillips and Lipsey did address cost-of-living effects on $\dot{W}$, these real wage changes were never formally incorporated into their models. Phelps (1967) and Friedman (1968) were the first to formally model the Phillips curve in terms of real wages. A basic starting point for this new analysis was the recognition that, in an economy with positive price inflation, $\dot{W} > 0$ could imply both positive or negative real wage growth, depending on whether it was greater or less than the rate of price inflation ($\dot{P}$). Therefore, if labour market decisions are made in terms of real wages, any change in the nominal wage rate will first be compared with the expected change in the inflation rate ($\dot{P}_e$) before the labour market responds.[8] The Phillips curve of equation (1) must therefore be changed to:

$$\dot{W} - \dot{P}_e = w\,(U^* - U) \tag{2a}$$

or, the form in which it is usually written,

$$\dot{W} = w\,(U^* - U) + \dot{P}_e \tag{2b}$$

An important ingredient of this analysis is some theory of how expectations are formed. Here we shall merely follow Friedman and Phelps in suggesting that inflationary expectations are formed by a weighting of past inflationary experience with the most recent experience receiving the highest weighting. Equation (2b) can thus be used to show how an increase in the actual rate of inflation may lead to the formation of expectations[9] and, ultimately, to an outward shift of the Phillips curve, e.g. from $\dot{P}_e = 0\%$ to $\dot{P}_e = 10\%$ in Figure 2.

This conventional model of the Phillips curve has proved useful in helping policy-makers to assess the social opportunity costs associated with different macroeconomic policies. In terms of the analysis presented here, for example, one might imagine a developing economy experiencing both high rates of un-

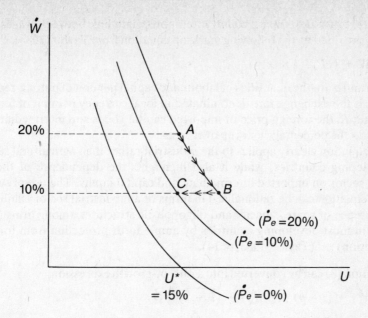

Figure 2

employment and inflation and a shortage of skills which, as indicated above, tends to raise the slope of the Phillips curve. Such a situation is shown by point A in Figure 2, where $\dot{W} = 20$ per cent and $U^* = 15$ per cent. If an attempt is made to bring down the rate of wage inflation through contractionary monetary policy, the economy will slide down the same Phillips curve from point A to point B. The cost in terms of unemployment of reducing inflation to 10 per cent is not excessive *because of the steep Phillips curve*. Moreover, as $\dot{P}_e$ adjusts to the lower rate of wage inflation, the Phillips curve will shift to the left until a new equilibrium is established at point C. Clearly, this scenario encourages the use of a strong anti-inflationary policy because of the low cost of the policy. It is scenarios like these which have pressured policy-makers in developing countries into experimenting with harsh contractionary policies over the last two decades.

3. MOVING FROM WAGE INFLATION TO PRICE INFLATION

Thus far the analysis has focused on the relationship between the rate of change of wages (whether nominal or real) and the unemployment rate. Samuelson and Solow (1960) were the first to point out that the Phillips curve could be translated into a price inflation/unemployment relationship by recognising the fact that movements of the wage rate have an effect on the inflation rate. There are many competing explanations of the exact nature of this relationship. In the context of a developing country an appropriate link between wages and prices is provided by the following mark-up equation from Taylor (1983):[10]

$$P = (aW + beR_f) (1 + x) \qquad (3)$$

where a and b are the quantities of labour and capital per unit of output, respectively; e is the exchange rate denominated in local currency per unit of foreign exchange; R_f the foreign price of imported capital goods and intermediate inputs, and x the percentage markup over costs.

This equation clearly applies to the industrial rather than agricultural sector in developing countries, while it also highlights the dependence of the industrial sector on imported intermediate and capital inputs. The use of such a linking equation can be rationalised in terms of an industrial sector exhibiting 'the presence of spare capacity and oligopolistic structures among firms (buttressed in most developing countries by ample tariff protection from foreign competition) ...' (Taylor, 1983, p. 14).

Equation (3) can be converted into a rate-of-growth expression,

$$\dot{P} = p(\dot{W}) + (1 - p) (\dot{e} + \dot{R}f) + (\overset{\cdot}{\overline{1 + x}}) - \dot{Q} \qquad (4a)$$

where p and $(1 - p)$ are the shares of labour and capital in unit costs, and $\dot{Q}$ reflects productivity growth. By assuming constant markups and productivity levels, $(\overline{1 + x})$ and $\dot{Q}$ can be set equal to zero and (4a) simplified to:

$$\dot{P} = p(\dot{W}) + (1 - p) (\dot{e} + \dot{R}f) \qquad (4b)$$

Substituting (2b) into (4b),

$$\dot{P} = p(w (U^* - U) + \dot{P}e) + (1 - p) (\dot{e} + \dot{R}f) \qquad (4c)$$

which represents the Phillips curve expressed in terms of price (rather than wage) inflation.

It seems reasonable to assume that for the typical developing economy $0 < p < 1$, indicating that unit costs are only partly determined by wages and perhaps largely by foreign input prices and the exchange rate. This follows from our earlier contention that productive activities in developing countries are heavily reliant on imported intermediate and capital goods.

The implications for the Phillips analysis of the previous sections are essentially twofold. Firstly, *the slope of the Phillips curve* is now smaller than before. Initially the curve was steep because of the skill constraint operating in the labour market. However, these labour market dynamics only act on $\dot{P}$ to the dampened degree that is defined by p. As p moves from 1 to 0 the relationship between $\dot{P}$ and U becomes weaker and, hence, the slope of the Phillips curve smaller.

Secondly, $\dot{e}$ and $\dot{R}f$ are important exogenous influences on $\dot{P}$ (except to the extent that they cause changes in $\dot{P}$ which in turn influence $\dot{P}e$). For example, a devaluation ($\dot{e} > 0$) will increase the price of imported (non-labour) intermediate inputs and so have a direct, positive effect on $\dot{P}$. Similarly, sharply rising oil prices ($\dot{R}_f > 0$) would also have a direct, positive effect on $\dot{P}$ for oil-importing developing countries. Equation (4c) makes it clear that in both these cases the effect would be to *shift the Phillips curve* upwards. This is illustrated in Figure 3, where a growth-induced depreciation of the currency moves the economy from point A to point C (rather than point B). When inflationary expectations adjust, the economy may move to point D, where the inflation rate is higher than it would have been in the absence of the depreciation.

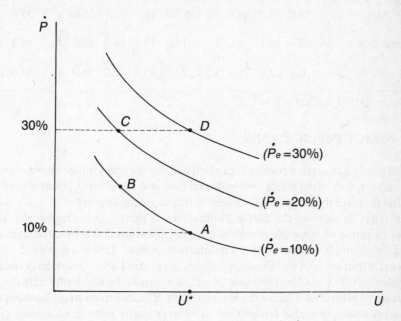

Figure 3

On an empirical level, evidence was cited earlier in the paper to support the assumption that U^* is high and rising in developing countries. The evidence on inflation rates is similarly sobering. As can be seen from Table 1, developing countries have a vastly different inflation position to the industrialised countries. Inflation rates are significantly higher and the rising trend pattern of inflation did not reverse itself after 1980 in developing countries as it did in the case of the industrialised countries. It would be hard to argue that these differences are due to differential wage rate patterns (as argued in section 2 above). Indeed, the significance of the fuel exporter/non-fuel exporter breakdown adds considerable support to the scenario outlined in this section, and specifically to equation (4c). In terms of this model, the rising inflation rates are exogenous to the Phillips curve and are therefore shifting it upwards whilst the rising structural unemployment is pulling it to the right.[11]

125

Table 1 INFLATION RATES OF INDUSTRIAL VERSUS DEVELOPING COUNTRIES AND FUEL AND NON-FUEL EXPORTERS

	Average 1967-76	1977	1978	1979	1980	1981	1982	1983	1984	1985	1986
Industrial Countries	6,7	7,5	7,6	8,0	9,2	8,7	7,2	4,9	4,1	3,9	3,7
Developing Countries	13,8	24,8	18,8	21,5	27,3	26,1	24,7	33,0	37,3	34,8	22,6
Fuel Exporters	9,7	18,1	12,5	11,8	15,9	16,4	18,0	25,5	20,1	15,3	12,1
Non-fuel Exporters	16,2	28,0	21,4	25,7	32,2	30,6	28,0	36,9	47,1	45,0	27,9

Source: IMF, 1985, Table 7, p. 212.

4. POLICY IMPLICATIONS

This paper has argued for the superiority of the second Phillips curve scenario of section 3 over the more conventional one in a developing country context. What then are the policy implications of this second scenario?

Firstly, because of the flatter Phillips curve, there is a far higher short-run cost in terms of unemployment in bringing inflation down by even a modest degree through contractionary stabilisation policy. This is supported by the recent experience of stabilisation policies in several Latin American countries. Foxley (1983) found that the rate of inflation remained resiliently high despite sustained efforts to stabilise these economies. The fact that unemployment rose sharply and wages also fell proved to be very costly indeed, especially in the light of high levels of structural unemployment and the widespread poverty which had already existed. Similarly, Truu (1986, p. 348) had this to say about the South African economy in 1976–77:

> At the time the authorities were pursuing a restrictive demand management policy during a cyclical downswing in economic activity, which is sufficient to account for the observed rise in unemployment. The fact that inflation did not fall suggests that it was now influenced by the supply rather than demand side of the economy. Alternatively put, demand inflation had been replaced by core inflation ...

Theoretically, once expectations begin to adjust to a lower inflation rate, the Phillips curve should shift inward. This has often led policy-makers to suggest that the higher level of unemployment should be tolerated as it will only be temporary. Modigliani (1977, p. 8) has offered a counter-argument by suggesting that this adjustment process 'will have more nearly the character of a crawl than of a gallop'. The experience of many developing countries seems to support

126

Modigliani. In an empirical study of 16 developing countries, Bomberger and Makinen (1976) found that in almost all the cases expectations adjusted very slowly to any change in the inflation rate. In explaining this, the adaptive expectations model that has been used in this paper thus far is useful. Given that the contractionary stabilisation policy only effects a small change in the inflation rate, there is no real reason to expect a swift adjustment of inflation expectations.

Finally, the analysis in Section 3 also highlights a serious policy dilemma facing developing countries today. This is illustrated in Figure 4 where a typical debt-ridden country is shown to experience both a high rate of inflation and extensive unemployment at point A. Without an adequate supply of foreign exchange, an expansionary policy aimed at reducing unemployment to U_1 may well entail a devaluation of the currency which, as described above, would move the economy from point A to point C (rather than B). Under these circumstances the costs in terms of inflation may be considered too high in relation to the benefits associated with a lower unemployment rate.

Domestic policy-makers would naturally prefer to have enough foreign exchange at their disposal to ease the pressure on the balance of payments, and enable them to reach point B (rather than C) in Figure 4. In the absence of adequate export earnings, however, most developing countries have to rely on foreign assistance which is not always available in unlimited supplies, and usually not forthcoming on an unconditional basis either. The assistance

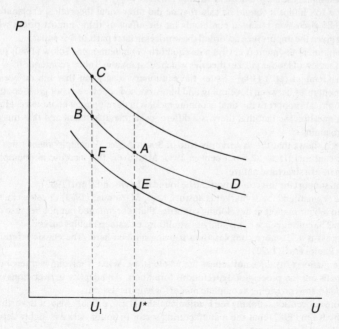

Figure 4

rendered by the International Monetary Fund (IMF), for example, is often made conditional upon the adoption of contractionary monetary and fiscal policies aimed at reducing the average inflation rate in recipient countries. This can be shown in Figure 4 as a movement from point A to point D along the same Phillips curve and, once the slow process of expectations adjustment has occurred, to point E on the lower curve. The granting of foreign assistance at this point might enable the economy to reach point F (rather than B). The long-term effect is thus a movement from point A to point F, or a reduction in unemployment without a concomitant rise in the inflation rate.

There is clearly a serious conflict of interest here. While the developing country is prepared to exchange a higher inflation rate for a lower unemployment rate by moving from point A to point B in Figure 4, this cannot be accomplished without the foreign exchange necessary to maintain a stable exchange rate. On the other hand, the IMF will not provide such assistance unless the developing country shows a commitment to fighting inflation by accepting a higher rate of unemployment. In short, developing countries are caught on the horns of a dilemma: they cannot afford the consequences of either going it alone (point C) or of getting to where others want them to be (point F), and neither can they get where they want to be (point B).

NOTES

1 See, for example, the list provided in Taylor (1983, pp. 8–9).

2 In fairness to Phillips it should be said that he did offer some theoretical explanations of his results. His discussion included comments on the effect of rising import prices which is interesting given the importance accorded these prices in later parts of this paper.

3 For Tobin, unemployment is always a disequilibrium phenomenon. Solow (1980) provides an excellent review of labour market theories which substantiates Tobin's contention.

4 Berry in 'Gemmel (ed.) (1987) issues the cautionary suggestion that the difference in unemployment rates between developing and industrialised countries is not great enough to lend much empirical support to the dual economy models in development economics. However, he does not question the fact that there *is* a difference in unemployment and that this difference needs explaining.

5 Bell (1985) shows that this is certainly true of South Africa. Unemployment rates rose from 16,2 per cent in 1975 to 22,5 per cent in 1985. Moreover, this increase in unemployment is shown to be of a structural nature.

6 Empirical support for this contention can be found in Levin and Horn (1987).

7 Clearly a segmented labour market is at work here. Mazumdar (1983) develops an analysis of the urban labour market in developing countries that is segmented but not because of skill differences. The consequence of his analysis would also be a steep Phillips curve.

8 This process is a lot more complex than is being implied here. The classic reference in this regard is Phelps *et al.* (1972).

9 Clearly equation (2b) does not reflect the whole story. What is missing is a second equation which spells out the process of expectations formation. An adaptive expectations equation is easily added, thus providing a complete model for empirical work.

10 For a more conventional linking see Hadjimichalakis (1986, p. 366). Also, it is worth noting the finding by Kahn (1987) that the manufacturing sector in South Africa is highly dependent on imported capital equipment.

11 The presence of rising unemployment and inflation has led many economists to suggest a posi-

128

tively sloped Phillips curve. A paper by Nugent and Glezakos (1982) provides perhaps the most interesting argument for such a Phillips curve. Whereas the emphasis in the current paper is on urban labour markets and the industrial sector in developing countries, Nugent and Glezakos focus on rural labour markets. They justify the positive slope by assuming that money illusion is impossible in rural markets and that price expectations adjust almost instantaneously to price changes. The current paper explains the same empirical scenario in terms of a shifting Phillips curve. See also Truu (1986).

REFERENCES

Bell, R.T., 1985. 'Issues in South African Unemployment', *South African Journal of Economics*, Vol. 53, No. 1.
Bomberger, W.A. and Makinen, G.E., 1976. 'Inflation and Unemployment in Latin America', *Southern Economic Journal*, Vol. 43, No. 2.
Foxley, A., 1983. *Latin American Experiments in Neo-Conservative Economics*. Berkeley: University of California Press.
Friedman, M., 1967. 'The Role of Monetary Policy', *American Economic Review*, Vol. 58, No. 1 (March).
Hadjimichalakis, M.G., 1982. *Modern Macroeconomics*. New Jersey: Prentice-Hall Inc.
Hines, A.G., 1972. 'The Phillips Curve and the Distribution of Unemployment', *American Economic Review*, Vol. 62 (March).
IMF, 1985. *World Economic Outlook*. Washington D.C.: IMF.
Kahn, S.B., 1987. 'Import Penetration and Import Demands in the South African Economy', *South African Journal of Economics*, Vol. 55, No. 3.
Levin, M. and Horn, G., 1987. 'Phillips Curves for Selected South African Labour Markets, 1969–1986,' *Studies in Economics and Econometrics*, Vol. 11, No. 2.
Lipsey, R.G., 1960. 'The relationship between unemployment and the rate of change of money wage rates in the UK, 1862–1957: A further analysis', *Economica* (February).
Mazumdar, D., 1983. 'Segmented Labour Markets in LDCs', *American Economic Review* (Papers and Proceedings), Vol. 73, No. 2.
Modigliani, F., 1977. 'The Monetarist Controversy or, should we forsake stabilisation policies?' *American Economic Review* (March).
Nugent, J.B. and Glezakos, C., 1982. 'Phillips Curves in Developing Countries: The Latin American Case', *Economic Development and Cultural Change*, Vol. 30, No. 2.
Phelps, E.S., 1967. 'Phillips curves, expectations of inflation and optimal unemployment over time', *Economica*, Vol. 34 (August).
Phelps, E.S. *et al.*, 1972. *Microeconomic Foundations of Employment and Inflation on Theory*. London: Macmillan.
Phillips, A.W., 1958. 'The relation between unemployment and the rate of change of money wage rates in the United Kingdom 1861–1957', *Economica*, Vol. 25 (November).
Samuelson, P.A. and Solow, R.M. 1960. 'Analytical aspects of anti-inflation policy', *American Economic Review* (Papers and Proceedings), Vol. 50 (May).
Solow, R.M., 1980. 'On Theories of Unemployment', *American Economic Review*, Vol. 70, No. 1.
Taylor, L., 1983. *Structuralist Macroeconomics*. New York: Basic Books.
Tobin, J., 1972. 'Inflation and Unemployment', *American Economic Review*, Vol. 62, No. 1.
Truu, M., 1986. 'Economics and Politics in S.A. today', *South African Journal of Economics*, Vol. 54, No. 4.

Part 2

Macroeconomic Policy in South Africa

4

Monetary Policy

4.1 INTRODUCTION

The term monetary policy conventionally refers to that branch of macro-economic policy aimed at influencing monetary magnitudes such as the supply of money, the level and structure of interest rates, and other conditions affecting the availability of credit in the economy. In South Africa the primary institution concerned with formulating and implementing monetary policy is the South African Reserve Bank.

Broadly speaking, the South African Reserve Bank has two kinds of policy instruments at its disposal. On the one hand, it can employ direct policy instruments in its conduct of monetary policy by simply using its legal power to instruct commercial banks and other participants in the financial system to behave in certain ways. Direct, or non-market-orientated, policy instruments include instructions to banks on the maximum limit of credit that may be extended, the maximum deposit rates which may be paid, and the maximum interest rates charged on loans. On the other hand, the Reserve Bank can employ indirect instruments to provide the necessary incentives for financial institutions to voluntarily change their behaviour in appropriate ways. In South Africa, it is possible to identify three major indirect, or market-orientated, instruments of monetary policy. Firstly, in its capacity as bankers' bank or lender of last resort the Reserve Bank can alter its discount rate — that is, the rate at which it deals with the commercial banks. More specifically, by changing its lending or bank rate the Reserve Bank can significantly influence the cost of credit in the South African economy. Secondly, the Reserve Bank can exert control over the money supply, and hence liquidity, by means of open-market operations. Open-market operations refer to the purchase and sale of financial paper, particularly Government bonds, by the Reserve Bank. Thus, should it desire to apply restrictive monetary policy, the Reserve Bank would sell Government bonds, thereby reducing the supply of money. Thirdly, the Reserve Bank can alter liquid asset and cash reserve requirements as an instrument of monetary policy. In terms of the Banks Act, commercial banks and some other financial institutions are required to hold a certain proportion of their liabilities in the form of cash reserves and various forms of liquid assets. By using its statutory powers, the Reserve Bank can require banks to hold additional liquid assets, or it can vary the cash reserve requirements. Since variable cash reserve and liquid asset requirements affect the ability of commercial banks to make loans, the Reserve Bank can influence the level of liquidity in the South African economy by modifying these requirements.

Monetary policy in South Africa has undergone a rather gradual evolution over the years. Indeed, it is possible to identify five broad phases of monetary policy, according to the emphasis the De Kock Commission report placed on the use of particular instruments of monetary policy. Generally speaking, however, the evolution of monetary policy in South Africa may be described as a process of transition from reliance on direct control measures to the present emphasis on market-orientated, indirect instruments.

Six readings are provided in this chapter. The first of these, by Faure, provides a valuable overview of the institutional framework within which monetary policy in South Africa is conducted. Indeed, so interwoven are institutional characteristics and the operation of monetary instruments, that a firm grasp of the former is essential for an understanding of monetary policy. The second reading is an extract from the De Kock Commission report, in which the main findings of the Commission are summarised. It is fair to say that this landmark document, submitted in 1985, represents a historical watershed in the development of monetary policy in South Africa.

The articles by De Wet and Kantor both represent critical appraisals of the findings and implications of the De Kock Report. In the fifth reading Whittaker provides an assessment of the efficacy of monetary policy in South Africa in the post-De Kock era, and argues that it possesses certain definite limitations. Finally, the paper by Innes represents a radical critique of the conduct of monetary policy in South Africa in recent times, in which he sets out to demonstrate the damage monetarism in its South African guise has inflicted on the local economy.

4.2 AN OVERVIEW OF THE SOUTH AFRICAN FINANCIAL SYSTEM

A.P. Faure*

INTRODUCTION

The South African financial system has undergone marked changes over the past few years. These changes have been brought about by both the monetary authorities and the private financial sector against the background of the liberalisation of the financial markets. Developments have included a changed attitude toward the implementation of monetary policy, the emergence of new financial instruments, new financial intermediaries and brokers (as well as the overlapping of their functions), and substantially higher levels of activity in the securities markets.

Against this background it is perhaps timely to provide an overview of the operation of the financial system. Insight into financial and monetary matters greatly depends on knowledge of the elements (the institutions, instruments and markets) which make up our financial system.

DEFINITION

The financial system may be defined briefly as a complex set of arrangements embracing the lending and borrowing of funds by non-financial economic units and the intermediation of this function by financial institutions to facilitate the transfer of funds, to provide additional money when required and to create markets in debt in order that the price of funds, and therefore the allocation of funds, is determined efficiently.

From this definition one may identify four essential elements of the financial system. Firstly, we have the lenders and borrowers, i.e. the non-financial economic units. Secondly, we have the financial institutions which intermediate, to a large degree, the lending and borrowing process. The third element is the wide array of financial instruments which are created to satisfy the various needs of the participants. Finally, we have the financial markets, i.e. the institutional arrangements and conventions which exist for the issue and trading (dealing) of the financial instruments.

FINANCIAL INTERMEDIATION

Surplus and deficit economic units

It is unlikely that saving performed by non-financial economic units out of in-

* Director of Securities Discount House Holdings Limited and editor of *The Securities Markets*. This paper was first published in *The Securities Markets*, No. 3, First Quarter, 1987.

come will be matched by desired investment. Some economic units will find that their savings out of income will exceed their planned investment, while others find themselves in a position where their saving is insufficient to meet desired internal investment. We can refer to the former as surplus units or ultimate lenders and to the latter as deficit units or ultimate borrowers (see Figure 1).

The ultimate lenders can be further described as non-financial economic units which generate investable funds. They can be split into various categories, i.e. the household sector, the corporate sector, the general government sector and the foreign sector. Exactly the same non-financial economic units also appear on the 'other side' of the financial system as ultimate borrowers. This situation arises as different members of the four categories, or even the same members at different times, may be either surplus or deficit units.

For purposes of the National Financial Accounts, the Reserve Bank[1] defines these four sectors as follows:

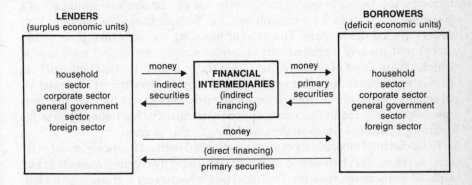

Figure 1 THE FINANCIAL SYSTEM

Household sector

The household sector consists of individuals and families, but also includes private charitable, religious and non-profit bodies serving households. It also includes unincorporated businesses such as farmers, retailers and professional partnerships, as the transactions of these businesses cannot be separated from the personal transactions of their owners.

Corporate sector

The corporate sector consists of all companies not classified as financial institutions and thus covers business enterprises directly or indirectly engaged in the production and distribution of goods and services.

135

General government sector

The general government sector consists of the central government, provincial administrations and local authorities.

Foreign sector

The foreign sector comprises all organisations, persons and assets resident or situated in the rest of the world.

Financial intermediation

Given the existence of surplus and deficit economic units or a supply of and a demand for loanable funds, some financial conduit is necessary if the excess funds of surplus units are to be transferred to deficit units. The needs of these units may be reconciled either through direct financing or through financial intermediaries. Direct financing involves the use of a broker who would act as a go-between in return for a commission, i.e. he distributes the claims of borrowers among the lenders. This type of financing can only take place to the extent that lenders' requirements in terms of risk, return, and term can be matched with those of the borrowers. Generally, a conflict exists between borrowers and lenders. Lenders would tend to require investments (financial instruments) which differ from those which borrowers prefer to issue, and borrowers generally require accommodation (issue financial instruments) on terms differing from those which lenders are willing or able to grant.

Financial intermediaries, performing so-called indirect financing, assist in resolving the conflict between lenders and borrowers by creating markets in two types of financial instruments, i.e. one type for borrowers and one type for lenders. They offer claims against themselves, tailored to the liquidity and maturity needs of the lenders, and in turn acquire claims on the borrowers. The former claims are usually referred to as indirect securities and the latter as primary securities (see Figure 1). The financial intermediaries receive a 'fee', of course, and this is represented by the difference between the cost of their indirect securities and the revenue from the primary securities held.

The functions of financial intermediaries

A number of benefits for the economic system are produced by the ability of financial intermediaries to transmute the unacceptable claims on borrowers into acceptable claims on themselves. Firstly, through aggregating small amounts of funds for on-lending in larger packets, liquidity is created for the lender. Secondly, through investing in a diverse portfolio of primary securities, a financial intermediary can achieve a more efficient diversification of risk than an individual lender. Thirdly, by providing liquidity and reducing risk, financial intermediaries are able to tap savings which otherwise would not have been a-vailable. In the fourth place, by facilitating the availability of finance, these institutions ease the constraint of income on expenditure, and thereby enable the consumer to spend in anticipation of income and the entrepreneur to acquire physical capital. Finally, through their expertise, financial intermediaries help to ensure that the flow of funds is allocated in the most efficient manner.

SOUTH AFRICAN FINANCIAL INTERMEDIARIES

General

As noted earlier, financial institutions exist primarily because of the conflict between lenders' and borrowers' requirements in terms of risk, return and term to maturity. They issue financial liabilities which are acceptable as assets to the lenders and use the funds so obtained to acquire claims which reflect the requirements of the borrowers. In so doing they facilitate the flow of funds from surplus to deficit economic units. Certain financial institutions also have the unique ability to first acquire financial claims and thus increase the financial liabilities in the system — the so-called money-creating institutions.

Financial institutions do not only perform the intermediation function as explained above. Certain of them are in the business of making markets in financial instruments, allowing investors to change the composition and nature of their portfolios and borrowers to access funds more readily. In so doing, they assist in the rapid adjustment in the price of funds in response to changing supply and demand conditions and in the efficient allocation of this scarce commodity.

The nature of financial intermediaries

The intermediation function is performed by many different types of institutions. As regards the essential function of intermediation there is little distinction between banks, finance houses, insurance companies, building societies, or any other type of intermediary. The distinguishing features lie in the nature of the claims and services offered to lenders and in the nature of the claims on and services offered to the borrowers. In these respects there are very wide differences between intermediaries. Since financial institutions tend to be more specialised on the liabilities side of their balance sheets, it would be appropriate to classify them according to the nature of the indirect securities they issue.

Classification of financial intermediaries

Financial institutions may be classified in two broad categories, i.e. deposit and non-deposit intermediaries. The first category may be split into two sub-

137

categories, i.e. banking and non-banking intermediaries, while the second category may be split into three sub-categories, i.e. contractual intermediaries, portfolio institutions and other specialised financing intermediaries. These are shown below.

DEPOSIT INTERMEDIARIES	NON-DEPOSIT INTERMEDIARIES
Banking intermediaries	*Contractual intermediaries*
South African Reserve Bank	Insurers
Corporation of Public Deposits	Pension and provident funds
Land and Agricultural Bank	Public Investment Commissioners
Private banks	*Portfolio institutions*
Discount houses	Unit trusts
Development Bank of Southern Africa	Investment trusts
	Participation mortgage bond schemes
Non-banking intermediaries	*Other financial intermediaries*
Building societies	Finance companies
Post Office Savings Bank	National Housing Fund
	Local Loans Fund
	Housing Trust

The main financial institutions, as well as their intermediation functions and relationships to one another, are depicted simply in Figure 2. As is evident from this presentation, the Reserve Bank intermediates between ultimate lenders (mainly the government in its capacity as government banker and the private sector in its capacity as sole issuer of bank notes) and the banks and building societies (i.e their cash reserves required to be held for monetary policy purposes) on the one hand, and ultimate borrowers (as represented by the Bank's holdings of foreign exchange and domestic securities) and the private banking sector on the other. The latter would represent the Reserve Bank in its function as the lender of last resort.

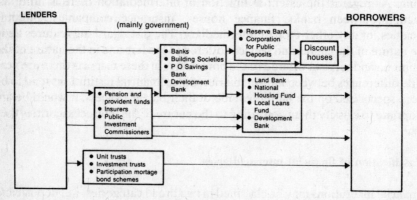

Figure 2 FINANCIAL INTERMEDIARIES

The Corporation for Public Deposits, a relatively new institution, intermediates mainly between the government on the one hand, and ultimate borrowers and the discount houses (when such funds are made available) on the other. An element of loans to other financial institutions, such as the Land Bank, in the form of Land Bank bills and debentures held, does exist from time to time.

The private banks, building societies and Post Office Savings Bank intermediate mainly between the ultimate lenders (in the form of deposits and loans) and ultimate borrowers (in the form of loans, hire-purchase and leasing contracts, mortgage advances and purchasing of securities). However, an element of intermediation between financial intermediaries does exist. They do issue liabilities to insurance companies and pension funds and make loans to and/or hold the securities of other financial intermediaries such as the Land Bank, the National Housing Fund, the discount houses (in the form of call loans representing the ultimate liquidity of the banking system) and the Reserve Bank (in the form of cash reserves required to be held).

Pension and provident funds and insurers intermediate between the public (in the form of so-called contractual savings) on the one hand, and ultimate borrowers (mainly in the form of equities and securities) and financial intermediaries on the other. The latter would be represented by bank and building society deposits and the holding of the securities of the Land Bank and the National Housing Fund. The Public Investment Commissioners are similar to the pension and provident funds and insurers in their intermediation function, but they are restricted to certain investments and are prohibited from holding equities. The so-called portfolio institutions intermediate almost entirely between ultimate borrowers and ultimate lenders. While the Land Bank's liabilities are almost entirely forthcoming from financial institutions (in the form of bank loans and bills and debentures issued), it lends only to ultimate borrowers (in the form of individual farmers, co-operatives and regulatory boards).

The specialised financing intermediaries fund themselves from ultimate lenders and financial intermediaries while providing finance almost exclusively to ultimate borrowers. Possibly the most unique group of institutions are the discount houses. They intermediate exclusively between other financial institutions on the one hand, and ultimate borrowers and financial institutions on the other. They accept as liabilities call loan deposits from banks and building societies (and mining houses, which could be regarded as financial intermediaries) and invest only in fixed-interest securities. This places them in a unique position as regards the execution of monetary policy, i.e. when call deposits are substituted by Reserve Bank loans.

FINANCIAL INSTRUMENTS

As a result of the process of borrowing and financial intermediation, a wide array of primary and indirect securities exist in the financial system.

Generally, a financial instrument or claim is defined as a claim against a person or institution for the payment of a future sum of money and/or a periodic payment of money. The 'and/or' in the definition implies that either of the payments will be sufficient, but that both may be promised. In many cases there is no periodic payment, such as with Treasury bills or bankers' acceptances which are issued at a discount and repaid at par.

Similarly, there may be no promise to pay a definite sum in the future, such as in the case with undated stocks. The more common financial claim is one where the issuer carries an obligation to pay interest periodically and to redeem the claim at a certain value in one of three ways, i.e. on demand, after giving a predetermined period of notice or on a definite date, or one of several predetermined dates. One of the most important characteristics of financial claims is that of reversibility, i.e. the ease with which the holders of financial claims can recover the funds they have surrendered to the issuers of the claims. This can be achieved in one of two ways: either by recourse to the issuer, as in the case with, for example, a bank deposit, or by recourse to a secondary market in which the holder can sell the claim held.

Examples of non-reversible (or non-marketable) financial instruments or claims would include savings deposits, other fixed deposits, mortage loans, life policies and lease agreements. There are many types of securities which are reversible, i.e. marketable, but the degree of marketability will vary substantially. These instruments are detailed below.

PRIMARY SECURITIES
(issued by ultimate borrowers)
Representing the obligations of the private sector
Bankers' acceptances
Trade bills
Promissory notes
Commercial paper
Company debentures
Representing the obligations of the public sector
Treasury bills
Government stocks
Stocks of the national states
Representing the obligations of the semi-public sector
Capital project bills
Bridging bonds
Municipal stocks
Public corporation stocks
Stocks of educational institutions

INDIRECT SECURITIES
(issued by financial intermediaries)
Representing the liabilities of private banks
Negotiable certificates of deposit
Representing the liabilities of public or semi-public banks
Reserve bank debentures
Land Bank bills
Land Bank debentures
Development Bank debentures

REPURCHASE AGREEMENTS

As noted above, all these instruments (with the exception of repurchase agreements) represent the financial obligations of the issuers. Repurchase agreements, on the other hand, represent the obligations of the makers of such agreements. Simply defined, a repurchase agreement is the sale of a previously issued security for a specified period of time at a certain rate of interest.

FINANCIAL MARKETS[2]

The economic function of financial markets is to provide channels through which the excess funds of surplus units can be transferred to deficit units. Put slightly differently, financial markets are the mechanism that link surplus and deficit units, providing the means through which surplus units can finance deficit units either directly, or indirectly through financial intermediaries. However, financial markets provide surplus and deficit units with additional options. Surplus units may purchase primary or indirect securities or reduce their debt by purchasing their own outstanding securities. Deficit units, on the other hand, may sell securities or dispose of some financial asset.

It will be evident that the participants in the financial markets are the borrowers (issuers of securities), the lenders (buyers of securities), the financial intermediaries (buyers and issuers of securities and other debt obligations) and brokers. The term financial market therefore encompasses the participants and their dealings in particular financial claims or groups of claims and the manner in which their demands and requirements interact to set a price for it (the interest rate).[3]

A fundamental distinction has to be made between the primary and secondary market in securities. The market for the issue of new securities for the purpose of borrowing money for consumption or investment is referred to as the primary market. This market would include the issue of both primary and indirect securities. It will be evident that the markets in non-negotiable instruments, such as mortgage loans, savings deposits and life policies, are entirely primary markets.

Secondary market is the term used for the markets in which previously issued financial claims are traded. There exist active markets in many of the securities referred to in the previous section, but they differ in terms of so-called 'breadth' and 'depth' or 'liquidity'. When talking about the secondary market, it is important to distinguish between brokers and market-makers. Brokers generally act on behalf of other financial market participants in return for a commission, and as such cannot be regarded as financial intermediaries. Market-makers, on the other hand, are comprised of certain of the financial institutions, such as the discount houses and certain banks, who have assumed this function, i.e. they are prepared to quote buying and selling prices simultaneously in certain securities and are prepared to deal in reasonable volume. It will be clear that because these institutions are prepared to hold portfolios of securities for this purpose, they need to be adequately capitalised.

An active secondary market in securities is important for a number of reasons. Firstly, it assists the primary market, i.e. the ease with which issuers may place securities, through providing investors with the assurance that they are able to dispose of securities if they so desire. Secondly, a secondary market provides the basis for the determination of rates which need to be offered on new issues. In the third place, it registers changing market conditions rapidly and thus indicates the receptiveness of the market for new primary issues. Finally, an active secondary market enables investors to rapidly adjust their portfolios in terms of size, risk, return, liquidity and maturity.

The financial market is usually split into the money and capital markets. These markets embrace the primary or 'new issues' market and the secondary market. The line demarcating the money and capital markets is usually drawn on the basis of term to maturity of the securities traded in, and is arbitrarily determined to be one year. Broadly speaking then, the capital market is defined as the market which exists for the issue and trading of long-term securities, while the money market is the market which exists for the issue and trading of short-term securities.

CONCLUDING REMARKS

After an extensive investigation, the Commission of Inquiry into the Monetary System and Monetary Policy in South Africa concluded that South Africa can boast of a relatively advanced and sophisticated financial system and broad and active financial markets. There are two main reasons why the Commission considered this to be desirable: 'The first is the significant contribution such markets can make to the growth and general soundness of the economy. And the second is the key role they can and must play in the application of effective stabilisation policies in a basically free-enterprise and reasonably developed economy.'[4]

NOTES

1 Uys, D.J. and Van der Walt, S.J., 'National Financial Accounts for South Africa, 1970 to 1979', *Supplement to Quarterly Bulletin*, September 1981, pp. 4–6.
2 This section draws heavily on Faure, A.P., 'The Liability and Asset Portfolio Management Practices of the South African Money Market Institutions and their Role in the Financial System', unpublished D. Phil. thesis, University of Stellenbosch, 1976.
3 Committee to Review the Functioning of Financial Institutions: *Report*, Her Majesty's Stationery Office, London, 1980, p. 25.
4 Commission of Inquiry into the Monetary System and Monetary Policy in South Africa: *Final Report*, RP 70/1984, p. 1.

REFERENCES

Dougall, H.E., 1970. *Capital Markets and Institutions*, 2nd ed., Foundations of Finance Series. New Jersey: Prentice-Hall, Inc.
Furness, E.L., 1972. *An Introduction to Financial Economics*. London: Heinemann.

Gurley, J.G., 1965. 'Financial Institutions in the Saving-Investment Process', reprinted in: Ketchum, M.D. and Kendall, L.T. (eds.), *Readings in Financial Institutions*. Boston: Houghton, Mifflin Co.

—— 1966. 'The Market in Loanable Funds, Creation of Liquid Assets and Monetary Control', in: Carson, D. (ed.), *Money and Finance*. New York: John Wiley & Sons, Inc.

Polakoff, M.E., 1970. *Financial Institutions and Markets*. Boston: Houghton, Mifflin Co.

Revell, J., 1973. *The British Financial System*. London: Macmillan.

Smith, P.F., 1971. *Economics of Financial Institutions and Markets*. Homewood, Illinois: Richard D. Irwin, Inc.

4.3 MONETARY POLICY IN SOUTH AFRICA: MAIN FINDINGS

De Kock Commission*

1. Like their counterparts in most other countries, the South African monetary authorities have in recent decades been confronted by pernicious and varying combinations of inflation, balance of payments fluctuations, cyclical instability and unemployment. Since the early 'seventies they have also had to cope with the effects of extremely volatile international exchange rates and marked fluctuations in the gold price. The Commission finds that, in dealing with these problems, the monetary authorities in South Africa have achieved many positive results and have made a valuable contribution towards counteracting both internal and external economic instability.

2. At the same time, the Commission has reached the conclusion that monetary policy[1] as applied in South Africa during most of the period since 1946 suffered from certain basic deficiencies. These shortcomings help to explain why only partial success was achieved in attaining the policy objectives of relative stability of the price level, reasonably sustained equilibrium in the balance of payments and optimal and relatively stable economic growth and employment.

3. The reasons why these objectives were attained only to a limited degree are manifold and by no means all of a cyclical or monetary nature. They include a number of structural features of the South African economy, such as a relative shortage of skilled labour, low productivity, an insufficient degree of competition, and recurring agricultural problems. Such features, which are of particular importance to growth and employment, do not fall within the Commission's terms of reference and are not discussed in depth in this Report.

4. The Commission has nevertheless concluded that the inadequate degree to which the abovementioned policy objectives were attained must to a significant extent be attributed to certain deficiencies in broad monetary policy. This applies particularly to the objectives of price stability and balance of payments equilibrium.

DEFICIENCIES OF MONETARY POLICY

5. The Commission has identified the following closely interrelated deficiencies in South African monetary policy which have at times contributed to the excess, the insufficiency or the instability of aggregate monetary demand,

---

* *Commission of Inquiry into the Monetary System and Monetary Policy in South Africa,* Final Report, RP 70 : 1984. Pretoria: Government Printer, May 1985. Cross references are to chapters and paragraphs in the main *Report*.

and therefore to inflation, balance of payments difficulties, and unstable growth and employment:

- The rates of increase of the monetary aggregates (such as M1, M2 and M3) were not adequately moderated and stabilised.[2]

- Control measures were applied which led to abnormal 'disintermediation' and 'reintermediation' and other developments causing marked fluctuations in the velocity of circulation of the monetary aggregates.

- Interest rates were not always allowed to rise to levels that would have been reconcilable with, or would have contributed to, the appropriate degree of moderation and stability in the rates of increase in bank credit, money supply(M) and aggregate monetary demand (MV, i.e. the money supply multiplied by its velocity of circulation). Instead, interest rates were frequently prevented from increasing to the required extent by means of central bank credit creation and/or direct controls of one kind or another. In addition, the *structure* of interest rates was not always allowed to reflect fully the 'natural' interrelationship between the rates of return on financial assets in accordance with the intrinsic quality, liquidity and maturity of these assets.

- Following the breakdown of the Bretton Woods par value system in 1971, the spot and forward exchange rates for the rand were not always allowed to adjust to levels that would have been reconcilable with the appropriate level of aggregate monetary demand. In part, this stemmed from inadequate co-ordination between exchange control policy and other policies forming part of the official monetary strategy.

The money supply, inflation and the balance of payments

6. The Commission finds that the excessive and unstable growth of the monetary aggregates has not only *permitted* or *accommodated* the relatively high rate of price increases in South Africa during the past twenty years or more, but has also been a major *cause* of this inflation. It is certainly significant that the increase of 651 per cent from 1960 to 1984 in the general price level, as measured by the gross domestic product deflator, was accompanied by a twenty-three-fold increase in the annual average of the broadly defined money supply (M3).

7. The Commission also finds that the marked cyclical fluctuations that occurred during this period in the growth rate of the money supply and in interest rates, initiated in many instances by external developments, were major causes of the observed cyclical fluctuations in the rate of increase in total domestic spending and in the balance of payments. Rates of monetary expansion and domestic inflation frequently in excess of those of South Africa's main trading partners were also an important element in explaining the longer-run downward pressure on the effective exchange rate of the rand in recent years.

8. The Commission finds that the income velocity of circulation of the various monetary aggregates has shown substantial short-term, cyclical and longer-term variations during the period since 1960.[3] Over the past ten years, in particular, these variations have been so extensive that the behaviour of the money supply statistics has been extremely misleading as a guide to monetary analysis and monetary policy. During this period the money supply aggregates have not correlated well with actual spending of total monetary demand, even after allowing for possible time lags. Of particular importance was the substantial increase in the velocity of circulation of the monetary aggregates M1, M2 and M3 from 1976 to the first quarter of 1980 and the subsequent sharp decline from the first quarter of 1980 to the first quarter of 1985.

9. The Commission believes that these marked changes in the velocity of circulation of the monetary aggregates are of crucial importance to an understanding of monetary developments and policy in South Africa during the past ten years. Between 1976 and the first quarter of 1980, *both* M and V increased rapidly. This meant that MV increased *even faster* than M. Subsequently, from the first quarter of 1980 to the first quarter of 1985, M continued to increase *but V declined sharply*. This meant that MV increased *at a much lower rate* than M. In other words, since 1980 the money supply statistics have given an exaggerated impression of the increase in actual spending or total monetary demand. During this period, monetary policy has actually been much less accommodative and, at times, more effective in curbing total spending than a superficial examination of the money supply figures by themselves would suggest.

10. The abnormal rise in velocity from 1976 to 1980 was mainly attributable to 'disintermediation', and the subsequent sharp decline from the first quarter of 1980 to the first quarter of 1985 to substantial 'reintermediation'.

11. *Disintermediation* is defined as the replacement of credit normally or previously extended through the intermediation of a bank or other financial institution, by non-intermediated credit extended directly by primary lenders to ultimate borrowers. This definition includes a shift by banks from on-balance-sheet to off-balance-sheet financing. *Reintermediation* refers to the reverse process, i.e. the return of disintermediated credit to the balance sheets of banks or other financial institutions.

12. Apart from artificially inflated intercompany borrowing and lending, disintermediation in South Africa has consisted mostly of a switch by non-banking parties from holding deposits with banking institutions to increased direct holdings of standard money market instruments, such as bankers' acceptances, bank-endorsed trade bills and promissory notes, and short-term securities.

13. In South Africa the banks themselves have come to participate in dis-

intermediation on a large scale. They have done this by entering the money broking field and arranging *off-balance-sheet financing* for their clients. This kind of disintermediation has mainly taken the following forms:

- The arranging by the banks of intercompany borrowing and lending and the matching of the requirements of other borrowers and lenders outside the books of the banks;
- the selling by banks of assets under repurchase agreements to the non-banking private sector;
- the creation of acceptance facilities and the rediscounting of such acceptances *outside* the banking system by companies seeking to invest their liquid funds; and
- the discounting of bank-endorsed trade bills with large depositors, rather than by banks for their own account.

Causes of disintermediation between 1976 and 1980: direct policy instruments

14. The Commission finds that the main cause of the large-scale disintermediation and the consequent rise in the velocity of circulation of the monetary aggregates that occurred between 1976 and 1980 was the application during that period of *direct* and *semi-direct* instruments of monetary policy, such as bank credit ceilings, deposit rate control and high liquid asset requirements.

15. The *direct quantitative restrictions or 'ceilings' on bank credit to the private sector* applied by the Reserve Bank between 1965 and 1972, and again from 1976 until 1980, forced the banks into sub-optimally small lending portfolios and correspondingly large holdings of liquid assets and prescribed investments. Since the use of this direct method of credit control was also accompanied by a lower level of interest rates, and therefore a stronger *demand* for credit, than would have prevailed under more market-oriented policies, the inevitable outcome was that unsatisfied borrowers turned to alternative sources of short-term credit. This resulted in large-scale disintermediation and a sharp rise in the velocity of circulation of money. It therefore greatly reduced the effectiveness of monetary policy.

16. A similar effect was exerted by the *deposit rate controls* imposed by the Reserve Bank from March 1965 to July 1966, from December 1969 to August 1970 and from March 1972 until March 1980. The effect of these controls was to keep deposit rates below free-market levels. The result was a diversion of funds from deposits subject to rate control to more attractive investments outside the banking system. This, of course, also resulted in substantial disintermediation, a rise in velocity and reduced effectiveness of monetary policy.

17. The fact that until February 1982 *the clearing banks' prime overdraft rate was linked by convention to the Reserve Bank's rediscount rate and that both these rates remained relatively rigid over many years,* also contributed to disintermediation during periods when these rates were maintained at levels that were *too high* in relation to other short-term rates, as during the 'gold boom' of

1979 and 1980. At such times, borrowers naturally turned to cheaper *non-inter-mediated* forms of credit. At the same time, the banks' inability to lend sufficiently large amounts on overdraft reduced their demand for deposits. In addition, borrowers' shifts to non-intermediated credit markets served to hold up the interest rates in those markets relative to the rates the banks were able and willing to offer on deposits. This also reduced the *supply* of deposits to the banks.

18. Finally, the *abnormally high cash reserve and liquid asset requirements that applied to banking institutions* in South Africa until 1982 significantly reduced the banks' competitiveness as intermediaries in the financial markets by artificially widening the gap between their lending and deposit rates. In this way, the scope for borrowers and lenders to meet each other directly at rates within this wider margin was greatly increased, leading inevitably to disintermediation.

Causes of reintermediation between 1980 and 1985: the transition to market-oriented policies

19. The huge decline in velocity of circulation between early 1980 and early 1985 to a large extent reflected the substantial reintermediation that occurred during this period. This return of disintermediated credit to the balance sheets of banks and other financial intermediaries was mainly the logical and inevitable consequence of the transition during this period from predominantly 'direct' to more market-oriented instruments of monetary policy, accompanied at times by tightening business liquidity.

20. The main steps which marked this transition were the *abolition of deposit rate controls in March 1980 and of bank credit ceilings from September 1980*. In addition, *a more flexible interest rate policy* was applied. Among other things, the Reserve Bank abolished the direct link between its rediscount rates and the clearing banks' prime overdraft rate in February 1982 and allowed the latter to rise to more realistic market-determined levels. The maximum interest rates laid down under the Limitation and Disclosure of Finance Charges Act (the so-called Ladofca rates) were also adjusted upwards from September 1980. In addition, the Reserve Bank applied more flexible techniques, conditions and rates in its rediscounting operations and other ways of granting accommodation to discount houses and banks. The move to a more market-oriented monetary policy was also given impetus by the increased use of tap issues of government stock and other open-market operations by the Reserve Bank at realistic market-related interest rates.

21. These various developments constitute the main explanation of the combination of continued rapid growth of the monetary aggregates and declining velocity of circulation since 1980, i.e. they explain why the actual spending of money — that is the money supply multiplied by its velocity of circulation — did not rise nearly as much as the money supply itself during this period.

In the course of analysing the various deficiencies of monetary policy set out above, the Commission identified certain 'ratchet effects' in South African monetary developments that contributed materially to the relentless growth of the money supply and the persistent inflation of the past twenty-four years. These ratchet effects arise from a basic asymmetry in the cyclical and seasonal behaviour of the money supply, the liquidity base and the cash reserves of the banking system: increases in these monetary quantities due to cyclical and seasonal influences are prevented from being reversed during subsequent cyclical or seasonal phases to the extent that might normally have been expected — hence the term 'ratchet'. The result is an exaggerated upward trend in the monetary quantities concerned.

23. In the case of the money supply the ratchet effect typically takes the following form: When a balance of payments surplus arises, the Reserve Bank and the other banks take foreign exchange into their reserves, partly suppressing the tendency of the rand's exchange rate to rise. This exerts a strong expansionary effect on the money supply. But when the balance of payments duly turns into deficit during subsequent cyclical phases and the net foreign reserves of the banking system decline, the commensurate contractionary effects on the money supply tend to be offset almost automatically by a substantial rise in the banking system's 'domestic credit extension', i.e. in the total of bank credit extended to the private sector and net bank credit extended to the government sector. This increase is usually made possible and supported by an increase in Reserve Bank credit, as the Bank finds it necessary to 'accommodate' the money market shortage resulting from the decline in foreign reserves at 'reasonable' rates of interest.

24. The Commission believes that one major reason for these ratchet effects was the reluctance of the authorities to accept the full interest rate and related consequences that the periodic balance of payments deficits and accompanying declines in net foreign reserves would have had in the absence of offsetting domestic credit creation by the Reserve Bank and the other banks.

THE UNDERLYING REASONS FOR THE DEFICIENCIES OF MONETARY POLICY

25. In the view of the Commission, the deficiencies of monetary policy set out above were largely the product of a number of shortcomings in the underlying approach to monetary policy in South Africa during the sixties and seventies. These were the following:

An inadequate recognition of the need for market-oriented methods of monetary policy

26. The Commisson believes that a basic shortcoming has been an inadequate

recognition of the need for market-oriented methods of monetary policy. One reason for this was an inadequate appreciation of the significance of the rapidly developing financial markets and particularly of their implications for monetary policy. A second contributory factor was a lack of faith in the ability of these markets to produce optimal economic results. And a third reason was the fear that the untrammelled operation of the financial markets would have certain socially unacceptable consequences, such as high interest rates on housing and agricultural finance. Undue reliance therefore came to be placed upon 'direct' methods — such as bank credit ceilings, deposit rate control, exchange control and import deposits — and, to a lesser extent, upon 'semi-market-oriented' methods in the form of variations in liquid asset and cash reserve requirements. To some extent this preference for 'direct' methods was associated with the relatively immature stage of development of the financial markets in earlier years. Nevertheless, these methods failed to give the monetary authorities adequate influence over the amount and velocity of circulation of the monetary aggregates, interest rates, exchange rates and credit generally, and therefore over monetary demand, income, output, prices and the balance of payments.

27. In reaching this conclusion, the Commission was influenced by the results of its investigation into the working of the various short-term financial markets in South Africa. As set out in Part I of this Report, the Commission finds that South Africa now has a relatively advanced monetary and banking system and a set of reasonably broad, active and expanding financial markets. Moreover, the Commission deems it desirable that these markets function efficiently and that their further development be encouraged. This is because they make a significant contribution to the growth and general soundness of the economy, and because they can and must play a key role in the application of effective monetary stabilisation policies in South Africa's basically free-enterprise and reasonably developed economy.

28. For these reasons, the Commission believes that monetary policy in South Africa should as far as possible be applied in a manner which does not undermine the development and functioning of sound financial markets. The Commission also accepts that these financial markets function best in the national interest if they are reasonably free, competitive, active and broad, and if they produce realistic market-related interest rates.

29. The essence of the matter is that the very existence of reasonably developed markets — such as those for Treasury bills, public sector stock debt, bankers' acceptances, trade bills, promissory notes, deposits, overdrafts and other bank loans, interbank loans and call loans to discount houses — means that monetary policy can be fully effective in influencing monetary demand *only* if it is basically market-oriented. Non-market-oriented or 'direct' methods of monetary policy, particularly credit ceilings and deposit rate controls, cannot achieve the desired results in such circumstances. This is partly because, as indicated above, they inevitably lead to large-scale disintermediation.

An unduly narrow view of monetary policy

30. The second underlying reason for the deficiences of monetary policy has been the tendency to equate 'monetary policy' largely with the control of credit extended by *the banking sector to the private sector*. The weakness of this unduly narrow view of monetary policy was that it tended to focus attention mainly on instruments of monetary policy aimed at controlling bank credit to the private sector, such as higher cash reserve and liquid asset requirements and credit ceilings, and to divert attention from other and more basic influences affecting money, credit, interest and exchange rates, and therefore aggregate monetary demand. This resulted in insufficient attention being given to such strategically important areas of broad monetary policy as public debt management, open-market operations, discount policy, and both exchange rate and exchange control policy. And it is precisely in these areas that the battle for *monetary stability* is often won or lost. These are the areas in which the monetary authorities must operate if they wish to exert an adequate influence over the monetary aggregates, interest rates and actual spending.

The lack of a clearly defined and consistent approach to either the monetary aggregates or interest rates

31. The third underlying reason has been the absence of a clearly defined approach to either monetary aggregates or interest rates, and therefore also to the relationship between them. No use has been made of either published or unpublished targets for M1, M2, M3, cash base or any other monetary aggregates, except where this was a precondition for drawing on the International Monetary Fund. In addition, for long periods at a time up to 1980, interest rates were not used as an instrument for influencing monetary and banking conditions and aggregate demand, but were instead kept artificially low.

Weaknesses in exchange rate and exchange control policy as an integral part of official monetary strategy

32. Another underlying reason for the policy deficiencies has been a lack of adequate co-ordination at certain times between exchange rate and exchange control policies and other policies forming part of the overall official monetary strategy.

33. Monetary policy can operate effectively only if full account is taken of the close relationship that exists between the money supply, interest rates, exchange rates and exchange control. In the extreme case of strict adherence to a target money growth rate, for example, the exchange rate is largely co-determined along with interest rates and the money supply. But these variables, in turn, are influenced by exchange control. And past experience has shown that the application of strict exchange control often prevents the most desirable

combination of money supply growth, interest rates and spot and forward exchange rates from being attained.

34. A good example of this was provided by the experience during the gold boom of 1979 and 1980, and again during the second half of 1982 and early 1983, when the existence of exchange control at a time of current account surplus contributed to a 'bottling-up' of funds in the economy and, consequently, an excessive rise in the money supply and an artificially low level and distorted structure of interest rates. This subsequently served to bring about new balance of payments difficulties. Instead of improving the balance of payments and reserve position, exchange control therefore in the end had the effect of weakening it.

35. The notion that exchange control 'helps to keep capital in the country' and therefore always has a beneficial effect on the balance of payments and the domestic economy is clearly fallacious. Outflows as well as inflows of capital can, depending upon circumstances, exert a beneficial stabilising effect upon economic conditions. Capital moves into and out of a country in response to a variety of influences, including actual and anticipated interest and exchange rates. When the balance of payments on current account is in surplus, a net capital outflow (in the form of either a reduction of foreign liabilities or an increase in foreign assets) may be desirable in order to prevent an undue appreciation of the spot exchange rate or an excessive rise in the money supply. Alternatively, when the current account is in deficit, a capital inflow attracted by sound fiscal and monetary policies, including high interest rates and realistic exchange rates, may be extremely beneficial. It is important, therefore, that the capital account of the balance of payments be allowed to play its part in overall economic stabilisation.

The inadequate implementation and inherent weaknesses of the liquid asset system of bank credit control

36. A fifth underlying reason for the deficiencies of monetary policy was the inadequate implementation and inherent weaknesses of the liquid asset system of bank credit control as applied during most of the post-war period. In addition to using various 'direct' instruments of monetary policy, the authorities attempted to control the banks' credit-creating ability by operating on their liquidity base, i.e. their actual total holdings of liquid assets and/or by *varying* the ratios of their *required* liquid assets. This technique was used rather than the alternative one of *operating* on the banks' *cash base* (defined in South Africa as reserve balances with the Reserve Bank), for example through open-market operations, and/or *varying* the banks' *required* cash reserve ratios.

37. The Commission finds that under the liquid asset control system the monetary authorities did not always achieve their objective of exercising adequate control over the banks' liquidity base and therefore over their credit creating ability. The use of *variations* of the liquid asset requirements as a

means of overcoming the problems experienced in controlling the banks' *actual holdings* of liquid assets also met with only limited success.

38. The Commission finds two main reasons why the liquid asset system proved relatively ineffective. The first is that, as a direct reflection of the closely interrelated shortcomings of monetary policy analysed above, the system of liquidity base control was at times inadequately implemented in South Africa. And the second is that the liquidity base control system itself suffers from certain inherent weaknesses.

39. The Commission wishes to emphasise that the same interrelated shortcomings of monetary policy that at times reduced the effectiveness of control over the banks' liquidity base would also have ruled out effective control over the banks' cash base. A cash reserve system depends just as much as, if not more than, a liquid asset system upon market-oriented interest rates and other monetary policies for its success. A cash reserve system can be made to work effectively only if the central bank is in a position to prevent undue increases in the cash base of the banking system. This means that it must be able to prevent undue increases in its own total domestic and foreign assets. And that is precisely where the nub of the problem lay: Because of the under-lying shortcomings of monetary policy at the time, the Reserve Bank was unable to exert effective control over its own assets.

40. The only way in which the Reserve Bank could have acquired the required degree of control over its total domestic and foreign assets would have been through the application of strict market-oriented monetary policies involving, among other things, realistic market-determined interest rates on public sector securities, agricultural credit and home mortgage loans. Since such policies were not applied during the period under review, a cash reserve system could not have been implemented any more effectively than a liquid asset system.

THE RECOMMENDED FRAMEWORK FOR MONETARY POLICY IN SOUTH AFRICA

41. The Commission recommended the following framework for monetary policy in South Africa:

A market-related approach to monetary policy

42. The dominant general characteristic of the proposed framework is that it is basically market oriented. It is the Commission's *conviction* that in South Africa's sophisticated financial system a market-oriented monetary strategy will serve the national interest better than any set of non-market-oriented or 'direct' monetary controls.

43. There are two fundamental reasons for this conclusion: The first is the Commission's finding that, by promoting the efficient allocation of resources

153

and performing a number of other vital economic functions, the various sophisticated financial markets which have developed in South Africa make an important contribution in their own right to general economic growth and welfare. Moreover, they function best in the national interest if they are reasonably free, competitive, active and broad, and produce realistic market-related interest and exchange rates. It is important, therefore, that monetary policy should, as far as possible, be pursued in a manner which does not undermine the efficient functioning of these markets.

44. The second main reason is that the Commission firmly believes that such a market-oriented approach can to a large extent overcome the main deficiencies from which monetary policy has suffered in the past. Specifically, it should contribute to (1) the moderation and stabilisation of the growth of the monetary aggregates; (2) more effective control over disintermediation and other velocity-related developments; (3) the maintenance of realistic and market-related interest rates; and (4) the attainment of realistic and market-related spot and forward exchange rates. In these ways it should greatly improve the ability of the monetary authorities to influence aggregate monetary demand.

Ultimate objectives

45. The Commission recommends that in the long term the primary objective of monetary policy in South Africa should be the maintenance of relative stability of the domestic price level, with, of course, an effective measure of freedom for relative prices to change.

46. This does not, however, mean that other objectives such as balance of payments equilibrium, growth and employment are not also important. In the view of the Commission, they must also rank as legitimate aims of monetary policy. At the very least, they should be viewed as policy constraints on the monetary authorities in their efforts to achieve relative price stability. As far as the objectives of growth and employment are concerned, the emphasis in monetary policy should fall on the avoidance of undue instability and of the misallocation of resources. The Commission does not, of course, wish to imply that *only* monetary policy should be used to achieve these various aims. On the contrary, the Commission views monetary policy as forming part of a more comprehensive economic policy strategy that includes also many other types of economic policy, such as fiscal policy, agricultural policy, industrial policy and labour policy.

47. The Commission sees no fundamental conflict or 'trade-offs' between these various traditional goals of monetary policy in the long term. It does not believe, for example, that anything can be gained in the long run in terms of real growth or employment by accepting higher inflation rates. The opposite is more likely to be true: Higher inflation will in the long run militate against growth and job creation. The objectives of external balance, growth and

employment will over time be served best by creating and maintaining a climate of reasonable domestic price stability.

48. From time to time short-term conflicts between the above-mentioned objectives of monetary policy are clearly possible and indeed often occur in the real world. 'Trade-offs' are therefore possible in the short term between, for example, growth and inflation, or between growth and balance of payments equilibrium, or even between inflation and balance of payments equilibrium (to the extent that, say, exchange rate depreciation, import surcharges or tighter exchange control are used to protect the balance of payments).

49. The Commission therefore accepts that short-term policy priorities may have to be switched in certain circumstances, depending particularly on the stage of the business cycle in which the domestic economy finds itself or on international economic developments, such as sharp gold price fluctuations to which the open South African economy is particularly vulnerable.

Intermediate objectives: money supply targets

50. The Commission recommends that the Reserve Bank adopt specific *intermediate* objectives of monetary policy in the form of target rates of growth for one or more selected money supply aggregates. This recommendation is made in the full realisation that the adoption of such money supply targets would strictly limit the number of combinations of the level and structure of interest rates, on the one hand, and of spot and forward exchange rates, on the other, that the monetary authorities can hope to see realised simultaneously in the financial markets concerned. Indeed, the Commission would stress the importance of monetary analysis and policy of the close interrelationship between the money supply, interest rates and exchange rates and of the fact that they cannot be determined independently of one another.

51. It must be emphasised, however, that in proposing the use of money growth rate targets, the Commission is *not* recommending the adoption of a *rigid* and *overriding* 'money rule' that implies leaving interest rates and exchange rates *completely* free to find their own levels at all times — a course of action which the Commission rejects as undesirable for South Africa. The Commission believes that monetary targeting should be applied in South Africa with a fair measure of flexibility and with a 'low profile'. More specifically, it recommends that, in setting and changing money supply targets from time to time, or even intentionally permitting them to be breached, the Reserve Bank should openly exercise discretion based on its assessment of the general economic situation and prospects at the time, including its 'view' on the appropriate level and structure of interest and exchange rates at that stage:

Constrained discretion in combining money supply, interest rates and exchange rates

52. In recommending 'low profile' money supply targets while rejecting a rigid

'money rule', the Commission is, in effect, assigning to the Reserve Bank the task of exercising discretionary judgement in deciding what (internally consistent) combination of monetary aggregates, interest rates and spot and forward exchange rates to aim at in any given set of circumstances.

It is important, however, to recognise that within the policy framework recommended by the Commission this discretion is not unlimited but 'constrained'. The main constraints are —

- the need to avoid changing or breaching the monetary targets so extensively and frequently that they lose their meaning;
- the close interrelationship between money supply, interest rates and spot and forward exchange rates; and
- the injunction to use essentially market-oriented instruments of monetary policy and to avoid as far as possible any recourse to direct monetary controls.

The importance of realistic market-related interest rates

53. In setting out its views on the interrelationship between money supply, interest rates and exchange rates, the Commission wishes to emphasise that, with or without the use of money supply targets, monetary policy under present conditions in South Africa can be effective only if realistic, market-related and appropriately aligned interest rates can be attained in the various financial markets. If effective control is to be exercised over the monetary aggregates and total monetary demand, interest rates must be free to reflect accurately the varying degrees of tightness in financial markets resulting from the combined operation of natural economic forces and monetary policy actions. At times this may mean that interest rates will rise to relatively high levels. But such increases will have to be accepted as an essential ingredient in effective monetary policy.

54. In assessing the role and influence of interest rates in any given situation, it is, of course, important to take account of not only the *nominal* but also the *real* rates, i.e. the interest rates adjusted for the expected rate of inflation. It follows that the higher the expected rate of inflation, the higher the nominal interest rates required to deal with the situation will be.

55. If it is deemed necessary to mitigate the social effects of higher interest rates in 'sensitive' areas such as housing or agriculture, relief should be granted by way of open subsidisation by the Government of the relevant interest rates and not by restraints on interest rates generally or by direct controls on certain deposit or lending rates. For the reasons given above, such restraints and controls would greatly reduce the effectiveness of monetary policy. They would also tend to be counter-productive as far as the attainment of their social objectives is concerned, since the resultant higher rate of inflation would in due course put increased upward pressure on the nominal interest rates concerned and seriously distort the relative structure of interest rates.

Integrating exchange rate and exchange control policy into overall monetary policy

56. The Commission underlines the importance of co-ordinating exchange rate and exchange control policy with other policies forming part of the overall official monetary strategy. The Commission recommends neither completely free floating for the exchange rate nor, at least for the time being, the *complete abolition* of exchange control over residents. Instead, it proposes the continuation of the present system of *managed* floating for the rand and the retention, for as long as necessary, of limited exchange control over residents (although it places great stress on the importance of relaxing and simplifying such control). But this approach in no way detracts from the vital importance of taking full account of the close relationship between the monetary aggregates, interest rates, exchange rates and exchange control in formulating and implementing monetary policy. Whatever the combination of 'rules' or 'discretion' in monetary policy, the recognition of the relationship between these variables remains a prerequisite for the success of any official monetary strategy.

Nature of proposed flexible money supply targets

57. In accordance with its views on the desirability of 'low profile' targets, the Commission recommends that the money supply objectives be expressed in terms of *tolerance ranges* of rates of increase rather than *single* rates, and be set once a year for periods of twelve months at a time. One method of doing this would be to use three-month moving averages for the monetary aggregates in question, and to announce in February each year the target ranges for the increases between the fourth quarter of the previous year and the fourth quarter of the current year. Provision should be made for a revision of the prevailing targets between normal reviewing dates if considered desirable on the grounds set out earlier.

58. The Commission further recommends that the target rates be publicly announced. (Paragraph 17.23.)

59. From the outset, however, it should be made clear to all parties concerned that the targets are not to be treated as sacrosanct. Failure to meet them on any specific date should not, in itself, be viewed in a serious light, and over-reaction in the financial markets to any such overshooting or undershooting should be discouraged. To this end, two points about the targets should be publicly underlined. The first is that, for a number of reasons, strict stability of the money growth rate over short periods is clearly not attainable in South Africa. Undue significance should therefore not be attached to fluctuations in this rate from month to month or quarter to quarter. These reasons include weaknesses in the month-end monetary statistics that are largely produced by a number of short-lived random factors affecting the banks' and the public's financial position at month ends, and frequent shifts between 'intermediated' and 'non-

intermediated' credit. And the second point is that it is the declared policy of the monetary authorities to adjust the targets themselves from time to time to take into account interest rate or exchange rate considerations, as well as other new developments.

Targets for aggregate monetary demand (MV)?

60. In recommending the setting of money supply targets, the Commission is in no way departing from its view that monetary policy operates mainly through its effects on *aggregate monetary demand*, i.e. the flow of actual spending. For the reasons set out in paragraph 17.25, it merely accepts that aggregate demand as such does not lend itself particularly well to use as the intermediate target of monetary policy.

Targets for interest rates?

61. The Commission does not recommend the use of *interest rates* as an intermediate target for monetary policy. Apart from the technical reasons for this recommendation provided in paragraph 17.27, experience in many countries has shown that interest rate targets do not enjoy the same public support as money supply targets. There is a better understanding and therefore more ready acceptance by the public of the need to avoid excessive money creation than of the need for interest rates to rise in certain circumstances.

Targets for cash base, monetary base or domestic credit extension (DCE)?

62. In opting for moderate rates of growth of certain money supply aggregates as the prime intermediate targets of monetary policy, the Commission is also expressing its preference for these targets over three other well-known financial alternatives. The first is the 'cash base' of the banks, i.e. their reserve balances with the Reserve Bank. The second is the 'monetary base', i.e. the cash reserve balances of the banks plus bank notes and coin in circulation, whether held by the banks or by the non-bank public. And the third is total current domestic bank credit extension (DCE). (Paragraph 17.31.)

Targets for exchange rates?

63. In the present world of fluctuating exchange rates, the Commission does not recommend the use of exchange rate targets for monetary policy. It is possible that circumstances might again arise in future in which South Africa would, as under the Bretton Woods par value system, adopt an exchange rate 'target' of one kind or another. Any such decision would naturally then place constraints upon the setting of targets for either monetary growth rates or interest rates — South Africa would then have to accept the consequences of its

exchange rate policy for both these sets of variables. Under present conditions, however, the Commission believes that South Africa's interests would best be served by the adoption of intermediate targets for one or more monetary aggregates and by leaving the rand largely free to find its own level, subject only to Reserve Bank intervention in the foreign exchange market. Such intervention would normally have the limited objectives of ironing out short-term fluctuations in the market and countering disorderly market conditions. The Commission believes, however, that the door should be left open for the Reserve Bank to go further and to exercise (constrained) discretion in 'managing' the exchange rate as part of its overall monetary policy. Such 'management' would, of course, have implications for the money supply and interest rates and might require some adjustment of the money growth rate targets.

The choice of money supply aggregates for targeting purposes

64. After examining the available statistical and other evidence, the Commission finds that the present official definitions of M1, M2 and M3 are not entirely satisfactory for targeting purposes. The reasons for this conclusion are set out in paragraphs 17.37 to 17.42.

65. The Commission also finds that the monetary authorities have acted correctly in delaying the setting of publicly announced money supply targets until the South African monetary system has 'settled down' to the new market-oriented dispensation that has progressively been introduced since 1980. In the opinion of the Commission, it would have been unwise to have attempted to choose the most appropriate money supply aggregates for use as intermediate objectives until more experience had been gained of the behaviour of various aggregates under the new monetary strategy.

66. The Commission believes, however, that the time to institute monetary targeting is now at hand. It notes that a close study is being made by the Reserve Bank of the interrelationships under the new policy approach between the banks' cash reserves, the money supply on various old and new definitions, gross domestic expenditure and product at current prices, and the rate of inflation. On the basis of this study it should be possible to make a better choice of the monetary aggregates to be used for target purposes in South Africa than would have been possible in the past. This choice should be made and monetary targeting introduced as soon as possible.

Policy instruments

Recommended: Use of market-oriented rather than 'direct' methods of monetary policy

67. The Commission recommends that, in order to achieve the intermediate and ultimate objectives of monetary policy set out above, the monetary au-

thorities use mainly market-oriented instruments of monetary policy, i.e. instruments which operate *through* one or more of the financial markets. Such methods generally consist of technical 'intervention' by the monetary authorities in the various financial markets in the sense of buying and selling the relevant financial claims (such as government stock, Treasury bills, bankers' acceptances and foreign exchange) in order to influence prices (and therefore interest and exchange rates) and quantities in these markets.

68. Of these methods or instruments, the Commission specifically recommends the use of the following:
- Public debt management (including public borrowing policy);
- Reserve Bank open-market operations;
- Reserve Bank discount and general accommodation policy; and
- Reserve Bank 'intervention' in the spot and forward exchange markets.

69. The Commission also recommends that, in exceptional circumstances, these market-oriented methods be supplemented by the use of the semi-market-oriented technique of varying the banks' cash reserve requirements.

70. The Commission recommends further that non-market-oriented or 'direct' methods of monetary policy, which attempt to suspend or bypass the operations of the financial markets, be avoided as far as possible. This applies in particular to credit ceilings, deposit rate controls, lending rate controls (excluding usury rate restrictions), direct controls over private sector capital issues and import deposit schemes. For the reasons given above, these controls not only obstruct the efficient operation of many financial markets but inevitably lead to large-scale disintermediation and other distortions in the flow of funds in the economy. They therefore vitiate the attempts of the monetary authorities to exercise adequate influence over monetary demand.

A cash reserve system of bank credit control; proposed new liquid asset and cash reserve requirements

71. As a basic part of its set of proposals regarding policy instruments, the Commission recommends the use of a cash reserve system of controlling bank credit rather than a liquid asset system. The Commission notes with approval that considerable progress has already been made in recent years in moving to such a cash reserve system.

72. As far as the various *minimum liquid asset and cash reserve requirements* for banking institutions are concerned, the Commission recommends:

- That the minimum *basic* liquid asset ratios as laid down by the Banks Act be reduced from 30, 20 and 5 per cent of short-term, medium-term and long-term liabilities to the public, respectively, to 20, 15 and 5 per cent, respectively. (The first two of these requirements have already been reduced by the Reserve Bank — using its powers under Proclamation R 184 of 1967 — to 22 and 16 per cent, respectively);

160

- that the Reserve Bank's powers to impose *supplementary* liquid asset requirements be revoked;
- that the minimum *basic* cash reserve balance with the Reserve Bank be set at 8 per cent of short-term and 4 per cent of medium-term liabilities;
- that the Reserve Bank be given the right to call for *supplementary* cash reserve balances against both short-term and medium-term liabilities, as well as the power to reduce the basic cash reserve requirements; and
- that the Reserve Bank be authorised to pay interest on reserve balances. (This recommendation has already been accepted and the Reserve Bank Act amended accordingly in 1984.)

73. If these recommendations are acceptable to the authorities, the Commission repeats the proposal it made in its *Second Interim Report* that building societies then be required to comply with the same (reduced) cash reserve and liquid asset requirements as banking institutions.

74. The purpose of the recommendation that the Reserve Bank be given the power to vary the minimum cash reserve requirements for banking institutions and building societies is to provide the Bank with a semi-market-oriented policy instrument that might at times prove useful as a *supplement* to the more basic market-oriented methods recommended in this Report. The Commission proposes, however, that this supplementary instrument be used only as a temporary measure in exceptional circumstances.

75. The Commission believes that because a cash reserve regime would help to eliminate the weaknesses in monetary policy identified above, it would be superior to a liquidity base regime as a means of controlling bank credit creation. This will only be the case, however, if it is properly implemented as part and parcel of the kind of market-oriented policy framework recommended by the Commission. In particular, the effective application of a cash reserve regime requires that the banks should either be restricted in their ability to convert their (non-cash) liquid assets into cash balances with the Reserve Bank (either directly or via the discount houses) or should be able to do so only at interest rates which are appropriate for monetary policy purposes. *In either case* this may at times mean that interest rates have to rise sharply and to relatively high levels, including interest rates on such liquid assets as Treasury bills, Land Bank bills and short-term government stock. The Reserve Bank will not be able to operate effectively on the banks' cash base if the banks are able to offset any drain on their cash reserves by monetising their non-cash liquid assets on terms favourable enough to prevent interest rates from rising substantially.

Recommended for South Africa: The 'classical' cash reserve system

76. The Commission recommends that the Reserve Bank use the so-called 'classical' cash reserve system as a means of controlling bank credit creation, rather than the so-called 'American' cash reserve system.

77. Under the 'American' system, the central bank uses such policy instruments as open-market sales or purchases of government securities in order to destroy or create cash reserves in the hands of banking institutions. It does so for the express purpose of exerting some desired quantitative effect on the *amount* of either the banks' *total* cash reserves or their *non-borrowed* reserves. Thus, if the banks' cash reserves are deemed to be too high, the central bank reduces these reserves by selling government securities in the market. If the reserve are considered to be too low, the central bank augments them by buying government securities in the market. In this approach, the central bank may set itself a target for what it believes the amount of the banks' total or non-borrowed cash reserves should be at future points in time, in order to bring about some target rate of growth of the money supply. The determination of the level and structure of interest rates in this system may then be left essentially to the free operation of market forces, as was in essence done in the United States for some time after October 1979.

78. Under the 'classical' system proposed for South Africa, the central bank again uses policy instruments such as open-market operations to hold down the banks' total cash reserve holdings and the associated money supply. The more immediate purpose of these operations, however, is not to have some direct and predetermined effect on the *amount* of the banks' cash reserves. Instead, it is to compel banking institutions (whether directly or via the discount houses) to make use of the central bank's accommodation facilities at the discount window *at the interest rates that are charged by the central bank for such accommodation*.

79. In this cash reserve system, the interest *cost* of cash reserves at the discount window constitutes a prime element of control. In forcing the banks to have recourse to its accommodation facilities at the discount window, the central bank may be responding to unduly rapid rates of increase in the money supply. At the same time, it may also wish to raise its accommodation rates in order to discourage excessive longer-term use of its credit facilities. Once the banking system has to make use of discount window accommodation, a change in the central bank's accommodation rates (traditionally the Bank rate) normally has a quick and roughly commensurate effect on the market rates on the rediscountable instruments that are used for obtaining such accommodation. The central bank is therefore able to exercise a major influence on these market interest rates. In a reasonably developed financial system, the rates on other financial instruments and forms of credit extension will, in turn, adjust to the rates on the rediscountable instruments. The generally higher level of interest rates will then slow down the rate of growth of bank credit, the money supply and the banks' required cash reserves.

80. In the classical cash reserve system, in other words, the high *cost* of cash reserves at the discount window — rather than the limited *amount* of cash reserves made available — acts as the prime deterrent to unduly rapid expansion of the banks' balance sheets and the money supply. However, as the rate of

growth in the money supply is held down, so is the rate of increase in the amount of the banks' required and actual cash reserve holdings.

81. In recommending the classical system for South Africa the Commission is, in fact, proposing that the Reserve Bank control the cash reserves of the banks by applying public debt management, open-market operations, foreign exchange market transactions and other policy instruments to compel the banks to use its refinancing facilities (mainly via the discount houses) at the Bank rate and other interest rates it deems necessary for the attainment of its monetary targets.

82. At the same time, the Commission wishes to point out that in practice the difference between the 'American' and 'classical' cash reserve systems is not as great as might be supposed. Firstly, under both systems, the central bank in the final analysis influences the banks' cash reserves and the money supply. Secondly, under both systems, 'net money market shortages' have, in practice, to be accommodated in one way or another by the central bank in its capacity as lender of last resort. This is necessary in order to avoid serious financial disruption. Thirdly, under both systems, attempts by the central bank to resist or minimise such increases in its accommodation in order to exert more effective control over the banks' cash reserves and the money supply, inevitably imply higher interest rates in the short term. Of course, once the banks' cash reserves and the money supply have been brought under control and both inflation and inflationary expectations significantly reduced, nominal interest rates will decline again. But that, too, will be the case under both cash reserve systems.

83. The reasons why the Commission recommends a classical rather than an American cash reserve system for South Africa are set out in detail in paragraphs 17.63 to 17.68.

PUBLIC DEBT MANAGEMENT

84. The first instrument of monetary policy recommended by the Commission is that of public debt management. The Commission believes that public debt management be viewed and used as an integral part of monetary policy in South Africa. 'Public debt management' is defined as decisions and actions by the relevant public entities to attain premeditated effects with regard to the *size,* the *composition* by type of debt instruments or variety of borrowing, the *maturity structure* and the *ownership distribution* of the public debt, notably the debt of the central Government. Public debt management is taken to include the *loan financing and incremental borrowing policy* of public entities, and in particular, the way in which the government sector finances its budgetary 'deficit before borrowing'.

85. The Commission recommends that the application of public debt management be guided by the following principles:
- The central Government's 'deficit before borrowing' or the broader 'public sector borrowing requirement' should at all times be restricted to an amount

that can be financed without either undue money creation by the banking system or undue upward pressure on interest rates.

- Interest rates on government securities should be basically market determined and always at levels adequate to finance the deficit before borrowing without undue money creation.
- In financing the deficit before borrowing, the use of net credit extended by the Reserve Bank and the Corporation for Public Deposits (CPD) should either be completely avoided or effectively curbed. Such credit extension not only increases the money supply directly but also provides the banks with the additional cash reserves required to support their larger deposit liabilities, as well as some surplus cash to be deployed as call money with the discount houses.
- In financing the deficit before borrowing, the issuing of Treasury bills and short-term government stock to the banks other than the Reserve Bank and the CPD should also be curbed by means of appropriate 'funding', i.e. by maintaining a sound balance between short-term and long-term public debt.
- Excessive issues of short-term debt to non-bank private parties should also be avoided, since some of these debt components, such as Treasury bills and Post Office savings instruments, essentially form part of the broader monetary aggregates.
- If the above principles are not fully adhered to and if the resultant expansion of net bank credit to the public sector and the (unduly low) level of interest rates contribute to an excessive expansion of *total* bank credit and the money supply, the Reserve Bank should act to neutralise these undesirable effects. To this end it should make full use of discount policy and open-market operations to bring about the rise in interest rates required to ensure adequate control over the monetary aggregates. If the problem arises through excessive credit extension to the government sector *by banks other than the Reserve Bank and the CPD,* the banks will probably make good the resultant shortfall in their cash balances with the Reserve Bank by withdrawing call money from the discount houses or by monetising other liquid assets via the discount houses. This will force the discount houses to make (more) use of Reserve Bank accommodation. In such circumstances, the Bank should raise its discount rates in order to achieve the desired level of interest rates, i.e. a level which will adequately restrain the *demand* for credit and therefore the expansion of banks' deposit liabilities and their required cash reserve balances. If the problem is caused by excessive use by the Government of net central bank credit, the Reserve Bank should still attempt to use discount policy and open-market operations in the manner indicated above.
- Such 'neutralising' operations by the Reserve Bank, however, would clearly represent a 'second-best' solution. Indeed, given the prevailing market imperfections and socio-political resistance to sudden, belated and disruptive increases in interest rates in South Africa, they are unlikely to achieve the

desired results. It is true that in the final analysis interest rates have to be at appropriate levels anyway if monetary policy is to be effective. But the authorities can make a key contribution to achieving those levels, and thus to effective monetary policy, by applying sound government borrowing policies in the first place.

- In addition to ensuring appropriate financing of the deficit before borrowing, public debt management should be used in two main ways, in particular:
  — New 'tap' and other issues of government securities made to finance expenditures should be timed and 'tailored' in such a way as to assist the monetary authorities in their efforts to attain the desired growth rates of the various monetary aggregates.
  — Whenever necessary in the interest of monetary stability, the Treasury should borrow in excess of its own financing requirements, 'sterilise' the funds in a stabilisation account and accept the increased interest rate burden as a small price to pay for the benefits of increased monetary and economic stability.

OPEN-MARKET OPERATIONS

86. The second major market-oriented instrument of monetary policy recommended by the Commission is that of open-market operations. *Open-market operations* are held to consist of sales or purchases of domestic financial assets by the central bank to attain premeditated effects on the banking system's cash or liquidity base, interest rates, the availability of credit, and/or the money supply.

87. The Commission finds that, provided the monetary authorities are prepared to accept realistic market-related interest rates, open-market operations can be a powerful and effective instrument of monetary policy under the new cash reserve regime. In the case of open-market *sales* of securities, for example, the essential point is that whereas certain transactions (those with non-bank parties) will directly reduce the money supply, *all* transactions (including sales of liquid assets to the banks) will, by creating a need for the banks' cash holdings to be replenished through Reserve Bank accommodation, enable the Bank to exert a strong influence on monetary conditions through its effects on interest rates. In other words, in addition to influencing the money supply directly in certain cases, open-market operations will serve the important purpose of making the Reserve Bank's discount rates effective. By influencing the money supply and interest rates, open-market operations will, of course, indirectly also affect spot and forward exchange rates.

88. On the basis of the above findings, the Commission recommends that, in close co-ordination with public debt management and discount policy, the Reserve Bank make increased and extensive use of open-market operations as a means of influencing the money supply and interest rates, and therefore in-

directly also exchange rates. The Commission's investigations have led it to the conclusion that the markets for Treasury bills, Land Bank bills, government stock and bankers' acceptances have reached a stage of development which affords ample scope for effective operations of this kind. It is also confident that this scope would be further broadened by the implementation of the various recommenations made in Part I of this Report to improve the working of these markets.

89. In regard to open-market operations, the Commission further recommends —

- that the Reserve Bank make more use of open-market transactions as a means of smoothing out seasonal fluctuations in money market conditions, instead of relying almost exclusively on rediscounting and overnight loans for this purpose;
- that the Reserve Bank conduct open-market operations mainly in government stock, Treasury bills, Land Bank bills and bankers' acceptances, and not in securities of other public entities such as the South African Transport Services, the National Housing Commission, municipalities or public corporations;
- that the Reserve Bank conduct open-market operations in the *full range of maturities* of Treasury bills, Land Bank bills, bankers' acceptances and government stock; and
- that the Reserve Bank make increased use of repurchase and matched sale-purchase agreements and that these be viewed as part of its open-market operations.

90. The Commission wishes to place particular stress upon the need for close co-ordination between public debt management and open-market operations in South Africa. For the reasons given in Chapter 18, these two instruments of monetary policy are so closely interwoven under South African conditions that, if they are to be applied effectively, the broad strategy underlying their use has to be determined by the Treasury and the Reserve Bank in close consultation and at the highest level.

BANK RATE AND DISCOUNT POLICY

91. As an integral part of its proposed monetary policy framework, the Commission recommends that increased and more clearly defined use be made of discount policy as a means of influencing the money supply, interest rates and exchange rates.

92. 'Discount policy' is defined in this Report as the Reserve Bank's policy in regard to its extension of financial assistance or 'refinancing' to discount houses and banks *at their instance,* either in the form of *rediscounting* of Treasury bills and other acceptable financial instruments or in the form of *collateral lending* against the security of such instruments. Key elements in this

policy are the rates of interest and other terms and conditions applied by the Bank to the provision of such refinancing through the 'discount window'.

Recommended: A more meaningful demarcation between Treasury/Reserve Bank operations in the open securities markets and discount policy

93. As a basic step towards making more effective use of discount policy, the Commission recommends that the monetary authorities achieve a more meaningful demarcation of the respective roles assigned in their broad monetary strategy to, on the one hand, public debt management and open-market operations and, on the other, discount policy. The principal aim of this demarcation should be to reduce the volatility of the amount of refinancing assistance provided by the Reserve Bank to discount houses and banks through its discount window and to bring about a closer association between changes in this amount and shifts in the official monetary policy stance.

94. This recommendation entails the ordering by the Reserve Bank of its open-market operations, including its repurchase transactions, in such a way that the amount of refinancing required by the discount houses and the banks through the discount window only rises substantially when the Reserve Bank wishes to tighten monetary policy and bring about a rise in interest rates (or when it wishes to prevent an undue easing of market conditions and a marked decline in interest rates). If no change in policy stance is desired and, in particular, if the level of interest rates is deemed high enough, any tightening of money market conditions that would tend to bring about a significant increase in discount window refinancing should be counteracted by such means as repurchase transactions or other open-market operations.

95. If this approach is followed, the term 'money market shortage' would unambiguously be confined to the amount of Reserve Bank refinancing assistance required and provided through the discount window. By permitting this 'shortage' to rise substantially in certain circumstances, the Reserve Bank would normally be giving the market a signal that it was adopting a more restrictive policy involving higher interest rates. Alternatively, by preventing the 'shortage' from rising, the Bank would be signalling that it did not desire a higher interest rate level and that it was not changing its policy stance.

Recommended: Reintroduction of Bank rate as the Reserve Bank's basic rediscount rate

96. As a further step in giving discount policy a more important and clearly defined role, the Commission recommends that the Reserve Bank reintroduce 'Bank rate' as its rate for rediscounting Treasury bills *for the discount houses*. This rate should be set and varied at the Bank's own initiative and discretion within the monetary policy framework proposed in this Report. It is also recommended that the Reserve Bank set rates for rediscounting Land Bank bills

and bankers' acceptances for discount houses, as well as rates for overnight loans to discount houses against the security of short-term government stock, Treasury bills, Land Bank bills, bankers' acceptances and other acceptable paper. The rates quoted on overnight loan and rediscounting facilities *for banks* may, however, be set at somewhat different levels for different banks (as noted in paragraph 20.35) and would not, therefore, be announced for information of the money market and the public generally.

97. In determining and varying Bank rate and the related set of other rediscount and overnight lending rates, the Reserve Bank should be guided basically by the need to attain its intermediate money supply targets and ultimate policy objectives. It should, however, also take into account conditions and tendencies in the financial markets, including the foreign exchange market, and in the economy generally. The unavoidable element of discretionary judgement that this entails is, of course, constrained by the close interrelationship between the money supply, interest rates and exchange rates.

98. By managing both the *amount* and *cost* of refinancing provided through its discount window along the lines indicated above, the Reserve Bank should be able to exert a strong influence on the general level of interest rates as an integral part of its policy of controlling the monetary aggregates.

99. The Commission recommends that the proposed new rediscount rate for Treasury bills to be determined by the Reserve Bank should be called by its traditional name — 'Bank rate' — because that is precisely what it is. The Commission believes that the tradition of Bank rate is worth preserving, and sees little merit in avoiding the use of the term merely for fear of 'repoliticising' the Reserve Bank's basic rediscount rate and thereby placing constraints on the Bank's ability to vary its refinancing rates in accordance with the needs of monetary policy. Such politicisation and constraints would indeed be harmful, but could, in the Commission's view, largely be avoided by using Bank rate in the manner proposed below.

100. The Commission further recommends that, to the extent warranted by changing conditions in the short-term financial markets, Bank rate and the Reserve Bank's other related rediscount and overnight lending rates be changed frequently and by small amounts. This should be done in a low key and as a technical matter, of interest principally to money market experts. As a rule, changes in Bank rate should not be accompanied by major policy statements and care should be taken not to magnify their importance. Although this 'low profile' approach might at times entail the loss of some useful announcement effects, it should, on balance, be conducive to more effective monetary policy.

101. In much the same vein, the Commission does not favour the reintroduction of any fixed link between Bank rate and the prime overdraft rates of the commercial banks. Such a link would not only tend to repoliticise Bank rate but also conflict with the Commission's general market-oriented approach. In practice, of course, the behaviour of prime overdraft rates is likely to be greatly influenced by changes in Bank rate. But the Commission recommends that

each bank be allowed and encouraged to determine its own prime overdraft rate in response to market forces and in competition with other banks. The banks would nevertheless be expected to discuss intended prime rate changes with the Reserve Bank.

102. The Commission further proposes that the interest rates charged by the Reserve Bank on the various categories of accommodation that it normally extends to public sector entities also be based on Bank rate, with provision for varying margins depending upon the status of the borrower, the collateral provided and other normal banking considerations.

Recommended: Abolition of the seven-day/fourteen-day rediscounting arrangement

103. The Commission further recommends that there should be no return to the currently suspended seven-day/fourteen-day rule applied by the Reserve Bank in its rediscounting operations over extended periods in the past. The reasons for this recommendation are provided in paragraphs 20.70 to 20.74. In this regard the Commission emphasises that what matters in any given situation is not the extent to which the money market is 'in the Bank', but whether the combination of money supply growth rates, interest rates and exchange rates is 'right' from the point of view of achieving the objectives of monetary policy. And such a 'right' combination may be obtained at varying levels of discount window refinancing.

Recommended: Preferential treatment of discount houses

104. In line with its findings and proposals regarding discount houses set out in Chapter 5, the Commission recommends that the Reserve Bank accord preferential treatment to discount houses in its discount policy. This special treatment should take the form mainly of lower rediscount and overnight lending rates than for other banking institutions rather than discriminatory quantitative restrictions.

105. The possibility of extending discount window assistance *directly* to banks, i.e. for purposes other than to rectify their 'unintentionally' overdrawn positions on current account with the Reserve Bank, should be kept open. Such assistance should take the form mainly of overnight loans at interest rates based on Bank rate, but differentiated according to the kind of security pledged as collateral. The collateral should consist of short-term government stock, Treasury bills, Land Bank bills or debentures, bankers' acceptances or other acceptable paper. Such assistance could be provided in cases where a bank has exhausted its call deposits or where it has a statutory liquid asset shortfall. But direct assistance to banks through the discount window should be discouraged by quoting preferential discount and lending rates to discount houses. The normal way for banks to meet a cash shortfall would be by withdrawing call

money from the discount houses. But no objection should be raised to banks' outright selling of rediscountable assets to discount houses for the latter to rediscount with the Reserve Bank.

EXCHANGE RATE POLICY

106. As the fourth major market-oriented method of broad monetary policy, the Commission recommends an exchange rate policy of managed floating in which, given the prevailing stance of the authorities' domestic monetary and fiscal policies, spot and forward exchange rates for the rand will essentially be determined by the free operation of market forces — with no exchange control applying to non-residents and only limited exchange control in the case of residents. This means that, under the domestic and external economic conditions prevailing at any point in time, the spot and forward exchange rates should essentially be a reflection or 'concomitant result' of the authorities' domestic monetary and fiscal policies.

107. It follows that an exchange rate policy of this nature cannot explicitly be made to serve the purposes of the development of manufacturing industry or be geared to the promotion of any other specific sectional interests. But this does not make it less desirable from a national economic point of view. On the contrary, the Commission is of the opinion that industrial development and economic development generally will ultimately be best served by —

- economic policies that are aimed primarily at establishing a relatively high degree of stability of the general price level; and
- rates of exchange of the rand that realistically reflect the underlying forces of supply and demand in the foreign exchange markets.

108. Moreover, as already stated, the Commission recommends that, in applying monetary targeting, the Reserve Bank should openly exercise discretion based on its assessment of the prevailing and prospective economic conditions, *including specifically its 'view' on the exchange rate.* In other words, the way should be left open for the Reserve Bank to intervene in the foreign exchange market not only to 'smooth out' but also to moderate exchange rate movements whenever it deems this to be in the national interest.

109. The Commission specifically recognises that in the case of a major gold price rise or similar extraneous event it may not always be desirable to allow such a development to exert its full effect on the exchange rate within a relatively short period of time. The difficulties that would be experienced by various sectors of the economy in such a situation have come to be referred to as the 'Dutch disease'. This 'disease' relates to the depressing effect on domestic aggregate real output and employment of high levels of the exchange rate that are essentially attributable to a large rise in the world price, or in the volume of domestic production, of a single internationally traded commodity. Symptoms of the 'Dutch disease' essentially arise from the limited short-run

adaptability of output and employment patterns.

110. The Commission accordingly recommends that in the event of a large gold price increase or any similar extraneous development, appropriate steps be taken to avoid an unduly sharp appreciation of the rand that might disrupt economic activity in important sectors of the economy. Such steps should include the encouragement of offsetting capital movements by means of the further relaxation of exchange control, the adjustment of fiscal incentives, interest rate policy and forward exchange intervention.

NOTES

1 For purposes of this Report, the Commission defines monetary policy as 'all deliberate actions by the monetary authorities to influence the monetary aggregates, the availability of credit, interest rates and exchange rates, with a view to affecting monetary demand, income, output, prices and the balance of payments'.
2 Definitions of these monetary aggregates are given in a footnote to paragraph 15.27 of the full *Report*.
3 The velocity of circulation of a monetary aggregate is defined for present purposes as the ratio of the nominal gross domestic product, at a seasonally adjusted annual rate, in a particular calendar quarter to the average value of the seasonally adjusted monetary aggregate during that quarter.

4.4 MONETARY CONTROL AS SEEN BY THE DE KOCK COMMISSION: AN ASSESSMENT

G.L. de Wet[*]

In this article an assessment is made of the potential effectiveness of the monetary control measures recommended in the final report of the De Kock Commission.[1] The policy aims and instruments recommended by the Commission are first summarised and analysed. Next the underlying analytical features of the recommended control system are studied. To this end the money demand and supply relationships implicitly underlying the Commission's reasoning are formulated in the context of a simple interdependent model. From the dynamics of this model the difficulties on the road to monetary control awaiting the recommendations of the Commission are identified and scrutinised. It is concluded that effective control of the stock of money in the South African economic system will still not be possible.

1. POLICY AIMS AND INSTRUMENTS RECOMMENDED BY THE COMMISSION

The Commission distinguishes between the ultimate and the intermediate aims of monetary policy (Report, pars 17.6 and 17.69, and Chapter 13). The ultimate aims of monetary policy coincide with those of economic policy in general, namely price stability, balance of payments equilibrium, optimal and stable economic growth and an optimal and stable level of employment. At the same time the Commission regards price stability as the most important ultimate or long-term aim of monetary policy (par. 13.22). In this respect an appropriately low and relatively stable rate of growth in the money supply is regarded to be of major importance (par. 13.22). Consequently, target growth rates with respect to one or more selected definitions of money supply become the intermediate aim of monetary policy. Yet the Commission is of the opinion that such monetary targets should be unobtrusive and flexible in character. It recommends that interest rates and exchange rates must therefore not be allowed to find their own levels at all times (par. 17.7). Instead, subject to the evaluation by the monetary authority of the economic situation, it should be able to influence interest and exchange rates directly in order to manipulate them towards whatever levels the authority considers appropriate. To effect this, the monetary target growth rates must necessarily be flexible and adjustable. The Commission's view and recommendation boil down to accepting some sort of monetary targeting, whilst at the same time leaving discretion with the monetary authority as to the appropriate levels of interest and exchange

* Professor of Economics, University of Pretoria. This paper was first published in *The South African Journal of Economics*, Vol. 54, No. 1, 1986.

rates, the appropriate growth in money supply and, in effect, the appropriate value of any other economic variable.

With respect to instruments of monetary policy or control, the Commission recommends that direct control measures be avoided as far as possible (pars 17.48 and 17.49). Instead, it recommends that so-called market-oriented instruments be used. These may, under exceptional circumstances, be supplemented by semi-market-oriented measures (par. 17.47). These so-called market-oriented measures operate, according to the Commission, through one or more of the financial markets (par. 17.45). These indirect measures change the prices and volumes which influence the decisions of economic subjects without directly restricting or prescribing the subject's choice. More specifically, the monetary authority sells and buys in financial markets, thereby influencing the decisions of the economic subjects (par. 17.40). The Commission specifically recommends the use of the following so-called market-oriented measures (par. 17.46):

- government debt policy;
- open-market operations of the Reserve Bank;
- rediscount and general accommodation policy of the Reserve Bank;
- intervention in the spot and forward exchange markets.

The Commission's recommendation that the liquid asset system of control over bank credit be replaced by a cash reserve system is fundamental (par. 17.50., and pars 17.53 to 17.55). However, although the emphasis of control shifts towards the cash reserve requirements, required liquid asset reserves are not to be totally abandoned, although they are to be diminished (par. 17.51). The liquid asset reserve requirements will still put an additional restraint on monetary expansion, although cash reserve requirements will constitute the primary restraint. The Commission mentions two possible variants of the cash reserve system, namely the American version and the Classical version, but expresses a preference for the Classical version (Report, pars 17.57 to 17.68). The essential difference between the two versions, according to the Commission is:

In the American system the emphasis falls on the amount of cash reserves in the banking system. In order to control money supply this amount is targeted directly through open market operations. A low profile is kept with regard to rediscounting or lending to the market at the discount window when fulfilling the central bank function of lender of last resort. Penalty rates are rarely imposed and market interest rates are not directly influenced.

In the Classical system the main action takes place at the discount window. The central bank attempts to control the money supply by manipulating the rate at which it fulfils its function as lender of last resort, namely the Bank rate. Market interest rates are directly affected. Interest rates in turn affect the volume of bank credit, the stock of money and finally the required amount of cash reserves. When necessary open market operations are used to drive the banks to the discount window where they pay whatever Bank rate the monetary authority considers appropriate at the time.

The analytical features of the particular cash reserve system of monetary control recommended by the Commission have important implications for the potential effectiveness of monetary policy. Will the monetary authority gain control over the stock of money or not?

2. UNDERLYING ANALYTICAL FEATURES OF THE RECOMMENDED CASH RESERVE SYSTEM

The supply of money of which the rate of growth is an object of monetary policy, is actually an equilibrium value[2] resulting from the interplay of money supply and demand relationships and the many forces behind these relationships. When attempting to influence the equilibrium value of money, the route taken will be very important, since there are distinct kinds of side-effects attaching to the demand and supply function routes, respectively.

In what the Commission calls the American system the emphasis falls on the *amount* of cash reserves, which is primarily determined through the money *supply* relationships. These are structural economic relationships and mainly of a specific kind, namely *institutional* or *legal* relationships. In the American system a mere watchdog is put at the discount window in order to prevent escape through that route.

In the Classical system the emphasis falls on the cost of borrowing from the central bank at the discount window. In this way the cost of borrowing from the private banks is influenced, so that the equilibrium amount of money is determined through other kinds of structural relationships in the economy, namely the money *demand* functions. These structural relationships are of an entirely different nature, since they are *behavioural* relationships. In this case a watchdog is placed at the supply or cash reserve side, in order to drive the banks to the discount window.

The two major control routes identified by the Commission differ in respect of both their functional characters and their linkages to the rest of the economy. Behavioural relationships are more elusive and also more likely to change in the process of control than institutional relationships. Choosing to operate through behavioural relationships and their central variables like interest rates, which are often endogenous, has different implications for the entire economy than operating through institutional relationships and their central variables, which are often exogenous and under direct control of the monetary authority. Choosing a cash reserve system and furthermore choosing any particular variant of it, such as the Classical variant, confronts one with the diverging implications attached to different routes of influence.

To analyse the effect of the Commission's recommended choice of route on the effectiveness of monetary policy, we need to take a closer look at the relationships determining the demand and supply of money as featured in the model which implicitly underlies the reasoning of the Commission.

3. THE MONEY DEMAND AND SUPPLY RELATIONSHIPS IMPLICITLY UNDERLYING THE COMMISSION'S ARGUMENT

Although the Commission recommends a cash reserve system as the central element of the control infrastructure it has in mind, it retains liquid asset reserve requirements (Report, par. 17.51). Liquid asset requirements continue to play a functional role in the money creation process for at least two reasons. The first is that such requirements place a secondary restraint on money creation, in the sense that should the banking sector have surplus cash reserves it can still not create money freely before having complied with the liquid asset requirements. The second, and for present purposes more important reason, is that non-cash liquid reserves pose a threat to control through cash reserves to the extent that liquid reserves can be changed into cash reserves at the discount window. The Commission is naturally fully aware of this threat so that a central theme of its argument is that the cost of borrowing at the discount window should be used to fend off this threat effectively.

In the light of the foregoing, we should make provision in our model for liquid asset reserves in such a way that their secondary restraining role, as well as their threat to cash reserve control may be studied. The primary role of cash reserves should stand clear.

For present purposes we take a broad view of money, namely M3, comprising short-, medium- and long-term deposits. This is done for two reasons: firstly to accommodate all the cash and liquid asset requirements which the Commission judged to be of importance (Report, pars 17.51 and 17.69) and secondly simply in order to accommodate a wide interpretation of money in our analysis. In the end narrower definitions like M1 and M2, as well as wider definitions, may be accommodated without changing the essence of the model, the analysis or the conclusions.

Banks create money on the basis of the liquidity *base*, consisting of all liquid assets including all forms of cash,[3] while having to comply with both *cash* and *liquid* asset requirements.

Liquid asset reserves, denoted by L, therefore consist of cash reserves, denoted by L^c, and non-cash liquid reserves, denoted by L^b.

$$L = L^c + L^b \tag{1}$$

Non-cash liquid reserves may originate from government borrowing operations, open market operations, private money market operations, the Land Bank or other miscellaneous sources. Their issue will in general depend upon agricultural conditions, policy decisions and the state of the economy, which is represented by aggregate real production or income, denoted by Y. We write

$$L^b = L^b \ (Y, \text{others}) \tag{2}$$

Cash reserves must essentially originate from the Reserve Bank, either through the issuing of notes and coins,[4] through its lending to the banks at the discount window, through buying operations in the open market, through government debt financing or through the foreign exchange market. The amount of cash to be obtained at the discount window will depend on two factors. These are the amount of liquid assets in possession of the banks against which they may obtain cash at the discount window, and the Bank rate, which is the cost at which the banks borrow from the Reserve Bank. It is not the Bank rate on its own, but the Bank rate in relation to the rates at which banks lend to the public, which is important.[5] *For present purposes we focus on two factors, namely the availability of liquid assets and the relative Bank rate, since operations at the discount window form the main thrust of the campaign to control money growth to be found in the Report.* The Commission, nevertheless, stresses the importance of other aspects of monetary policy and this is precisely why we analyse its recommendations in the context of a model. Let us denote the effect of the open market, foreign exchange market and other operations of the Reserve Bank on cash reserves by RB. Let us further denote the interest rate at which banks lend to the non-banking sector by r.[6] We then have

$$L^c = L^c (L^b, \text{ Bank rate}/r, RB) \tag{3}$$

Required liquid assets consist of cash and non-cash assets to be held against short-, medium- and long-term deposits.

$$L^r = L_1^{ncr} + L_1^{cr} + L_2^{ncr} + L_2^{cr} + L_3^r \tag{4}$$

The components of L^r are prescribed (Report, par. 17.51).

$$L_1^{ncr} = t_1 D_1 \tag{5}$$
$$L_1^{cr} = v_1 D_1 \tag{6}$$
$$L_2^{ncr} = t_2 D_2 \tag{7}$$
$$L_2^{cr} = v_2 D_2 \tag{8}$$
$$L_3^r = w_3 D_3 \tag{9}$$

The subscript 1 denotes a short-term variable, while 2 and 3 denote medium- and long-term variables respectively. L denotes liquid assets and D denotes deposits. The superscript r denotes 'required'; ncr denotes 'required non-cash'; and cr denotes 'required cash'. In the case of short- and medium-term deposits, both cash and non-cash liquid assets are required, whilst in the case of long-term deposits only non-cash liquid assets are required (equation (4)). However, the cash reserves required to be held against short- and medium-term deposits may be counted as part of the required liquid assets to be held against these deposits. Thus, if we use w_1, w_2 and w_3 to denote the required liquid asset ratios in the case of short-, medium- and long-term deposits, we have

$$L_1^{ncr} = w_1 D_1,$$
$$L_2^{ncr} = w_2 D_2, \text{ and}$$
$$L_3^r = w_3 D_3$$

Yet, if v_1 and v_2 denote the required cash reserve ratios in the case of short- and medium-term deposits, we may write

$L_1^{ncr} = (w_1 - v_1)D_1$ and
$L_2^{ncr} = (w_2 - v_2)D_2$

Defining $t_1 = (w_1 - v_1)$ and $t_2 = (w_2 - v_2)$

we arrive at the expressions used in equations (5) to (9).

The amount of excess liquid reserves in the banking sector necessarily consists of the difference between the actual amount of liquid assets and the required amount of liquid assets:

$$L^c = L - L^r \tag{10}$$

Let us denote the amount of credit flowing from the private banks to the non-banking sector by E. The amount of credit which the non-banking sector demands from the private banks depends upon the state of the economy, once again represented by aggregate real production or income, and on the rate of interest at which the non-banking sector can borrow from the banks. We can thus formulate the credit demand function

$G(E,Y,r) = 0 \text{ (credit demand)}.$

Since the major component of total income is wage income, we may postulate

$G(E,W,YT,r) = 0$

$$\left(\frac{\delta E}{\delta W} > 0; \quad \frac{\delta E}{\delta r} < 0; \quad \frac{\delta E}{\delta YT} > 0 \right)$$

W denotes wage income and YT denotes other income. The amount of credit which the banks wish to supply depends on the interest they may earn, as well as on the amount of excess liquid reserves they possess. The more excess liquid reserves they possess, the more they would want to extend credit. The higher the interest they could earn, the more they would want to extend their credit. The credit supply function may be formulated as follows:

$$H(E, L^c, r) = 0 \qquad \left(\frac{\delta E}{\delta L^c} > 0; \frac{\delta E}{\delta r} > 0 \right)$$

In equilibrium the supply and demand will be equal and we will have a relationship

$J(E, L^c, W, YT, r) = 0$

which may also be written

$$E = E(L^c, W, YT, r) \tag{11}$$

Expression (11) represents the amount of actual lending by the private banks to the private non-banking sector. The effect of L^c, W and YT on E will be

177

positive. The effect of r on E will depend on the relative strength of the negative effect of r on the demand for credit and the positive effect of r on the supply of credit. *The less sensitive the private sector becomes to the cost of credit, the higher the possibility that r may have a net positive effect on E in equation (11).*

Since the banks will always attempt to cover their costs, the interest rate, r, will depend upon their cost of borrowing, viz. the Bank rate. This is an essential element in the Commission's argument.

$$r = r \ (Bank \ rate). \tag{12}$$

$$\frac{\delta r}{\delta \, Bank \ rate} > 0$$

From a macro point of view, all deposits at the banks originate from credit given by the banks. Leakages may take place, possibly on a small scale only, depending on interest rates. The spread of deposits in the portfolio from the short to the long end will depend upon relative interest rates. Thus we may postulate

$$D_1 = D_1 \ (E,r) \tag{13}$$
$$D_2 = D_2 \ (E,r) \tag{14}$$
$$D_3 = D_3 \ (E,r) \tag{15}$$

and finally

$$D = D_1 + D_2 + D_3 \tag{16}$$

E denotes total credit by the private banks to the non-banking sector, r denotes the relevant interest rate, D denotes total deposits and D_1, D_2 and D_3 denote short-, medium- and long-term deposits respectively.

Equations (1) to (16) now constitute a model containing the essential relationships underlying the suggested method of money supply control to be found in the Commission's recommendations. Using this model, we can analyse the potential success of its suggested method of control. This model replaces the traditional money multiplier which does not exist in the complicated South African monetary system. In addition, the model also incorporates the money demand relationship in a simple way.

4. DYNAMICS OF THE DEMAND AND SUPPLY RELATIONSHIPS

Let the non-cash liquid assets increase for any reason, for example as a result of an increase in Land Bank bills due to a good maize crop. This means that L^b (equation (2)) and L (equation (1)) increase. This in turn implies an automatic increase in L^c (equation (10)), namely excess liquid assets in the banking sector. Some money creation has already occurred in financing the maize crop against the security of Land Bank bills, and against these demand deposits cash and liquid assets must be held. This implies an increase in required reserves, L^r (equations (4), (5) and (6)). Yet the increase in L^r is not as much as the increase in L, since L^r is only a fraction of the increase in deposits. Consequently, the banking sector remains in possession of excess liquid assets. It would therefore attempt to extend credit to the private sector, which would take up more credit as long as its incremental demand for credit remains positive at the existing level of income and at the going rate of interest. Credit expansion takes place, which means that E increases (equation (11)) and further monetary expansion occurs. The money flows back to the bank in the form of short-, medium- and long-term deposits. Thus D, D_1, D_2 and D_3 (equations (13) to (16)) increase. Against these liabilities the banks must hold cash and liquid asset reserves, so that L^r and its components L_1^{ncr}, L_1^{cr}, L_2^{ncr}, L_2^r and L_3^r (equations (4) to (9)) increase. We see that cash reserves become effective through equations (6) and (8), but as long as the banks have excess cash reserves, equations (6) and (8) put no end to the monetary expansion process. When they reach their cash limits, they can exchange liquid assets for cash at the discount window (equation (3)). They will continue to do so as long as they can lend out at rates which still provide them with acceptable profit margins. If the Bank rate is increased, they will simply increase their lending rates (equation (12)). Credit extensions and therefore monetary expansion (equations (11) and (13) to (16)) will carry on until the lending rate, r, has a negative marginal effect on E which is stronger than the positive marginal effect of excess liquid reserves and income in the form of wages and other income in equation (11). If this does not happen, monetary expansion may continue indefinitely, since excess reserves will never vanish and the banks will continue to lend out on the basis of their excess reserves.

5. PROBLEMS OF CONTROL OF THE MONEY SUPPLY

The first difficulty on the road to control of the money supply lies in the possible unlimited availability of liquid asset reserves (equation (2)) which may be exchanged through the discount window for cash in order to overcome the cash reserve restraint (equation (3)). In this respect the sources of liquid asset reserves are important. The Commission realises this and therefore recommends close co-ordination between monetary policy and government debt policy (Report, pars 13.13, 13.14, 24.2, 25.4). Yet there are sources of liquid asset reserves, such as agriculture and the private banking sector, which lie outside the immediate influence of the monetary and fiscal authority. The Commission hopes that the monetary authority will be there to regulate the total amount of liquid assets by appropriate open market operations. This necessarily relies heavily upon the judgement of the relevant authorities. A lack of co-ordination between monetary and fiscal policy, non-economic considerations with regard to government debt, the exchange rate, agriculture and related matters, may cause difficulties in this respect. To prevent unwanted excess liquid assets from entering the banking sector, the Reserve Bank will have to display good judgement with regard to its buying and selling operations in the open market at all times. Human judgement is hardly likely to be infallible. Yet the biggest potential difficulties lie elsewhere, not with the availability of liquid assets.

A much graver problem awaits the monetary authority when operating through the discount window. The recommendations of the Commission indicate that the cost of supplying cash to the banks through the discount window must play a leading role in controlling the stock of money. It is to be hoped that this will be effected through raising the cost of credit supplied by the banks, which should discourage the demand for credit and in this way play a major role in checking undue expansion in the level of the money stock. The difficulty lies in the dynamics of the system as presented in the previous section. Control is channelled through equation (12), which relates the market rate to the Bank rate, and equation (11), which shows the effect of the market rate on the equilibrium amount of credit. Yet we saw earlier that the effect of interest cost on E will depend upon the interest rate sensitivity of the private sector's demand for credit. Just when the monetary authority would most urgently like to control the money stock, the rate of interest may become of minor importance in the credit function, equation (11). During times of high economic activity and especially during times of high inflationary expectations, high interest rates may not deter economic subjects from taking up additional credit. As long as people *expect* an increase in income, and especially in wages, they will simply argue that they will be able to pay the higher interest. Even if the net effect of r in equation (11) is negative, the positive effect of wages, other income, and excess liquid assets may outweigh it. Furthermore, if the negative effect of r on the *demand* for credit is not strong, r may have no negative effect at all in equation (11). On balance then, it is highly likely that credit will increase continuously, despite increases in the Bank rate, until the demand for credit declines for reasons other than a mere increase in interest cost. Under these circumstances the supply of money becomes infinite at the ruling rate of interest. The equilibrium value of the money stock is determined by the demand for money, which depends on wages and other income or in effect on the general level of economic activity. The monetary authority determines the level of interest rates only through the Bank rate.[7] To the extent that interest payments form part of the costs in the private sector, the raising of the interest rate level will fuel inflationary expectations and cause wage and price increases, more credit expansion through equation (11) and a perpetuation of the process.

The only way in which this upward spiral in the level of interest rates, economic activity, inflation and inflationary expectations, wages and the stock of money can be broken will be to create a situation where the demand for money breaks down completely, with dire implications for the economy.

There may be times when the problem will not arise and when the cost of credit will be an effective restraint on the demand for credit and ultimately on the equilibrium amount of the money stock. Yet this is more likely to be the case when people do not expect increases in wages, profits and other income with which to pay the higher interest, when the rate of inflation will be declining

180

and when the economy in general is in a declining phase or in a severe recession. Ironically when this happens the monetary authority may believe that it has gained control. Yet it implies that the economy must constantly be in a semi-depressed condition if the monetary authority would want to run no risk of losing control at the discount window. Another very important question to be asked is to what depth of recession the economy will have to slide in order to eliminate all risk that Bank rate manipulation will be ineffective on account of the behaviour of the economic subjects underlying equation (11).

Another major problem with the Commission's choice of attempting to control the stock of money from the demand side, which is closely linked to the previous difficulty, is the fact that behavioural equations change over time. Such behavioural relationships play an important role in the working of the system which determines, *inter alia*, the equilibrium stock of money. Equation (11) is a reduced form, originating from two important behavioural relationships, namely the demand and supply of bank credit. Behind these two functions lie a host of other important behavioural relationships such as the consumption, investment, import, labour demand and other functions. There are many factors which may change the behaviour of economic subjects. One of these factors is their reaction to policy meaures. Another is the general psychological climate, influenced positively or negatively by the general state of the economy, by politics, by weather conditions and many other circumstances. We see this happening quite often in the structure and coefficients of econometric model equations which change over time. The monetary authority is therefore faced with the situation that it operates through a channel which may change in length and width. Unfortunately it would become aware of a change only when it has already occurred.

This difficulty ties up with another one. Although we know a lot about the specification of economic relationships, we do not have perfect knowledge about them. This is especially true in the case of behavioural relationships such as the demand for bank credit. One does not know what the exact form of the function is and one also does not know precisely what variables enter such a relationship. There is still much uncertainty about the length and structure of the time lags involved. These difficulties occur in respect of almost all the economic relationships, which aggravates the problem in the light of the interdependence between economic variables. The monetary authority, operating from the discount window through the money demand functions, thus faces an uncertain world.

The Commission was probably aware of some of these problems. This may be the reason why it sought so much room for discretionary decision-making on the part of the monetary authority with regard to interest rates, money growth and so forth (Report, pars 17.8 and 17.9). The Commission specifically recommends that the monetary authority uses its discretion with regard to the optimal level and structure of interest rates in the light of its interpretation of the general economic situation and outlook. However, this subjects the economy not only to its imperfect knowledge, but also to possible judgemental errors on the part of the monetary authority. It is notable that the Commission evades definite targets (pars 17.8 and 17.24). Instead, it chooses low profile targets, judgement over the optimal level of monetary variables and operation through behavioural relationships. The question is whether an economy can afford to allow the possibility of judgemental errors in respect of such important variables as interest and exchange rates and the change in the money stock. The question becomes even more serious when one considers the fact that even in the absence of judgemental errors, the other problems mentioned above render control difficult if not impossible.

A subtle and largely unrecognised difficulty in control over the money stock in South Africa lies with the different cash and liquid asset requirements applicable to liabilities or deposits with different maturity structures. It is not always appreciated that, even when all other factors remain unchanged, a mere shift in the composition of the monetary asset portfolio of the private sector may change the equilibrium stock of money. This becomes clear when studying equations (4) to (9) and then (10) to (16). Moving from D_1 to D_2 means moving to a type of deposit where the cash and liquid asset requirements are less than before. Such a movement releases some cash and liquid assets tied up under legal requirements. The same happens when moving from D_2 to D_3. Required cash and liquid reserves diminish and excess reserves increase, opening the way for credit and deposits to increase. *In fact, if the supply side of the money creation process is to be effectively controlled, the same cash and liquid asset requirements will have to be set against all types of deposits which may enter one's definition of money.*

To all the aforementioned problems, which make *effective technical* control over the stock of money impossible, should finally be added some other non-economic factors. They are, nevertheless, quite important. First we have the vagaries of agricultural conditions and the financing of the crop which put additional strain upon open market operations and operations at the discount window. Furthermore we have the influence of the world economy on the balance of payments, and especially on the exchange rate, which may at any time evoke political reaction and politically inspired action with regard to the Reserve Bank's actions on the foreign exchange market. Finally we have the unfortunate but real situation that government expenditure and government debt policy cannot be separated from broader political issues. This means that there will always be changes in the amount of liquid assets and cash reserves to upset monetary policy.

The main difficulty with the recommendations of the Commission lies in its choice to work from the demand side, which the Commission does not really perceive in such terms. It argues in terms of market-oriented instruments, working through one or more of the financial markets, influencing prices and volumes and thereby the decisions of the economic subjects. In exceptional circumstances, cash reserve requirements will be varied (pars. 17.45 to 17.48).

There are two main deficiencies in this approach. The first is that the monetary authority has to influence and steer quite important prices, such as interest rates and exchange rates, in order ultimately to influence quite important behavioural equations. As was argued above, this is for various reasons a very uncertain way of attempting to exercise control. The second deficiency in the demand-side approach of the Commission is that it places too much reliance upon subjective evaluation by the monetary authority on what the appropriate values of certain key economic variables should be. Although this approach shelters behind the notion of a market-oriented policy, it is in principle not much different from the old direct control methods, which the Commission denounces. In fact, the only true difference between the approach recommended by the Commission and the direct control approach lies in the *nature* of the economic variables which the monetary authority attempts to control according to its perception of what is appropriate. In the case of the Commission's approach, these variables are certain interest rates, exchange rates and other related variables. In the direct control approach, the variables include other types of interest rates, credit volumes and so forth. In both cases reliance upon human judgement about what is appropriate and what not, and the ultimate inability to control economic behaviour are weak elements. When applying the approach of the Commission, errors of judgement may remain concealed somewhat longer, since they may be ascribed to market forces.

Some of the difficulties encountered in the demand-side approach of the Commission may be avoided by working directly on the cash reserves. This will be a supply-side approach. Most of the structural money supply equations are of an institutional nature and the effect of action through institutional relationships is much more certain. Yet, the effect is still not perfectly predictable and other, different problems may arise. However, space does not allow an adequate analysis of the possible effects of a supply-side or other approach to monetary control. This leaves us in a somewhat uncomfortable position. We have established that the Commission's approach does not offer effective monetary control, without being able to determine whether effective control is possible at all. Such a study still needs to be done.

6. CONCLUSION

Given the framework of control measures which the Commission recommends, effective control over the stock of money in the South African economic system will still not be possible. The monetary authority will have an influence on the equilibrium amount of money, but no control. The fact that the Commission chose to work from the demand side makes control virtually impossible in view of the imperfect knowledge about the structure of the relevant behavioural relationships and the length of the time lags involved, as well as on account of the changing nature of these behavioural relationships. It also places too much judgemental power over key economic variables in the hands of the monetary authority. At times the authority may be under the impression that it has control; in reality it will simply be the working out of the economic system bringing temporary relief. In the end the supply of money becomes infinite at the ruling rate of interest, while the demand for money, dependent upon income and especially wages, determines the equilibrium amount of money. The monetary authority then merely sets the level of interest rates through the Bank rate. In its attempt to gain control it may seriously hurt the economy. The authority may continue to try to gain control from the demand side, driving up interest rates until the whole economic system is disrupted.

NOTES

1 *Commission of Inquiry into the Monetary System and Monetary Policy in South Africa*, Final Report. RP70: 1984, Pretoria Government Printer, May 1985. This will be referred to as the Report. The Commission of Inquiry, chaired by Dr G.P. de Kock, Governor of the South African Reserve Bank, will be referred to as the Commission.
2 The Commission invariably refers to this equilibrium value as the *supply* of money. We prefer to call it the *stock* of money and to use the notion *supply of money* when referring to a structural economic relationship.
3 These forms of cash consist of banks' balances at the Reserve Bank and coins and notes in circulation.
4 The South African Reserve Bank is not formally responsible for the issuing of coins. Yet *functionally,* the issuing of coins moves in harmony with that of notes which is the responsibility of the Reserve Bank.
5 The Bank rate as such has no bearing upon the private banks' willingness to borrow from the central bank. No matter how high the Bank rate, if private banks can lend out at higher rates, they will continue to borrow at the discount window.
6 In practice we have a whole structure of lending rates, but it is common practice in a basic analytical approach to reduce this structure to one interest rate. The model can be relatively easily extended to accommodate more than one lending rate. However, this will complicate the analysis without changing the basic results.
7 In this way interest rates other than the Bank rate lose much of their endogeneity and become virtually exogenous. (The Bank rate is exogenous by nature.) The problems related to inherently endogenous variables such as interest rates becoming exogenous are discussed below in the context of imperfect knowledge and judgemental errors. It furthermore introduces unnecessary and unwanted rigidity into the economic system.

4.5 THE DE KOCK COMMISSION REPORT: A MONETARIST PERSPECTIVE

B.S. Kantor*

There is much in the De Kock Commission Report and in the De Kock reforms to encourage a monetarist. With monetarists, the Report shares a deep dissatisfaction with the recent history of monetary policy practice in South Africa. For a monetarist, the advocacy in the Report of market forces for the efficient allocation of credit and the case made for a market in foreign exchange represent a major advance in official thinking. Furthermore, a monetarist could find little fault with the explanation in the Report of inflation as a monetary phenomenon:

> The Commission views monetary and fiscal policies designed to control the money supply and aggregate monetary demand as the essence of anti-inflationary strategy. Indeed, its inquiry has led it to the firm conclusion that the only effective way to restore and maintain reasonable stability of the price level in South Africa is to exert better control over money creation and total spending, with full acceptance of the implications this will have for interest rates and exchange rates (Main Findings: Para. 138, pp. A25–A26).

Nevertheless there are fundamental differences between a monetarist's prescription for South African monetary policy and the solutions proposed by the De Kock Commission. The monetarist argues for rules to bind economic policies, particularly rules for money supply growth. The Commission argues for discretion for the Reserve Bank over interest rates, exchange rates, exchange control and money supply. The Report makes the case for Reserve Bank freedom from political interference with interest rates and exchange rates. The 'market-oriented' interest rates argued for in the Report are not market-determined rates in the usual sense of that term. What is recommended is that all interest rates be closely aligned with those short-term interest rates controlled directly by the Reserve Bank through its more or less continuous interaction with the money market, banks and the discount houses.

The Report therefore is not a monetarist document. It should rather be understood as a testament for modern discretionary central banking. Modern central bankers regard the supply of money as important, as they do other instruments of control. Accordingly, the case for rules rather than discretion for policy is nowhere seriously addressed in the Report.

The main purpose of this discussion is to indicate precisely why it will not be possible for the South African Reserve Bank to exercise the management discretion proposed for it in the Report and to control money supply closely in the interests of economic stability, as the Commission would wish. A proper recog-

* Director, School of Economics, University of Cape Town. This paper was first published in *The South African Journal of Economics*, Vol. 54, No. 1, 1986.

nition of such difficulties would surely have led the commissioners to different conclusions about the appropriate structure of the South African financial system. In particular, moves towards what are described in the Report as an American-type relationship between the central bank and the money market, rather than the London-type or 'classical' arrangement prevailing in South Africa, might have commended themselves (paras 17.59 and 17.60).

THE CASE FOR A MONEY SUPPLY RULE

It would perhaps be helpful if the monetarist case for money supply rules were briefly stated here. The case for controlling money supply rests upon the existence of empirically reliable links between money supply changes and changes in spending. Money is one of the arguments in the expenditure functions of economic actors. Monetarists argue that more money held and owned will mean more spending and more spending will, in turn, bring higher prices. Money is a component of wealth and changes in money have effects on wealth which, in turn, influence spending. It should, however, be recognised that it is money and not credit that constitutes part of individual wealth. For every domestic financial credit there is a domestic debit. Domestic financial credits and debits cancel out. Or in other words, for every borrower there is a lender, for every investor, a saver. Foreign credits may facilitate more domestic spending; however, foreign credits also represent domestic liabilities that have to be repaid. They clearly do not represent wealth but are a charge on it.

Recognising the distinction between money and credit is vital for the purposes of understanding money supply causes and effects. Monetarists argue that changes in the nominal supply of money, which are equivalent to changes in nominal wealth, need to be controlled in the interest of controlling spending. Excess supplies of money, in particular excess supplies of what is described in the literature as 'outside money', that is to say money unencumbered by repayment schedules or interest commitments, lead to additional spending. Outside money is the non-interest-bearing debt of the government sector, i.e. the notes and deposits supplied by the central bank which form a part of individual wealth. Outside money is more usually described as high-powered money or the money base. Interest-bearing government debt will not be a component of wealth, unless taxpayers fail fully to discount the future interest payments on government debt.

When the present value of interest payments on government debt is regarded by taxpayers as equal to the value of government debt newly issued on their behalf, then so-called Ricardian equivalence holds. That is to say, under Ricardian equivalence, financing government expenditure through debt issues is no more stimulatory of private spending than financing such expenditure through taxation (Barro, 1974). Nor will bank deposits be a component of net wealth unless the issuers of these deposits, the shareholders of the banks, disregard such liabilities.

186

A full explanation of why money and not debt is important as an influence on spending is provided by Don Patinkin in his scholarly *Money, Interest and Prices* (Patinkin, 1965). Patinkin (1972) has also considered the wealth effects of banking. These issues are further considered below.

The case for a money supply rule rather than money supply discretion is based upon what would now be understood as a Rational Expectations view of the world. The argument may be briefly stated as follows: If the expectations of economic actors are rational then actual money supply or any other policy actions taken by the authorities do not have real effects. It is only the difference between actual and expected money supply developments that will affect the real economy. Expected money supply developments will have been incorporated into decisions to produce, consume, hire labour, borrow or lend capital, buy or sell foreign exchange, etc. Thus expected money supply is fully reflected in the prevailing structure of wages, prices, interest and exchange rates. Unexpected changes in money will affect these prices and so the real economy. However, given rational expectations, there is no justification for unexpected action by the authorities. The system will stabilise itself at a full employment equilibrium. Unexpected action by the authorities simply adds uncertainties about policy to the uncertainties of nature with which economic actors have to cope, and about which the economic authorities will not have superior information.

It is therefore best if the authorities act predictably to minimise uncertainty. This is the case for a money supply rule. Furthermore, since low inflation implies lower information costs about relative prices than does higher inflation, since high inflation will be expected and so will not stimulate economic activity, and because inflation is a monetary phenomenon, the money supply rule should be consistent with very low rates of inflation in the long term. That is to say, money supply should be made to grow at a rate that will satisfy additional demands for money arising from real activities so that inflationary or deflationary pressure will not emanate from the money market (Kantor, 1979).

THE CASE AGAINST DIRECT CONTROLS

As is well known, the central bank may not wish to control the supply of money at all. It may prefer to manage interest rates without regard to the money supply. In such circumstances, given the chosen structure of interest rates, changes in money supply become a function of changes in demands for bank credit, which will in turn be dependent on the state of the economy or inflationary expectations. The essential monetarist argument is that money supply need not be made dependent on the state of the economy and that it will become so dependent only if the authorities prefer it that way. The logical corollary of money supply policies that are independent of demands for credit is market determined interest and exchange rates. Thus excess demands for or supply of bank credit, given the supply of high-powered money, will mean higher or lower interest rates combined with a currency that is expected to depreciate or appreciate as the case may be.

If the money supply is made dependent upon demands for bank credit, then one method the authorities may use to restrain credit demands, other than to increase interest rates, would be to impose direct controls on the demands for and supplies of bank credit. Direct controls on demands for credit and on deposit and other interest rates were very much a feature of monetary policy in South Africa before the De Kock reforms. The Commission is strongly opposed to such controls and proposes its own 'market-oriented' policies for money supply control as an alternative. The justification that the Commission advances for market-oriented policies is summarised as follows:

43. There are two fundamental reasons for this conclusion: The first is the Commission's finding that, by promoting the efficient allocation of resources and performing a number of other vital economic functions, the various sophisticated financial markets which have developed in South Africa make an important contribution in their own right to general economic growth and welfare. Moreover, they function best in the national interest if they are reasonably free, competitive, active and broad, and produce realistic market-related interest and exchange rates. It is important, therefore, that monetary policy should, as far as possible, be pursued in a manner which does not undermine the efficient functioning of these markets (Report, p. A9).

44. The second main reason is that the Commission firmly believes that such a market-oriented approach can to a large extent overcome the main deficiencies from which monetary policy has suffered in the past. Specifically, it should contribute to (1) the moderation and stabilization of the growth of the monetary aggregates; (2) more effective control over disintermediation and other velocity-related developments; (3) the maintenance of realistic and market-related interest rates; and (4) the attainment of realistic and market-related spot and forward exchange rates. In these ways it should greatly improve the ability of the monetary authorities to influence aggregate monetary demand (Report, p. A9).

Avoiding direct controls will, it is agreed, mean more efficient financial markets and hence lower real costs of investment and higher real rewards for savers out of a better allocation of loanable funds. The efficiency argument against direct controls is overwhelmingly strong. One can agree with the Commission that it is possible to control money supply, and so aggregate demand, without direct controls. What is doubtful is the ability of the Reserve Bank to control the money supply in the manner suggested by the Commission. In this respect a money supply rule is preferable to discretionary control.

INTERMEDIATION, DISINTERMEDIATION AND REINTERMEDIATION

The views of the Commission on disintermediation and other velocity-related developments cannot be accepted without reservation (par. 44, Main Findings, p. A9). It would appear that the analysis of the Commission was influenced by the fallacy that credit demand (and therefore debits) are important for their own sake as an influence on spending rather than as potential determinants of the supply of money.

Clearly the imposition and then the relaxation of direct controls will influence movements of funds from and to the balance sheets of banks and will therefore influence the monetary aggregates, as is explained in Chapter 9 of the Report. Such movements complicate the interpretation of reported money supply developments, or in other words, M1, M2 and M3 may be less reliable as indications of the directional effects of money supply policies. Clearly also, if the actual money supply that influences spending is different from the money supply recorded in the books of the banking system, then 'money' may matter less or more than the economy-watchers, including the Reserve Bank, believe. In other words, the velocity of 'money' as defined may be unreliable as a basis for economic forecasting or management. It is the apparent instability of measured velocity or of the demand for money that has made the Commission reluctant to commit itself to a specific money supply aggregate to manage.

The case for controlling the supply of money rests squarely on the stability, that is the predictability, of the demand for money or its reciprocal, the velocity of circulation of money. As indicated above, the money properly included in the expenditure function is outside money, being a component of wealth. Monetary theory suggests that it is changes in demand for and supply of non-interest bearing notes and deposits issued by the central bank (high-powered money) that is the relevant monetary aggregate. Of course, other monetary aggregates will be dependent upon the supply and demand for high-powered money.

Reintermediation, intermediation, and disintermediation, which are the results of the evolution of the financial system or influenced by the imposition or removal of direct controls, may change the relationship between high-powered money and other 'monies' and between the different monies and expenditure. Nevertheless, in principle, disintermediation and reintermediation can only affect spending through their effects on wealth. The supply of credit, including the supply of bank credit, as indicated previously, is not a component of wealth. Thus the impact of a reintermediation or disintermediation on spending may be much less important than the Commission believes.

The case against direct controls is best made on grounds of the efficiency losses incurred through them. The distortions of monetary statistics may be less important for spending than the Commission believes. Nevertheless, the Commission is perfectly correct to warn against naive interpretations of money supply statistics. That is why a highly visible, high-powered money supply rule is preferable. Changes in high-powered money supplied to the system indicate unambiguously the influence of the authorities on the financial system. If the supply of high-powered money were well controlled, changes in the financial structure could be safely left alone.

THE IMPORTANCE OF MONEY

What is required to establish the importance of high-powered money for South

Africa is a monetary policy experiment. That is to say, the Reserve Bank could control high-powered money according to some rule quite independently of the state of the credit market or the economy, and the outcomes for economic activity could be observed. Conclusive evidence will, however, require an initial act of faith. Evidence of the relationship between 'money' and expenditure taken from a system where the supply of money has been made to respond to the state of the economy through official intervention may not be convincing.

Unfortunately the De Kock Commission recommendations are not going to provide us with such an experiment. The discretion the Reserve Bank will exercise over money supply will complicate any efforts to discover whether money supply changes were the cause or the effect of changes in economic activity.

Incidentally, it is not at all obvious that the relevant velocities of circulation of money are as unpredictable as the Report implies. Certainly, expenditure velocities of circulation of money have declined recently but such declines would not necessarily have been unexpected.

Money, as has been mentioned, is an argument in the expenditure function. Money affects expenditure which, in turn, influences output. Gross domestic expenditure and output are not, however, identities. The difference between GDE and GDP is the trade balance. Exports and so output may be affected by foreign demands, which are independent of domestic monetary policies. Therefore it is the relationship between money and expenditure, or the expenditure velocities, that are of importance for the South African monetary authorities; and so it is the stability of expenditure velocities and not output velocities that will determine the importance of money in South Africa.

This point is conceded by the Commission, but none the less it is the output velocities that receive closest attention in the Report (Chap. 15, especially no. 4, p. 158. See also Barr and Kantor, 1982).

The relationship between changes in high-powered money, defined as currency plus required reserves of the banking system, and changes in gross domestic expenditure over different time periods, was analysed by way of regression analysis, using the Almon lag procedure. As may be seen below, high-powered money has been and remains important in explaining gross domestic expenditure in South Africa. The equation tested was

$$GDE = \text{Constant} + \sum_{i=0}^{3} M_{t-1}$$

Fourth percentage changes of gross domestic expenditure (GDE) and high-powered money (M) were used to avoid seasonal factors. An Almon polynomial was applied with both end points constrained. The t statistics appear in parentheses after the coefficients.

Clearly it can be concluded that high-powered money has been and remains important in South Africa.[1]

Table 1 CHANGES IN HIGH-POWERED MONEY AND GROSS DOMESTIC EXPENDITURE IN SOUTH AFRICA. ESTIMATES OF THE PARAMETERS OF THE EQUATION*

$\dfrac{M_o}{GDE}$	1969 I – 1984 IV	1980 II – 1984 IV
Constant	9,7446 (6,53653)	11,65285 (5,42453)
Mt_0	0,49210 (3,9101)	0,48477 (3,3267)
Mt_1	0,22053 (2,9810)	0,14847 (1,76805)
Mt_2	−0,17177 (−1,0364)	−0,2357 (−1,19592)
Mt_3	−0,04191 (−0,26023)	0,10544 (0,55546)
M_i	0,49896 (5,4495)	0,50298 (5,0642)
$\bar{R}^2$	0,45198	0,64565

* The author wishes to thank Mr G. Toms, Graduate Assistant, University of Cape Town, who was responsible for the calculation of the figures.

MONEY SUPPLY CONTROL: THE PROBLEM WITH AN INTEREST RATE TARGET IN AN OPEN ECONOMY WITHOUT A DEVELOPED FOREIGN EXCHANGE MARKET

The conventional approach to the difficulties of using interest rates as a target for money supply control purposes concludes that the authorities have to be able to estimate the demand for money. The point is well illustrated with the help of the following diagram.

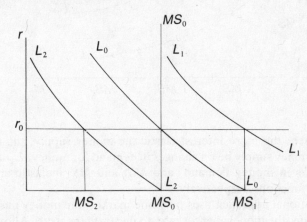

Figure 1

The objective of monetary policy is a money supply level MS_0. If the authorities are to achieve this objective by means of an interest rate target, they

191

have to be able to predict the demand for money. In Figure 1, if demand for money is expected to be L_O, an interest rate target r_O will prove successful for the purpose of satisfying the money supply objective. However, if demand for money is unexpectedly high at L_1, money supply inadvertently will increase to MS_1. Alternatively, if money demand is unexpectedly low, money supply will fall unintentionally to MS_2.

The monetarists' argument is in favour of ignoring interest rates and concentrating upon a target for high-powered money. The high-powered target is preferred to the non-borrowing reserve target because it gives fewer opportunities for banks to influence money supply via accommodation from the central bank. In general the less interest-elastic the demand for reserves, or in cases where accommodation is available, the less interest-elastic the banks' demands for borrowed reserves, the closer will be the links between the high-powered money targets and the supply of money. Interest-elasticity of demand for notes is another potential point of slippage (Thornton, 1982). The importance of the interest-elasticity of the money supply under base targeting can be illustrated in Figure 2.

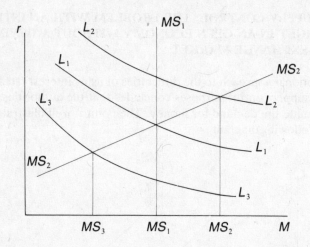

Figure 2

As may be seen, the more interest-elastic the money supply, the more dependent will money supply be on changes in demand for money. L_1, L_2 and L_3 represent shifts in money demand, and MS_1 and MS_2 inelastic and elastic money supply functions, respectively.

The conventional approach uses only one market, the money market, and one interest rate, the money market rate, to illustrate the issue. Allowing for a further market, viz. the market for bank credit, can reveal how much more complicated is the task of controlling money supply via interest rate targeting in practice. The importance of disaggregating the money and credit markets has been central to the monetary analysis of the pioneering monetarists, Karl

Brunner and Allen H. Meltzer (1968, 1974). The problems are further compounded when credit and money markets are open to capital inflows and outflows.

These complexities can be demonstrated by widening the conventional model to include explicitly equations for the supply and demand for bank credit and solving the two equation models for money supply and the bank credit or overdraft rate. The credit and money market model includes, as an additional dependent variable, the bank overdraft rate. This model is surely much more representative of the money supply process in South Africa and provides a much better insight into the difficulties of money supply control, given interest and exchange rate targeting, than the simple money market model illustrated above.

For the purposes of simplicity, a linear model of the money and credit supply process is presented. The model is introduced by two simplified balance sheets, one for the Reserve Bank and one for the commercial banking system, as follows:

RESERVE BANK

Notes	N	Foreign Assets	FA
Bank Deposits	CR	Government securities	GS
Government Deposits	GD	Loans and advances to commercial banks	BR

COMMERCIAL BANKS

Deposits	D	Cash Reserves	CR
Accommodation from Res. Bank	BR	Government securities	LA
		Private securities	OD
Time deposits	T		

THE MODEL

Identities and definitions

$$NDA \text{ (net domestic assets)} = GS - GD \tag{1}$$
$$HPM \text{ (high-powered money)} = N + CR \tag{2}$$
$$M \text{ (money supply)} = N + D \tag{3}$$
$$N = nM \tag{4}$$

where n is the proportion of notes in the money supply.

Behavioural equations

The foreign exchange reserve position of the Reserve Bank is represented as

$$FA = FA_1 rm + FA_2 r^* \text{ with } FA_1 > 0 \text{ and } FA_2 < 0 \tag{5}$$

193

where rm is the money market interest rate in South Africa, and r^* is the effective cost of offshore borrowing. As indicated by the signs on the partial derivatives of the variables, an increase in the money market rates will improve the balance of payments and increase the foreign reserves held by the Bank while an increase in the effective cost of offshore finance will cause outflows of capital or smaller inflows and a loss of reserves.

r^* is defined as equal to the exogenously determined offshore interest rates (r_o) plus or minus the expected changes in the dollar value of the rand, i.e.:

$$r^* = r_o + e \tag{6}$$

and where

$$e = (SR^e - SR)/SR \tag{6'}$$

SR^e is the greater of the spot rate expected by the market and the forward rate quoted by the Reserve Bank (measured in rands per dollar). If the quoted forward rate exceeds the spot rate expected by the market, then borrowers will cover forward. If the forward rate quoted by the Reserve Bank is less than the expected spot rate, then a greater proportion of offshore borrowing will be uncovered (Barr and Kantor, 1984). r^* is assumed to be exogenous to the model.

In a well-developed foreign exchange market, which would include a well-developed market for forward exchange, market forces would simultaneously establish spot and forward exchange rates and short-term interest rates. The forward rate by definition would be the spot rate of exchange expected in, say, three months' time. Interest parity would hold; that is, the cost of local and offshore borrowing, after adjusting for differences between spot and forward rates of exchange, would be expected to be the same. Furthermore, in well-developed money and exchange markets, changes in expectations about the future value of the currency cause adjustments to interest and exchange rates without influencing the supply of foreign exchange reserves held by the central bank. In other words, unless the central bank intervenes, the exchange and money markets equalise the demands for and supplies of foreign exchange and the balance of payments will not influence the money supply. Clearly, this is not the case in South Africa, where a well-developed forward market in foreign exchange has not yet been developed despite some encouragement from the De Kock Commission. The Reserve Bank provides forward exchange at a rate that is consistent with its interest rate and foreign exchange reserve objectives. Unless the Reserve Bank wishes to augment its foreign exchange reserves, such rates will be set to avoid opportunities for profitable arbitrage that would be available if interest differentials were greater than the effective cost of forward cover. However, such forward (as quoted) rates may and are often not regarded as equalising the expected costs of offshore and onshore finance. Offshore borrowers or lenders, importers or exporters do not necessarily cover against the risk of changes in the foreign exchange value of the rand. The supply of foreign exchange reserves held by the Reserve Bank and therefore the high-powered money supply may change accordingly. Such possibilities are reflected in equation (5) (Barr and Kantor, 1984; Part II of the Report, Chapters 11 and 12).

The demand for money function takes the usual form

$$Md = L_1 rm + L_2 Y \tag{7}$$
with $L_1 < 0$ and $L_2 > 0$

where Md is money demand and Y the exogenously determined level of economic activity.

The supply of money function is represented as a multiple of the sources of high-powered money, as follows, where

$$M = g[FA + NDA + BR] \tag{8}$$

and where g is the money multiplier (Kantor, 1982).

NDA, the open market position of the Reserve Bank, is regarded as exogenously determined. Equation (8) also reflects the fact that the banking system is continuously indebted to the Reserve Bank and borrowed reserves (BR) may be regarded as a permanent source of high-powered money. BR is referred to in South Africa as the money market 'shortage'.

The demand for accommodation by the banks from the Reserve Bank (BR) is written as

$$BR = Br_1 rOd + Br_2 rm \tag{9}$$
with $Br_1 > 0$ and $Br_2 < 0$

where rOd is the overdraft or bank credit rate.

Thus the banks are assumed to borrow more from the Reserve Bank as the level of overdraft rates rises. The overdraft rate indicates the return to bank lending. The money market rate, rm, is regarded as reflecting the opportunity cost of borrowing reserves. The discount rate of the Reserve Bank will approximate the money market rate. Other things being equal, including the overdraft rate, the higher the returns in the money market or the higher the cost of borrowing reserves, the less inclined will the banks be to borrow. Clearly the willingness of banks to borrow reserves depends upon the difference between the costs of borrowing and the rewards for lending. Irrespective of the level of rates, any gap between the bank lending and borrowing rates will encourage the banks to borrow additional reserves from the Reserve Bank.

However, it should be understood that higher lending rates charged by the banking system, again with other things equal, including inflation and inflationary expectations, imply greater credit risks to be assumed by the banks. Therefore, even if the customers of the banks are willing borrowers at high levels of interest rates, or in other words demands for credit are relatively interest-inelastic, the banking system may be unwilling to supply additional credit, given greater risks of default. It is interest rates and credit-worthiness that determine the supply of bank credit. The influence of risks of default is not included specifically in the supply of bank credit function of the model. In equation (11) below the supply of bank credit is simply regarded as a multiple of the reserves held by the banks.

The demand for bank credit function of the private sector (Od) is described as

$$OD = OD_1 r^* + OD_2 rOd \text{ with } OD_1 > 0 \text{ and } OD_2 < 0 \tag{10}$$

The demand of the government sector for bank credit (LA) is regarded as determined independently of interest rates.

The supply of bank credit may be described as

$$BC = h.CR \tag{11}$$

where h is the credit supply multiplier.

SOLUTION OF THE MODEL

Equilibrium conditions

In the money market the demand for money is made equal to the supply of money, $Md = M$ and by substitution

$$L_1 rm + L_2 = g[FA_1 rm + FA_2 r^* + NDA + BR_1 rOd + BR_2 rm] \tag{12}$$

Equilibrium in the credit market is defined as $OD + LA = BC$ and by substitution

$$LA + OD1r^* + OD2rOd = h[FA_1 rm + FA_2 r^* + NDA + BR_1 rOd + BR_2 rm - nM] \tag{13}$$

(*Note: $CR = FA + NDA + B - nM$, from the Reserve Bank's balance sheet.*)

The problems facing the Reserve Bank in its desire to control both short-term interest rates and the supply of money can be demonstrated by assuming that rm, the money market rate, is determined exogenously by Reserve Bank intervention. The model then reduces to a system with two dependent variables, the overdraft rate rOD, and the supply of money, M, and is solved as follows:

$$r_{OD} = \frac{L_1 rm + L_2 \bar{Y}}{gBR_1} - \frac{1}{BR_1} FA_1 r_m + FA_2 r^* + N\bar{D}A + BR_2 r_m \tag{14}$$

and

$$M = -\frac{1}{nh}(LA + OD_1 r^*) - OD_2[r_{OD}] + hFA_1 r_m + FA_2 r^* + NDA$$
$$+ BR_2 r_m + h[r_{OD}] \tag{15}$$

In order to achieve money supply objectives, the authorities would not only have to be able to estimate the income elasticity of demand for money, and at least all the other elasticities indicated in equations (14) and (15). This is clearly

196

a most formidable task and one which might be judged to be beyond the capabilities of the Reserve Bank.

CONCLUSION

Applying the model has, it is hoped, revealed how difficult it would be for the South African Reserve Bank to control the supply of money by exercising its discretion over interest and exchange rates. The model also indicates how much easier it would be for the Reserve Bank to control interest rates and money supply if the exchange market were well developed and the balance of payments did not affect the supply of high-powered money. Regrettably, after the South African foreign debt crisis of 1985, the full development of the foreign exchange markets has been interrupted and the influence of balance of payments flows on the money supply remains as important, or has perhaps become even more important, than it was before.

It is probable that the Reserve Bank, while enjoying the greater freedom recommended for it by the De Kock Commission Report, will continue to fail to make money supply growth a stabilising force in the economy. Money supply growth rates are likely to continue to be too rapid in the upward phases of the business cycle and too slow in the downward phases, as experienced in 1984 and 1985. If so, the monetarists' hope is that the Report of the Commission may be an important waystation on the road to a money supply rule for South Africa. Their fear is that the revealed failures of discretionary-type policies would in due course lead to a greater reliance on direct controls.

NOTE

1 For an earlier application of this method see Barr and Kantor, 1982.

REFERENCES

Barr, G.D.I. and Kantor, B.S., 1984. 'Interest rates, the exchange rate and money supply in South Africa', *The Investment Analysts Journal*, No. 23, June, pp. 45–49.
Barr, G.D.I. and Kantor, B.S., 1982. 'Money and economic activity', *South African Journal of Economics,* Vol. 50 (4).
Barro, R.J., 1974. 'Are Government Bonds Net Wealth?', *Journal of Political Economy,* Vol. 83, December, pp. 1095–1118.
Brunner, K. and Meltzer, A., 1968. 'Liquidity traps for money, bank credit and interest rates', *Journal of Political Economy, 76,* January, pp. 1–37.
—— 1974. 'Money, debt and economic activity', *Journal of Political Economy, 80*, pp. 951–977.
Kantor, B.S., 1979. 'Rational expectations and economic thought', *Journal of Economic Literature,* Vol. XVII, No. 4, pp. 1422–1441.
Kantor, B.S. and Rees, D., 1982. *South African Economic Issues.* Cape Town: Juta, Chapter 5, pp. 95–99.
Patinkin, Don, 1965. *Money, Interest and Prices: An Integration of Monetary and Value Theory* (2nd ed.). New York: Harper & Row. Esp. Chaps. II & IX.
—— 1972. *Money and Wealth, Studies in Monetary Economics.* New York: Harper & Row, Chap. 9.
Thornton, D.L., 1982. 'Simple Analytics of the Money Supply Process and Monetary Control', *Federal Reserve Bank of St Louis Review,* October, Vol. 64, No. 8.

4.6 MONETARY POLICY: ITS SCOPE AND LIMITATIONS

J. Whittaker*

Based on observation of the institutional practices of the Reserve Bank, this paper argues that domestic monetary policy is nothing more nor less than setting the interest rate for short-term loans. The effects in South Africa of recent interest rate changes are then studied, and it is deduced that whilst the rate of price inflation can be successfully controlled by suitable choice of interest rates, this objective has not been satisfactorily fulfilled in South Africa because it has not been consistently pursued. Doubts are raised as to whether monetary policy can be usefully applied to other purposes such as stimulating expenditure, and it is found that attempts to do so interfere with the inflation objective.

INTRODUCTION

It is commonly accepted that, whatever the *causes* of price inflation, monetary policy has a role to play in subduing it. Another common notion is that monetary policy should be able to stimulate the economy in a recession. It is also sometimes thought that there is scope within monetary policy for providing subsidised finance for particular favoured groups. This paper aims to show the extent to which these notions are correct and mutually compatible.

As a matter of definition, monetary policy comprises the use of all means for influencing the economy which are at the disposal of the Central Bank (the Reserve Bank in South Africa). The Central Bank's powers of influence arise because (a) it is the monopoly issuer of the nation's currency, (b) it is empowered to regulate the activities of other financial institutions, and (c) it holds the major part of the nation's foreign exchange reserves. This paper concentrates specifically on South African *domestic* monetary policy. This classification excludes the Reserve Bank's activities of regulation and intervention in the foreign exchange markets.

The methodology of the paper is *not* the evaluation of competing theories, but rather the observation and analysis of existing and past monetary policy techniques and their effects. It is found that, despite the unnecessary complexity of the institutional practices by which monetary policy is applied, a few simple results can be derived. *Inter alia* it is argued that:

- all domestic monetary policy actions combine to influence the economy through a single variable, the short-term interest rate. Monetary policy *is* interest rate policy. It follows that:

* School of Economics, University of Cape Town. This paper was first published in *Social Dynamics*, Vol. 13, No. 1, 1987.

- monetary policy is not practised by setting the money supply, as is implied in much orthodox macroeconomic theory, although one of the *objectives* of the choice of interest rates may be a particular growth rate of the money supply;
- inflation can be successfully controlled by appropriate choice of interest rates provided this objective is pursued consistently;
- if monetary policy is to be successfully used for some other motive such as stimulation of demand, then this conflicts with its use for controlling inflation.

CURRENT DOMESTIC MONETARY POLICY PRACTICES

A description of the current techniques of the Reserve Bank (hereinafter 'the Bank') is now presented in order to show that the Bank exerts its influence by setting the interest rate for short-term borrowing (hereinafter 'the interest rate'). Technical intricacies are avoided as far as possible (a fuller account is presented in Whittaker and Theunissen (1987), where it is also shown that the Bank's interest rate instrument derives from its monopoly over currency issue).

The current tactic of the Bank is to ensure that financial institutions collectively remain indebted to it. This debt is variously known as 'accommodation', 'discount window' borrowing, or the 'money-market shortage'. Changes in the money-market shortage can have several causes. For instance, when tax is paid, the Treasury deposits this into its accounts at the Bank. Individuals and firms paying the tax draw from their accounts at commercial banks, and the net consequence of these events is a greater indebtedness of the commercial banks to the Reserve Bank. To make good their loss of funds, the commercial banks have to sell assets to other financial institutions, or to borrow, and this must culminate in some institution(s) obtaining accommodation from the Bank. The converse changes occur when the government spends out of its Reserve Bank accounts; this causes the money-market shortage to fall.

The Reserve Bank, at its own initiative, causes the shortage to change when it buys assets (e.g. Treasury bills) from the private sector or sells assets to the private sector. It is by means of these 'open market operations' and by other methods (details are available in Meijer (1986)) that the Bank counteracts other causes of changes, and is enabled to control the shortage (the volume of accommodation) at some positive level. The rules for granting accommodation and the interest costs are set by the Bank. The interest rates charged extend over a narrow range of about 1 per cent, depending on the type of assets offered for sale to the Bank or as collateral. The lowest rate is known as 'bank rate'.

The effect of these arrangements is that the interest rate in financial markets for 'call funds' (very short-term loans) is approximately equal to bank rate. No institution will borrow at a higher rate when it can freely obtain funds from the Bank; conversely, no institution which is indebted to the Bank at bank rate would be prepared to lend at a lower rate. Given then that bank rate is closely equal to the cost of funds in financial markets, commercial banks are prepared to lend on overdraft at a rate which is sufficiently *above* bank rate to cover risks and transaction costs, and their rates offered for deposits are set at a margin *below* bank rate depending on the type of deposit. In this way, all short-term market interest rates take their lead from bank rate, and longer-term rates are similarly formed in financial markets as an approximate average of expected future short-term rates. Thus, in determining long-term rates, market participants are implicitly forming a view of the Reserve Bank's *reaction* to future expected values of the inflation rate, output, and other variables. If for instance, inflation is expected to rise in the future, then the Bank may be expected to react by raising bank rate, and this general expectation would be reflected by higher current long-term rates than short.

The volume of the shortage (accommodation) does not independently influence the economy. Clients of banks, both borrowers and depositors, make their decisions according to the interest rates charged or offered; they are not influenced by the changing magnitude of inter-institutional debt. Hence the money-market activities of the Reserve Bank all exert their influences via interest rates. The interest rate *is* the only domestic monetary policy instrument.

HOW DOES THE RESERVE BANK CHOOSE THE INTEREST RATE?

In general, reducing the interest rate is stimulatory and raising it is deflationary, although theories differ as to the causal mechanisms. A lower interest rate leads to higher nominal expenditure in the economy than would otherwise have occurred ('nominal' expenditure refers to the rand value of expenditure), but the magnitude of this change in expenditure is unpredictable and follows only after a lag of unknown duration. It is also not known whether the increment in nominal expenditure will reflect rising *real* expenditure (i.e. more goods purchased) or merely a rise in prices, although the division between these two components is supposed to depend on the existing state of unemployment or underemployment of manpower and physical capital. If resources are already 'fully utilised', a lower rate of interest is expected to cause price inflation.

Despite the difficulties of predicting the response to interest rate changes, the following stimulatory effects of a *fall* in interest rates can be identified: (a) it is cheaper for individuals to borrow for the purpose of spending on consumption and investment goods; (b) individuals owning financial assets (lenders) receive a lower return and are therefore inclined to reduce their asset holding by spending; (c) the value of financial assets and real assets like land and machinery rises as the percentage return from such assets moves towards equality with the new lower rate of interest. As an example, a fall in the cost of mortgage finance tends to raise the demand for houses and thereby raises house values. This extra perceived wealth also promotes spending.

Unfortunately, however, the interest rate is not the only causal influence on expenditure, nor probably the strongest. Current expenditure is also influenced, *inter alia*, by past expenditure habits, by expected future interest rates, and expected future political stability. These influences are difficult to quantify, and this is why the response of the economy to interest rate changes is unpredictable.

Not knowing the precise response to its interest rate policy at any time, the Bank has to rely on the feedback of information and on its own judgement (see also Goedhuys, 1982). For instance, if lower inflation is the priority, it is not known to what level the interest rate should be raised, nor for how long this treatment should be applied. In practice the Bank keeps in view a variety of economic variables besides the inflation and growth rates. For example, in line with the precepts of the monetarist school of economic thought, the money supply figures are considered to be important because of their known approximate association with nominal expenditure. Since 1986, this has been formalised by the Reserve Bank's adoption of announced target ranges for the growth rate of one of the reported measures of the money supply (M3). In addition, many other variables such as the volume of bank credit, the rate of unemployment and bankruptcies, the balance of payments and the exchange rate, are all surveyed by the Bank as indicators of the degree of success of its interest rate policy and of possible unwelcome side-effects.

The reaction of the Reserve Bank to these different signals varies over time as it changes its policy stance in the face of changing economic and political pressures. Amongst the Bank's declared objectives, it aims to foster stable high real growth of the economy at the same time as maintaining a stable low rate of inflation. Clearly it is not possible for monetary policy to reduce inflation whilst stimulating demand since these effects would indicate opposite adjustments to the interest rate. In practice, either of these objectives may assume precedence as priorities change from time to time. In 1984, the reduction of inflation was seen as the most important objective and interest rates were accordingly moved to high levels; since 1986, the inflation problem has been put aside in favour of stimulating demand, and rates have accordingly been considerably reduced.

These lower rates have, however, not had the desired effect on demand. Clear evidence of this was the 10,1 per cent growth rate in the money supply (M3) during 1986 as against its target range of 16–20 per cent. It will be argued later that one of the reasons why the target was not achieved is the expectation, based on Reserve Bank announcements and past performance, that a further reversal of policy direction will follow in the near future, i.e. interest rates will be raised again. The general inference may be drawn that when the direction of monetary policy is changed too frequently, this aggravates the difficulty of effective use of the policy.

MONETARY POLICY DURING THE 1970s: THE LIQUID ASSET SYSTEM

During the 1970s, interest rates were held generally low, often below the prevailing rate of inflation. Inflation was seen as a significant problem from about

1973 onwards, but relatively little importance was attached to the interest rate as a corrective tool (De Kock Commission, 1985: 147). The purpose of this section is to describe some direct controls which were used in this period in the attempt to contain inflation, and to argue that these controls were largely ineffective.

Part of the reason for the interest rate patterns of the 1970s was the mistaken notion of the authorities that the level of interest rates could be market-determined. As has been demonstrated above, under a positive money-market shortage, market rates adjust to approximate equality with the Reserve Bank's accommodation rates, yet in the period 1973–1983, the Bank's self-imposed operating rules tied their accommodation rates (e.g. bank rate) at a margin above rates which had existed in the market in the previous week. This led to indeterminacy as market rates were following accommodation rates which were, in turn, following market rates. The observed result of these rules was that, at times of money-market shortage, rates 'ratchetted' upwards (De Kock Commission, 1985: 214); at other times, the shortage was allowed to fall to zero and rates fell to very low levels (see Fig. 1). As one example, in 1979 short-term market rates moved down to about 4,5 per cent whilst inflation was running at some 14 per cent. The fall in the shortage (or rise in 'liquidity') in this case arose because the Reserve Bank was buying foreign assets in order to hold down the foreign exchange value of the rand under a high gold price. In fact, it was entirely within the power of the Bank to prevent this occurrence. It could have allowed the rand to appreciate further, or it could have re-established the shortage by open market sales of bonds or by other means, or it could have offered interest on excess reserves thus absorbing the liquidity.

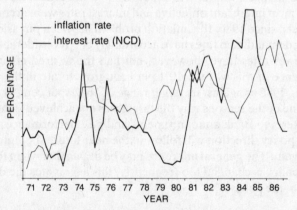

Figure 1 THE SHORT-TERM INTEREST RATE AND THE INFLATION RATE

The action of the authorities during the 1970s and early 1980s to curb inflation amounted to the imposition of a number of measures other than raising the interest rate. Notable amongst these regulatory measures were periodic quantitative limits on bank credit (credit ceilings) and liquid asset requirements. Under these requirements, banks must hold particular assets defined as 'liquid', such as Treasury bills or bills or stocks of the Land Bank, as a specified minimum proportion of deposits. The supposition was that the limited supply and/or low yields of these assets classified as 'liquid' would serve to curtail bank lending and money growth.

As is acknowledged (De Kock Commission, 1985: 221), the outcome from applying credit ceilings and liquid asset regulations was 'disintermediation'. The service which banks perform is to 'intermediate' between borrowers and lenders (depositors). If banks are forced to use some of their deposits to buy low-yielding statutory liquid assets, then this causes them to offer lower interest for deposits and to charge more to borrowers of that portion of deposits which remains after satisfying the regulations. Liquid asset regulations thus render banks' intermediation services more expensive, whilst credit ceilings directly inhibit these services. This provides opportunities for intermediation by other agents who are not constrained in the same way as banks; alternatively, deals can be arranged directly between borrower and lender. With such 'disintermediation', lending activity therefore continues largely as before and there is little impact on inflation. However, since only bank-mediated deals are included in the official money supply figures, the control techniques succeed in reducing *measured* money supply growth, and thus appear to have worked. Evidence consistent with the occurrence of disintermediation in the late 1970s was the rise in the velocity of circulation of money (i.e. nominal output divided by money supply) and its subsequent decline as the direct controls were relaxed. The peak rate of growth of 42 per cent recorded for the M2 measure of money supply in April 1981 can be attributed to reintermediation associated with the decline in velocity.

THE PROVISION OF CHEAP FINANCE VIA THE LAND BANK

By having its liabilities officially labelled as 'liquid' the Land Bank could obtain funds and grant loans at rates below those ruling in the market. The liquid asset system thus seemed to be a costless way to subsidise farmers, a group deemed worthy of such assistance, besides seeming to aid monetary control. In fact, as explained above, the cost of these subsidies was borne by the other customers of the banking system in terms of higher charges for overdrafts and lower interest received on deposits. The consequences would have been identical if the subsidies had been financed by a tax on banking activity rather than by the liquid asset regulations.

The effects on the agricultural sector of this cheap finance are well known. In general, the relative value of farm property rose, and capital expenditure was undertaken which otherwise would not have been viable, and which became unviable when the cost of finance was later brought closer to prevailing market rates. The consequent distress then brought forth pressure for further assistance.

Three important general points have been illustrated by the foregoing example:

(a) monetary policy is not an appropriate channel for redistribution by using regulations which provide for differential costs of finance between favoured and non-favoured groups;
(b) when some group receives financial assistance, unless it is understood that the assistance is only for some finite term, the distress at the future termination of assistance should be anticipated, or otherwise it must be expected that the assistance will continue indefinitely at whatever cost is required;
(c) the budget constraint applies; if one group receives subsidised loans, then some other group is paying for them.

The direct methods of monetary control have now been discredited and curtailed; credit ceilings have been dismantled and liquid asset requirements significantly reduced. The 'market-oriented' principles of the De Kock Commission are an admission that these direct methods were a failure; the Commission acknowledged and condoned the Reserve Bank's use of the short-term interest rate as the control instrument but expressed general dislike for regulatory interference in financial markets.

WHY NOT CONTROL THE MONEY SUPPLY?

Before criticising the authorities' recent interest rate policy, and before assessing the scope for future policy, it is appropriate briefly to address the issue of *why* the control is exercised via the interest rate. Why does the Reserve Bank not directly control the money supply instead?

According to orthodox theory, the money supply is, or can be, controlled by the Central Bank's choice of the money base, using the empirically reliable 'money multiplier' relationship between these two variables. The notion that it *should* be controlled in this way is sometimes associated with 'monetarist' economic theory. However, since accommodation is a component of the money base, such a system would require that accommodation be quantitatively limited. This implies that the Central Bank's 'discount window' would be closed, or open only to the extent of allowing truly 'last resort' assistance to banks when they are potentially unable to meet demands for withdrawals of deposits. The difficulty is that this would require continual judgement of the circumstances under which 'last resort' lending should be granted.

If access to accommodation is withheld totally, there is always a finite probability of banks as a whole becoming unable to supply cash on demand, not necessarily as a result of imprudent business, but, for instance, because of unexpected net withdrawals of deposits as currency. This implies that some limited access to accommodation is essential. On the other hand, as soon as it is known that some accommodation is available, profit-maximising banks will accordingly adjust their portfolios to take advantage of this. In the end the arrangements become the same as the existing South African system in which the interest cost of accommodation is the instrumental variable.

When these arguments are extended, it can be convincingly demonstrated (see e.g. Goodhart, 1984) that money base control is unworkable. Control of the money supply by means of the money base has been rejected by the De Kock Commission (1985: 177) and is not practised, so far as is known, by Central Banks anywhere. Control by means of the interest rate instrument is then the only option; moreover, as has been shown, this method cannot usefully be supplemented by the types of direct control which were used in South Africa during the 1970s.

THE SCOPE FOR DOMESTIC MONETARY POLICY

We have found, in broad agreement with the De Kock Commission, that the only instrument available for domestic monetary policy is the interest rate. The present low rates of interest (e.g. prime rate at 12,5 per cent as against inflation (CPI) of 16,8 per cent), are consistent with the current aim of encouraging higher growth, the problem of inflation having assumed a lesser priority.

The question therefore arises as to why bank credit (and hence money supply) is not growing faster. Why are individuals and firms not borrowing heavily at the cheap rates available in order to raise consumption expenditure and investment? The reason for this is apparent from the level of longer-term interest rates. At present, long-term rates are considerably higher than short, indicating that short-term rates are expected to rise in the future. If and when higher growth and some confidence return the monetary authorities will be expected to raise short-term rates in order to resume their attack on inflation. Potential borrowers are consequently reluctant to commit themselves to debt since the current low costs of finance are not expected to be maintained. If, on the other hand, business conditions remain depressed or become worse, then potential returns to investment will not be forthcoming and borrowers will be less able to service their debts. This combination of (a) expected higher costs of borrowing and/or (b) the low level of expected returns from investment, is sufficient to dissuade individuals and firms from incurring more debt. It is clear that monetary policy has little to offer to solve the current problems. Even if bank rate were reduced close to zero, it is doubtful whether this would cause any significant improvement in aggregate expenditure.

A symmetrically opposite position occurred during 1983–1984 when credit growth (and money supply growth) continued to rise in the face of high and rising interest rates. Among the reasons advanced for this perverse response of credit was 'distress' borrowing by firms with large unsold inventories and by others with various accumulated debt obligations, who now needed extra finance to support higher interest payments. Moreover, at the time, longer-term rates were lower than short, and thus short-term rates were expected to fall, discouraging individuals from liquidating their debts disadvantageously.

With hindsight, the high rates during 1983–1985 (prime overdraft rate peaked at 25 per cent in August 1984) may be seen to have been unnecessarily severe. Perhaps too much significance was attached to the rapid growth at that time of the money supply figures since this growth rate was then exaggerated by reintermediation. The monetary authorities were however faced with chronic inflation which was partially attributable to the spending and borrowing habits cultivated by the low interest rates during 1977–1980 (see Figure 1). Moreover, in the early 1980s the authorities were progressively moving away from direct control techniques under the realisation that raising the interest rate was a better method for containing the growth of money supply, credit and inflation. When these variables failed to respond in the desired way, the authorities were faced with a problem of credibility. In their determination to see the success of their high interest rate policy, the authorities may well have paid too little attention to the generally depressing effects of this policy. As it happened, any benefits from this policy turned out to be short-lived, since inflation has subsequently continued at a high level as a result of the fall in the foreign exchange value of the rand. With the hard experience of high interest rates during 1984–1985 still fresh in memory, it is not surprising that there is a reluctance by individuals and firms to incur debt at the present time.

These recent events emphasise some of the difficulties of using the interest rate instrument, and lend support to those economic theorists who question the usefulness of attempts to apply countercyclical monetary policy. As observed above, there is no objective method by which the authorities are able to judge with any precision which path of interest rates is consistent with their goals. Yet the recent experience overseas is that appropriate interest rate policy has been able to reduce the inflation rate (e.g. in Britain), and to maintain it at low levels (e.g. in Germany), when these goals have been consistently accorded priority. In the case of South Africa, however, it may be argued that such a single-minded approach is politically unfeasible. Control of inflation must, from time to time, imply upward adjustments to the interest rate, and raising the interest rate is always unpopular since it causes discomfort for borrowers and inhibits economic growth.

These points suggest that the poor record of inflation control in South Africa is not a result of any inherent weakness in the system of control via interest rates, but rather because the use of the interest rate instrument has not been consistent. This assertion is well illustrated by the recent large changes in the *real* interest rate (i.e. the difference between the actual or nominal interest rate and the inflation rate: a measure of the real cost of borrowing money). In 1980 the real interest rate was about –9 per cent (as may be derived from Figure 1). As already discussed, this was due to foreign asset inflows whilst reliance was placed on the liquid asset system of control. The sharp rise to about 0 per cent in 1981 and the subsequent advance to +10 per cent during 1983–1984 signalled the change in technique; the interest rate was now being used with determination to combat inflation. The subsequent fall to about –8 per cent in 1986 was the result of the shift in objective, from reducing inflation to stimulating demand.

If the monetary authorities henceforth were to use their interest rate instrument exclusively for the purpose of holding a low steady rate of inflation, then this objective should be achievable and one important source of economic uncertainty would be removed. If, on the other hand, they continue to pay attention to a multiplicity of goals, or if the direct controls of the 1970s are resurrected, it is unlikely that the achieved results with respect to any goal will be satisfactory.

CONCLUSION

There is little doubt that a major cause of the current depressed economic conditions is political uncertainty, and that a restoration of perceived future stability is an important priority. The outflow of foreign capital, whilst contributing to the low level of expenditure via the weak foreign exchange value of the rand and consequent higher price level of imports, is one symptom of this uncertainty and not its cause.

Against that background, this paper has found that domestic monetary policy is largely impotent as a means of alleviating the current economic difficulties. It has, moreover, been argued that the main responsibility of the monetary authority should always be to use its interest rate instrument to maintain a stable purchasing power for its currency; it should therefore be generally insulated from pressure which would cause deviations from this responsibility. If monetary policy is diverted towards providing a temporary stimulus by means of lower interest rates, the cost of this must be future inflation, or else the stimulus will later have to be reversed in order to forestall inflation.

The other observation, made above in the context of monetary policy techniques of the 1970s, is that the monetary authority is not the appropriate agent for undertaking redistribution. It is not possible for the Reserve Bank, somehow without cost, to procure subsidised finance for some favoured group, and attempts to do so interfere with the proper conduct of monetary policy. Any subsidies or transfer payments which are deemed desirable should rather be financed via the Treasury in the usual way.

In view of these negative conclusions, let us comment briefly on the possibility of relieving the current recession by *fiscal* stimulus, as the other arm of macroeconomic policy. If the private sector is reluctant to borrow and spend because of uncertainty, the government can take the initiative. The task then becomes that of assessing what patterns of further expenditure would provide the greatest advantages. The wisdom or otherwise of deficit financing (state expenditure not matched by revenue) should also be brought into consideration.

Government has, of course, already taken fiscal action by allocating further expenditure specifically for job creation. Whilst this policy may have its merits, surely greater benefit would follow from the *reduction of non-productive state expenditure*. If the government could, for instance, reduce the costs of maintaining the new parliamentary arrangements and the homelands policies along with their associated bureaucratic structures, then taxation could be reduced to help restore the incentives for investment and consumption expenditure.

REFERENCES

De Kock Commission, 1985. 'The Commission of Inquiry into the Monetary System and Monetary Policy in South Africa'. Government Printer, Pretoria, RP 70/1984.

Goedhuys, D.W., 1982. 'Monetary Policy and the Flow of Spending'. *South African Journal of Economics*, Vol. 50, No. 2, 195–207.

Goodhart, C.A.E., 1984. *Monetary Theory and Practice*. London: Macmillan, Ch 7, reprinted from the Bank of England *Quarterly Bulletin*, Vol. 19, No. 2, 1979, 144–159.

Meijer, J.H., 1986. 'Monetary Policy and the Instruments of Monetary Policy', pp. 450–507 in Falkena *et al.* (eds). *The Mechanics of the South African Financial System*, 2nd ed. Johannesburg: Macmillan.

Whittaker, J. and A.J. Theunissen, 1987. 'Why Does the Reserve Bank Set the Interest Rate?' *South African Journal of Economics,* Vol. 55, No. 1, 16–33.

4.7 MONETARISM AND THE SOUTH AFRICAN CRISIS

Duncan Innes*

The monetarist economic policies adopted by the South African government in the early 1980s were intended to combat the destructive pattern of short, unstable upswings and increasingly severe recessions which had bedevilled the economy since the early 1970s. However, during the turbulent course of 1984–85, these policies have failed disastrously. Rather than depressing inflation and gearing the economy for a sound and sustained upswing, the particularly severe austerity measures introduced towards the end of 1984 led South Africa into a debt crisis. This was exacerbated by the political conflict that arose in part as a response to the official decision to drive the economy into recession. The two disastrous drops in the value of the rand, in November 1984 and again in August 1985, intensified constraints on economic growth and rendered futile the major object of the monetarist exercise by contributing to 1985 inflation levels as high or higher than those in 1984. South African monetarist policies have exacted a high price in political instability and, partly as a consequence, have failed to attain their economic objectives. The economic outlook in the last quarter of 1985 was bleaker than it had been a year earlier.

THE MEASURES OF 1984

During 1984, South Africa's financial authorities faced a number of problems. The fall in the dollar price of gold was eroding state revenues. Together with unbridled consumer spending, the falling gold price fuelled a dangerously high deficit on the current account of the balance of payments, which had reached R2,86 billion in the first quarter of 1984. This deficit was undermining investor confidence, inhibiting imports and rendering it difficult to pay for borrowing which would be needed in due course for the economy to reflate.

The monetarist response focused on inflation and the balance of payments deficit as the two primary evils to be righted in order to gear the economy for sound growth in the long term. Attention was focused on South Africa's rapidly growing state expenditure, which rose from 22 per cent of the gross domestic product in 1981 to 29 per cent in 1984, and which was highly inflationary. Cutting state expenditure and raising interest rates to unprecedented heights, it was argued, would cure both evils. South African interest rates were already almost double those of the United States, at a time when American interest rates were regarded as excessively high. Following the abandonment of exchange controls on foreign investors in 1983, high domestic interest rates were

* Professor of Sociology, University of the Witwatersrand. This article was first published in S.A. Research Service (SARS), *S.A. Review III*. Johannesburg: Ravan Press, 1986.

needed to prevent foreign investors exporting capital to take advantage of the high profits on investment available in the United States.

In August 1984, the Reserve Bank raised its discount rate steeply, with the result that the crucial prime lending rate rose to 25 per cent. Bond rates also climbed, with Barclays' rate hitting 26 per cent, and the rate of interest on hire purchase agreements soared to 32 per cent. As planned, the immediate consequence was to drive the economy into recession. The high cost of credit caused consumer spending to drop sharply and inhibited company borrowing. Thus both the drop in consumer demand and the reduction in company spending placed producers under pressure to cut back on expansion plans and to contract production.

High interest rates also necessitated cuts in state and parastatal expenditure. Since the South African state is the country's largest single consumer of goods and services, these cuts affected a number of sectors. Civil engineering and heavy industrial companies saw immediate contraction of demand. Sales and development in the property sector also fell because of the prohibitive bond rates, and the construction industry was hard hit. Unemployment began to rise.

THE RECESSION TAKES EFFECT

An important consequence of the August austerity measures — one that within a year was to have unforeseen and disastrous effects — was the sharp increase in South African borrowing abroad. Because interest rates in South Africa were so high, it was logical for banks, businesses and the state itself to borrow in the US and Europe, where interest rates stood at about 11 per cent.

South Africa's debt burden, already high, rose sharply. As a percentage of the gross domestic product, foreign debt rose to 26,8 per cent by the end of 1984, compared with 8,4 per cent in 1980. Similarly, by the end of 1984, the country's debt was equivalent to 94 per cent of the value of its exports, compared with 23 per cent in 1980. Thus following the August rise in interest rates, outstanding foreign bank credit rose perilously close to equalling the country's total export income. Still worse, much of this spate of borrowing was short term, and would fall due within a year.

The surge in foreign indebtedness after August 1984 combined with the strong dollar on international currency markets to cause the rand's first dramatic drop in November 1984. The South African Reserve Bank deliberately refrained from supporting the rand, allowing it to fall to approximately $0,50. The official attitude was that a sharp drop in the value of the rand relative to the dollar would be the equivalent of a devaluation. This would make imports more expensive, but income from South Africa's predominantly mineral exports would double in rand terms, while its manufactured products would be cheaper and more competitive in foreign markets. As a consequence, the balance of payments deficit would begin to right itself.

At the same time, however, those banks, companies and state institutions which had borrowed overseas found their debt and service charges doubled. Despite this, the current account of the balance of payments began to move into surplus as consumer and industrial expenditure on imports dropped. For most of 1985, the current account of the BoP has been running at an average surplus of R400m per month.

In time, the growing surplus enabled the Reserve Bank to begin bringing down interest rates after July 1985, mitigating the extreme recessionary effects of the August package. The prime rate, for example, fell from 25 per cent to 18,5 per cent in October 1985. But while a 6,5 per cent drop sounds impressive and had lightened some of the debt servicing costs which companies faced, interest rates still remained far too high to stimulate growth, and remained much higher than those overseas.

On closer inspection, too, the BoP surplus did not indicate the degree of economic health that Finance Department officials repeatedly asserted. The improved export revenue did not reflect a strong rise in exports, but was simply a result of the fall in the rand. Much of the income was from mining revenues that were now worth more in rand terms. The increased export revenue therefore did not indicate that a strong economic foundation was being laid for future growth.

This is disturbing, as one of the South African economy's most serious weaknesses is the failure of its manufactured goods to compete internationally. Only substantial improvements in productivity can achieve this over the long term, laying the basis for a sustained economic recovery. Without such a productivity rise, economic upswings are likely to be short-term affairs.

The surplus on the current account of the balance of payments concealed another drawback: most of it was going to service foreign debt. Month by month during 1985, much of the income was spent on interest payments due on established debt, whereas the intended purpose of the surplus was ultimately to finance new borrowing to generate a phase of economic growth. In addition, continued political instability, combined with the contraction of economic demand, caused foreign-owned companies in South Africa to remit increased dividends to their parent companies rather than reinvesting their profits to the same extent as before. Like the debt repayments and service charges, such remittances served to reduce the surplus on the current account.

STATE EXPENDITURE AND INFLATION

Despite a number of declarations of intent, state expenditure failed to fall. After mid-1985, the government had some success: while fiscal spending continued to rise, its *rate* of increase had eased somewhat. In July 1985 government spending was 38 per cent higher than in July 1984, while the figure for August was merely 21 per cent higher than the equivalent month in 1984. Overall, after the first four months of the 1985 financial year, fiscal spending was R850 million over budget. However, 1985 tax revenue rose sharply to a level 34 per cent higher than in 1984. This was probably due to increased revenue from the mining sector, which has been earning record profits due to the low value of the rand.

While the falling rate of increase in government spending coupled with increased tax revenue may well ease the fiscal crisis, the fact remains that the government appears committed to continuously rising expenditure. State commitment to high expenditure on its repressive apparatuses of defence and police is inflexible, and has risen with the tide of unrest in the course of 1985. High expenditure on black education, industrial decentralisation programmes and small business development is dictated by the government's perception that these programmes are crucial to the long-term political and economic restructuring of South Africa's social relations. Similarly, 'homeland development', agricultural subsidies, and sheltered employment for a large white bureaucracy are each in its way regarded as essential for political stability.

Added to this are the cost of financing the state of emergency; the cost of escalating military adventurism beyond South Africa's borders; and the rising cost of servicing the foreign debt, given the rand's failure to recover against other currencies. Faced with these increases in expenditure, the rise in tax revenue is unlikely to resolve the fiscal problem.

Ironically, but not surprisingly, the state's record in reducing inflation — the central object of the austerity exercise — is unambiguously negative. Rising state expenditure, coupled with the monetarist commitment to reduce or withdraw subsidies on basic goods such as maize and bread, continued to put upward pressure on the inflation rate, as did the cheap rand. And just when South Africans were told that the inflation rate had peaked at 16,9 per cent at the end of August 1985, the rand fell below $0,35. Unless the rand recovers from its current low levels (below $0,40) the inflation rate is highly unlikely to come down in the immediate future. In fact, with the recent price increases in petrol, bread and parastatal tariffs still to feed through the system, it is possible that inflation could rise further. There is an additional danger that governmental attempts to reflate the economy may well be inflationary. The 10 per cent import surcharge already imposed is a case in point. Should there also be a substantial rise in fiscal spending the possibility of hyperinflation cannot be ruled out.

DAMAGE TO THE INDUSTRIAL BASE

In the course of 1985 not only has the state's monetarist policy failed in its stated aims, but it has seriously damaged South Africa's industrial base. The government's means of 'eliminating excessive demand' have put crushing pressure on industrial and commercial capital, as well as on the labour force: African unemployment is now estimated at around 25 per cent of the economically active population. Between August 1984 and June 1985, white, coloured and Indian unemployment doubled (from 30 000 to 69 691). For the first five months of

1985, insolvencies (at 1 123) were 105 per cent higher than for the corresponding period in 1984, when the recession was already under way. And in the first six months of 1985, company liquidations (at 1 581) were 27 per cent higher than for the last six months of 1984.

Nor is it just smaller concerns which have been battered by the monetarist onslaught. Virtually every major industrial and commercial company has suffered losses over the past year, arising from the drop in income following the contraction of demand, combined with doubled foreign debt obligations due to the fall in the rand. The near-collapse of the Kirsh group, which in 1985 was seventeenth in the *Financial Mail's* list of Top 100 Companies, is a case in point. Only a rescue operation by Sanlam, involving a cash injection of R190m, could salvage the group. Even Gencor incurred huge losses in its industrial division, in which four companies alone lost over R54m. Only Gencor's massive mining profits (up by 58 per cent in six months) enabled the group to declare a profit. South Africa's most successful automobile manufacturer, Toyota, which declared pre-tax profits of R23m in the second half of 1984, produced a R9m rand loss in the first six months of 1985, mainly as a result of the fact that the new car market has collapsed by one-third since 1981 (from 300 000 units sold per year to 200 000).

Economic pressures on companies also contributed to the build-up of foreign debt. Companies were forced into ever greater borrowing to stave off collapse, but because of exorbitantly high local interest rates began borrowing more abroad. As the value of the rand fell against other currencies, so borrowers found it increasingly difficult to meet repayment obligations. The present foreign debt crisis is an outgrowth of monetarist policies.

If allowed to continue, such policies may well begin to destroy South Africa's industrial base. An important indicator of the effects of economic attrition is the physical asset-stripping forced upon cash-short companies. Operating well below capacity, some companies have resorted to selling equipment abroad. In the course of 1985 the civil engineering industry, for example, has been exporting its assets at the rate of more than R100m worth monthly. While such asset-stripping might well serve to generate cash from unused equipment in the short term, it poses serious problems for the future. Should the economy begin to pull out of recession, producers who have sold off equipment will find replacement extremely expensive. For example, a unit of capital equipment used in the cement industry which cost R1m in 1984, cost almost R8m rand a year later. Such asset-stripping and gearing-down, a product of the monetarist-induced recession, means that future industrial expansion will face serious hindrances.

IMPEDIMENTS TO SOCIAL RESTRUCTURING

Until the middle of 1985, business interests supported the austerity package, despite its high toll. Most business spokesmen saw the recession as a period of economic restructuring that would remove the drag of high inflation, thereby preparing the economy for a more sustained upswing. The austerity measures were presented, and endured, as the economic component of a process of social restructuring. The other crucial part of this was of course a successful process of political reform. Such reform would mean that South Africa was beginning to conform to at least some of the characteristics of a capitalist democracy, thereby moving towards long-term social stability.

However, as the effects of the recession began to intensify from the beginning of 1985, unemployment rose ominously in the context of unabated inflation. Elsewhere we have argued that: 'The major priority of the state and leading business sectors is to carry through these (monetarist) restructuring policies. To do this, they have to inflict severe damage on various social groups, especially workers and the poor in general.'[1] The escalation of social unrest in the course of 1985 indicated that these 'social groups' were not prepared to take this lying down.

By the middle of 1985, it seemed that the process of restructuring was threatened by the government's inability to put forward and implement political reforms that would gain it widespread legitimacy, thereby defusing the mounting unrest. In view of South Africa's high degree of dependence on foreign trade, investment and finance, business leaders were becoming concerned about foreign perceptions of South Africa as a high-risk banana state. Such concern was fuelled by the increasingly successful and respectable disinvestment campaign, especially in the United States.

But the official view was still optimistic. In July 1985, the governor of the Reserve Bank, Gerhard de Kock, still bubbled with enthusiasm for the success of the official policy: 'Prosperity and growth for all sectors of the population could be expected next year,' he said, adding that 'the country's painful austerity measures were pulling the economy back into line'.

He admitted that allowing the prime rate to rise from 14 per cent to 25 per cent to prevent the economy from overheating had been an unpopular move which had damaged industry, had a recessionary influence, and, through its effect on unemployment, had contributed to the current unrest, but he stated emphatically that 'it had been necessary and it had worked'. The improvements on the economic front 'would bring good times for all in 1986'.

In fact, South Africa was in an extremely vulnerable position economically. Its high degree of foreign indebtedness, and especially the extremely high proportion of short-term debt (66 per cent of the total debt burden, compared with a more normal 44 per cent in Western industrialised countries) rendered South Africa doubly vulnerable to the loss of international financial confidence following political instability.

Under these circumstances, the declaration of the state of emergency in July might well appear inexplicable. Perhaps it may best be explained as an attempt on the part of the state to smash its way out of the vicious circle in which it was trapped by decisive, confident action. The official view was best summed up by the director-general of finance, Chris Stals, who, in one of his less intelligent predictions, argued that the emergency would be viewed positively by those abroad.

Business interests represented by the Federated Chamber of Industries, the Association of Chambers of Commerce, the Afrikaanse Handelsinstituut and other institutions cautiously welcomed the emergency, evidently believing that the 'reimposition of law and order' would precede the announcement of far-reaching political reforms. The joint statement by Assocom and the FCI, issued shortly after the emergency was declared, emphasised that repression must be accompanied by reform: 'The business community has been greatly concerned at the escalating violence in South Africa and acknowledges the need to re-establish law and order in certain areas ... However, organised commerce and industry also believe that security action alone will not resolve the serious conflict in black townships. To be effective, the restoration of law and order must be backed by a package of substantial reforms, to recognise black aspirations and to redress legitimate grievances.' Evidently foreign financial interests shared this view.

This hope, on the part of investors, foreign banks and local business interests, was decisively killed by President P W Botha in his notorious mid-August 'Rubicon' speech. It became obvious that the government's commitment to major reform — the political aspect of restructuring — was half-hearted, to say the least. An end to political instability was not in sight.

THE POST-RUBICON CRISIS

In the wake of Botha's speech, the rand, which had clawed its way up to $0,50, began to fall again. Prospects for repayment, and even for servicing, the foreign debt diminished as the rand fell. Rumours began to circulate that US bankers would refuse to roll over, or extend the repayment date of, the billions of dollars of short-term debt that would fall due in the coming months. And so it proved. At the beginning of September, US banks led the move to call in much of South Africa's foreign debt, estimated at about $24 billion or some R55 billion. This was no less than a massive vote of no confidence in Botha's political policy and led to the immediate collapse of the rand, which fell to $0,35.

In the face of this financial crisis, the government was forced to act: the Minister of Finance announced a package of far-reaching financial measures. First, trade on the Johannesburg Stock Exchange was briefly suspended so as to prevent foreign investors moving capital out of the country through the sale of shares. A few days later the financial rand was reintroduced to impede repatriation of foreign capital. A four-month moratorium on SA's foreign debt repayments was declared, to allow officials to negotiate terms of repayment. Significantly, these moves represented a complete reversal of previous monetarist policies aimed at introducing a 'free market' in financial and exchange markets.

In fact, it was only in 1983, as part of the monetarist programme, that the financial rand had been abolished. Now it was back, playing its original role of hampering the flight of foreign capital from the country. Foreign investors are obliged to buy foreign currencies through the financial rand system. Since the value of the financial rand is quoted at a discount to the commercial or ordinary rand, foreign investors must pay more and therefore take a loss if they want to move capital out of the country. Conversely, because the financial rand is cheaper than the ordinary rand, foreign would-be investors are theoretically encouraged to buy in.

The foreign debt crisis, and the intransigence on reform that sparked it, spurred local business leaders onto the offensive — this time in open confrontation with the government. Organised commerce and industry began expressing anti-government views and making more strident calls for reform, even taking their case to the United Nations where they openly denounced apartheid. *Business Day* called for P W Botha's resignation, and then for the resignation of the whole government. Leading Afrikaner businessmen like Louis Luyt and Anton Rupert, who had previously not spoken out, now joined the chorus of criticism, while Gavin Relly and other business leaders flew to Lusaka to consult with the ANC. Overall, local business interests were making plain their disillusionment with the government's capacity to carry through the necessary political restructuring.

The government itself did not remain immune from these pressures. The Minister of Law and Order, Louis le Grange, indicated that the state would not further escalate physical repression, while P W Botha committed himself in principle to single citizenship and a universal franchise in South Africa. As usual, though, it was too little, too late, and government equivocation on precisely how these changes would be implemented did little to increase confidence.

On the economic front, the Minister of Finance announced a package of measures designed to encourage economic reflation. These measures — especially the increase of fiscal spending to ease the unemployment crisis and a 10 per cent surcharge on imports to finance it — represent a reversion to Keynesian reflationary tactics and are a further rejection of monetarism. But the government's economic turnaround has not won it many friends. Christie Kuun, vice-president of the AHI, pointed out that government steps to stimulate the economy could lead to runaway inflation and the decline of the surplus on the current account of the balance of payments. This would choke off economic revival before it activated employment to any meaningful extent. 'Political expediency,' Kuun argued, 'rather than sound economic considerations, appears to have led to the announcement of these steps.'

Kuun has correctly identified one side of the double bind or vicious circle the state finds itself in. Abandoning monetarism and reflating the economy cannot produce a sustained upswing, since the fundamental restructuring of social relations which monetarist policy aimed at has not been completed. Yet if

216

monetarist policy is continued and the economy allowed to remain in recession, political unrest will intensify, and foreign confidence in South Africa's prospects will diminish further. As unemployment rises and industry runs down, foreign investors in the country will double their efforts to withdraw and the government's political support will be further eroded, even among its own constituency.

The government finds itself pushed increasingly into a corner as the vicious circle tightens. Monetarism, after all, is not merely a technical economic theory, but, as we have argued before, it is also a broader theory aimed at achieving 'a major change in the balance of power and a restructuring of the system of production'. So far, the government has failed to achieve these broader goals in South Africa. Faced with intense local resistance, increasing overseas pressure and growing division in its ranks, the government now finds itself on the defensive, to a large extent because it failed adequately to calculate the social consequences of its monetarist programme. It is now reversing many of the policies it introduced earlier. As Kuun puts it: 'This type of action indicates a lack of positive economic strategy.'

The outlook for the economy is bleak: new foreign investment on any scale is out of the question while confidence in the country's future is low. As a result of the debt crisis, South Africa will find it very hard to borrow, both because its international credit rating is damaged, and because the cost of its existing debt is almost prohibitive. As a result, financing an upswing will be a major problem. Further, with the foreign debt crisis restricting South Africa's capacity to borrow abroad, any attempt at reflation via increased fiscal spending may well put upward pressure on domestic interest rates as local borrowing would increase. This would inevitably impede reflation.

The only glimmer of hope for the government is that the dollar price of gold will rise. This could occur in response to a substantial fall in the value of the US dollar against other currencies, an international debt crisis, a resurgence of international inflation or a major international political crisis. A rise in income from gold could bring temporary relief from some of the serious economic pressures South Africa faces and lead to an economic upswing. But on its own, such relief will be at best only temporary.

CONCLUSION

The South African government's fling with monetarism has, it appears, left the country's economy facing worse prospects of combined high inflation and economic stagnation than it did a year ago. And this time it faces them with a weakened industrial base, an increasingly politicised labour force and a crippled currency.

Even if the catalytic political events of the past year had not had such an extreme impact, South African monetarism was unlikely to succeed. Unlike the far larger and more complex economies of the US and capitalist West, South

Africa has an open economy: its imports and exports of capital and commodities have a far greater relative impact on the total economy. Hence the massive effects of the depreciation of the rand on its industrial base, which is not as resilient as that of the US or even of Britain. The South African economy — with its low productivity, dependence on mineral exports, competitive weakness in manufactured exports, and its reliance on imports of capital goods — was far more vulnerable than its policy-makers realised.

Then, too, industrialised Western nations have a welfare system that enables them to blunt the effects of unemployment on their populations. Equally, they have a far higher degree of popular political legitimacy. While unable to avoid some of the violent consequences of monetarist recession and repression, they are able to contain them. South Africa, with its more vulnerable economy, its absence of a welfare safety net, and its oppressive racial policies, cannot.

NOTE

1 Stephen Gelb and Duncan Innes, 'Economic crisis in South Africa: monetarism's double bind', *Work in Progress, 36*, April 1985, 39.

5

Balance of Payments and Exchange Rate Policy

5.1 INTRODUCTION

The South African economy does not exist in a vacuum. It trades extensively with other nations and cannot expect to achieve rapid growth without an inflow of capital and skilled labour from abroad. All foreign transactions in a given year are recorded in the balance of payments, which is published in the *Quarterly Bulletin* of the South African Reserve Bank. Broadly speaking, the balance of payments is divided into a current or trading account in which the country's exports and imports of goods and services are included, and a capital account which keeps track of short- and long-term capital movements between South Africa and the rest of the world. The balance of payments is said to be in equilibrium when the stock of gold and foreign exchange remains unchanged, or when a current account deficit (or surplus) is matched by a net inflow (or outflow) of foreign capital. In the absence of such capital movements, however, the deficit (surplus) on current account must be counterbalanced by a corresponding decrease (increase) in the gold and foreign exchange reserves of the central bank. The state of the country's balance of payments is perhaps best reflected in the so-called *basic balance*, which requires that an excess of imports over exports must be matched by a net inflow of long-term rather than short-term capital. This is considered to be a more sustainable way of maintaining a current account deficit.

In a free market system with perfect capital mobility, there is a natural tendency for the stock of gold and foreign exchange to remain more or less unchanged. During periods of economic upswing when imports tend to exceed exports, the accompanying deficits on the current account are likely to be matched by a net inflow of foreign capital prompted by rising interest rates in the domestic money and capital markets. Conversely, a current account surplus can be expected to offset the outflow of capital resulting from a recessionary decline in domestic interest rates. Balance of payments equilibrium is therefore more or less assured in the long run, leaving the authorities free to pursue their domestic goals by means of conventional monetary and fiscal policies.

From a macroeconomic standpoint, the openness of the South African economy renders it particularly vulnerable to changes in the world economy. A sudden decrease in the gold price, for example, will lower our export earnings and thwart any attempt by the authorities to boost the domestic economy during a severe recession. Likewise, speculative increases in the gold price will have the opposite effect on the domestic economy during a period of inflationary price rises. To counter such disturbances, the authorities must either maintain a fixed exchange rate, in which case a stronger dose of monetary and fiscal policy may be required, or adopt a free exchange rate and allow the rand to find its own equilibrium value on the foreign exchange markets.

Free exchange rates provide an automatic means of stabilising the economy in the face of outside disturbances. In the example of a drop in the gold price, the resultant decrease in the supply of foreign currency will induce a depreciation of the rand and an increase in the rand value of our exports and imports, thus partly forestalling a prolonged recession. Such adjustments in the exchange rate may therefore help to limit the destabilising effects of exogenous changes on the domestic economy. Despite its theoretical appeal, however, a free exchange rate does tend to be at the mercy of unscrupulous speculators capable of manipulating it to the detriment of local exporters and importers. On the other hand, a fixed exchange rate renders the economy vulnerable to unforeseen disturbances and places an inordinate burden on domestic policy-makers. It is largely for these reasons that most countries have adopted a system of managed floating, in order to spread the burden of adjustment between the exchange rate and domestic monetary and fiscal policies.

Some of these issues are discussed at greater length in the first three readings included in this chapter. The first paper, by De Kock, explains how recent changes in the gold price have affected the rand exchange rate and the domestic economy, and identifies several ways in which the Reserve Bank can intervene to smooth out excessive fluctuations in the exchange rate. Shuttleworth's paper deals with the financial rand market, in which financial rands can either be used to purchase quoted shares and gilts locally, or sold to foreigners at a substantial discount to the commercial rand. He points out that the dual exchange rate system is primarily aimed at inhibiting disinvestment and encouraging foreigners to invest in the domestic economy. Strijdom investigates the implications of the De Kock Report for the South African foreign exchange market, and argues for the retention of the current dual exchange rate system.

The subsequent readings by Kahn, Cloete and De Kock all focus on recent policy changes in the South African economy. Following on from the recommendations of the De Kock Commission, South Africa adopted a free exchange rate system and temporarily abandoned the financial rand during the early part of the 1980s. It is unfortunate that the country experienced a massive net outflow of capital during this same period: whilst capital inflows were much too small to finance the current account deficit during the boom period of 1981–84, the subsequent outflow far exceeded the surplus on current account in 1985. The result was a massive depreciation of the rand which, according to De Kock, represented an unavoidable readjustment to an extraordinary set of circumstances. The subsequent reintroduction of the financial rand and the debt standstill did succeed in curbing capital outflows and stabilising both the commercial and financial exchange rates.

The paper by Kahn examines the effects of exchange controls and exchange rate policy on the South African economy. He argues that exchange rate policy is not sectorally neutral, and that the existing undervalued rand benefits those sectors with low import propensities. Moreover, given the volatility of the political situation in South Africa, he maintains that the authorities have little choice but to continue their control of the exchange rate. Likewise, Cloete maintains that the unprecedented fall in the rand could have been partly avoided by an appropriate mix of monetary, fiscal and incomes policies. In the final contribution to this chapter, De Kock is given the chance to answer his critics. He argues that the abolition of the financial rand did not put undue pressure on the balance of payments, and that the South African economy was never overborrowed but merely experienced a shortage of liquidity due to the withdrawal of short-term bank credits.

5.2 THE GOLD PRICE AND THE SOUTH AFRICAN ECONOMY

G.P.C. de Kock*

The recent large fluctuations in international exchange rates and the accompanying increase in the US dollar price of gold have created renewed interest in the influence of the gold price on the exchange rate of the rand and the economy as a whole.

THE GOLD PRICE AND THE ECONOMY SINCE 1974

That fluctuations in the gold price have on occasion had a decisive influence on the weal and woe of the South African economy is clearly evident from the events of the past decade.

First, the facts. Since 1974 the average annual gold price in US dollars has behaved as follows:

	USA$ per ounce
1974	159
1975	161
1976	125
1977	148
1978	193
1979	307
1980	613
1981	460
1982	376
1983	424
1984	361
1985	317
1986	368
1987 (until 27 April)	413

In reality the gold price reached a peak of $850 on 21 January 1980, then declined to a low point of $297 on 21 June 1982, then increased to an upper turning-point of $512 in February 1983, then declined to a low point of $285 in February 1985, and then recovered to as high as $477 on 27 April 1987, before declining again later in the day.

It is well known that, like many other countries, South Africa has been adversely affected since the early seventies by a succession of unfavourable

---

* Governor of the South African Reserve Bank. This paper was delivered as an address to the Cape Town Sakekamer on 28 April 1987, and first published in *The Securities Markets*, No. 4, Second Quarter, 1987.

economic developments. Moreover, in South Africa's case the situation was later exacerbated by political developments. This all led to a decline in the *average* annual growth rate of the real gross domestic product from 4,9 per cent between 1946 and 1974 to 1,9 per cent between 1974 and 1985.

The unfavourable economic developments since 1974 included a decline in the ratio of exports to gross domestic product and a weakening in the terms of trade, i.e. in the ratio of export prices to import prices (except during the 'gold bonanza' years from 1978 to 1980 when the gold price increased sharply).

The slowing down of South Africa's export growth since 1974 was, in turn, related to a levelling-off in world production during this period following the oil price increases of 1973. In the decade up to 1973 total world production increased at an annual average rate of 6 per cent. During the ten years up to 1983 it increased by an annual average rate of only 2 per cent. There was also a shift in world economic growth from raw-material-intensive to service and high-tech industries.

The sharp increase in the gold price between 1970 and 1980 temporarily neutralised the adverse effects of these long-term factors, especially as it was accompanied by good rainfall and increased agricultural crops. This 'bonanza' helped us both economically and politically and gave the South African economy three very good years, namely 1979, 1980 and 1981.

But the underlying unfavourable trends in the South African economy were continued when the gold price moved sharply downwards from January 1980 and the droughts of the early eighties exerted their influence.

With the aid of monetary and fiscal policy the South African economy nevertheless adjusted well to these new setbacks in 1982–83 and a solid foundation was laid for economic recovery. Matters improved further when, largely as a result of an increased realisation that the world was moving towards an international debt crisis, the gold price increased from $297 per ounce in June 1982 to $512 per ounce in the middle of February 1983. This increase contributed materially to the new upswing that occurred in the South African economy from April 1983 to June 1984.

But there was more to come. The gold price declined again from its peak of $512 per ounce in February 1983 — this time to as low as $285 per ounce in February 1985. Together with the drought this exerted serious adverse effects on South Africa. Painful corrective measures accordingly became unavoidable — especially since government and private expenditure increased excessively during the 1983/84 upswing and helped to bring about a large deficit on the current account of the balance of payments as well as demand inflation.

It is now a matter of history that these corrective measures proved successful. They were painful but effective. Excess spending was eliminated and the deficit on the current account of the balance of payments was transformed into a large surplus in 1985. The exchange rate of the rand, which had in the meantime declined to a low point of 43 American cents in January 1985, recovered and stabilised around 50 American cents between January 1985 and late July 1985.

The net gold and foreign exchange reserves increased by about R1 billion in the second quarter of 1985. And in the course of 1985 the rate of inflation started to decline — from an annual rate of 20,0 per cent in the first quarter to 13,6 per cent in the third quarter.

But further exogenous shocks were on the way. Just as the foundation for new growth had been well and truly laid, new socio-political storms burst loose over South Africa from July 1985 onwards.

Events such as the social unrest, the emergency situation and the increasing threat of disinvestment and economic sanctions resulted in a deterioration of overseas perceptions of the domestic political and economic prospects. However absurd and distorted these perceptions were, they resulted in a withdrawal of credits by foreign banks from South African banks and other private enterprises, a net capital outflow in other forms, a depreciaton of the rand, the introduction of a 'debt standstill' and the re-imposition of exchange control over the equity investments of non-residents, in the form of the financial rand system. Because this had an unfavourable influence on domestic business and consumer confidence, it also contributed to the apathy that prevailed in the economy at that time.

It is old hat by now that the nature of South Africa's short-term economic problems changed dramatically under the influence of these unfavourable political developments. After July 1985 there was little danger of a return of demand inflation or excess spending. In fact, the new cyclical upswing which started from a low level in the middle of 1985 was very sluggish from the beginning and was interrupted during the first quarter of 1986 before it recovered somewhat during the rest of the year.

Against this background the Reserve Bank and the Treasury applied a more expansionary monetary and fiscal strategy of encouraging investment and consumption with a view to increasing production, employment and real economic growth.

In retrospect it is clear that the South African economy adjusted extremely well to these various economic and political shocks. The adjustment process entailed sacrifices but proved very effective. This is attested to by the achievement and maintenance of a large surplus on the current account of the balance of payments, the repayment of large amounts of foreign debt, the large increase in the official gold and foreign exchange reserves, the appreciation of the rand, the marked increase in the real growth rate since the middle of 1986, and the decline in the rate of inflation from an annual rate of 26,0 per cent in the first quarter of 1986 and 20,7 per cent in the third quarter to 15,1 per cent in the first quarter of 1987.

Once again movements in the gold price had a significant influence on the course of events. From a low point of $285 per ounce in February 1985 the gold price increased to a peak of $443 in September 1986, then declined again to a low point of $390 in February 1987, but subsequently increased to a level of between $440 and $477 during the past few days.

IMPLICATIONS OF THE HIGHER GOLD PRICE FOR THE ECONOMY IN THE COMING MONTHS

If maintained for a full year, each $50 per ounce increase in the gold price means an increase of more than $1 billion in the value of South Africa's annual gold production. At an exchange rate of R1 = $0,50 this is equivalent to an increase in the rand value of South Africa's gold production of more than R2 billion.

It is difficult to predict the exact influence of the gold price increase of recent months on the South African economy in the period ahead. But there is little doubt that it will have an extremely favourable overall effect.

Firstly, the higher gold price should exert a positive 'multiplier' effect on spending and income via the increased rand value of gold exports. It should also have an expansionary financial impact. For example, the money supply will tend to rise faster, which would be desirable under current circumstances. In addition, the increased domestic liquidity will probably keep interest rates low for the time being, while the Government's tax revenue from gold mining should rise substantially. All of this should serve to promote real economic growth.

Secondly, the higher gold price should initially tend to make the surplus on the current account of the balance of payments larger than it would otherwise have been. But since it would also increase the growth rate it would most probably bring about an increase in the imports of goods and services. It would probably also tend to keep the rand relatively strong in the exchange market. All of this might serve to limit the increase in the current account. But the net result would probably be a combination of a real growth rate of about 3 per cent and a current surplus of more than R4 billion.

Thirdly, in the absence of new unfavourable political developments, the recent improvement in the capital account of the balance of payments will probably be sustained. This is not only because the higher gold price should have a favourable influence on the leads and lags in current payments and receipts, but also because the higher rate of domestic economic growth might keep capital in the country which would otherwise have flowed out.

Fourthly, the maintenance of a stronger rand should make an important contribution towards the gradual lowering of the rate of inflation.

Most of these favourable effects of a higher gold price have already been experienced during recent months. They have more than neutralised the adverse effects of trade sanctions and have undoubtedly contributed towards greater business and consumer confidence.

THE GOLD PRICE AND THE EXCHANGE RATE

The implications of the higher gold price for the exchange rate of the rand deserves further attention. Does the higher gold price mean that the rand will ap-

225

preciate further and, if so, would such an appreciation be good or bad for the South African economy?

In answering these questions it must be stressed that *South Africa's exchange rate policy has remained essentially unchanged since 1979.* Exchange control over non-resident equity capital movements was abolished in February 1983 and again reintroduced in September 1985. There was accordingly a period of about two and a half years during which South Africa had a *unitary* exchange rate system instead of a *dual* system with a commercial rand and a financial rand. But with regard to the commercial rand itself, the policy has since 1979 basically remained one of *managed floating.* The spot exchange rate is mainly determined by market forces, but the Reserve Bank regularly 'intervenes' by buying or selling dollars in the exchange market with a view to eliminating unnecessary exchange rate fluctuations.

A year or two ago the question was often asked why South Africa does not apply a policy of 'exchange rate stability' in order to provide businessmen with greater certainty. But today it is more generally understood that in the present world of floating exchange rates this policy option simply does not exist for South Africa. The rand may well be pegged to one foreign currency, such as the US dollar, at a fixed rate. However, even such pegging would only be possible if the Reserve Bank were able to buy and sell as many dollars as necessary to maintain that predetermined exchange rate. Even then, of course, the rand would still float with the dollar against most other currencies. Floating in one form or another is therefore unavoidable in present circumstances.

It is self-evident that, all other things remaining equal, a more stable exchange rate would be preferable to a less stable one. But if the choice for South Africa lies, as it does at present, between *general economic stability* and *exchange rate stability*, the official policy is to give preference to general economic stability.

In any event, exchange rate policy cannot be determined independently of monetary and fiscal policy in general and interest rate policy in particular. In South Africa, as in most other countries, the exchange rate is today fundamentally a reflection of the official monetary and fiscal policy which is aimed at increasing total spending at the desired rate, namely a rate that would lead to the attainment of the ultimate objectives of curbing inflation and maintaining a healthy balance of payments — as prerequisites for a higher average economic growth rate and the creation of adequate employment opportunities. In terms of this policy, priority is given to domestic economic growth and stability, and the exchange rate has to adjust to this, not the other way around.

The importance for sound economic growth of exchange rates that realistically reflect the underlying supply and demand in the foreign exchange market *and are accepted as realistic by the market* can hardly be overemphasised.

It is therefore clear that the exchange rate of the rand can never be the main barometer or indicator of economic prosperity or of the success or failure of economic policy. In any analysis of either the state of the economy or the results of economic policy, the exchange rate is only *one* of many economic indicators to be investigated. What is decisive in the final analysis is the behaviour of production, employment, salaries and wages, profits, exports, imports, prices and other basic economic variables. And these basic indicators will definitely perform better with a realistic rather than an overvalued or undervalued rand.

What has, in fact, happened recently to the exchange rate of the commercial rand under this policy of managed floating? After reaching a low point of about $0,36 on 12 June 1986 the rand increased to about $0,50 on 27 April 1987 — an appreciation of about 40 per cent. Over this period the rand increased by nearly 30 per cent against a weighted basket of important currencies.

CHANGES IN THE EXCHANGE RATE OF THE RAND (%)

	12/06/86 to 22/09/86	22/09/86 to 31/12/86	31/12/86 to 19/01/87	19/01/87 to 11/03/87	11/03/87 to 27/04/87	12/06/86 to 27/04/87
Weighted average	23,1	0,6	4,7	−2,6	2,5	29,5
US dollar	26,7	0,8	7,9	−2,8	5,1	40,4
British pound	32,3	0,6	3,5	−6,4	0,2	29,3
German mark	17,6	−4,0	–	−0,6	1,0	13,6
Swiss franc	14,5	−0,3	0,8	–	−2,4	12,0
Japanese yen	17,8	4,6	1,4	−0,7	−5,6	17,0
French franc	19,1	−1,5	1,2	−0,7	1,2	18,9
Financial rand	14,2	−8,2	7,8	15,7	19,6	58,0

With regard to the coming months, there is no intention to deviate from the present exchange rate policy of managed floating. The monetary authorities do not have any fixed target for the rand/dollar exchange rate. The recent level of around $0,50 is neither a floor nor a ceiling for the rand. If the US dollar were to depreciate further against the other major currencies and if this were to be accompanied by a further increase in the gold price, it is possible that the rand will appreciate further against the dollar.

This does not, however, mean that the Reserve Bank will adhere slavishly to its announced money supply targets and be indifferent towards movements of the exchange rate as such. In fact, it is fully recognised that an appreciation of the rand is not always good and a depreciation not always bad for South Africa. For an open economy such as that of South Africa there are always important advantages and disadvantages attached to any appreciation or depreciation of its currency. These advantages and disadvantages must be weighed up carefully in any attempt to determine whether the *net* effect of a change in the exchange rate would be favourable or unfavourable in any given situation.

The Reserve Bank would welcome some further appreciation of the rand against other currencies because this would contribute towards a further lowering of the rate of inflation. The rand is at present still undervalued on a purchasing power parity basis. However, it is certainly true that over the past few years the depreciation of the rand has materially assisted the South African economy in adjusting to the exogenous economic and political shocks to which it was exposed. The depreciation served, *inter alia*, to maintain the rand value of the gold output and of many other South African exports at a high level and thereby also boosted tax revenue. At the same time it granted additional protection to many domestic manufacturers that have to compete with imports. It also served to strengthen the balance of payments on both current and capital accounts and to increase the official gold and foreign exchange reserves.

If, therefore, the gold price were to remain high or to increase further *without any significant depreciation of the US dollar against other currencies,* the monetary authorities will take steps to prevent the value of the rand from increasing too much and too fast against the dollar and the other major currencies. It is true that such an appreciation would help to curb the rate of inflation, but it would also undermine the present policy of promoting growth and creating employment. This is because it would reduce the rand value of non-gold exports and expose domestic manufacturers to increased foreign competition.

Accordingly, if the rand should tend to become too expensive, the Reserve Bank would continue, as it has done during recent months, to be a net buyer of dollars in the market in order to curb the tendency towards appreciation. If these dollar purchases tended to augment the money supply too much — which at present seems unlikely because the current rate of increase in the broad money supply — M3 — is still well below the target range of 14 to 18 per cent — instruments such as open-market sales of government stock and other money market paper could be used to prevent such an excessive increase. In the meantime the repayment by the private sector of foreign debt in terms of the new debt arrangements will naturally also help to prevent an undue appreciation of the rand or an excessive increase in the money supply.

The Reserve Bank is therefore in a position to prevent an undesired appreciation of the rand. And owing to the large surplus on the current account of the balance of payments, the recent improvement of the capital account and the large increase in the official gold and foreign exchange reserves, the Bank is also in a better position than it has been for some years to prevent an undesirable depreciation of the rand or excessive fluctuations in the exchange rate.

In accordance with the official exchange rate policy of managed floating this, of course, in no way implies that the exchange rate of the rand in terms of the dollar or any other currency will or should remain stable in the months ahead. But it does mean that the movements of the various rand exchange rates are capable of being properly integrated with the present monetary and fiscal policy, which continues to aim at maintaining a balance between the promotion of growth and the curbing of inflation.

5.3 THE MECHANICS OF THE FINANCIAL RAND MARKET

A.B. Shuttleworth*

BACKGROUND

The present financial rand era began on 2 September 1985 when the dual exchange rate system was reintroduced in South Africa.[1] The financial rand provides a vehicle through which non-residents may disinvest from South Africa, or invest in certain types of assets in this country. Non-residents may freely trade financial rands between themselves; residents' activities in the financial rand market are severely circumscribed.

SUPPLY AND DEMAND

A large proportion of the turnover in the financial rand market is motivated by arbitrage and position taking. Before discussing these activities it is essential to examine the activities that underlie the supply (or creation) of, and demand for, financial rands.[2] This may take the form of the sale of quoted shares and securities, or the sale of non-quoted shares, plant and equipment. The rand proceeds are required by Exchange Control regulations to be deposited in bank accounts designated as 'financial rand accounts'. These financial rands can be used only for a very limited range of purposes. They certainly cannot be used to purchase foreign currency at the commercial rate. Financial rands are usually used to purchase quoted shares, gilts, or semi-gilts in which case the certificates are stamped 'non-resident'.

Alternatively the financial rands can be sold to other non-residents at a mutually agreed price — normally a substantial discount to the commercial rand rate. At present prices, the discount is over 50 per cent.

The underlying demand for financial rands has two components. Non-residents buy financial rands—

- in order to make payment in rands for shares, gilts or semi-gilts bought from residents in South Africa, or,
- subject to Exchange Control approval, to purchase fixed assets or property in South Africa.

It is important to note that in both cases, financial rands are actually destroyed. When a non-resident buys shares from a resident, the buyer receives a certificate marked 'non-resident', while the financial rands paid over to the seller become unrestricted, ordinary rands. Similarly, when a non-resident's appli-

---

* Financial Economist, Standard Bank Investment Corporation Ltd. This paper was first published in *The Securities Markets*, No. 3, First Quarter, 1987.

cation to purchase, for example, property through the financial rand market is approved, he purchases financial rands which become ordinary rands when paid over to the seller. The property must, of course, become registered in the name of the non-resident. The attraction to the non-resident of investing in South Africa through the financial rand market is that interest and dividends may be remitted through the commercial rand market. Given the present financial rand discount of over 50 per cent, this means that non-residents receive a yield before tax that is double the yield available to residents on the same investments.

To summarise: apart from arbitrage activities and the taking or unwinding of speculative positions, the financial rand *supplied* to the market are *created* by the sale of assets by non-residents. Conversely, the *demand* for financial rands results in the *destruction* of financial rands as non-residents buy approved assets from residents.

THE PLAYERS

The financial rand market operates mainly in two centres, Johannesburg and London. For analytical purposes it is more helpful to examine two parallel markets, namely the 'cash market' and the stock exchanges (both Johannesburg and London). The cash market is made by a few local banks, with The Standard Bank of South Africa Limited, French Bank of Southern Africa Limited and UAL Merchant Bank Limited being among the most active. Strictly, the banks are not allowed to deal as principals, but the Reserve Bank appears to tolerate market-making activity as long as positions are kept small (the banks report their financial rand dealings to the Reserve Bank on a daily basis). Two-way rates are quoted, good for R500 000, with a spread of 0,5 US cents. These parameters give an indication that the market is thin, volatile and risky.

The local banks deal extensively with London stockbrokers, of whom about half-a-dozen appear to be the most active. Dealings with Johannesburg stockbrokers are much more limited. The local banks also deal with or on behalf of non-residents who have obtained exchange control approval to invest in South Africa through the financial rand market. Similarly, non-residents disinvesting from South Africa can obtain foreign currency by selling their financial rand in the cash market. The flurry of corporate disinvestment late in 1986 has given rise to a suspicion that large parcels of financial rands are being transacted for foreign currency on a principal-to-principal basis. Given the thinness of the cash market, this makes sense.

Of course, non-residents investing in, or disinvesting from, South Africa need not trade in the cash market for financial rands. They have the option of using the stock exchanges. Investors would create financial rands by buying shares for foreign currency in London and selling them in Johannesburg. Disinvestors would do the opposite. The use of the stock exchanges as a vehicle for investment and disinvestment naturally brings in stockbrokers as players in the financial rand market, and it is the brokers, especially the London ones, who provide the link between the stock exchanges and the cash market.

ARBITRAGE AND POSITION TAKING

To illustrate an arbitrage opportunity let us take as an example a non-resident who has received exchange control permission to make an investment in South Africa through the financial rand market. He can either buy financial rands from a local bank and pay in dollars, or he can use his dollars to buy shares in London, and sell those shares in Johannesburg for financial rands. He will use whichever method enables him to buy his financial rands more cheaply.

For example, he may be able to buy financial rand at $0,22 in the cash market. Alternatively, if the ruling price of De Beers in London is $9,43 and in Johannesburg R41,00 then by using the stock exchange he may obtain his financial rand at $9,43/R41,00 = $0,23 per financial rand. Clearly the former is preferable. However, such significant discrepancies do not last for long — somebody (probably a London broker) will take advantage of the situation to arbitrage the markets. The arbitrageur will quickly buy financial rands in the cash market at $0,22 and use them to buy De Beers in Johannesburg at R41,00. Simultaneously he will sell De Beers in London at $9,43 to end up with more dollars than originally laid out to buy the financial rands. His actions will affect all three prices: in the cash market the financial rand will rise above $0,22; the price of De Beers will tend to rise above R41,00 in Johannesburg and to fall below $9,43 in London. The process will continue until the price of the financial rand in the cash market is so close to the ratio between the dollar and rand prices of a given share that there is no longer an incentive to arbitrage.

In practice, arbitrage takes place in both directions but is limited to some extent by the 0,5 US cent spread between the banks' buying and selling quotes for financial rand. Nevertheless, the ratio between the Johannesburg and London prices for any given share is usually within the financial rand buying and selling range. This is illustrated by the following example of ruling prices on 5 February 1987:

Share	Price in London ($)	Price in Johannesburg (R)	Ratio ($/R)
De Beers	9,50	42,00	0,2262
Kloof	8,03	35,50	0,2262
Randfontein	92,00	402,00	0,2289
Rustenburg	12,00	54,25	0,2212
Anglo	15,75	70,00	0,2250
GFSA	15,0625	67,00	0,2248

The closing quotes for the financial rand on that day were $0,2238 and $0,2288. Randfontein was marginally outside of this range, but Rustenburg was sufficiently far out to make arbitrage worthwhile, assuming that the prices were accurately recorded and at the same time. A profit could have been made by buying Rustenburg in London and selling in Johannesburg, producing financial rand at a cost of $0,2212 to the arbitrageur, and which he sells to a local bank for $0,2238. The profit would be $1 300 per R500 000 transaction.[3]

Because Exchange Control regulations prohibit residents from taking positions in financial rand, local brokers can only perform arbitrage operations which are perfectly matched. This is the purest form of arbitrage, in which no risk is involved, but it is difficult to arrange. In the above example, the Johannesburg broker would have to line up a foreign seller of Rustenburg (in dollars) with a local buyer (in rands) while simultaneously keeping an open line to a bank to hold a financial rand quote that makes the entire deal viable. London brokers, on the other hand, can keep a working balance in a financial rand account to facilitate payment and can go long or short of financial rand for hours or days if they wish to take a view on the rate.

THE EFFECT OF THE FINANCIAL RAND ON SHARE PRICES

There have been a number of occasions when external events have had an effect on the financial rand rate and this has had disturbing and unexpected effects on share prices. For example, the Comprehensive Anti-Apartheid Act passed in the United States Congress last year, forbade new investment in South Africa by Americans after 15 November. This led to increased demand for financial rand ahead of the deadline, and the financial rand rate rose to a peak at $0,2525 on 13 November. To take advantage of this, arbitrageurs began buying shares in London and selling them in Johannesburg. This depressed Johannesburg share prices. In fact it appears that the creation of financial rand was overdone on 13 November by non-residents wishing to take a long position in anticipation of an even stronger rate on 14 November. In the event, liquidation of positions caused the financial rand rate to fall on that day to close at $0,2238/88, while Johannesburg share prices recovered their losses.

The above example illustrates the well-known inverse relationship that exists (at least in the very short term) between the financial rand rate and Johannesburg share prices. However, it is necessary to put this relationship into perspective. On 14 November 1986 when the financial rand rate closed at $0,2238/88, De Beers stood at $7,50 in London and R34,00 in Johannesburg. On 11 February 1987, when the financial rand rose to $0,2400/50, the ruling prices for De Beers were $9,65 and R40,20, respectively. De Beers had risen significantly in both markets as a result of the excellent 1986 sales figures published by the Central Selling Organisation, and the improving outlook for the diamond market.

Another example of the link between the financial rand share prices is the often quoted view that when the gold price drops, gold share prices in Johannesburg are cushioned by the financial rand. Of course, if the financial rand rate were to remain unchanged, share prices in Johannesburg and London would drop by the same proportion. But there is, however, some relationship between fluctuations in the gold price and fluctuations in the financial rand itself. A significant drop in the gold price is normally accompanied by a drop in the financial rand rate. When this happens there is an incentive for arbitrageurs to buy gold shares in Johannesburg and sell in London. This to some extent cushions gold shares on the Johannesburg Stock Exchange.

CONCLUDING COMMENTS

The whole purpose of the dual exchange rate system is to separate non-residents' holdings of rands into a restricted pool, in order to discourage disinvestment. The rands in this pool are traded between non-residents at a price in dollars far below the commercial rand exchange rate. This penalises those who are disinvesting from South Africa, while providing an attractive entry yield to those non-residents who are willing to invest in this country.

The potential supply of financial rands is very large in relation to turnover. All quoted securities owned by non-residents could in principle be turned into financial rands. So too, could foreign-owned property, fixed assets and non-quoted securities, provided buyers could be found. The demand for financial rands hinges on the willingness of non-residents to invest in South Africa, and the rate at which the Exchange Control approves applications for the release of financial rand. Given these parameters, the future direction of the financial rand rate depends crucially on the foreign perceptions of the risk of doing business and owning assets in South Africa.

NOTES

1 The historical background is well summarised in Gidlow, R.M., 'The Financial Rand Market', *The Securities Markets*, No. 1, Third Quarter, 1986, pp. 37–39.
2 Emigrants' settling-in allowances (R100 000 per family) also form part of the supply of financial rands. However, emigrants' assets in excess of the allowance do not become financial rands, and must remain in South Africa as blocked rand.
3 A complication was that Rustenburg was *cum* a 90 cent dividend, and the Johannesburg price would have been bid up by dividend strippers.

5.4 A CRITICAL ASSESSMENT OF THE EQUILIBRIUM APPROACH TO THE RATE OF EXCHANGE

P.D.F. Strydom*

The Commission of Inquiry into the Monetary System and Monetary Policy in South Africa (hereafter referred to as the Commission) submitted its final report[1] during 1985 and made a substantial contribution towards official thinking by following a market-oriented approach. The Commission was not in favour of direct controls over monetary or financial magnitudes, but preferred to have the monetary authorities influence these magnitudes primarily as a market participant rather than as a market regulatory body. In developing this line of thought the Commission followed an eclectic approach, but failed to develop a coherent analytical framework in terms of which to present its policy proposals. It proposed the following market-related instruments of monetary policy: public debt management (including public borrowing), Reserve Bank open-market operations, Reserve Bank discount and general accommodation policy, and Reserve Bank 'intervention' in the spot and forward exchange markets. These four monetary policy instruments were to be supplemented by a variable cash reserve requirement while the Commission saw a limited but useful role for moral suasion. This paper is concerned with the Commission's policy proposals regarding the foreign exchange market.

1. THE SOUTH AFRICAN FOREIGN EXCHANGE RATE REGIME

Following the adoption of flexible exchange rates by the major trading countries during the 1970s in the wake of the collapse of the Bretton Woods system, South Africa adopted a dual exchange rate system[2] in January 1979. The 'commercial rand' was a market-determined rate of exchange for current account and loans transactions while the 'financial rand' was a freely floating rate for equity capital. The Reserve Bank participated actively in the commercial rand market by quoting buying and selling rates for US dollars to authorised dealers. The Reserve Bank also quoted rates for forward dollars at a premium or discount for different maturities up to 12 months. This system of variable dollar pegging evolved gradually as the Reserve Bank varied its buying and selling rates for dollars more freely in response to market forces while the authorities liberalised the foreign exchange market. The dual exchange rate regime was terminated during February 1983 and simultaneously exchange controls on non-residents were abolished. A unitary floating exchange rate regime with Reserve Bank intervention was adopted. Apart from certain concessions, exchange controls over residents and emigrants remained in force. During Sep-

* Chief, Strategic Research, Sankorp, Johannesburg. This paper was first published in *The South African Journal of Economics*, Vol. 54, No. 1, 1986.

tember 1983 the Reserve Bank stopped quoting a spot exchange rate for the rand against the US dollar, except for its own customers, and started influencing the unitary rate of exchange as a buyer and seller of US dollars.

2. ANALYTICAL FRAMEWORK

Although the Commission accepted the well-established interrelations between monetary, fiscal and exchange rate policies it did not propose an active exchange rate policy. This is, of course, in line with international experience confirming the difficulties and inefficiencies associated with such an approach. The Commission envisaged the exchange rate policy of the Reserve Bank as an interventionist policy in the sense that the 'Reserve Bank intervene directly in the foreign exchange market in a *stabilising* or generally more "defensive" manner in order to *moderate* or "smooth out" exchange rate movements whenever it deems this to be in the national interest' (par. 21.13). The Commission saw this interventionist policy as a smoothing-out action in the event of 'minor fluctuations and irregularities that occur in the exchange rate in a random fashion ...' (par. 21.14). Furthermore, the Commission supported intervention owing to 'long-term rises or declines in the exchange rate which are judged to be essentially temporary' (par. 21.15). Finally, intervention could attain 'a *more gradual* transition of the exchange rate to a new level that, in the estimation of the authorities, is likely to be a long-lasting if not a "permanent" one' (par. 21.16). The interventionist smoothing-out policy is clearly envisaged within a relatively stable environment where market forces are well structured to attain equilibrium. Therefore the Commission maintained that intervention by the Reserve Bank would not be recommended to '*exacerbate* exchange rate movements that would have resulted from the operation of market forces' (par. 21.10). In similar vein the Commission would not recommend intervention which would '*reverse the direction of change* in the exchange rate that would have resulted from the free operation of market forces' (par. 21.10). This is a typical equilibrium approach, assuming sufficient information in the system to attain equilibrium and, more importantly, the assumption is that once equilibrium is attained the system is stable so that deviations from equilibrium could be of a temporary nature. In such a framework the smoothing-out interventionist policy applied to a floating exchange rate is defensible. The stability assumption underlying this exposition is of course in line with the monetarist stance which the Commission adopted in analysing the foreign exchange market. It has been demonstrated convincingly in the literature that a basic tenet of monetarism is that the economic system is inherently stable (see Wilson, 1984 and Du Plessis, 1979). The approach of the Commission is clearly in line with this stability assumption and therefore intervention by the Reserve Bank is envisaged as a smoothing-out operation of minor fluctuations occurring in a random fashion within an equilibrium system.

At this juncture it is in order to point out that this monetarist stance in respect of the rate of exchange contradicts the Commission's proposed Keynesian monetary framework which is based on monetary control through interest rates.[3] The contradiction arises since the Commission viewed the rate of exchange as being determined by market forces within a framework where the price variable is a policy variable. In respect of monetary policy the Commission subscribed to a Keynesian approach while the exchange rate policy is defended within a monetarist framework, and the Commission failed to derive a synthesis of these two approaches to support its total policy exposition. This logical inconsistency casts doubt on the effectiveness of the proposed exchange rate policy. As long as these contradictory analytical frameworks form the basis of policy, one can expect little success from any intervention and smoothing-out activities on the foreign exchange market by the monetary authorities.

The equilibrium approach is not very helpful in understanding markets, particularly not foreign exchange markets, which have been characterised by a high degree of volatility during recent years. The assumption of optimal equilibrating forces is typical of such a system and the Commission's belief in the operation of these optimal processes is evident from its claim that 'a free-market mechanism is generally conducive to the optimal allocation of available funds among competing uses, which ensures the production of goods and services most fully in accordance with the nation's wants, needs and priorities' (par. 1.13). The assumption of these optimal equilibrating forces is defensible within an equilibrium system but has little bearing on the real world. In the real world one is rather concerned with the 'degree of success with which market forces can be relied upon to generate spontaneous corrections in the allocation patterns prevailing at times of disequilibrium' (Kirzner, 1973, pp. 6–7). The adjustment process in markets could rather be characterised by economic rivalry in the terminology of Lavoie (1985). The prime reason why we support a market economy as opposed to a centrally regulated economy is that we are convinced that economic rivalry within a market framework is more advantageous than a centrally regulated economy, since it enables market participants to co-ordinate their plans. The process of co-ordinating human plans through abstract rules whereby individuals exploit and interpret the available information has been referred to by Hayek as a spontaneous order (Hayek, 1967).[4] This means that in a market-oriented economic system, economic agents try to co-ordinate their plans in a spontaneous way. In such a system all plans are not always carried out; some plans fail, but this system is nevertheless preferred to an economic order where individual plans are centrally planned or regulated by an official body. Plans should be carried out spontaneously while market participants are aware of the risk that some plans might fail. In this analytical framework the failure of some plans is an important obstacle to the optimal processes propagated by equilibrium analysis. Optimal equilibrating processes are absent in the spontaneous order where market forces are characterised by economic rivalry.

This dynamic framework is far more helpful in analysing the foreign exchange market than the equilibrium approach adopted by the Commission. Within its equilibrium framework the Commission maintained that 'equilibrating inflows and outflows of capital would, of course, occur and spot exchange rates would probably also move to new equilibrium levels' (par. 12.19). If we argue in terms of a spontaneous order while allowing for economic rivalry in the absence of optimal equilibrating capital flows since in this non-equilibrium framework there will be equilibrating as well as non-equilibrating forces, we cannot claim a dominant position for equilibrating capital flows. In the real world capital flows have disrupted foreign exchange markets to a significant extent, and in many instances disequilibrating capital flows have been a dominant force in disrupting these markets.

The mere liberalisation of the foreign exchange market in itself will do little to improve the situation. In this respect the arguments of the Commission are not convincing. It claimed that: 'By abolishing exchange control over non-residents it (South Africa) has removed an important deterrent to foreign investment and has demonstrated not only its favourable disposition to foreign capital but also its ability to provide a suitable and equitable environment for productive and profitable investment' (par. 12.25). In terms of our dynamic analysis we claim that foreign capital inflows into South Africa are primarily determined by the real rate of return. Furthermore, if the real rate of return is relatively unattractive while foreign investment in South Africa is not supported by 'safe haven' considerations as suggested by Murphy (1985), the mere liberalization of the market will not in itself generate capital inflows or, for that matter, equilibrating capital flows. While pursuing the liberalization issue the Commission overstated the British case by maintaining that Britain abolished exchange control in 'one decisive step' (par. 12.36). In fact the UK exchange controls were abolished in several stages.[5]

Another instance of the equilibrium approach adopted by the Commission is the claim that 'the flexible rand exchange rate rapidly increases the cost of transferring funds abroad and discourages speculation by forcing speculators, once the rand has floated down to a certain point, to take into account the possibility of a rand appreciation as well as depreciation from that point onwards ...' (par. 12.16). In equilibrium analysis information is distributed freely and therefore the Commission's claim regarding rapid adjustments is defensible as long as we adhere to the static framework of equilibrium analysis. In the real world this conclusion is not valid. In the real world information changes and is unevenly disseminated while the interpretation of information may diverge, and the system may not adjust rapidly towards equilibrium.[6] The Commission identified a 'certain point' where market forces could start moving in a particular direction. Such perfect knowledge is only possible within the framework of equilibrium analysis. In the real world this exposition is not very helpful since we lack perfect foresight and cannot identify these 'certain points' in a framework of economic rivalry.

It is primarily because of its static equilibrium analysis that the Commission uncritically accepted the conventional arguments in favour of floating exchange rates. Economic theory claims that a system of freely floating exchange rates removes the balance of payments constraint and consequently domestic policy is more successful in attaining the policy goals of employment, economic growth and a low inflation rate. Black (1977) demonstrated that a stable floating exchange rate system is only feasible under conditions of stable targets for monetary and fiscal policy backed by the political ability to enforce them. These conditions are not readily met in the real world and Black analysed these issues in detail. Furthermore, in the modern world it became even more difficult to satisfy these conditions because of the extensive liberalisation of banking activities in the major industrial countries since 1979. Monetary authorities appear to have less and less control over the monetary aggregates as international money and capital markets became more integrated, and an important argument in favour of freely floating exchange rates has been impaired. It could well be that monetary authorities have lost their independence in conducting monetary policy, as has been demonstrated by De Grauwe (1985) and Wilson (1985). The intellectual argument in favour of freely floating exchange rates has become exposed to severe criticism. This does not imply that the world will start adopting a fixed exchange rate regime, but it is clear that the intellectual tide in favour of freely floating exchange rates has probably run its course.

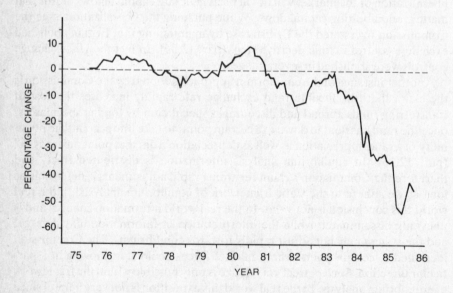

Figure 1 PERCENTAGE CHANGE IN THE WEIGHTED VALUE OF THE RAND FROM THE SEPTEMBER 1975 = 100 LEVEL

3. ASSESSMENT OF THE FOREIGN EXCHANGE RATE REGIME

Certain characteristics of the South African economy, such as its relatively high degree of openness and the dominant influence of a few commodities, particularly gold, on its foreign trade, make the rand exchange rate vulnerable to large fluctuations. Thus for relatively long periods the rand exchange rate tended to move in one direction. These observations are clearly illustrated in Figure 1 depicting the percentage change in the weighted values of the rand. As is evident from the graph, the rand depreciated sharply since September 1983. Owing to the fact that South Africa's inflation rate deteriorated markedly *vis-à-vis* its major partners from 1981, as is illustrated in Table 1, the rand exchange rate came under substantial downward pressure on a weighted basis.

Table 1 INFLATION: CONSUMER PRICES (PERCENTAGE CHANGE ON PREVIOUS YEAR)

	1980	1981	1982	1983	1984	1985
US	13,5	10,4	6,2	3,2	4,3	3,7
UK	18,0	11,9	8,6	4,6	5,0	6,1
West Germany	5,4	6,3	5,3	3,3	2,4	2,2
South Africa	13,8	15,2	14,1	12,3	11,6	16,2

A closer examination of the value of the rand, the British pound, the Japanese yen and the West German mark against the US dollar confirms the relatively poor performance of the rand. As illustrated in Figure 2, the rand depreciated more than the major currencies against the US dollar from September 1983 to December 1985. During the second half of 1984 the rand weakened progressively more against the US dollar than the other currencies under consideration. This progressively weakening pattern of the rand exchange rate was interrupted during the first half of 1985, as is illustrated in the graph, but as from the third quarter of 1985 the rand depreciated markedly against the US dollar while, on average, the other currencies appreciated against a weakening US dollar. The sharp depreciation of the rand will, no doubt, have substantial adverse effects on the economy. These effects will not be analysed here and it suffices to summarise them along the lines suggested by the President of the Bundesbank in his 1983 Annual Report,[7] viz. 'a depreciation of one's currency … is not, as past experience has shown, a promising strategy over the longer term. Depreciation results in a deterioration in the terms of trade … and leads to a reduction in real income and a rise in domestic prices … the exchange rate is not a suitable instrument for ensuring external competitiveness in the long run'.

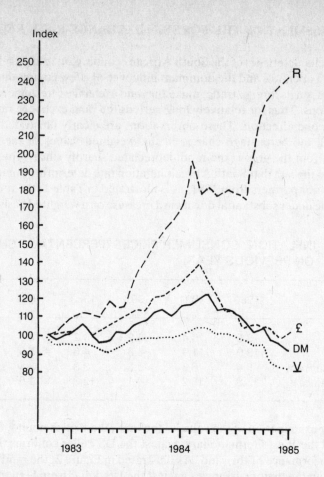

Figure 2 THE VALUE OF SELECTED CURRENCIES AGAINST THE
US DOLLAR (INDEXES SEPTEMBER 1983 = 100)

We shall now describe the performance of the rand *vis-à-vis* other currencies through its relatively overvalued or relatively undervalued position in terms of the real effective exchange rate, i.e. the trade weighted value adjusted for international inflation differentials. As is evident from Figure 3, during 1983 the rand and the US dollar tended to be overvalued *vis-à-vis* the German mark, the British pound and the Japanese yen, but during 1984 the situation changed as the rand moved more into line with the other major currencies while the US dollar remained relatively overvalued. During 1985 the rand depreciated to such an extent that it became undervalued *vis-à-vis* all the other currencies depicted in the graph. More importantly, over a period of less than two years the rand switched its relative position from the most overvalued to the most undervalued currency.

The Commission submitted its Report during May 1985, and therefore did not have access to the full data range discussed above. The major problems regarding the exchange rate had nevertheless been evident during 1984. In assessing the foreign exchange market the Commission concluded that the exchange regime has been successful. It claimed that 'The important reforms introduced in the course of 1983 proved their mettle immediately when they were severely tested by the $100 drop in the gold price in the last week of February 1983 and again by the price decline after September 1983. The outflow of equity capital during much of that year and the sharp reversal of exchange rate expectations were successfully accommodated by the new mechanism' (par. 11.28).

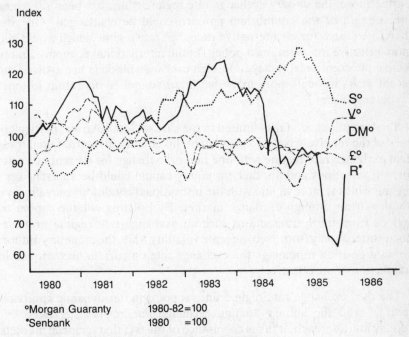

°Morgan Guaranty   1980-82=100
•Senbank   1980   =100

Figure 3 REAL EFFECTIVE EXCHANGE RATES

The evidence submitted above shows that subsequent events did not support this conclusion. As a matter of fact the new exchange regime did not contain speculative capital movements including leads and lags as claimed by the Commission (par. 12.6). Leads and lags had already been prominent prior to the submission of the Report and they expanded so rapidly during the fourth quarter of 1984 and early 1985 that the Reserve Bank had to take special measures. In view of this experience and developments subsequent to the submission of the Report it would appear that the Commission's assessment of the performance of the foreign exchange market is out of line with the evidence. One is inclined to infer that its assessment is akin to 'value judgements parading as statements of fact', in the terminology of Blaug (Blaug, 1980, p. 138).

It is clear that the foreign exchange market has put up a dismal performance since September 1983. It would therefore appear that the rand exchange market does not satisfy the stability assumptions of a normal market. This state of affairs has been aggravated by the events subsequent to the submission of the Report such as the political unrest and the state of emergency which was declared in July 1985. In these circumstances the rand is unlikely to be considered a 'safe haven' investment, which means that the exchange rate is extremely vulnerable to volatile capital movements. The equilibrium approach is clearly not applicable and the smoothing-out interventionist exchange rate policy suggested by the Commission on the basis of that approach falls apart. Furthermore, the unitary exchange rate regime which has been suggested on the strength of the equilibrium aproach could be challenged. One should therefore search for an alternative exchange rate regime which would allow a more effective interventionist policy. In the international economy a more effective interventionist policy in foreign exchange markets has evolved during recent years through more extensive international co-operation in terms of economic policies.[8]

Similar options are fairly limited in the case of South Africa, particularly in view of the relatively isolated position of this country in international trade. A dual exchange rate regime with one rate of exchange for current account and loans transactions and another for equity capital could be an exchange rate regime which is more in line with the institutional conditions prevailing in the South African foreign exchange market. By isolating volatile capital transactions from trade transactions such an exchange rate regime protects the domestic economy from exchange rate volatility while the monetary authorities are in a position to manage the exchange rate on current account and loans transactions more effectively.

The dual exchange rate regime finds support in our dynamic approach. In contrast with the unitary floating exchange rate regime suggested by the equilibrium approach, it takes cognisance of the fact that financial markets are speculative markets and since market participants do not have perfect foresight there is no reason to believe that these markets will approach an equilibrium state of affairs.

The solution to the disrupting effect of volatile capital movements suggested by the dual exchange rates regime is to demarcate the foreign exchange market into two separate sections, thereby isolating trading transactions and the domestic economy from disruptive exchange rate instability. We nevertheless hasten to qualify that this method of isolating unstable speculative transactions does not guarantee a total isolation since one has to accept that market participants are likely to exploit the loopholes in the system whereby its effectiveness is reduced. The dual exchange rate regime is nevertheless a superior solution to outright exchange controls since it involves markets in a forceful manner.

4. SUMMARY AND CONCLUSIONS

During recent years flexible exchange rates have become a common feature of international financial markets and in view of the fact that South Africa is a major trading country it had to introduce a flexible exchange rate system to facilitate foreign trade payments. The market-oriented approach of the Commission should be acclaimed since it proposed a policy framework opposing direct controls over monetary or financial magnitudes while encouraging the authorities to influence these magnitudes primarily as a market participant rather than as a market-regulatory body.

While the Commission moved in the right direction, in the final analysis it proposed a foreign exchange rate regime based on contradictory fundamentals, thus rendering exchange rate policy ineffective. The Commission followed an eclectic approach but failed to develop a synthesis for its policy framework. Besides lacking a coherent theoretical base the unitary exchange rate regime proposed by the Commission has also been brought into question by the evidence, particularly by events subsequent to the submission of its Report.

The theoretical framework applied by the Commission is a static equilibrium framework which is not sufficiently realistic in an analysis of foreign exchange markets. Under South African conditions a dynamic analysis suggests that a dual exchange rate system would be preferable to a fluctuating unitary system based upon equilibrium assumptions.

NOTES

1 *The Monetary System and Monetary Policy in South Africa: Final Report of the Commission of Inquiry into the Monetary Policy in South Africa.* Pretoria, Government Printer, RP 70/1984.
2 The dual exchange rate system was adopted following the Interim Report (RP 112/1978) of the Commission. For a review see Strydom and Dagut (1979).
3 See Chapter 17 of the Report.
4 See also Lavoie (1985) for an application of this approach.
5 See Bank of England (1979, p. 260, p. 274, and pp. 370–371).
6 See Strydom (1984).
7 Deutsche Bundesbank (1984, p. 55).
8 For a discussion of these issues see Aliber (1983).

REFERENCES

Aliber, R.Z., 1983. 'Exchange-rate Intervention: Arbitrage and Market Efficiency' in Machlup, F., Fels, G. and Müller-Groeling, H. (eds). *Reflections on a Troubled World Economy: Essays in Honour of Herbert Giersch.* London: Macmillan, pp. 171–87.
Bank of England, 1979. *Quarterly Bulletin,* Vol. 19.
Black, S.W., 1977. *Floating Exchange Rates and National Economic Policy.* New Haven: Yale University Press.
Blaug, M., 1980. *The Methodology of Economics.* Cambridge: Cambridge University Press.
De Grauwe, P., 1985. *Internationale Monetaire Verhoudingen Concurrentie of Coördinate?* De Roos-Lezing 1984, Amsterdam. Nederlands Instituut voor het Bank- en Effectenbedrijf.

Deutsche Bundesbank, 1984. *Report for the year 1983,* Frankfurt am Main.

Du Plessis, F.J., 1979. 'Monetary Policy in South Africa', *South African Journal of Economics,* Vol. 47, pp. 331–42.

Hayek, F.A., 1967. 'The Principles of a Liberal Social Order', reprinted in Nishiyama, C. and Leube, K.R. (eds) (1984), *The Essence of Hayek.* Stanford: Hoover Institution, pp. 363–81.

Kirzner, I.M., 1973. *Competition and Entrepreneurship.* Chicago: University of Chicago Press.

Lavoie, D., 1985. *Rivalry and Central Planning. The Socialist Calculation Debate Reconsidered.* Cambridge: Cambridge University Press.

Murphy, J.C., 1985. 'Reflections on the Exchange Rate System', *American Economic Review Papers and Proceedings,* Vol. 75, pp. 68–73.

Strydom, P.D.F. and Dagut, M.B., 1979. 'Exchange Rates in South Africa', *The South African Journal of Economics,* Vol. 47, pp. 115–35.

Strydom, P.D.F., 1984. 'The Economics of Information', *The Investment Analyst Journal.* No. 24, pp. 11–15.

Wilson, J.S.G., 1985. 'How Assets and Liabilities are Managed Around the World', *The Banker,* June, pp. 54–62.

Wilson, T., 1984. *Inflation, Unemployment and the Market.* London: Oxford University Press.

5.5 EXCHANGE CONTROLS AND EXCHANGE RATE POLICY IN THE SOUTH AFRICAN ECONOMY

Brian Kahn*

Because South Africa's balance of payments are vulnerable to changes in the gold price and to political crises, foreign exchange control and exchange rate policy is of crucial importance. The first section of this paper analyses the structure of the balance of payments and outlines the adjustments that are required to overcome shocks to both the current and capital accounts. The second section analyses recent exchange rate policy and argues that the policy preference for undervalued exchange rates has the effect of benefitting profits at the expense of wages. The third section looks at exchange control policy and the liberalisation of capital flows in the 1980s. Declining rates of profit and political uncertainty made it increasingly attractive for South African companies and individuals to invest abroad resulting in pressure for exchange control relaxation. Because access to international financial markets is uncertain, liberalisation does not appear to be appropriate for a country subject to volatile flights of capital in the wake of political crises.

INTRODUCTION

International trade and investment play a crucial role in the South African economy, and over the past two decades imports plus exports as a percentage of GDP have fluctuated between 60 and 70 per cent. Given this openness of the economy, the exchange rate policy is of critical importance not only in its effects on the overall balance of payments (BOP) but also on the distribution of income between different sectors of the economy and between wages and profits.

With the breakdown of the Bretton Woods system in the early 1970s, the South African authorities experimented with a variety of alternative exchange rate regimes, eventually opting for a more flexible exchange rate policy and a liberalisation of exchange controls. This emphasis on the market mechanism and freeing of capital flows had drastic consequences for the balance of payments and the economy as a whole when confronted with the recent political crisis. While such policies may be appropriate for industrial countries with relatively stable political systems, they can have adverse effects for countries subject not only to political shocks but also to sudden exogenous changes in their terms of trade, particularly of primary exports. In this respect South Africa is not significantly different from the Southern Cone countries of Latin

* School of Economics, University of Cape Town. This paper was first published in *Social Dynamics*, Vol. 13, No. 1, 1987.

America where most of the balance of payments related liberalisation experiments were failures and were eventually reversed.

This paper is divided into four sections. Section 1 provides a brief analysis of trends in the structure of South Africa's balance of payments with particular emphasis on how shocks, in the form of gold price changes and changing political perceptions, affect the BOP. Section 2 looks at the recent conduct of exchange rate policy and also at the likely distributional effects of exchange rate changes. It is argued that exchange rate policy has been aimed at protecting the interest of export industries, particularly mining and agriculture, which also has the effect of benefitting profits at the expense of wages. Section 3 critically assesses exchange control policy in South Africa, and the final section draws together the conclusion.

1. THE STRUCTURE OF SOUTH AFRICA'S BALANCE OF PAYMENTS

South Africa's balance of payments has been characterised by cyclical features which exhibit an apparently stable structure over time. Figure 1 shows the movements of the current and capital accounts over the past 20 years.[1] It can be clearly seen that these accounts have moved in opposite directions. This regular pattern is normally explained as follows: during an upswing in the business cycle, increased demands for imports and increased investment bring about a deficit on the current account which is then financed by borrowing from abroad.

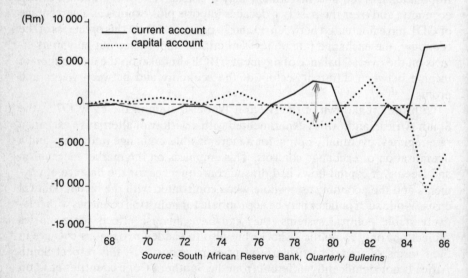

Source: South African Reserve Bank, *Quarterly Bulletins*

Figure 1 CURRENT AND CAPITAL ACCOUNTS OF THE BOP 1967–1986

Higher rates of growth also attract more foreign investment. During a downswing, imports decline, the current account moves into surplus (or the

246

deficit declines) and this allows for a repayment of loans, resulting in the deficit on the capital account. Although the BOP appears to be self-correcting over time, merely looking at the overall aggregates hides the severe adjustments required to bring about such stability. The two accounts have not always balanced each other out, as can be seen from the fluctuations in net gold and foreign reserves (Fig. 2). In particular, net reserves fell substantially in 1976, 1981 and 1985, which required Reserve Bank foreign borrowing to stabilise the level of reserves. In addition, structural problems of the South African economy and the susceptibility of capital and current accounts to exogenous stocks, have important implications for the BOP and the conduct of exchange rate policy.

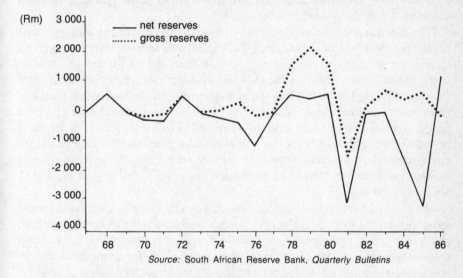

Source: South African Reserve Bank, *Quarterly Bulletins*

Figure 2 CHANGES IN NET AND GROSS FOREIGN EXCHANGE RESERVES

Imports into South Africa tend to move procyclically. As incomes and economic activity increase, because of South Africa's dependence on imported technology, expansion of output requires the importation of capital equipment. This is due to the marked tendency over the past two decades for the capital intensity of production to increase, particularly in the manufacturing sector (Black and Stanwix, 1986; Kleu, 1983). In recent years, capital equipment and intermediate goods have comprised approximately 80 per cent of all imported goods. Despite the policy of import substitution (see Archer, 1987, elsewhere in this issue), import penetration ratios (imports as a proportion of domestic sales) have remained high and followed an upward trend in the fields of machinery and motor vehicles and transport equipment (Kahn, 1987).

Exports on the other hand do not exhibit the same cyclical features as imports. During the 1980s, approximately 70 per cent of exports (excluding gold)

have been agricultural and mineral, with gold alone averaging 47 per cent of total exports. Mineral prices are determined on world commodity markets and their volatility, particularly that of gold, results in 'shocks' to the current account which requires adjustments in the rest of the balance of payments, in the exchange rate and in the economy as a whole. For example, an unexpected fall in the gold price could result in an increase in a current account deficit which would require either a depreciation of the exchange rate or an accommodating capital inflow through foreign borrowing. From a balance of payments point of view, the important aspect is that such movements in the gold price are *not* predictable and do not follow a cyclical pattern; rather, gold price changes impinge on the business cycle, which in turn determines imports, the exchange rate and accommodating flows on the capital account.

The *capital account* reflects the flows of foreign investment and foreign loans. Except for 1977-80 and again since 1983, capital inflows have been necessary to finance the excess of investment over savings. Until the 1970s most of the flows in the capital account were either long-term direct investment[2] or short-term trade credits. By the early 1970s the expansion of private international money and capital markets meant that the South African state could embark on its programme of strategic infrastructural expenditure (Escom, Sasol, Iscor, etc.) financed through loans from the Euro-currency markets. This emphasis on loans rather than direct investment resulted in an increase in the proportion of indirect investment to total foreign investment from 32 per cent in 1970 to 61 per cent by 1984.

The increased reliance on foreign loans implies that South Africa has become more vulnerable to external 'shocks' to the capital account. A current account shock, e.g., a fall in the gold price or an increase in the price of oil, can be dealt with by increased foreign borrowing in order to allow for a smoother adjustment, but a capital account shock usually comes about as a result of political instability which restricts South Africa's access to international capital markets. Such shocks occurred in the aftermath of Sharpeville (1960), Soweto (1976) and again after the recent debacle in 1985. These crises not only result in capital flight but also make it difficult for South African borrowers to raise new loans to offset the effects of the capital outflow. Thus, in 1977 not only was there a large outflow of capital, but no new loans were made available until the international bankers' perceptions of South Africa's risk rating improved. A capital account shock involving restricted access to new loans implies that the deficit on this account will have to be overcome by increasing domestic savings, i.e. bringing about a current account surplus through reductions in consumption. This requires a policy of deflation which reduces income and expenditure, employment and imports.

The need for deflation can, however, be reduced if an appropriate exchange rate policy is followed. After the 1979 shock, the rand/dollar exchange rate was kept constant and a severe recession followed, eventually bringing about the improvement on the current account. The effects of the recession would have

248

been even more long-lasting had the gold price not begun fortuitously to increase dramatically in 1979. This took the pressure off the current account, and the increased investor confidence it brought with it helped reopen the doors to South African borrowers abroad. During the more recent crisis which began in mid-1984, the need for drastic deflation was lessened because of the depreciating exchange rate. Of course, a year later some deflation *did* occur, but that was partly due to the collapse of investor confidence. Besides, as will be discussed below, exchange rate depreciation is not necessarily a painless alternative.

2. EXCHANGE RATE POLICY

The degree to which shocks to the current and capital accounts of a country can be accommodated depends to an important degree on the nature of its exchange rate policy. Under the Bretton Woods *fixed exchange rate system* established after World War II, all the authorities had to do was to maintain the exchange rate at a given level by buying and selling foreign currency to accommodate any excess supplies and demands. Since the breakdown of the system in 1971, countries have had to decide on the degree of flexibility of their exchange rate. In a world of *floating exchange rates*, even if a country decides to peg its own currency to a key currency it will effectively be floating against all third-party currencies.

In the 1970s South African exchange rate policy was characterised by indecision. From August 1971 the rand was pegged to the dollar, then sterling and back to the dollar. After a brief period of 'independent managed floating'[3] the rand was repegged to the dollar in June 1975. Apart from the 17,9 per cent devaluation against the dollar in 1975, this peg was maintained until the publication of the Interim Report of the Commission of Inquiry into the Monetary System and Monetary Policy in 1978. This resulted in the adoption of a form of variable dollar pegging, with the authorities adjusting the exchange rate more freely. In August 1983 the Reserve Bank ceased its policy of quoting the spot exchange rate and instead began to allow a more market determined rate in which they intervened, only when considered desirable, by buying or selling US dollars.

The direction of exchange rate movements has been dictated to a large extent by the gold price and political developments. However, in following the gold price the authorities have adopted a definite downward bias in their determination of the exchange rate for reasons to be explained. In general, sustained falls in the gold price are followed by marked and rapidly falling exchange rates; whereas during periods of a rising gold price the authorities have tended to prevent the rand from appreciating as much as it might have under a freely floating regime. Such policies have important real effects which are now considered.

In analysing the effects of exchange rate changes it is necessary to distinguish between real and nominal exchange rates. The nominal rate is the relative price of domestic and foreign monies, whereas the real rate is the nominal exchange rate adjusted for inflation differentials between the two countries. Thus if inflation in South Africa is 10 per cent higher than in the US and the rand depreciates by 10 per cent against the dollar, the real rate remains unchanged. It follows that there are real effects of exchange rate changes, such as changes in export competitiveness, only if a depreciation is not completely offset by rising costs. Real changes arise when commodity and factor prices adjust slowly relative to exchange rate changes, or when there are changes in real variables such as productivity, labour costs, consumer tastes, as well as discoveries of new mineral resources and alterations in the price of a major export commodity such as gold.[4] Figure 3 shows the behaviour of the nominal and real trade-weighted exchange rate over the past 11 years. It can be seen that both rates appreciated in response to the rising gold price in 1980 and 1982, and depreciated significantly following the political events of 1984.

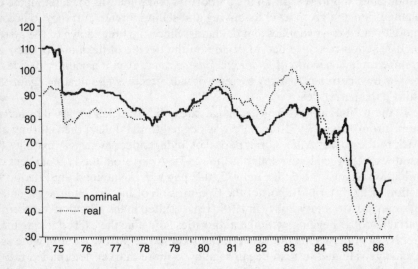

Figure 3 REAL AND NOMINAL RAND EFFECTIVE EXCHANGE RATE (1980 = 100)

Because real exchange rate changes come about when wage and price increases in the domestic economy do not match a nominal depreciation, the initial distributive effect of such a currency depreciation is to reduce real wages of workers, but the precise length of such a wage lag will vary from situation to situation and be affected at any point in time also by such factors as the level of unemployment and the power of trade unions. At the same time it implies higher profits for exporters. Diaz-Alejandro (1965: 20) and Krugman and Taylor (1978) have also shown that regardless of the effect of a depreciation on

250

total profits, the profit *share* in the national income will necessarily improve after devaluation. Given the bias towards depreciation rather than appreciation in the conduct of South African exchange rate policy, such a stance tends to discriminate against wages in favour of profits.

Apart from the effect on income flows, there are also changes in wealth which affect social classes in different ways. When there are inputs in the production of exportables that cannot readily be expanded or contracted (e.g. land), the change in relative prices brought about by a depreciation will not only increase the real income of the producers of such exportables, but it may also increase the wealth of the owners of these inputs by increasing the value of their assets. Furthermore, if it is assumed that the depreciation does not change the aggregate wealth of the country, the gains by owners of land must be offset by a wealth loss from the rest of society, such a transfer being realised through changes in relative prices of the different types of assets. Such effects are particularly relevant in a country like South Africa with a large agricultural sector and a highly unequal racial pattern of wealth ownership.

A further wealth effect results from foreign currency debts. A depreciation increases the local currency value of the debt and debt servicing. This means for the economy as a whole that more resources have to be given up in order to repay the existing debt. Between 1983 and 1984 debt rose by 6,6 per cent in dollars, but because of the currency depreciation the rand value of this debt increased by 65,6 per cent and the proportion of total debt to GDP rose from 32,6 per cent to 45,7 per cent (Table 1).

Table 1 SOUTH AFRICA'S FOREIGN DEBT 1980–1985

	1980	1981	1982	1983	1984	1985
Dollar value of debt ($ billion)	16,7	18,7	22,4	23,9	25,5	27,0
Rand value of debt (R billion)	12,6	18,1	24,3	29,1	48,2	60,1
Rand value of debt as % of GDP	20,3	25,4	30,4	32,6	45,7	50,1
Short-term debt as % of total debt	49,1	57,9	56,5	65,8	68,0	72,0

Source: South African Reserve Bank, *Quarterly Bulletins.*

The extent to which different sectors of the economy benefit from a real depreciation depends on whether they are export-oriented, import-competing and the degree of their dependence on imported inputs. A real depreciation makes South African exports cheaper in foreign currency terms and imports more expensive in rand terms. However, the competitive advantage gained will be reduced to the extent that these industries depend on imported technology and intermediate inputs which will also have increased in price. The Kleu Committee report shows that manufacturing, being far more capital-intensive than both mining and agriculture, is the highest net user of foreign exchange and has the highest import content in its exports (1983: 74).

Clearly mining and agriculture benefit most from a depreciation. Given the strength of the farmers as a political pressure group, and the importance of mining exports to the economy in terms of employment, foreign exchange earnings and tax revenues for the government, it is not surprising that exchange rate policy has implicitly been used to protect the fortunes of these sectors. The downward bias in exchange rate policy means that, because the rand is allowed to depreciate markedly following a gold price fall, mining profits in rand terms are maintained or even increased. Preventing the rand from appreciating by as much as it should during periods of a rising gold price allows even greater rand profits for the mines and, at the same time, protects export industries otherwise adversely affected by the appreciating rand. However, these steps also have a cost effect in as far as inflation will not fall by as much as it otherwise might have. The agricultural sector in particular would lose from an appreciation because it has relatively low imported input requirements.

3. EXCHANGE CONTROL POLICY

An integral part of South Africa's exchange rate policy is exchange *control* policy. Foreign exchange controls were first instituted in 1961 following the Sharpeville shootings which precipitated a large outflow of capital. Controls were imposed on both residents and non-residents, the latter having to use the blocked rand mechanism if they wished to repatriate capital. Essentially, this meant that the capital account was insulated from volatile flights of equity capital because sales of blocked rand could be only to other non-residents. There was thus effectively a pool of investment currency, the price being determined by foreigners' supply and demand for South African securities. If foreigners were pessimistic about the future, the blocked rand rate would fall, creating a discount against the commercial rand rate. This would increase the return on South African securities as shares would be bought at a discount, but dividends could be repatriated at the commercial rand rate. This system remained more or less intact until 1983, except for a few technical changes which widened the scope of blocked rand transactions with the change to securities rand (1976) and the financial rand (1979). An important feature of the latter change was that foreign direct investment could now take place through the financial rand mechanism, thereby giving the foreign direct investor more rand for every dollar.

The liberalisation trends occurring in the financial and foreign exchange markets in the late 1970s and early 1980s also affected exchange control. The Franzsen Commission Report of 1970 had argued strongly in favour of maintaining exchange controls, specifically in view of political factors that could cause capital flight and thereby put strain on the level of foreign exchange reserves. By 1978, with the changing attitude towards the market mechanism and the increasing influence of Dr Gerhard de Kock in the Reserve Bank, this approach had changed. The De Kock Commission[5] stressed the inefficiency and ineffectiveness of controls and proposed the complete elimination of exchange controls on non-residents and only limited controls for residents. The Commission was thus clearly putting its faith in the ability of the market to eliminate capital flight through exchange rate depreciation, which would decrease the value in foreign currency of the repatriated capital and therefore inhibit it.

Exchange controls on non-residents were lifted in 1983, but had to be reimposed in August 1985 following the debt crisis. With regard to residents, the Commission had recommended a gradual relaxation of controls, since a sudden lifting of such controls might have had a large impact on real estate and stock market prices and interest rates. Some adjustments were made but, in general, exchange control remained intact except that a far more liberal attitude was adopted towards applications by local firms to borrow abroad as well as towards certain types of investments abroad. However, when granted, such permission is still subject to *ad hoc* rules by the Reserve Bank.

In recent years we have witnessed numerous examples of capital account liberalisation, including South American countries and Israel. In most cases the experiments failed and were eventually reversed.

A major problem with opening up the capital account is that, although liberalisation might lead to increased *net* inflows, the aggregate flows may hide the changing *composition* of inflows and outflows, which can at a later stage lead to a potential debt problem. The phenomenon of simultaneous borrowing and investing in international capital markets has been analysed, *inter alia*, by Kahn and Ul Haque (1985). Capital flight has been shown, in a number of countries, to have caused a build-up of gross foreign debt, an erosion of the tax base and, to the extent that there has been a net real resource transfer out of the country, a reduction in domestic investment. Typically, when controls are lifted residents invest their own money abroad and invest at home with borrowed foreign capital because of a larger perceived risk at home than abroad. Given the uncertainty surrounding private property in a post-apartheid economy, the incentives for capital flight are high and rising as political instability increases, whereas the risk on assets held abroad is negligible.

Thus, although opening up capital flows may encourage a net inflow into the country, domestic *private* capital may be flowing out. A sudden political crisis would then result in an outflow of borrowed capital, with no likely return of the locally owned capital abroad. An increased foreign debt and the simultaneous rise in investment abroad indicate that this pattern has been evident in South Africa.[6]

Although exchange control was not completely lifted for residents, its relaxation had severe consequences for the structure of South African foreign debt. In 1981–82 the authorities adopted a liberal attitude towards foreign borrowing by private companies. 'The Reserve Bank encouraged overseas borrowing without keeping tabs on the amount. "The Reserve Bank's reporting systems were inadequate. Its free market philosophy seemed to extend to not requiring information" said the managing director of one South African bank ... They had no idea of corporate foreign debt' (Grant, 1985: 71). As seen from Table 1, between 1980 and 1985 total foreign debt increased from $16,7b to $27b and the proportion of short-term debt to total debt increased from 49,1 per cent to 72 per cent. This bunching of maturities exacerbated the problems of the Reserve Bank when American banks began to recall their loans in 1985.

The rationale for lifting exchange controls was based on two fundamental arguments in the De Kock Commission Report: (a) that exchange control appears to work when it is not needed, yet fails precisely at times when it is needed; and (b) enforcing exchange control results in conflict with broader monetary and exchange rate policy. Both these arguments deserve further consideration.

Despite exchange controls, there is evidence of leakages of foreign exchange from the country, particularly during times of crisis when political risks increase the incentives to evade controls. An indication of this evasion, following the 1976 unrest, was the rise in the 'error and unrecorded transactions' item of the balance of payments from R77m in 1975 to R585m in 1977. When this latter figure is compared to the Reserve Bank's gross gold and foreign exchange reserves of R837m in September 1977, it is clear that the size of these transactions must have been significant. Although not all of these unrecorded transactions are illegal outflows, the large and sudden increase makes it reasonable to assume that a sizeable proportion was due to exchange control evasion.[7]

There can be little doubt that exchange control can achieve its objectives in the short run. However, there is less confidence about its long-run effectiveness. Clearly, the existing controls have not been completely successful in stopping outflows, though it is impossible to say what the outflows would have been without controls. Exchange controls should provide a *degree* of protection to reserves; in this respect it is significant that the financial rand was reintroduced and most of the previous relaxation reversed when outflows began to increase on a large scale in 1985. De Kock sums up very clearly the ambivalent feelings about controls: 'In my experience at this bank, every time we try direct controls, it's failed ... Controls take a lot of work — and they don't work. I wasn't happy to bring back forex controls, but you have to be realistic' (Grant, 1985: 65).

The Commission's second argument against exchange control was that it often conflicted with the general thrust of monetary and exchange rate policy. The argument throughout the Report is based on examples of conflict during periods of high gold prices (1979–80 and 1982–3) when exchange controls caused a 'bottling up' of funds in the country which in turn resulted in excessive monetary growth, an artificially low level of interest rates and high inflation. What was needed was both allowing the capital account 'to play its part in overall economic stabilisation' (1984: 132) and 'strong upward pressure on the exchange rate ... to be counteracted by relaxing exchange control' (1984: 219).

These bold assertions raise various problems. First, to allow the capital account to 'play its part' requires open access to world capital markets. It is precisely at times of crisis that these markets are closed to South Africa, as occurred in 1976 and 1985. This means that all the burden of adjustment is placed on either the current account (and accompanying deflation) or the exchange rate.

Secondly, the converse of the argument is that strong downward pressure on the exchange rate would have to be counteracted by tightening up exchange control, which would of course negate the whole policy of liberalisation. If the object of exchange control relaxation was, in the first place, to attract foreign investment, the reimposition of controls discredited any future liberalisation. Credibility formation is an asymmetric process: once eroded, it is hard to restore. Reimposition of controls did indeed occur when the capital account came under pressure, despite the assurance of Dr Chris Stals, then Senior Deputy Governor of the Reserve Bank that '[t]he abolition of the Financial Rand System is a permanent and non-reversible decision' (Nedbank 1983: 197).

On the question of capital flight, the Report was confident that the absence of controls would not bring about either a substantial loss of foreign reserves or an unacceptable depreciation of the rand during periods of political unrest. '[I]t is in precisely such circumstances that some depreciation is called for to counter the effect of a decline in confidence in private domestic investment. A depreciation of the exchange rate would then cushion the effect on the real economy by making investment in export industries and in import replacement much more attractive. To the extent that it succeeds in these sectors, it would also encourage investment elsewhere in the economy' (1984: 133).

The views of the Commission are consistent with our argument above about a downward bias in South Africa's exchange rate policy. Whilst it is argued that exchange control causes the exchange rate to appreciate excessively when the gold price rises, it is not readily acknowledged that controls might prevent the rate from falling excessively when the gold price or confidence fall. The dominant view seems to be that exchange rate flexibility and the market mechanism only produce the efficient allocation of resources when the exchange rate is depreciating and not when it is appreciating. There is concern for the distortions of excessive appreciation but not for excessive depreciation. In addition we see a one-sided optimism that the exchange rate on its own could prevent capital flight.

The Commission's report was written at a time when there were balance of payments surpluses, and when pressure was being brought to bear on the government by local conglomerates wishing to diversify investments abroad. Declining rates of profit and political uncertainty have made it increasingly attractive for South African companies and individuals to invest in other countries, resulting in increasing pressure for exchange control relaxation. Yet, because access to international financial markets is uncertain, particularly so when it is most needed, liberalisation of capital flows does not appear to be appropriate. Lifting exchange control could help facilitate an outflow of funds when there is excess liquidity as a result of high gold price-induced current account deficits, but does not ensure inflows at times of capital account shocks.

4. CONCLUSION

This paper has attempted to show that exchange rate policy in South Africa has tended to favour the low import content industries such as mining and agriculture; at the same time the preference for an undervalued exchange rate tends to redistribute income in favour of profits at the expense of wages. Because of the reliance of manufacturing on imported components, the exchange rate is not a simple tool for encouraging the competitiveness of the manufacturing sector. Its effectiveness clearly differs from industry to industry, but, if the intention is to stimulate manufacturing output, more direct methods should be used to raise productivity in manufacturing rather than distorting the exchange rate as an instrument for industrial protection.

It has, furthermore, been argued that the policy of foreign exchange liberalisation is inappropriate for a country subject to political crises like South Africa. It is clear that full liberalisation primarily serves the interests of those who wish to hold their assets outside the country. Given the necessity hitherto of supplementing domestic savings with foreign capital, it also seems highly questionable that scarce investment funds should be allowed to be invested elsewhere. At the same time, even if lifting exchange controls did relieve the pressure on monetary policy on certain occasions, it raises new problems as well. Experience with liberalisation in LDCs and semi-industrialised countries has not been a success: the Southern Cone countries, Israel and South Africa have all reversed these policies in time. Following the reimposition of the financial rand and the continuing debt crisis in South Africa, liberalisation does not seem to be an option for the foreseeable future either.

NOTES

1 The current account reflects imports and exports of goods and services; the capital account reflects inflows and outflows of capital which include foreign loans and direct investment.
2 Direct investment is an investment by a non-resident in a South African enterprise in which he has a controlling interest. Indirect investment implies no controlling interest and includes equity investment (shares) and foreign loans.
3 This practice involved the Reserve Bank setting the rate and changing it every few weeks. In effect the Bank was pegging to a fixed basket of currencies which resulted in speculative pressures as private operators found they could fairly accurately predict changes in the rand-dollar link on the basis of movements in the component currencies of the basket used by the Reserve Bank.
4 See Korteweg (1980) for a detailed analysis.
5 An interim report was published in 1978 which dealt specifically with exchange rate and exchange control policy. The final report (1984) dealt with monetary policy and the monetary system as well as exchange rate issues. Although the views of the Commission cannot be iden-

tified without qualification with official orthodoxy, De Kock's influence on the report and the fact that by the time the final report was published most of the recommendations of the interim report had been implemented, indicate that the Commission and official views did not differ significantly.

6 By 1980 South African investment abroad was in excess of one-third of foreign investment into South Africa (Kaplan, 1983).

7 In 1978 the Reserve Bank discontinued the practice of reflecting 'errors and unrecorded transactions' as a separate entry and instead these amounts were combined with those of short-term private capital movements. This makes it impossible to see how this former item behaved during the recent intensification of the crisis.

REFERENCES

Black, A. and Stanwix, J., 1986. 'Crisis and Restructuring in the South African Manufacturing Sector'. Paper presented at the Workshop on Macroeconomic Policy and Poverty in South Africa. SALDRU: UCT.

De Kock Commission: Reports of the Commission of Inquiry into the Monetary System and Monetary Policy in South Africa, 1978. 'Exchange Rates in South Africa'. Interim Report (RP 112/1978).

—— 1985. 'The Monetary System and Monetary Policy in South Africa'. Final Report (RP 70/1984).

Diaz-Alejandro, C.F., 1965. Exchange Rate Devaluation in a Semi-Industrialised Country. M.I.T. Press.

Grant, C., 1985. 'The Banks Abandon South Africa', *Euromoney* (December).

Kahn, S.B., 1987. 'Import Penetration and Import Demands in the South African Economy'. Unpublished mimeograph, UCT.

Kaplan, D., 1983. 'South Africa's Changing Place in the World Economy', *South African Review*, One.

Kahn, M., and N. Ul Haque, 1985. 'Foreign Borrowing and Capital Flight: A Formal Analysis'. *International Monetary Fund Staff Papers*, Vol. 32, No. 4.

Kleu Study Group, 1983. Report of the Study Group on Industrial Development Strategy. (Government Printer for the Department of Industries and Commerce.)

Korteweg, P., 1980. Exchange-Rate Policy, Monetary Policy, and Real Exchange Rate Variability. *Essays in International Finance,* Princeton, No. 140.

Krugman, P., and L. Taylor, 1978. 'Contractionary Effects of Devaluation', *Journal of International Economics* (August).

Nedbank, 1983. *South Africa: an Appraisal.* Nedbank Group Economic Unit (Second edition).

5.6 RECENT EXCHANGE RATE POLICY IN SOUTH AFRICA — A CRITIQUE

J.J. Cloete*

The more troublous the times, the worse does a laissez-faire system work. I believe the times are likely to remain troublous for a generation and that the magnification of the evils of monetary instability which we have suffered in the past five years are likely to continue unless we do something about it.

John Maynard Keynes (1923)

In a situation where funds can flow freely over the capital account of the balance of payments and where domestic interest rates are also free to move, the exchange rate can be expected to remain reasonably stable. In such circumstances, surpluses and deficits on the current account of the balance of payments, arising from imbalances between aggregate domestic demand and supply, would drive down or drive up domestic interest rates. The interest rate changes, in turn, would generate outflows and inflows of funds over the capital account of the balance of payments that would roughly equal the funds in full accruing or lost on the current account. The gold and foreign exchange reserves of the country would accordingly not change and neither would the exchange rate.

The circumstances surrounding the rand exchange rate, however, are very different from this 'ideal' situation. In the first place, because of the uncertain political future of the country and also because of the predominance of mining shares in the equity portfolios of foreign investors in South Africa (together with the susceptibility of goldmining shares to fluctuations in the gold price), foreign capital funds other than perhaps trade finance do not necessarily flow into the South African economy in sufficient volume fully to offset the substantial current account deficits which are accumulated from time to time and which arise from the high import propensity of the economy and the unfavourable effect which large decreases in the gold price can have on export earnings. As a developing economy, in which new jobs have to be created at a rapid rate to match rapid population growth, South Africa also cannot afford intermittent substantial capital outflows to offset the large current account surpluses which develop from time to time under the impact of the country's high propensity to export.

In the second place, the prevailing conditions governing the demand for and supply of credit and capital in the domestic economy might be such that interest rates do not adjust fast enough or to the extent necessary to induce the foreign capital flows required to balance the deficits and surpluses arising on current

* Formerly Chief Economist, First National Bank. This paper was first published in *The South African Journal of Economics*, Vol. 54, No. 3, 1986.

account. This means that appreciable changes in the exchange rate can take place (generating expectations which can drive the currency away from its equilibrium rate to a considerable extent) before the interest rate adjustment mechanism comes into operation.

In the third place, because of the pressing social need to create new jobs and a rising standard of living for the Black population, South Africa also cannot afford the high level of domestic interest rates required to finance the persistent current account deficits which, because of the high propensity to import, would tend to develop if the economy were to operate reasonably close to its full potential growth rate, even though this rate is considerably restricted by the limited supply of skilled labour available in the country. On the contrary, the rate of economic advance needed in the South African economy actually requires the maintenance of a relatively low interest rate structure during the course of the business cycle, otherwise new fixed investment in the private sector as well as in essential social and economic infrastructure would not take place at the required pace.

Given the high import and export propensities of the South African economy and the resultant high degree of instability of the current account of the balance of payments, the rand exchange rate will be subject to sharp appreciations and depreciations, if the interest rate is relied upon to balance the current account deficits and surpluses, especially in the prevailing political situation.

This is borne out by developments over the past five years. From 1981 to 1984, net deficits amounting to R9 699 million were incurred on the current account of the balance of payments. As a result, there was a substantial drain of liquidity from the domestic banking system and domestic interest rates moved to sharply higher levels well above corresponding rates overseas. While the higher domestic rates did attract a net inflow of funds over the capital account the amount involved was only R3 581 million. The result was that an acute shortage of foreign exchange prevailed during the greater part of the period, which pushed the rand down by 48 per cent against the U S dollar between 1980 and 1984.

More recently, net capital outflows have substantially exceeded the very large current account surpluses which have accumulated in the wake of the renewed recession in the economy from mid-1984 onwards. The balance of payments figures show a current account surplus of R7 112 million for 1985 against a capital outflow of R10 418 million. The resultant shortage of foreign exchange caused a further substantial depreciation of the rand by 43 per cent against the dollar during the course of 1985.

While the unprecedentedly large capital outflows over the past year or so can be attributed mainly to the deteriorating political situation in the country, it does show the vulnerability of the exchange rate to foreign capital flows, which could also result from a sharp fall in the gold price and a sell-off of mining shares by foreign investors.

259

THE EXCHANGE RATE AS ADJUSTER

From 1981 onwards the South African monetary authorities consistently pursued a policy of allowing the rand exchange rate to float downwards under pressure from the large current account deficits and the accompanying constant reduction in the gold and foreign exchange reserves. It was only once extreme pressure had developed on the South African currency by September 1985 that they acted to protect the rand against the accelerating outflow of foreign capital by declaring a 'standstill' on foreign banking debt repayments and re-introducing the financial rand mechanism that inhibits the sale of South African assets by foreign investors from depressing the commercial rand rate.

In pursuing this exchange rate policy, it seems that the monetary authorities pinned their hopes, at least at first, on the operation of the interest rate mechanism to restore the necessary balance between aggregate domestic demand and supply and so balance of payments equilibrium, thereby preventing an unduly large depreciation of the rand. Hence their emphasis on a policy of market-related rates and their readiness to see the market take up interest rates to unprecedentedly high levels by 1982. When the interest rate mechanism failed to restore balance of payments equilibrium and the rand continued to slide, however, the monetary authorities started to see the exchange rate itself as adjuster. In other words, they argued that a depreciating rand itself would, in time, restore balance of payments equilibrium by discouraging imports and encouraging exports thus removing the deficits on the current account of the balance of payments.

Furthermore, they argued that the depreciating rand was making it possible for the South African economy to absorb and to adjust to the political and economic shocks (including a fall in the dollar price of gold and reduced agricultural export earnings resulting from prolonged drought) that were hitting the economy. They maintained that they did not have the necessary foreign exchange to protect the exchange rate and, by allowing the rand to float downwards, the exchange rate would sooner or later reach a low point from where expectations would start to take it up again. Confidence in the South African currency would return and the resultant renewed inflow of foreign capital would help to restore balance of payments equilibrium again. Meanwhile, the depreciating rand would boost rand export earnings and protect domestic manufacturers against foreign competition, thereby preventing the shocks to the economy from causing a severe slump in domestic growth and employment.[1]

POLICY PROBLEMS

However, in pursuing a policy of allowing the exchange rate and domestic interest rates to adjust to restore internal as well as external equilibrium the monetary authorities faced considerable risks.

260

(a) In the prevailing situation in South Africa (i.e. political unrest, the disinvestment campaign overseas, threats of trade sanctions, an inflation rate well above those in the industrialized countries overseas, rising unemployment and a very unsatisfactory growth performance), a depreciating rand would probably generate expectations of a continued further depreciation. The market would tend to push the exchange rate well below its purchasing power parity value and, once a currency has overshot to this extent, confidence in it is not easily restored.

(b) A substantial depreciation of the rand would have had a negative effect on domestic manufacturing industry in a situation where domestic importers had borrowed extensively overseas to take advantage of the large positive differential between domestic and overseas interest rates. Domestic manufacturing profits were not only being squeezed by increased rand costs of essential imports but also by the increase in the rand value of foreign debt. This two-part squeeze on manufacturers' profits meant that the favourable effect of the rand depreciation on domestic economic activity was largely offset by its negative impact on production and employment in the domestic manufacturing industries. The result was that, despite the sharp depreciation of the rand from 1981 onwards, growth was depressed to an average annual rate of only one per cent during the five years 1981–85. Employment increased at an even slower rate (0,7 per cent p.a.) over the period, with very unfavourable repercussions for unemployment and for social peace which, in turn, impacted further on the exchange rate. In the face of this dismal growth and employment performance, it is difficult to see how it can be argued that the interest and exchange rate policies pursued by the authorities could have allowed the economy to adapt to or to absorb the exogenous political and other shocks successfully.

(c) A substantial depreciation of the rand in a situation where double-digit inflation and inflationary expectations are strongly entrenched can easily engender an uncontrolled depreciation/inflation spiral, with disruptive results both for the real economy and the financial markets.

(d) Overseas investors in and lenders to South Africa (including overseas banks) would take a gloomy view of future prospects for investment and for business in this country in the wake of the substantial reduction in their South African profits and in the value of their South African assets expressed in their own currencies brought about by the rand depreciation. Both the fall in asset values and in profits have significantly impaired the safety of foreign investment in and loans to this country. This can only result in a further diminution of the future accretion of foreign capital, which is already inadequate to balance the substantial net current account deficits that would probably accompany the achievement of satisfactory growth and employment rates.

(e) Both exports and imports are strongly driven by income effects which normally swamp the effect of changes in the exchange rate on these quantities, unless the exchange rate changes should be appreciable. South Africa's export earnings normally increase and decrease in response to economic recovery and contraction in the industrialized economies overseas. The improvement in demand for South African exports tends, in turn, to initiate a strong business cycle upswing in the domestic economy which, because of the high propensity to import, tends to generate a substantial increase in imports particularly during the mature phase of the upswing when essential capital goods have to be imported to extend domestic production capacity. At that stage in the domestic business cycle, it should be noted, the business cycle overseas is normally starting to contract. South African export earnings accordingly also start to contract, thereby accentuating the adverse effect of the peak in imports on the current account of the balance of payments.[2]

Thus, both exports and imports tend to be subject to strong cyclical swings. These, in turn, cause and require very appreciable changes in the exchange rate to moderate in the face of the uncertainties surrounding the balancing foreign capital flows. As recent experience has shown, however, such substantial changes in the exchange rate tend to have very adverse consequences for internal price stability, for foreign investors' confidence in the South African economy and for stable growth in the export as well as import (manufacturing) industries.

AN INTEGRATED POLICY MIX

Recent exchange rate and accompanying interest rate policies pursued by the South African monetary authorities have resulted in extreme fluctuations in both the exchange and interest rates and have stabilised neither the balance of payments nor the domestic economy. In the process, business confidence has been seriously disturbed to a degree that new long-term investment in the economy by both foreign and South African businessmen has ceased or slowed down greatly. The misery index, in terms of unemployment, inflation, business insolvencies and depressed aggregate output, has never been higher.

The question arises whether, instead of allowing market forces to push the exchange rate and domestic interest rates to the levels required to restore and maintain internal and external stability, the South African authorities could not have pursued an alternative policy or policies that would have yielded better results, bearing in mind the political and other shocks which have impacted on the economy. The answer to this question appears to be in the affirmative. The key to such an alternative policy appears to be the realisation that, while the political difficulties facing South Africa continue, the country will simply be forced to maintain growth in aggregate domestic demand at a level at which the accompanying growth in essential imports can be financed by export earnings. This does not mean that no current account deficits or, for that matter, surpluses can be allowed to occur, but that deficits will have to be kept to moderate proportions in view of the limited supply of foreign capital that the country can expect to attract at reasonable interest rates to finance current account deficits that are in excess of export earnings.

Because it would be very costly (in terms of unemployment, insolvencies of smaller businesses and lost production) to control growth in aggregate domestic monetary demand to the extent necessary by applying an appropriately restrictive monetary and interest rate policy, there will have to be fairly heavy reliance on fiscal policy in the form of changes in taxation and in Government expenditure to keep domestic monetary demand growth in check. And, since salaries and wages paid by Government constitute one of its principal costs or items of expenditure, it would be necessary, in the first place, to maintain proper control over increases in Government salaries and wages not only to prevent the contribution of the Government towards aggregate domestic demand from rising too rapidly, but also to demonstrate to the private sector the extent to which salary and wage increases in that sector will need to be restricted in order to keep down the rate of increase in total domestic monetary demand to an acceptable level.

In the same way that the task of maintaining equilibrium between domestic demand and supply cannot be entrusted to monetary and interest rate policy alone, because of the extreme and damaging movements in interest rates that this entails, fiscal policy also cannot carry the burden of maintaining internal equilibrium by itself. Monetary and interest rate policy would still be required to reinforce the effect of fiscal policy on aggregate demand, otherwise the required changes in Government expenditure and in taxation might well have to be so large as to damage the economy. With fiscal and monetary policy reinforcing each other, however, the changes required in the policy variables to maintain the desired degree of control over aggregate demand can be more moderate and less damaging to the economy.

As indicated, an important part of the Government's fiscal policy is the control it exercises over the annual salary and wage increases it grants to its employees. The control in this respect, in fact, extends to salary and wage increases in the public sector generally, as well as to increases in prices of such important economic inputs as power, transport and agricultural produce. But it is not only increases in wages and in prices administered by Government that contribute to the annual increases in aggregate monetary demand and so to the continuous wage/price spiral embedded in the economy. Nominal salary and wage increases in the private sector make an even more important contribution.

To reduce the harmful effects that fiscal and monetary restrictions will have on output and employment, it will also be necessary to operate more directly on nominal salary and wage increases in the private sector. This can be done, for example, by Government having regular discussions with organised business and labour to indicate the kind of wage and price behaviour that is required on their part to maintain price stability as well as a high level of employment and output.[3]

To the extent that organised commerce and industry and labour can be persuaded to moderate their wage and price behaviour, aggregate monetary

263

demand in the economy can be restricted without the creation of unemployment and loss of production. The moderation of wage increases in this way means a simultaneous moderation of wage cost increases which, in turn, makes a simultaneous moderation in price increases possible. The voluntary moderation of wage and price increases in both the public and private sectors of the economy should accordingly be the third leg of the policy mix that should be applied in the prevailing circumstances.

Once internal equilibrium has been established through the application of an appropriate mix of fiscal, monetary, and prices and incomes policies to aggregate domestic monetary demand, the deficits and surpluses that would emerge on the current account of the balance of payments would automatically be smaller, and so would be the fluctuations in the exchange rate. In other words, as Keynes suggested so many years ago in 'A Tract on Monetary Reform' (1923), primacy should be accorded to the pursuit of internal balance and price stability, while the exchange rate should be managed to crawl as needed to support price stability (Williamson, 1983).

It cannot be argued that the financial authorities had no option but to allow the exchange rate to absorb the political and other shocks that were hitting the economy. On the contrary, by applying an appropriate mix of fiscal and monetary policy (reinforced by appropriate control over government-administered wage and price increases in particular), aggregate domestic monetary demand could have been controlled so as to have prevented in particular the excessive current account surpluses and deficits incurred during the 1979–82 period. This, in turn, would have considerably reduced the vulnerability of the balance of payments to uncertain foreign capital flows, which would not only have stabilised the exchange rate significantly but also liquidity in the domestic banking system and the demand for bank credit, and hence domestic interest rates.

With regard to exchange rate policy, the South African economy is still largely facing a situation that applied under the old IMF fixed exchange rate system up to 1971. The country cannot afford other than moderate depreciations of the rand because of the strong inflationary bias in the economy arising from the shortage of skilled labour, strong wage push on the part of the Black population aimed at redressing the unequal distribution of incomes, and strong upward pressure on profits in markets characterised by imperfect competition. The country also cannot afford immoderately large appreciations of the rand because of the important role of exports in the economy.

In the face of the strong inflationary bias in the economy, quite a high degree of exchange rate stability is required, otherwise growth and employment would be very detrimentally affected not only by an unstable price level but also by the disruptive effects that appreciable exchange rate changes have on both the export and the domestic manufacturing industries. Furthermore, to maintain the required degree of exchange rate stability, interest rates would need to move sharply upwards and downwards, given the uncertainties surrounding foreign capital outflows as well as inflows. But this would also be very harmful to growth and employment.

It seems that South African policy-makers have little option but to pursue a policy of removing imbalances that arise between total domestic supply and demand by directly reducing (or expanding) demand in the first place through appropriate fiscal measures (which include appropriate pressure on administered wages and prices in both the public and private sectors) and to assign to interest and exchange rate changes a more moderate role in the adjustment process similar to the part they did, in fact, play under the IMF fixed exchange rate regime but not necessarily so restrictive. This does not require an inflexible rate but merely the avoidance of sharp changes that are so disruptive to the economy and, instead, pursuance of a policy that allows the rand exchange rate to crawl downwards gradually against the major currencies at a rate that will preserve the competitiveness of South African exports in the overseas markets.[4]

Of course, even if the best monetary and fiscal policies had been applied over the past five years, growth in output and employment would probably still have been at an unsatisfactory level because growth in export earnings had also been depressed, except in 1984 and 1985 when the recovery overseas and the substantial depreciation of the rand started to exert a favourable effect on export volumes. There is also a limit to what can be accomplished with anti-cyclical monetary and fiscal measures in raising growth and employment to permanently higher levels. In order to achieve satisfactory rates of growth and employment, the political problems will have to be resolved, while considerable structural impediments to growth and stability will also have to be overcome or at least reduced. But without a proper anticyclical stabilisation policy that will at least maintain a reasonable degree of economic and price stability over the business cycle, it will be impossible even to make a start with the resolution of these structural problems.

The greater stability that an alternative policy conducted on the lines indicated (i.e. a policy of operating directly on total domestic demand by appropriate fiscal and prices and incomes policy) would have imparted to the exchange rate as well as to domestic interest rates and the price level would at least have reduced significantly the uncertainty and risk which confronted businessmen. To that extent, new investment, production and employment would have proceeded more smoothly and the average annual economic growth rate achieved over the past five years would almost certainly have been higher than that actually recorded. In contrast, the policy pursued by the fiscal and monetary authorities of allowing changes in interest rates and in the exchange rate to carry the main burden of adjusting the imbalances between total domestic demand and supply has been tantamount to merely allowing the business cycle to run its course. As was to be expected, the result was a 'boom' and 'bust' cycle, with considerable instability in both the real and financial markets, and very unfavourable consequences for growth and employment.

Recent changes in the direction of policy both in the Reserve Bank and in the Treasury give some hope that the South African authorities are now aware of the need to maintain a relatively stable exchange rate in the difficult circumstances facing the country — hence their willingness to reintroduce the financial rand mechanism to reduce volatility on the capital account of the balance of payments, and to impose a surcharge on imports to limit the impact of imports on the current account of the balance of payments. (Selective import controls to avoid the inflationary impact of an import surcharge would have been better.)

In deciding to adopt an explicit target for domestic monetary growth (following a recommendation to this effect in the Final Report of the De Kock Commission of Inquiry into the Monetary System and Monetary Policy in South Africa published in May 1985), the monetary authorities have also now firmly placed the emphasis of policy on controlling aggregate domestic demand and establishing 'internal' equilibrium in the first place. To the extent that the new monetary policy will succeed in achieving and maintaining internal equilibrium, greater external equilibrium will automatically follow and the exchange rate will also be more stable.

Furthermore, in deciding on an appropriate target to set for monetary growth, the monetary authorities would have to take a forward view of the likely performance of exports in the period ahead and on the likely outcome on the balance of payments, as envisaged in the policy mix outlined above. They would also have to take into account targets for Government expenditure and taxation as well as targets for the expected achievable growth rate and the inflation rate to be accepted, both of which have to be financed and have to be allowed for in their target for monetary growth.[5]

In other words, an appropriate mix of fiscal, monetary and incomes policies is at least implicit in the new policy of monetary growth targeting. The new policy, moreover, is also forward looking, which should overcome some of the difficulties of correct timing of policy measures inherent in the application of discretionary monetary and fiscal stabilisation policy.

The need for restoring more stable conditions to the South African economy is now urgent. Growth and employment are already being seriously affected by the unstable political environment. Price, interest rate and exchange rate instability and the uncertainties and risks accompanying this will merely depress growth and employment to an even greater extent. What is required from the monetary and fiscal authorities is a skilfully formulated policy mix that will be resolutely applied to stabilise internal monetary demand relative to export earnings in the first place and, in this way, prices, interest rates and the exchange rates.

NOTES

1 The Governor of the Reserve Bank has on a number of occasions spelled out the rationale for flexible and market-related interest and exchange rates and for a policy of allowing the exchange

rate to adjust rather than domestic output and employment. See, for example, his recent addresses to the meeting of the Executive Committee of the Federated Chamber of Industries (1986) and to a meeting of Forex R.S.A. (1986).

2 See Barclays Business Brief, August 1985, for a more detailed description of the extent to which aggregate domestic demand and output are driven by alternating surpluses and deficits that develop cyclically on the current account of the balance of payments.

3 This kind of co-operative wage and price policy was suggested by Paul McCracken *et al.* in a special report entitled 'Towards full employment and price stability', OECD, Paris, 1977.

4 It is significant to note that Colm Kearney (1984) concluded that by 1984 the Conservative Government in Britain had also effectively abandoned its monetarist experiment and had switched to a policy more consistent with the promotion of low interest rates without feeding inflation by a weaker exchange rate.

5 Vines, Maciejowski and Meade (1983) have detailed the kind of policy mix and assignment of financial instruments to financial targets that are required if demand management of an economy is to be effective.

REFERENCES

Barclays Business Brief, 1985. 'The next upturn: how and when?' Barclays National Bank Limited, Johannesburg.

De Kock, 1985. Final Report of the Commission of Inquiry into the Monetary System and Monetary Policy in South Africa. Pretoria: Government Printer.

De Kock, G., 1986. 'Monetary and Fiscal Policy in 1986 — Constraints and Objectives'. Address to an Executive Council Meeting of the Federated Chamber of Industries, Cape Town.

—— 1986. 'Money Supply Targets and Exchange Rate Policy in South Africa'. Address to Forex R.S.A., Johannesburg.

Kearney, C., 1984. The British Anti-inflationary Strategy: Implementing Monetarism or turning to Radcliff, published by Société Universitaire Européenne de Recherches Financières (SUERF), Paris.

McCracken, P. *et al.*, 1977. Towards Full Employment and Price Stability. Published by the OECD, Paris.

Vines, D., Maciejowski, J. and Meade, J.F., 1983. *Stagflation*, Vol. 2: *Demand Management*. London: George Allen & Unwin.

Williamson, J., 1983. 'Keynes and the International Economic Order', in D. Worswick and J. Trevithick (eds), *Keynes and the Modern World*. Cambridge University Press.

5.7 ECONOMIC GROWTH AND FOREIGN DEBT: THE SOUTH AFRICAN CASE

G.P.C. de Kock*

DEBT FATIGUE

The international issue of economic growth and foreign debt is very much in the news at present. In this regard the recent Annual Report of the Bank for International Settlements coined the apt phrase 'debt fatigue'. Signs of such 'fatigue' can be found among the indebted countries, some of which have decided to limit or suspend debt interest service, as well as among the many creditor banks that are now reluctant to play their part in the current international debt strategy as embodied, for example, in the so-called Baker plan.

THE CALL FOR GROWTH-ORIENTED ADJUSTMENT

Another phrase in vogue at present is 'growth-oriented adjustment'. In the view of most experts, appropriate 'balance of payments adjustment' by heavily indebted countries, which invariably implies restrictive monetary and fiscal policies, remains an essential part of any solution to the foreign debt problem. In deference to the developing countries, however, it is accepted that as far as possible this adjustment should be 'growth-oriented'. Understandably, some would underline 'growth-oriented' while others would underline 'adjustment'. But most accept that 'adjustment' is essential. Thus far, however, the 'adjustment' efforts of most indebted Third World countries have been sadly lacking. Governments have generally flinched from applying the required unpopular monetary and fiscal policies.

The major exception to this rule has been South Africa. Indeed, the main theme of this address will be that the South African economy has experienced a remarkable balance of payments adjustment during the past two years, which has not gone unnoticed in overseas financial circles and which has placed the country's foreign debt situation in a new perspective.

REASSESSING SOUTH AFRICA'S FOREIGN DEBT SITUATION

Twenty-two months have now passed since the imposition by South Africa of a partial debt standstill and the reintroduction of exchange control over non-residents in September 1985. At the time there was considerable misunder-

* Governor of the South African Reserve Bank. This paper was presented at an economic forum arranged by the Department of Economics of the University of Durban/Westville and the Natal Building Society Limited on 2 July 1987, and first published in *The Securities Markets*, No. 5, Third Quarter, 1987.

standing inside South Africa about the nature and causes of the country's 'debt problem'. Wild accusations were the order of the day. Some blamed the South African banks *en masse* for having borrowed too much abroad, particularly in the form of short-term credits. Some bankers, in turn, tried to shift the blame on to the Reserve Bank, claiming that the Bank had encouraged them to borrow abroad by quoting attractive forward exchange rates. Others blamed public entities like the Transport Services and the Electricity Supply Commission (Escom) for excessive overseas funding. At the same time it was alleged that the Department of Finance had not controlled foreign borrowing effectively and had not applied a proper 'strategy' in this regard.

Now that the dust has settled it is possible to reassess the whole sequence of events leading to the debt standstill and to clarify some of the issues still outstanding. The facts now indicate clearly that while there were serious deficiencies in the offshore operations of some South African banks, the specific allegations to which I have just referred were totally unfounded.

TWO ELEMENTARY POINTS

First, it might be useful to clear the decks by making two elementary points. The first point is that it is perfectly sound and normal for a developing economy to use foreign capital to promote economic development. This applies to both equity capital and loans. In Hamlet, Polonius advised his son Laertes: 'Neither a borrower nor a lender be.' This may have been good advice for a father to give his son, but it does not apply to foreign borrowing by a developing country or to the use of credit in business generally. The United States became the greatest economy on earth by making extensive use of foreign equity and loan capital. Similarly, South Africa became an important economy on the African continent by making good use of foreign capital to develop its mining, manufacturing, commerce and other forms of economic activity. For a developing country to have a substantial amount of foreign debt outstanding at any given moment is therefore quite in order. 'Debt' is not a dirty word. On the contrary, 'debt can be beautiful'.

Of course, it goes without saying that a country should not borrow *too much*. To determine what is an appropriate level of foreign debt for any developing country, economists and bankers use certain well established criteria, such as the ratio of foreign interest payments to exports, the ratio of foreign debt to gross domestic product and the ratio of foreign debt to exports. If these ratios become excessive the country in question is rightly held to be 'overborrowed'. But provided the various safety limits are not exceeded, it is not only acceptable but also sound and desirable for a developing country to have foreign debt. Indeed, a developing country can be *under*borrowed as well as *over*borrowed.

The second elementary point is that the foreign debt *of a country* is by no means the same thing as the foreign debt *of the Government*. In most countries it is not only or even mainly the Government that borrows overseas; the banks and other private sector entities also make extensive use of foreign loans or credits. In South Africa's case the foreign debt of the central government, including such public authorities as the South African Transport Services and the Department of Posts and Telecommunications, amounted to only 16,5 per cent of South Africa's total foreign debt in 1984 and 18,6 per cent in 1986 (see Table 1).

Table 1 FOREIGN DEBT OF SOUTH AFRICA

Year	Public authorities* (US$ billion)	Total (US$ billion)	Foreign debt of public authorities as percentage of total foreign debt
1980	1,7	16,9	10,1
1981	1,9	18,9	10,1
1982	3,7	22,6	16,4
1983	3,8	23,8	16,0
1984	4,0	24,3	16,5
1985	4,3	23,5	18,3
1986	4,2	22,6	18,6

* Central Government, local authorities and public business enterprises.
Source: South African Reserve Bank.

So much for the two elementary points. Let us now revisit the South African debt problem of July/August 1985.

DID THE SOUTH AFRICAN ECONOMY 'OVERBORROW'?

It is now clearer than ever that, as many international bankers and other financial experts have repeatedly pointed out, the post-July 1985 capital withdrawal and the resultant depreciation of the rand had their own special causes rooted in deteriorating overseas perceptions of socio-political developments in South Africa, and were *not* caused by 'overborrowing'. The South African case was totally different from that of debt-ridden countries such as Brazil, Mexico, Argentina, Chile and Poland. The South African economy was never overborrowed. It experienced a 'liquidity problem' because of the withdrawal of short-term bank credits.

What happened is now a matter of recorded history. Following the deterioration in socio-political conditions, the township unrest and the other developments that led to the declaration of a state of emergency on 20 July 1985, certain American banks announced their decision to withdraw credits previously extended to South African banks and other private enterprises. This brought about a form of confidence crisis and a capital flight that inevitably put downward pressure on the exchange rate of the rand. And it was this sequence of events that induced the authorities to declare a partial 'debt standstill' on 1 September 1985.

WAS THE ABOLITION OF THE FINANCIAL RAND THE CAUSE OF THE DEBT PROBLEMS?

In the months following the introduction of the debt standstill in September 1985 there was one line of criticism that was given much publicity at the time but which was always without any foundation. This line of criticism ran as follows:

In February 1983 the Government allegedly made the 'mistake' of abolishing exchange control over non-residents, i.e. the financial rand system, and returning to a unitary exchange rate system. This, so it was argued, resulted in a harmful outflow of capital as foreigners disinvested by selling their South African shares to South African residents.

It was further alleged that, to protect the foreign exchange reserves, the Reserve Bank then encouraged the banks to borrow excessive amounts abroad by quoting favourable forward exchange rates to them, i.e. rates which made it cheaper to borrow overseas than in South Africa, even after adding to foreign interest rates the cost of forward cover against exchange rate depreciation. This resulted in 'overborrowing', so the story goes, and it was this overborrowing that brought about the debt crisis of August 1985.

This simply was not the case. The return to a unitary exchange rate in February 1983, i.e. the abolition of exchange control over non-residents, was a positive forward step in the circumstances of the time and did *not* lead to a harmful outflow of capital. In calendar 1983 there was a net capital outflow of R1,3 billion in the form of net sales by non-residents of South African shares to residents — largely as a result of the sharp decline in the gold price from the middle of February 1983 onwards. But in 1984 and the first quarter of 1985 there was a net *inflow* of capital through the Stock Exchange of R1,3 billion. Thus, over the whole period of 27 months from the beginning of 1983 until March 1985, there was no net outflow through the Stock Exchange! Moreover, the initial Stock Exchange outflow during 1983 occurred mainly at a time when the current account of the balance of payments was in surplus, whereas the subsequent inflow came at just the right time to help finance the current account deficit.

For more than two years the abolition of the financial rand therefore had a useful stabilising effect on the money supply and the economy, and did not put any undue pressure on the overall balance of payments or the gold and foreign exchange reserves.

The credits withdrawn by foreign banks from July 1985 onwards were credits which, like all other loans, were always *commercial rand transactions* and never subject in any way to the financial rand arrangements. Their withdrawal would therefore have occurred *irrespective of whether or not there was a financial rand system in operation.* The financial rand was brought back in September 1985 only after it had become clear that the more drastic measure of the debt standstill would have to be imposed to deal with the credit withdrawals. It was then judged appropriate also to curb any possible accompanying outflow of non-resident equity funds.

DID THE RESERVE BANK ENCOURAGE THE BANKS TO BORROW ABROAD BY QUOTING FAVOURABLE FORWARD RATES?

The allegation that the Reserve Bank encouraged the banks to borrow off-shore by manipulating its forward exchange rates was also without foundation. Throughout the period in question the Reserve Bank's approach to foreign borrowing by banks was basically one of *neutrality*, provided, of course, that the banks complied with the various requirements of the Banks Act and Exchange Control. In accordance with this approach the Reserve Bank based its forward rates on the interest rate differentials between South Africa and other countries. This had the effect of more or less equating the average cost of domestic borrowing to the average overall cost of foreign borrowing, i.e. including the cost of forward cover.[1]

The only exceptions to this rule were made on occasions when South African banks were *repaying* foreign credits *too rapidly*. On such occasions the Reserve Bank adjusted its forward rates temporarily in a manner designed to provide the banks with some marginal incentive to roll over a part of their maturing foreign credits. But at no stage during the period in question did the Reserve Bank manipulate its forward rates in order to encourage banks to increase their foreign debts.

The truth is that, far from encouraging banks to increase their foreign borrowing, the Reserve Bank from the second quarter of 1983 onwards applied an increasingly restrictive domestic policy involving rising rates of interest in order to bring about a large current account surplus — with a view, among other things, to *reducing* South Africa's short-term foreign debt.

It is now a matter of history that this policy proved effective and that South Africa's foreign debt, in fact, started to decline well before the crisis situation of August 1985 came about. It is ironic that some of the very same commentators who criticised the Reserve Bank for allegedly encouraging banks to borrow abroad also criticised the tightening of domestic monetary policy that was designed to eliminate the current account deficit and to encourage the repayment of foreign debt.

FACTS SHOWING THAT SOUTH AFRICA WAS NOT 'OVERBORROWED'

The following facts can be adduced to show that, according to all accepted economic criteria, the combined foreign debt of South Africa's public and private sectors of US$23,7 billion at the time of the 1985 debt standstill was far from excessive:

- South Africa's total interest payments abroad in 1985 amounted to only 10,7 per cent of exports of goods and services, compared with an *average* of 26,8 per cent for developing countries with debt servicing problems and over 40 per cent in some cases.
- Even if dividends to foreigners are added to interest payments, the percentage of exports becomes only about 13,5 per cent — a level which has, moreover, remained more or less constant over the past 40 years.
- South Africa's foreign debt of $23,7 billion in August 1985 equalled about 171 per cent of one year's exports of goods and services, compared with an *average* of 247 per cent (in 1984) for developing countries with debt servicing problems and over 400 per cent in many cases.

Table 2 shows how favourably South Africa's foreign debt situation compared with that of a number of major foreign debtor countries in 1984/85.

These various facts and figures refute what is left of the allegation that the South African economy 'overborrowed' and that this was encouraged by the 'negligent' attitude of the authorities towards foreign borrowing in general and by the banks in particular.

Table 2 TOTAL FOREIGN DEBT AND SELECTED RATIOS FOR CERTAIN COUNTRIES*

	Total foreign debt (US$ billion)	Total foreign debt as percentage of GDP	Debt service ratio (Interest)	Total foreign debt as percentage of exports of goods and services
	(1984)	(1984)	(1984)	(1985)
Argentina	47,8	72,2	55,1	520,4
Bolivia	3,2	125,3	24,3	528,6
Brazil	102,3	45,2	31,8	356,7
Chile	18,4	96,1	42,3	519,2
Ecuador	7,2	69,4	28,1	278,8
Mexico	96,2	60,8	25,5	317,9
Morocco	14,8	120,0	56,5	465,6
Nigeria	18,5	24,9	10,5	120,5
Peru	13,4	74,7	27,7	400,0
Philippines	25,4	72,5	32,9	362,0
Poland	26,9	35,7	50,0	N/A
South Africa	24,3	45,7	9,9	148,9

Uruguay	3,7	62,2	26,5	323,1
Venezuela	32,8	57,2	21,6	203,0
Yugoslavia	20,2	41,4	11,9	N/A

* Latest available figures.

Sources: Organisation for Economic Co-operation and Development: *External Debt Statistics*, Paris, 1987.

International Monetary Fund: *International Financial Statistics*, Washington DC, June 1987.

RELATIVELY TOO MUCH SHORT-TERM DEBT?

There are some observers who would agree wholeheartedly with the broad conclusion that South Africa was not overborrowed but who would nevertheless question whether the *short-term* portion of South Africa's foreign debt, i.e. debt with an unexpired maturity of less than one year, which amounted to $13,4 billion out of the total of $23,7 billion in August 1985, was not on the high side. My own view at the time was that in relative terms the short-term portion was too large. In retrospect, however, I doubt whether even that was the case — judged, that is, by purely economic criteria and taking into account that the short-term debt included all foreign financing of the country's large exports and imports. Moreover, by 1985 the current account was already showing a large surplus, which subsequently became even larger. Of course, any amount of short-term debt is too large if many of the creditors suddenly demand repayment. But that is exactly the point: the problem of August 1985 was not one of either short- or long-term overborrowing but a liquidity crisis caused by the sudden withdrawal of short-term bank credits for basically non-economic reasons. And since no trading country can repay all its short-term foreign liabilities in a matter of months, the sudden withdrawal of bank credits would have precipitated the liquidity crisis even if the short-term portion of the total debt had been much smaller.

UNSOUND BANKING PRACTICES AND INADEQUATE BANKING SUPERVISION

Not that everything in the South African financial garden was lovely. Far from it. A serious weakness had developed in that some South African banks had in their foreign operations engaged in 'maturity mismatching', i.e. in 'borrowing short and lending long', and in the related practice of maintaining excessive uncovered foreign exchange positions. When the banks were suddenly denied adequate access to foreign credits, these cracks in the wall were exposed and complicated the handling of the overall debt situation. They represented a problem within a problem.

For these unsound banking practices improper bank management and inadequate banking supervision must take part of the blame. This was a deficiency in its own right which called for urgent remedial attention. Fortunately, such corrective action has now been taken. Comprehensive new banking legislation has been passed and is in the process of being implemented. In addition, banking and building society supervision has, with effect from April 1987, been transferred from the Office of the Registrar of Financial Institutions to the Reserve Bank.

It is important, however, not to confuse the weakness of unsound banking practices and inadequate banking supervision — which undoubtedly did exist — with the country's overall debt problem at the time — which was a liquidity problem and not one of overborrowing.

EFFECTIVE BALANCE OF PAYMENTS ADJUSTMENT

Turning now to more recent developments on the foreign debt front, it is evident that South Africa is one of the few developing countries that does not suffer from 'debt fatigue'. On the contrary, South Africa has not only continued to make all foreign interest and dividend payments punctiliously but has also repaid substantial amounts of foreign debt inside and outside the so-called 'standstill net'. In the process of doing so it has brought about precisely the kind of 'growth-oriented adjustment' sought by the international pundits. Consider the facts:

- The deficit on the current account of the balance of payments has been transformed into a large surplus. In 1985 this surplus amounted to R5,9 billion. In 1986 it increased to R7,2 billion or about 5 per cent of gross domestic product. During the first quarter of 1987 it amounted to a seasonally adjusted annual rate of R7,4 billion.
- South African banks, other private enterprises and public entities have made net repayments of foreign debt inside and outside the 'standstill net' of about R8 billion (US$4 billion) since the beginning of 1985. In Table 3 (p. 277) figures are given in US dollars for the debt at the end of August 1985 valued at the dollar exchange rates then prevailing, and for the end of December 1986 valued in one column at the August 1985 dollar exchange rates and in the other column at the December 1986 rates. This brings out the effect on the dollar value of South Africa's foreign debt of the depreciation of the dollar in terms of other major currencies between these two dates. It does not, of course, mean that because the dollar depreciated South Africa's debt burden was not reduced. Many other things also changed as a result of the exchange rate fluctuations, including the dollar and rand prices of South Africa's gold and other exports. The bottom line is clearly that South Africa's foreign debt in dollar terms is now substantially lower than it would have been in the absence of the repayments actually made, and that measured by all the accepted ratios the country's overall debt situation is much stronger now that it was in 1985. This is clearly illustrated in Table 4, (p. 278.)

- The Reserve Bank's own gold and foreign exchange reserves increased from R3,6 billion at the end of June 1986 to R6,5 billion at the end of June 1987. In US dollar terms this represented a rise from $1,4 billion to $3,2 billion.
- The commercial rand has appreciated from a low point of 36 US cents on 12 June 1986 to its present level of around 49 US cents, i.e. by about 37 per cent. Over the same period the financial rand has risen from about 18 US cents to about 29 US cents.
- From this position of relative balance of payments strength satisfactory debt arrangements were concluded in March 1987 under the leadership of Dr Chris Stals with foreign creditor banks.
- Since May 1985 both short- and long-term interest rates have declined substantially to their present low levels.
- Supported by a monetary policy designed to promote real economic growth, banks and building societies have for some time now been in a position to provide additional credit on a sound basis to underpin the current upswing in the economy.

Against this encouraging background it is evident that a solid foundation for accelerated economic growth and job creation has now been well and truly laid. The South African economy has gone through one of the most difficult periods in its history. The fiscal and monetary medicine at times had a bitter taste. But it worked. The sacrifices and belt-tightening were not in vain.

It would be naive to believe that South Africa's intertwined political and economic problems have now been resolved. We have won an 'adjustment' battle, but the 'growth' war is far from over. However, nothing can detract from the fact that the growth-oriented adjustment performance of the South African economy over the past two years has been remarkable. It has provided students of international economic relations with a classical case study of how an economy can achieve balance of payments and foreign debt adjustment if it has to.

Table 3 FOREIGN DEBT OF SOUTH AFRICA VALUED AT DIFFERENT EXCHANGE RATES (US$ MILLIONS)

	As at 31/08/85 Valued at the exchange rates as at 31/08/85	As at 31/12/86 Valued at the exchange rates as at 31/12/86	As at 31/12/86 Valued at the exchange rates as at 31/08/85
Payable in terms of the Proclamation:			
Bearer bonds	3 081	3 118	2 415
SA Reserve Bank	1 317	474	455
Other public sector	2 867	3 000	2 505
Private sector	2 828	2 054	1 726
Total	10 093	8 646	7 101
Not payable in terms of the Proclamation:			
Public sector	2 692	4 115	3 756
Banking sector	8 814	6 962	6 890
Private sector	2 122	2 870	2 638
Total	13 628	13 947	13 284
Grand total	23 721	22 593	20 385

Source: South African Reserve Bank.

Table 4 SOUTH AFRICA: COMPARISON OF EXTERNAL DEBT AND DEBT SERVICE WITH OTHER DEVELOPING COUNTRIES

	1980	1981	1982	1983	1984	1985	1986
External debt as percentage of exports of goods and services							
South Africa	55,7	87,8	111,2	125,7	170,7	148,9	108,4
Developing countries with recent debt servicing problems	151,2	185,8	241,5	254,3	247,2	263.9	302,4
Interest payments as percentage of exports of goods and services							
South Africa	3,3	4,7	6,2	6,8	9,9	10,7	9,5
Developing countries with recent debt servicing problems	15,9	22,7	30,8	30,0	28,8	26,8	27,3
External debts as percentage of GDP							
South Africa	20,3	25,5	30,4	32,5	45,7	50,0	35,2
Developing countries with recent debt servicing problems	33,6	38,5	45,5	50,0	51,1	52,2	54,8

Source: International Monetary Fund: *World Economic Outlook*, Washington DC, April 1987.

NOTE

1 There is, of course, not only *one* interest rate in South Africa and *one* interest rate overseas, but a whole spectrum of rates covering different kinds of paper and different maturities. It follows that there might well at times have been a differential between a particular interest rate in South Africa and a particular interest rate abroad that was not completely neutralised by the cost of Reserve Bank forward cover. But on average and in most individual cases the Reserve Bank's forward cover rates did fully equate the cost of domestic borrowing to the overall cost of covered foreign borrowing.

6

Fiscal Policy

6.1 INTRODUCTION

The term *fiscal policy* customarily refers to that branch of macroeconomic policy aimed at achieving macroeconomic goals by means of taxation and government expenditure. Fiscal policy thus implies the use of the state budget to regulate the level of economic activity. In South Africa, the principal institution concerned with formulating and implementing fiscal policy is the Treasury.

The effects of changes in government expenditure and taxation are transmitted to the economy through the operation of the fiscal multiplier. Thus increases and decreases in state expenditure and taxation may raise or lower national income by some multiple of the original change. However, even when state revenue exactly covers state expenditure, fiscal policy is not neutral. Given the lower propensity to save on the part of the government sector, a balanced budget will be slightly stimulatory in the short run. Thus a balanced budget multiplier is expansionary insofar as an equal amount of spending stimulates economic activity more than the corresponding amount of taxation restricts it.

It is clear that the major instruments of fiscal policy are the level and composition of government expenditure, and revenue-raising through both direct and indirect taxation. Since government expenditure constitutes an element of aggregate demand in the economy, variations in state expenditure have a direct effect on aggregate demand and hence on output and employment. Consequently, an increase in government expenditure will increase aggregate demand and thereby stimulate economic activity. Similarly, a fall in government expenditure will reduce the level of aggregate demand thus restricting output and employment. Although, in principle, changes in state expenditure may be used to manipulate the level of economic activity in the economy, in practice it is difficult to induce rapid changes in government expenditure. The reason for this lies in the nature of government expenditure; state expenditure programmes usually require much time to plan, implement and complete, while abandoning existing projects may be equally time-consuming and wasteful.

In contrast to government expenditure, tax rates are relatively quick and easy to change, and consequently variations in the level of taxation have historically formed the main instrument of fiscal policy. A distinction is usually drawn between direct taxes and indirect taxes. Direct taxes, which include income taxes, profits taxes and capital gains taxes, are those levied directly on specific economic units. Indirect taxes, on the other hand, are those levied on goods and services and include the general sales tax and excise and customs duties. The macroeconomic effects of changes in the level of taxation are analogous to changes in the level of government expenditure. Thus an increase in taxation will lower consumption expenditure, hence depressing aggregate demand and the level of economic activity. Similarly, a decrease in taxation will boost consumption expenditure thereby stimulating economic activity.

From the aforegoing discussion it is clear that by raising or lowering government expenditure and taxation, the fiscus can generate budget surpluses or budget deficits which are transmitted to the economy through the fiscal multiplier. In short, a budget surplus will have a contractionary influence on economic activity, whereas a deficit budget will be expansionary.

In practice, modern governments tend to generate budget deficits on a more or less permanent basis, and fiscal policy consists in varying the size of the deficit in accordance with macroeconomic policy objectives. The way in which these deficits are financed is thus of central importance. In attempting to finance the budget deficit, the authorities confront two possibilities. Firstly, the deficit may be funded by the creation of new money through the monetary system. The obvious problem with this option resides in its highly inflationary character. Secondly, the state may borrow funds from the public through the sale of gilt-edged securities. A problem with this approach is that it may require higher interest rates which are likely to crowd out some private investment.

Four readings are provided in this chapter. In the first paper, Mohr examines fiscal policy in South Africa for the period 1970 to 1985 against the background of developments in the theory of macroeconomics. After outlining various views on the importance of fiscal policy as an instrument of stabilisation policy, Mohr investigates government expenditure, the budget deficit, and taxation trends in South Africa. In the second reading, Black and Cooper draw an important distinction between the short- and long-run effects of fiscal policy. More specifically, they argue that the increasing reliance in South Africa on domestic loan financing of budget deficits is likely to have deleterious long-run consequences. The third and fourth articles in this chapter examine longer-term aspects of fiscal policy. Döckel and Seeber analyse government expenditure patterns in South Africa in recent years. They outline the structure of the public sector, examine various explanations for the secular growth of state expenditure, and provide empirical estimates of expenditure patterns in South Africa. In contrast, De Wet's contribution focuses on the revenue-raising aspects of the fiscus in South Africa, and more specifically examines the implications of the Margo Report for fiscal policy in this country.

6.2 FISCAL POLICY IN SOUTH AFRICA

P.J. Mohr*

INTRODUCTION

In this article we consider the use of fiscal policy as an instrument of economic stabilisation in South Africa between 1970 and 1985.

Fiscal policy deals with decisions regarding the finances of public authorities — their revenues and expenditures, and their borrowing and lending operations. Both the level and the composition of government spending, taxes and transfers are dealt with annually by the Minister of Finance in his Budget Speech (which is usually presented in March). Even a superficial reading of one of these speeches gives some indication of the scope of fiscal policy. Further evidence of the complexity of fiscal policy (and of the interrelationships between fiscal and monetary policy) can be found in the three reports published by the Commission of Inquiry into Fiscal and Monetary Policy in South Africa (the Franzsen Commission) in 1969 and 1970. Most of the issues addressed by the Franzsen Commission concerned the structure of government spending and taxation, rather than stabilisation (or anti-cyclical) policy. The tax structure was again comprehensively reviewed in 1985 and 1986 by the Commission of Inquiry into the Tax Structure of the Republic of South Africa (the Margo Commission).

The issues investigated by these two commissions include: the appropriate balance between direct and indirect taxation; the balance between the company tax and the personal income tax; the progression of the personal income tax; the appropriate unit of taxation; the choice between a general sales tax and a value-added tax; the possible introduction of a capital gains tax; and the use of tax concessions to stimulate particular types of economic activity. The debate on these matters involve questions of *equity* (i.e. the equitable distribution of the tax burden among the different taxpayers) and *efficiency* (i.e. the effects of various tax measures on the allocation of resources and/or on the propensity to work, save and invest), which fall beyond the scope of this article.[1]

VIEWS ON FISCAL POLICY

The broader, macroeconomic notion of an anti-cyclical fiscal policy is based on Keynesian-type macroeconomic models. During the heyday of Keynesianism in the 1950s and 1960s fiscal policy was generally regarded as an important instrument of stabilisation policy. If the economy was suffering from unemploy-

* Professor of Economics, University of South Africa. This paper was first published in *The Securities Markets*, No. 4, Second Quarter, 1987.

281

ment, an increase in government expenditure and/or a lowering of taxes was prescribed. On the other hand, if private sector spending was creating inflationary pressure and/or balance of payments problems, the reverse had to be applied. Moreover, the income tax and unemployment benefits were regarded as *automatic (or built-in) stabilisers*, in the sense that changes in income would automatically trigger changes in tax revenue and transfer payments, thus stabilising aggregate demand, income and output.[2]

In the 1950s and 1960s there was wide agreement on the need for such an anti-cyclical fiscal policy. The only real task, it seemed, was to make it work in practice. One of these problems, namely the long inside lag typically associated with fiscal policy, led to the recommendation that the Minister of Finance be granted greater authority to change fiscal policy between budgets. There are also limits to the extent to which government spending and taxes can be varied in an attempt to stabilise fluctuations in the level of economic activity. In 1975 the then Secretary of Finance described some of these problems as follows:[3]

Consider the possibility of a reduction in Government expenditure in order to counter inflationary pressures in the economy. A very large proportion of current Government expenditure consists of salaries, wages, allowances and ancillary payments which cannot easily be reduced without a reduction in personnel, which in itself is politically difficult to achieve. A further large proportion consists of social and civil pensions, provincial subsidies and other statutory commitments which cannot be changed except by amending legislation; here again a reduction would obviously be difficult for any government to propose. Other current payments are unavoidable in terms of contractual commitments, while still other expenditure, such as that on defence, may be regarded as irreducible for policy reasons.

On capital account ... an important limiting factor is that large projects, once under way, are frequently difficult to stop ...

Even an *increase* in public spending (if this should be desirable to counter a recession in economic activity) is not easy to accomplish within a short space of time. Plans must be drawn up, staff engaged, accommodation arranged, tenders invited and contracts awarded. It is sometimes suggested that a stockpile of plans for public investment should be kept in reserve against a time when increased public spending is desirable. Experience seems to show, however, that conditions and requirements tend to change so rapidly that plans drawn up in advance have to be considerably altered if there is a delay in their execution ...

It seems necessary to conclude that the variation of public expenditure has only a limited utility as an instrument of short- and medium-term fiscal policy, and this seems to be borne out by recent South African experience.

However, apart from these practical considerations, the very notion of an anti-cyclical fiscal policy was increasingly questioned during the seventies on theoretical grounds.

Monetarists denied any anti-cyclical or anti-inflationary role for fiscal policy. In terms of their analysis inflation can only be combatted through monetary policy, while an expansionary fiscal policy will merely crowd out private expenditure in the long run. The only aspect of fiscal policy which interests monetarists is the financing of the budget deficit, and in particular the degree to which government spending is financed by money creation.

In the face of cost-push, supply shocks and stagflation, *Keynesians* were also forced to re-examine their earlier views on fiscal policy. In 1975 Walter Heller, a prominent American Keynesian, admitted that: '... further work is needed to measure the cost-push effects of anti-inflationary tax increases ... this is a serious gap in our fiscal policy knowledge'.[4] Apart from the direct effects of increases in indirect taxes on costs and prices, it also became apparent in many countries that a rising personal income tax burden could be a major source of increased wage claims. As Weintraub [5] put it: '... wage earners were not avid readers of Keynesian textbooks, so as their pay envelopes thinned, the clamor for pay hikes to allay the tax bite touched off an enduring wage–price spiral.'

Three major implications emerged from this Keynesian rethink on fiscal policy:

- Given the nature of the inflation process, tax increases could no longer be regarded as an instrument of anti-inflationary policy.
- The notion of the income tax as an automatic or built-in stabiliser was no longer valid — in fact, it could operate as a built-in destabiliser, via its effect on the formation of wages.
- Government spending had to be kept in check, since the increasing tax burden associated with increased government spending could give further impetus to inflation.

A third approach to fiscal policy, which became very popular in the United States in the 1970s and 1980s, is that of the *supply-side* economists, who advocated a particular brand of fiscal policy as a cure for stagflation. Supply-siders focus on microeconomic incentives and they believe that government is too large. They therefore recommend a reduction in marginal tax rates (to increase the incentive to work, save and invest) and a concomitant reduction in government spending (to create more scope for private sector activity).

The different views on fiscal policy that emerged during the 1970s had one important element in common — *government spending had to be kept in check:* (1) to avoid crowding out and/or inflationary financing (the monetarist argument); (2) to avoid the cost-push effects of higher taxation (the Keynesian argument); and (3) to create the necessary scope for the tax cuts that were essential to increase the incentive to work, save and invest (the supply-side argument).

GOVERNMENT SPENDING IN SOUTH AFRICA, 1970–1985

In South Africa there was a rapid increase in government spending during the first half of the 1970s. This formed part of the period which Browne[6] has termed the 'years of fiscal expansion'. As indicated in Table 1, both consumption and investment spending by the South African government increased rapidly, and together they increased from 19,8 per cent of gross domestic expenditure (GDE) in 1970 to 25 per cent in 1976.

Table 1 TRENDS IN GOVERNMENT SPENDING, 1970–1985

Year	1 Growth in real consumption spending %	2 Growth in real investment spending %	3 Government spending as % of GDE
1970	8,0	11,1	19,8
1971	8,0	19,7	21,9
1972	–0,4	14,2	23,7
1973	4,6	–14,6	20,4
1974	7,6	2,1	19,6
1975	14,2	18,0	23,0
1976	7,9	5,7	25,0
1977	–0,2	–19,0	25,1
1978	1,5	–12,6	23,6
1979	3,1	0,1	23,6
1980	11,5	2,2	21,8
1981	3,4	12,7	21,5
1982	7,1	–0,2	23,6
1983	–0,2	–12,1	24,0
1984	7,4	–7,5	24,4
1985	–1,1	1,2	25,8

Notes
1. Percentage increase in consumption spending by general government at constant prices.
2. Percentage increase in gross investment by public authorities at constant prices. This does not include investment by public corporations.
3. Nominal consumption spending by general government plus gross investment by public authorities as percentage of gross domestic expenditure at current prices.
Source: South African Reserve Bank, *Quarterly Bulletin*; De Loor, 1984.

The 1976 Budget Speech heralded the start of a new era in South African public finance. In spite of the lowest growth rate since the Second World War — the real GNP had actually *declined* by 1,4 per cent in 1975 — the Minister of Finance introduced a particularly restrictive Budget and *financial (or fiscal) discipline* became the slogan. This major policy switch was the result of a number of factors, including the following:

- a widely held view (supported by the theoretical developments which we have outlined) that the rapid increase in government spending had been a major cause of the increase in the inflation rate during the first half of the 1970s;
- the philosophy of the new Minister of Finance (Horwood) and his economic advisers[7]; and

284

- the conditions attached to the loan which South Africa had obtained from the International Monetary Fund in January 1976.

In his 1976 Budget Speech Minister Horwood explicitly referred to the latter aspect:

> It is customary ... that the Fund requests the member country concerned to furnish certain undertakings in respect of its economic policy — undertakings which are actually in the country's own interest in order to strengthen its economy. I did not hesitate, therefore, to give the Fund the assurance, firstly, that State expenditure in 1976/77 would increase at a slower rate than in 1975/76, and secondly, that the budget deficit would not increase in real terms.[8]

This policy of financial discipline resulted in a significant slowdown in the rate of increase in government expenditure and a concomitant decline in government's share of GDE, as indicated in Table 1.[9] This in itself was a remarkable achievement, especially in view of the continued pressure for increased government spending. With respect to the latter Browne[10] stated that:

> Those who have not personally taken part in such an exercise may find it difficult to appreciate the tremendous pressures for higher expenditure to which the Treasury is exposed — pressures applied, for the most part, with the best of motives and for expenditure on services of unquestioned merit. The Minister of Finance and his aides are condemned to fight a lonely and thankless battle for a cause which is seldom adequately understood.

But how were these results achieved? A closer examination of government spending during the period 1976–1980 reveals three important factors: (1) a cutback in investment spending; (2) a lower rate of increase in public sector pay; and (3) the influence of the business cycle.

- The curtailment of *investment spending* by the public authorities between 1976 and 1980 is clearly indicated in Table 1. This had severe implications for certain industries, especially the construction industry. On average about 85 per cent of construction in South Africa is undertaken by the public sector (including the public corporations) and this in turn represents more than 40 per cent of public sector investment. The construction industry therefore clearly suffered from the cutbacks (and volatility) of public sector investment from 1976 onwards.[11]
- A large portion of *consumption expenditure* by general government consists of wages and salaries. In 1976 and 1977 there were significant real declines in the average remuneration of public sector employees which contributed to the slower growth in government spending. Unfortunately, this wage discipline could not be maintained and in the 1980s public sector pay was often a driving force behind the high growth in real government spending.
- A third important aspect of the fiscal discipline between 1976–1981 was the effect of the business cycle, especially the strong cyclical upswing during 1979 and 1980, which relieved some of the pressure on government spending.[12]

The significant fiscal restraint of the first half of the Horwood era could, however, not be maintained. From 1981 onwards government spending once more increased as percentage of GDP. Although this was again partly the result of fluctuations in the level of economic activity, and in particular the almost complete lack of economic growth between 1981 and 1985, a number of disconcerting features emerged during this period.

First, there was an increasing tendency to exceed budget estimates, as indicated in Table 2. Fiscal discipline was still regularly preached in the annual Budget Speeches, but it was not practised.[13] Although the overspending was invariably explained *ex post* (often quite plausibly), a serious credibility gap developed which undermined taxpayer morale and the influence of the fiscal authorities. This was particularly serious in 1983 and 1985. In both these years the fight against inflation was accorded the highest priority by the Minister of Finance. Restrictive budgets were introduced in an apparent attempt to dampen inflationary expectations. The fact that this did not have the desired effect can be attributed, in part at least, to considerable scepticism in the private sector that the envisaged fiscal discipline would be achieved. As it turned out, these fears were well-grounded.

Table 2 EXCESS GOVERNMENT EXPENDITURE, 1979–1986

Fiscal year	Budgeted amount Rm	Revised estimate Rm	Excess expenditure	
			Rm	%
1979/80	11 190	11 480	290	2,6
1980/81	13 083	13 590	507	3,9
1981/82	15 871	16 350	479	3,0
1982/83	18 238	19 205	967	5,0
1983/84	21 176	22 803	1 627	7,7
1984/85	24 945	27 194	2 249	9,0
1985/86	30 892	32 977	2 085	6,7

Note: Last column indicates excess expenditure as percentage of budgeted amount.
Source: Budget Speeches.

A second disturbing feature of fiscal policy during the eighties (which was related to the first) was the tendency to finance current expenditure out of loans. Until 1975 the Budget had consisted of two separate accounts, the Revenue Account and the Loan Account, the idea being that current expenditure should be financed from current revenue and capital spending from borrowing. In 1976 this distinction was abolished and a single State Revenue Account established. Nevertheless, sound financing principles still required that current expenditure be financed from current revenue. This principle was strictly adhered to until

1981, but during the ensuing four years current expenditure by general government consistently exceeded current revenue (by R248 million in 1982, R1 332 million in 1983, R2 537 million in 1984 and R1 327 million in 1985). In effect this meant that government was dissaving. The extent of this dissaving was, of course, related to the excess (over budgeted) expenditure indicated in Table 2.

As during the period of fiscal restraint, the emphasis in government spending was therefore still on *consumption*, rather than investment, spending. Moreover, a significant portion of the increase in consumption spending consisted of increases in the wages and salaries of public sector employees and increased interest payments on the public debt (due to increases in interest rates) and therefore did not represent a direct additional demand for goods.[14] The increases in the level of government spending during the 1980s thus did not really constitute an anti-cyclical fiscal policy.

This last point has to be underlined. In judging the stabilisation and growth effects of government spending, it is not only the *level* (or growth) of government spending that has to be considered. The *composition* of government spending is equally important. In particular:

- growth-inducing investment spending is preferable to consumption spending;
- a demand for new goods and services is preferable to increases in public sector pay; and
- spending on imported goods and services should be avoided, since it weakens the balance of payments without stimulating domestic economic activity.

As far as the future is concerned, high and increasing *levels* of government spending in South Africa seem unavoidable. Calitz[15] has identified six major sources of increasing pressure on government spending in the long run: the projected increase in the population; the extension of democracy; increased urbanisation; the provision of equal opportunities (such as education) to all sections of the community; the aging white population; and strategic and security needs. In these circumstances, the *composition* of government spending will assume increasing significance.

THE BUDGET DEFICIT

One of the key elements of the policy of financial discipline introduced in 1976 was the declared intention to keep the budget deficit, i.e. the difference between total government spending and current revenue, within certain limits. The emphasis on the so-called *deficit before borrowing* (which is usually expressed as a percentage of GDP) has been justified in a number of ways.[16] Basically, however, it reflected the monetarists' fear that large budget deficits either increase inflation (if they are financed through bank credit) or result in a crowding out of private investment (if they are financed through borrowing). Conventional macroeconomic models indicate that an expansionary fiscal policy will lead to higher interest rates if the money supply is not allowed to expand. From this line of reasoning it follows that the budget deficit has to be kept in check, so that both inflationary financing and crowding out can be avoided. This approach was adopted and advocated by the International Monetary Fund (IMF) and it became one of the main criteria employed by the IMF when judging the fiscal policy of member countries, including South Africa. However, as Browne[17] has pointed out, the deficit before borrowing *as such* has little meaning, since a given deficit can be achieved at various levels of government spending and taxation. It is only in conjunction with other criteria, pertaining to the level and composition of government spending and taxation, that the deficit assumes any real significance. Moreover, it has to be borne in mind that a significant portion of public sector loan financing is done by the public corporations and other extra-budgetary institutions, with the result that the budget deficit is no real reflection of the borrowing requirements of the public sector at large.

TAXATION IN SOUTH AFRICA, 1970–1985

Some of the most important trends in taxation between 1970 and 1985 are indi-

Table 3 TRENDS IN TAXATION, 1970–1985

Year	Tax revenue as % of GDP	Personal income tax as % of personal income	Direct taxes as % of tax revenue
1970	18,4	6,2	56,7
1971	18,5	6,6	55,8
1972	18,3	6,8	57,8
1973	18,4	7,5	61,3
1974	18,8	7,9	65,3
1975	19,4	7,9	64,3
1976	20,0	9,0	62,6
1977	20,2	8,9	60,1
1978	20,4	8,9	58,9
1979	20,5	7,6	57,5
1980	20,0	6,6	60,9
1981	20,2	7,5	58,3
1982	21,6	8,6	54,8
1983	22,3	9,3	57,4
1984	22,2	11,1	54,9
1985	24,4	11,7	56,8

Source: South African Reserve Bank, *Quarterly Bulletin*.

cated in Table 3. The most obvious of these is the almost monotonic increase in tax revenue as percentage of GDP. Note in particular that this ratio did not decline during the period of fiscal restraint (which was characterised by a decline in government spending as percentage of GDP). This can be attributed to the declared policy of keeping the deficit before borrowing to between 2 and 3 percent of GDP.[18]

The second column of Table 3 indicates the ratio between personal income tax and personal income. This ratio: increased steadily between 1970 and 1976; remained steady in 1977 and 1978; declined significantly in 1979 and 1980; and almost doubled between 1980 and 1985. The declines in 1979 and 1980 were the result of significant reductions in the rates of personal income tax. These were made possible by the introduction of a 4 per cent general sales tax (GST) in July 1978 and a substantial increase in revenue from gold mining in the wake of the sharp rise in the gold price. The gold price increased from a daily average of $193,26 per fine ounce in 1978 to $612,94 in 1980. State revenue from gold mining increased from R727 million in 1978 to R3 040 million in 1980, which provided ample scope for reductions in personal income tax. Note, however, that this amounted to a *pro-cyclical* tax policy, since the reductions were implemented during a particularly strong expansion in economic activity. When the gold price subsequently declined, effective tax rates were again increased (as indicated in Table 3) in spite of the deep and prolonged economic downturn. No anti-cyclical tax policy was thus implemented during the period under consideration.

The introduction of GST and subsequent increases thereof (to 5 per cent in February 1982, 6 per cent in September 1982, 7 per cent in February 1984, 10 per cent — excluding certain food items — in July 1984, and 12 per cent in March 1985) are also reflected in the third column of Table 3, which indicates a declining share of direct (income) taxes in total tax revenue. This was regarded as the major element of a process of tax reform outlined in the 1979 Budget Speech.[19] Another element of this process was a significant reduction in the top marginal rate of personal income tax from 72 per cent in 1972/73 to 47,5 per cent in 1986/87, based on the supply-side argument that high marginal tax rates have a disincentive effect on effort, saving and investment.

However, the most important aspect of taxation in South Africa since 1970 was the effect of inflation on a tax system that had originally been designed in a period of relative price stability and not for the high inflation rates experienced from 1973 onwards. As is well known, the combination of inflation and a progressive personal income tax results in *bracket creep*. As their nominal incomes increase, taxpayers are pushed into higher marginal tax brackets, with the result that their average tax rates increase, even if their real incomes remain unchanged. In many countries this phenomenon led to the *indexation* of the personal income tax, i.e. tax brackets, rebates and deductions were linked to an official price index (usually the CPI). This was done to avoid bracket creep and to ensure that tax increases remained *discretionary* and *visible*.

289

In South Africa the authorities decided against the indexation of the tax system and opted for *ad hoc* adjustments (depending on the circumstances). As we have seen, however, the significant downward adjustments in the personal income tax in 1979 and 1980 occurred at a time when the domestic economy was in a strong expansionary phase, with the result that these adjustments had a strong *pro-cyclical* effect. This effect was maintained during the 1980s in that no further downward adjustments were made, in spite of high inflation and a declining (often negative) rate of economic growth. The result was a significant increase in the overall personal income tax burden, as illustrated in Table 3. Moreover, the combined effect of (1) these *ad hoc* adjustments, (2) the significant reductions in the marginal rate of personal income tax, and (3) inflation was a significant increase in the relative tax impact on the middle-income group, as indicated in Table 4.

Inflation has also had significant effects on other taxes, notably the company tax. However, a detailed examination of these and other aspects of taxation policy in South Africa falls beyond the scope of this paper.

Table 4 AVERAGE TAX RATES OF MARRIED TAXPAYER WITH TWO CHILDREN IN SELECTED TAX YEARS

Taxable income in 1986 (Rands)	Average tax rate (%)			
	1972	1978	1981	1986
5 000	0	0	0	0
10 000	0,5	4,1	0,3	5,2
20 000	5,5	9,1	6,5	14,8
30 000	8,0	14,2	12,0	22,0
50 000	13,5	24,2	20,7	32,2
100 000	26,1	42,0	34,0	42,6
200 000	44,1	54,0	42,0	48,1

Notes
Only primary and child abatements (1972 and 1978) and rebates (1981 and 1986) were taken into account. Levels of taxable income in 1972, 1978 and 1981 were obtained by deflating the 1986 levels with the CPI.
Source: Calculated from tax tables.

CONCLUDING REMARKS

From this brief overview of trends in taxation it should, nevertheless, be clear that taxation was not employed as an instrument of stabilisation policy between 1970 and 1985. In fact, the increasing pressure on government spending in the 1980s and the declared policy of keeping the deficit before borrowing within the limits prescribed by the IMF effectively ruled out an anti-cyclical taxation policy.

Given (1) that the pressure on government spending will remain high (and probably increase) during the remainder of the century and (2) an unequal distribution of personal incomes in South Africa, which implies a very narrow income tax base, there also does not appear to be any scope in future for an anti-cyclical tax policy either. As a result, the debate on taxation policy in South Africa will probably continue to be dominated by *structural* issues, such as those mentioned in the introduction. The *level* of taxation will, in any case, be governed by the level of government spending.

NOTES

1 For a discussion of these issues, see: the various reports of the Franzsen Commission (RP24/1969, RP86/1970 and RP87/1970); Franzsen (1984); Browne (1975 and 1983); and the report of the Margo Commission which had not yet been published at the time of writing.
2 An automatic stabiliser can be defined as any mechanism in the economy that reduces the effects of changes in autonomous demand. In terms of the simple Keynesian model it stabilises the economy by reducing the multiplier effects of any disturbance to aggregate demand. However, the inflationary environment of the 1970s and 1980s and the apparent propensity of governments to spend all additional tax revenue, have rendered the concept of automatic stabilisers practically irrelevant.
3 Browne, 1975, pp. 7–8.
4 Heller, 1975, p. 14.
5 Weintraub, 1978, p. 196.
6 Browne, 1983, pp. 154–162.
7 See Lombard, 1979, p. 343; Browne, 1983, p. 162.
8 Further loans were obtained in 1977 and 1982. Although it is difficult to judge the extent of its influence, the International Monetary Fund undoubtedly had a significant impact on economic policy in South Africa from 1976 onwards, as in other countries (see Franzsen, 1984, pp. 197–198).
9 For a summary and discussion of fiscal policy during this period, see Horwood, 1980 and Lombard, 1979.
10 Browne, 1983, p. 164.
11 Calitz, 1986, p. 266.
12 See Calitz, 1986, pp. 261–268.
13 See Sadie, 1984; Sadie, 1985b.
14 See Sadie, 1984, pp. 7–8; Sadie, 1985a, pp. 21–24.
15 Calitz, 1986, pp. 285–289.
16 See Browne, 1984, pp. 180–185; Van Staden, 1984, pp. 208–214.
17 Browne, 1984, p. 181.
18 Van Staden, 1984.
19 See also Franzsen, 1984.

REFERENCES

Browne, G.W.G., 1975. 'Fiscal Policy in South Africa', *Economic Policy in South Africa*, edited by Lombard, J.A., Cape Town: HAUM, pp. 1–25.
—— 1983. 'Fifty Years of Public Finance', *South African Journal of Economics*, Vol. 51, No. 1, March, pp. 134–173.

—— 1984. 'Die Koördinering van Fiskale en Monetêre Beleid'. *Owerheidsfinansies in Suid-Afrika*, edited by Franzsen, D.G. Durban: Butterworth, pp. 163–188.

Calitz E., 1986. *Aspekte van die Vraagstuk van Staatsbestedingsprioriteite met Spesiale Verwysing na die Republiek van Suid-Afrika: 'n Funksioneel-Ekonomiese Ondersoek*. D. Comm thesis, University of Stellenbosch.

De Loor, J.H., 1984. 'Die Ekonomie van Owerheidsuitgawes'. *Owerheidsfinansies in Suid-Afrika*, edited by Franzsen, D.G. Durban: Butterworth, pp. 19–38.

Franzsen, D.G., 1984. *Owerheidsfinansies in Suid-Afrika*. Durban: Butterworth.

Heller, W.W. 1975. 'What is Right with Economics?' *American Economic Review*, Vol. 65, No. 1, March, pp. 1–26.

Horwood, O.P.F., 1980. 'Die Huidige Fiskale en Monetêre Beleid in Suid-Afrika', *South African Journal of Economics*, Vol. 48, No. 4, December, pp. 359–369.

Lombard, J.A., 1979. 'Fiskale Beleid in Suid-Afrika'. *South African Journal of Economics*, Vol. 47, No. 4, December, pp. 343–368.

Sadie, J.L., 1984. 'Observations on the 1984/85 Budget and its Times', *Opinion Survey*, No. 121, April, Bureau for Economic Research, University of Stellenbosch, pp. 6–10.

—— 1985a. 'Reflections on Economic Policy in South Africa', *Studies in Economics and Econometrics*, No. 21, March, pp. 9–40.

—— 1985b. 'The 1985/1986 Budget: An Appraisal'. *Opinion Survey*, No. 125, April, Bureau for Economic Research, University of Stellenbosch, pp. 10–15.

Van Staden, B., 1984. 'Die Koördinering van Fiskale en Monetêre Beleid'. *Owerheidsfinansies in Suid-Afrika*, edited by Franzsen, D.G., Durban: Butterworth, pp. 205–224.

Weintraub, S., 1978. *Capitalism's Inflation and Unemployment Crises*. Reading, Mass: Addison-Wesley.

6.3 THE SHORT- AND LONG-RUN CONSEQUENCES OF THE GOVERNMENT'S FINANCING REQUIREMENT

P.A. Black and J.H. Cooper*

1. INTRODUCTION

An understanding of the nature of government spending and the multiplier is vitally important to the comprehension of fiscal policy analysis. The multiplier is the mechanism which transmits and regulates the aggregate impact of changes in government expenditure on the level of income and employment in the economy. Consequently, it is essential to know the size and composition of government spending, and the factors determining the size of the multiplier, if fiscal policy is to be used as a means of altering certain macroeconomic variables.

Without this information it would be most difficult to predict the impact of given policy changes with any degree of accuracy. Such a 'blind' fiscal policy might well cause more problems than it solves. It may, for example, induce pro- instead of anti-cyclical changes in the level of government expenditure, thus harming the prospects for economic growth and hampering the fight against unemployment and inflation.

Whilst the effect on income of a change in government spending depends on the size of the multiplier, it is not always realised that the *composition* of that change may also have an important bearing on the final outcome. For example, current South African budgetary procedure is characterised by a statistical anomaly, whereby loan redemptions are excluded from the estimates of government spending. This practice not only tends to under-represent the true magnitude of government expenditure but may also have implications for its overall impact on the equilibrium level of income.

Conventionally, government spending (G) is greater than tax receipts (T), insofar as current expenditure by government (G_w) is usually associated with financing by T (or by money creation), and capital expenditure (G_c) by loans. The deficit is therefore,

$$D = G_c.$$

If allowance is made for loan redemptions (R), then the total financing requirement (F) is

$$F = G_c + R$$
$$= (G_w - T) + G_c + R$$
$$= G + R - T$$

* Department of Economics, University of Stellenbosch and Department of Economics and Economic History, Rhodes University, respectively. This paper was first published in the *South African Journal of Economics*, Vol. 56, No. 4, December 1988.

The expansionary effect of F will ultimately depend on how it is financed, i.e. either by an increase in the money stock or the sale of additional government securities (Black, 1981). But an important consideration in this regard — not always appreciated — is the size of R *relative* to G and G_c, which may have a significant effect on the outcome. The reasons for this include the differential impact of G_c and R on national income and net private wealth, and the role played by the creation of new debt in the long run. These reasons are considered in sections 2 and 3 below, and their implications for the South African economy in section 4.

2. SHORT-RUN CONSEQUENCES

As far as the *short run* is concerned, it is generally known that money creation is a more expansionary/inflationary method of financing F than borrowing from the public. But irrespective of how the financing requirement is met, the larger R is, relative to G_c, the smaller will be the multiplier effect on the level of income.

In the case of *bond financing*, for example, a given increase in G_c will normally induce a multiplied expansion in the aggregate level of income. An equal increase in R, however, will have only a marginal impact because new bonds are simply being substituted for old ones. However, this substitution still has a positive effect on income if the proportion of R spent on goods and services exceeds the corresponding proportion of money withdrawn from circulation through the sale of new bonds; that is, the effect on income will depend on the extent to which idle (speculative) balances are being activated in the process of replacing old with new government bonds. This is illustrated in Figure 1 by the

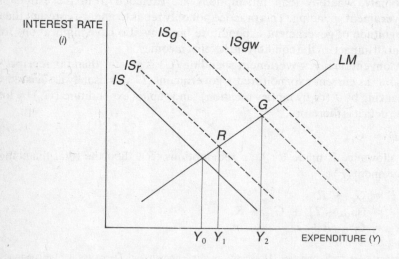

Figure 1

294

difference in the extent to which the *IS* curve shifts as a result of equal increases in G_c and R, and where crowding out moves the corresponding equilibria to points G and R respectively. It can be seen that a given increase in G_c induces a much larger expansion in the level of income than the same increase in R, i.e. the increase from Y_0 to Y_2 as opposed to Y_1.

A similar conclusion follows in the case where F is financed by the *creation of new money*. As far as loan redemptions are concerned, they have a larger impact on income than in the previous case because old bonds are replaced by money, not new bonds. Consequently, there is no offsetting withdrawal from the circular flow of income, and the net effect on income will depend on the entire portion of R spent on goods and services — shown in Figure 2 by the larger shift of the *IS* curve to IS_r. Equal increases in R and G_c still have a differential impact, however, because of differences in the way that the multiplier affects them. In the case of R, for example, the first stage of the multiplier process is missing because some of R is immediately saved, whereas with G_c the full amount is spent. This reduces the corresponding impact of R on the level of income.

For the rest, the analysis is similar to the previous one: equal increases in G_c and R produce outward shifts in the *IS* and *LM* curves in Figure 2, resulting in new equilibria at points H and S respectively. Once again a larger expansion is associated with G_c than with R, i.e. the increase from Y_0 to Y_4 as opposed to Y_3 in Figure 2.

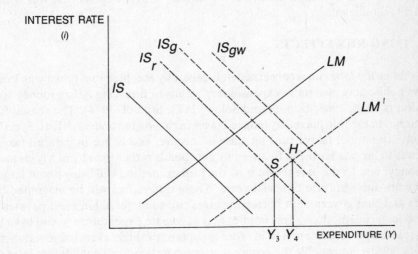

Figure 2

An additional source of short-run variation in the expansionary effect of government spending is the different impact of G_c and R on *net private wealth*.

Suppose, for example, that private consumption is a positive function of wealth, where wealth is given by

$$W = A + M + B$$

and where A represents real assets, M currency (excluding reserves) and B the value of outstanding government debt.

Changes in R have no effect on W irrespective of whether it is financed by newly created money (M) or by borrowing from the private sector (B), because loan redemptions simply entail a substitution of either M or B for B, thus leaving net private wealth unchanged in either case.

The financing of G_C, on the other hand, implies an increase in either M or B, which unavoidably causes an increase in W and hence in consumption expenditure and, via the multiplier, the level of aggregate expenditure. Consequently, the larger G_C is, *relative* to R, the greater will be the wealth effects associated with deficit financing, and hence the stronger the associated expansionary effect.

The impact of wealth effects can be illustrated diagramatically by an additional outward shift of the IS curve, to IS_{gw} in Figures 1 and 2, which represent the cases where G_C is financed by the issue of new bonds and new money respectively. *Ceteris paribus*, the impact of wealth effects then is further to boost the differential short-run impact of G_C relative to R. Although this simplified analysis ignores the impact of increases in wealth on crowding out when G_C is bond financed, which has the effect of weakening the expansionary impact of G_C, empirical evidence (Shaw, 1977; Currie, 1981) suggests that this is not highly significant.

3. LONG-RUN EFFECTS

As far as the *long run* is concerned, it is generally accepted that borrowing from the public may be a more expansionary means of financing F than money creation (Christ, 1968; Blinder and Solow, 1973; Steindl, 1974). The reason for this lies in the role played by induced taxes in closing the budget deficit. Specifically, the initial (short-run) increase in income, and hence in induced taxes, tends to be smaller if F is financed by new bonds rather than by newly created money; and to the extent that it is, the former method will bring about larger deficits during future financial years. These differences will be magnified by the fact that government borrowing gives rise to increased interest payments and loan redemptions. This implies that aggregate expenditure would have to increase by a greater amount in order to support the higher level of government expenditure and enable the economy to reach its 'long-run equilibrium level of income' (Blinder and Solow, 1974, p. 50).

Although the above analysis suggests that the increase in induced taxes will be larger in the short run if F consists of G_C rather than R, this does not necessarily imply that the expansionary effect of G_C in the long run will be weaker.

The impact of higher tax revenues on F is likely to be more than offset by the expansionary impact of an increased G_c arising from the growth of the government's debt. Irrespective of how F is financed, the larger G_c is, relative to R, the larger will be the value of outstanding debt and the interest payments and loan redemptions that have to be made during future financial years. It would therefore appear that in the long run too, the effect on income of a given increase in G_c is greater than that associated with an equal increase in R.

This argument is an extension of the orthodox Keynesian justification for advocating fiscal spending as the most efficient means to achieve the long-run equilibrium level of income (where $G + R = T$ and the budget is 'rebalanced'). It is based on the assumption that the issue of new securities today implies greater government expenditure later, and hence greater aggregate demand, a higher level of income, etc. Such reasoning applies *a fortiori* when capital outlays constitute a relatively large proportion of total government expenditure because of the higher interest and redemption payments so implied.

4. SOUTH AFRICA

The implications of the foregoing analysis for the South African situation can be explained with the aid of the information provided in Appendix 1: Firstly, the authorities' neglect of loan redemptions in their deficit estimates may convey a mistaken impression of the overall multiplier effect of government spending; secondly, the relatively large and growing deficit component of the total financing requirement tends to boost the expansionary/inflationary impact of government spending in both the short and the long run; and thirdly, as a result of rapid increases in the deficit relative to loan redemptions during the 1980s, the value of outstanding debt and the interest burden associated with servicing this debt continue to grow rapidly both in absolute and relative terms.

The growing interest burden is reflected in the fact that interest payments constituted 16 per cent of total government spending (excluding loan redemptions) in 1988/9 — exceeded only by the amounts budgeted for defence/police and education. As mentioned before, this is a direct result of continuous increases in the deficit relative to loan redemptions. Put differently, government expenditure in 1988/9 could have been much lower if the authorities had previously used the proceeds from bond sales to retire their past debt, rather than to finance additional capital (and current) expenses during the preceding years. The upshot is that the total financing requirement will in all likelihood continue to grow until the level of income is great enough to support a far higher level of tax receipts.

On the whole, there can be no doubt that the South African taxpayer is already having to pay for the growing deficit and the concomitant decline in the amount of loan redemptions made during the 1980s, both of which have boosted the size of the government's debt. It could thus be justifiably argued that South Africans today are living in the long run.

297

Appendix 1 GOVERNMENT FINANCES (R MILLIONS)

	Government revenue	Government expenditure	Deficit (Gc)	Loan redemptions (R)	Total financing requirement (F)	Gc F
1976/77	5 990,5	8 244,6	2 254,1	598,8	2 852,9	79,0
1977/78	7 016,4	8 960,5	1 944,1	1 144,5	3 088,6	62,9
1978/79	8 138,4	9 955,3	1 816,9	1 895,8	3 712,7	48,9
1979/80	9 787,5	11 441,0	1 653,5	1 285,3	2 938,8	56,3
1980/81	13 310,3	13 595,4	285,1	1 720,7	2 005,8	14,2
1981/82	14 416,3	16 431,3	2 015,0	3 084,8	5 099,8	39,5
1982/83	17 173,6	19 183,0	2 010,0	1 768,0	3 778,0	53,2
1983/84	19 087,7	22 316,8	3 229,1	2 148,7	5 377,8	60,0
1984/85	23 425,9	27 130,6	3 704,1	2 457,6	6 161,7	60,1
1985/86	29 320,1	32 908,4	3 588,3	2 045,0	5 633,3	63,7
1986/87	34 135,9	40 247,4	6 111,5	2 326,5	8 438,0	72,4
1987/88*	37 822,0	47 836,2	10 014,2	2 592,6	12 606,8	79,4
1988/89(1)	42 840,0	52 933,5	10 093,5	2 671,0	12 764,5	79,1
1988/89(2)	44 005,0	53 865,5	9 860,0	2 671,0	12 531,0	78,7

* Preliminary figures.
(1) Estimated prior to budget proposals.
(2) Estimated after budget proposals.
Source: Statistical/Economic Reviews: Budget Speeches 1980–81 and 1988/89.

REFERENCES

Black, P.A., 1981. 'On the Expansionary Effect of the 1981–82 Budget,' *Studies in Economics and Econometrics*, No. 12.
Blinder, A. and Solow, R.M., 1973. 'Does Fiscal Policy Matter?' *Journal of Public Economics*, November.
—— 1974. 'Analytical Foundations of Fiscal Policy,' in Blinder, A.S. *et al.*, *The Economics of Public Finance*. Washington DC.: The Brookings Institution.
Christ, C.F., 1968. 'A Simple Macro-economic Model with a Government Budget Constraint,' *Journal of Political Economy*, January–February.
Curry, S.A., 1981. 'Monetary and Fiscal Policy and the Crowding-out Issue,' in Artis, M.J. and Miller, M.H. (eds), *Essays in Fiscal and Monetary Policy*. Oxford: O.U.P.
Peacock, A.T. and Shaw, G.K., 1971. *The Economic Theory of Fiscal Policy*. London: George Allen & Unwin.
Shaw, G.K., 1977. *An Introduction to the Theory of Macroeconomic Policy*. London: Martin Robertson.
Steindl, F.G., 1974. 'Money and Income: The View of the Government Budget Restraint,' *Journal of Finance*, September.

6.4 THE BEHAVIOUR OF GENERAL GOVERNMENT EXPENDITURE IN SOUTH AFRICA 1948–1984

J.A. Döckel and A.V. Seeber*

1. INTRODUCTION

From time to time alarm is expressed at the size and rate of growth of the public sector. It is also true that a constant demand is made for more and better public services as an economy develops. It would seem that an economist should be able to determine to what degree resources should optimally be diverted to the provision of public and private goods. Many economists[1] have come forward with such normative solutions. Central to these solutions is the existence of some sort of social preference relation. The impossibility[2] of deriving an acceptable social welfare function is well known. This fact leaves the theory of social choice in a very unsatisfactory state.[3]

In explaining the actual tendencies of government expenditure[4] one can indicate a host of factors that would seem important, such as the specific needs of the citizens of a country, which are influenced among other things by cultural, ethnic, religious and other socio-economic factors; the stage of a country's development; the political process as well as budgetary procedures; and the efficiency of the public sector in providing services. To these factors one must add that many services provided by the authorities fall into the public goods category where non-exclusion can cause an overstatement of preferences for these services.[5]

It is apparent that the factors influencing the behaviour of government expenditure over time are only partly economic.[6] An economist can therefore, at best, only provide a limited number of guidelines in this area.

In this study a description of the public sector will be provided in section 2, followed by a brief review of the analytical techniques that have been applied to the analysis of government expenditure. This will be followed in section 4 by the development of a model, and the empirical estimates of expenditure patterns found in South Africa are discussed in section 5.

2. GROWTH IN CURRENT GOVERNMENT EXPENDITURE

In a discussion on the growth of government expenditure it is useful to disaggregate total government expenditure. A study of individual expenditure votes, although interesting in itself, would have been too detailed and was therefore not undertaken in this study. A functional classification of public ex-

* Department of Economics, University of South Africa. This is an extended and revised version of an article originally published in *The South African Journal of Economics*, Vol. 46, 1978, pp. 337–51.

penditure was thought appropriate because it allowed meaningful disaggregation and also corresponded to an analysis of the various hypotheses discussed later on, especially the Wagner hypothesis.

Accordingly, the votes of the central government, as detailed in the various reports of the Comptroller and Auditor-General[7] were classified into four functional categories: *Administration, Economic, Social Services* and *Law and Order*. The two votes *Public Debt* and *Defence* were kept separate. The method of functional classification was, to a certain extent, arbitrary, in the sense that the vote title was used to determine the category into which it fell.[8] The Department of Statistics[9] has begun to present data on this functional basis, but their records are limited to the period 1970 onwards. Once the categorisation had been decided upon expenditures were calculated for the 36-year period 1948–84.

Current provincial expenditure was not divided into functional categories. The classification of the expenditures of the local authorities was made impossible by the degree of disaggregation required, because of the many organisations involved.

The period of study was divided into three parts, since 1960 seems to represent the start of a new period in the pattern of central government activities, to be followed in 1976 by a period of concern about the high level of government expenditure,[10] which corresponds with a lower level of growth in the overall economy. This was confirmed in the prior graphical analysis as well as the analysis which follows below.

Table 1 ANNUAL PER CAPITA GROWTH RATES OF CURRENT
GOVERNMENT EXPENDITURE IN REAL TERMS

Category	1948–60	1960–75	1975–84	1948–84
Central government:				
Administration	1,45	7,48	2,85	6,05
Economic	–0,08	0,80	–2,33	0,50
Social services	0,11	0,04	0,98	0,38
Law and order	1,34	0,38	–1,47	0,16
Public debt	–1,79	5,55	2,86	1,87
Defence	0,96	5,76	–1,27	5,01
Total central government	1,08	1,85	–0,57	1,61
Total non-defence expenditure	1,09	1,56	–0,45	1,30
Provincial administration	2,11	1,52	–2,9	0,77
Local authorities	2,03	0,17	–1,03	0,78
All local govt (Prov. admin. and local authorities)	2,06	0,86	–1,97	0,78
Total government expenditure	1,41	1,53	–0,98	1,36

Table 1 shows the annual growth for the sub-periods 1948–60, 1960–75 and 1975–84, and the overall annual growth for the entire period. In order to assess the growth in the real level of government expenditure the implicit general government expenditure deflator was used.[11] Although this is not a perfect index for all expenditure categories it is superior to other published deflators.

As can be seen in Table 1 the annual growth rates in real government expenditure for the central government, with its various components, showed an increase during the period 1960–75 compared to the previous period. Local and provincial governments did not follow this trend. This high growth rate in the real levels of government services did not continue during the next period, 1975–84. Negative growth rates in the various categories are the most common, with positive growth rates limited to the administration, social services and public debt categories. There was a substantial decline in the growth rate of real defence expenditure from 5,8 per cent during 1960–75 to –1,3 per cent during 1975–84.[12] Total government expenditure also mirrors this tendency over the period 1975–84, with real total government expenditure showing a growth rate of nearly –1,0 per cent compared to 1,4 and 1,5 per cent over the periods 1948–60 and 1960–75 respectively.

The observation that public outlays are taking an increasing share of GDP is confirmed in Table 2. This table shows central, local and overall government expenditure as a percentage of GDP. The central government share rose from 9,2 per cent in 1948–50 to 11,3 per cent in 1973–75 and 16,8 per cent in 1982–84, while for the same period local government outlays represent 8,4 and 9,4 and 10,2 per cent respectively.

Table 2 GOVERNMENT EXPENDITURE CATEGORIES AS PERCENTAGE OF GDP[13]

Expenditure	1948–50	1960–62	1973–75	1982–84
Local government	8,39	9,54	9,43	10,18
Central government	9,22	8,83	11,31	16,80
Central govt (non-defence)	8,37	7,84	9,09	13,29
Total government	17,61	18,37	20,74	26,98
Local govt/central govt	0,91	1,08	0,83	0,61

A further ratio reflected in Table 2 is that between local and central government. This is usually interpreted as representing the degree of centralisation in public outlays. The evidence suggests that expenditures are becoming centralised. This percentage was 0,9 in 1948–50 and dropped to 0,83 in 1973–75 and 0,61 in 1982–84.

Finally, Table 2 reflects the growing share of GDP accruing to total public outlays. In 1948–50, public outlays as a proportion of GDP represented 17,6 per cent, rising to 20,7 per cent in 1973–75 and 26,9 per cent in 1982–84. It is worth noting that the expenditure patterns of the various public corporations have been excluded from this study. If they had been included this trend might have been confirmed still further. Calitz[14] reflects on these trends in general government expenditure by drawing attention to the fact that no single indicator exists which could tell the policy-maker that public expenditure is becoming too large or too small. The size of the government sector relative to the rest of the economy, as well as the composition of these expenditures, is the result of a complex set of factors — not all of economic origin — and might even sometimes appear to defy logic.

3. POSSIBLE EXPLANATIONS FOR GOVERNMENT EXPENDITURE BEHAVIOUR

No satisfactory positive theory exists that explains expenditure behaviour over time. Several attempts have been made to fill this gap, among which is that of Wagner.[15] Wagner's hypothesis is mainly demand orientated and proposes that as per capita incomes increase the public sector will grow in relative importance. This action is the result of the tendency of the administrative and protective functions of the state to increase more than proportionally, owing to the substitution of public for private activities; for example, protection. Wagner also proposed the relative expansion of cultural and welfare activities such as education and the redistribution of income. These activities were considered luxury goods and, as such, income elastic. The final factor proposed by this hypothesis is the notion that technological development will favour large-scale organisations leading to private monopolies, which in turn will be taken over by the state.

Although the income elasticity of government expenditure in various countries was found to be greater than one,[16] which seems to verify Wagner's hypothesis, great scepticism exists as to its value. The main criticism against the hypothesis is the fact that it is based on the originator's normative assumptions about the nature of the state and its behaviour. The hypothesis therefore represents an opinion on what ought to happen as an economy becomes industrialised. Furthermore, the empirical content of the hypothesis is suspect since it is not clear that the role of the state should necessarily increase through its takeover of private monopolies, if they exist, nor is it clear that certain goods and services provided by government are luxuries. The hypothesis is therefore not very helpful in understanding the growth in government expenditure, nor its future development. At best, Wagner's hypothesis helps to illuminate part of past reality, which did depend on the stage of development.

Wagner only stressed the demand for government services and ignored supply. He assumed that people's demand for public goods and services would be strong enough to overcome the possible inertia in willingness to pay for these services through taxation. Peacock and Wiseman[17] questioned Wagner's optimism and stressed the question of supply. They postulated that there would be an unwillingness to accept the higher tax burden required to finance an increasing level of government services. This unwillingness can only be overcome by a major exogenous shock, such as a war. A war economy requires larger sacrifices in terms of government revenue and people would get used to those levels of taxation. At the conclusion of hostilities, the drop in war expenditure would then be taken up by other government services.

Their stressing of the supply side of the 'market' is commendable but empirical verification of this hypothesis is inconclusive.[18] Little empirical evidence was found of significant discrete jumps in the trend in government expenditure as a result of large exogenous shocks such as war. Peacock and Wiseman's hypothesis is based on the tendency of taxpayers, under normal circumstances, to resist tax rate increases. The responsiveness of the tax structure itself must also be considered. Government revenue tends to have an income elasticity of greater than unity, implying a relative increase in the share of government revenue as GDP increases. To this it must be added that the willingness or unwillingness of the public, as well as its ability to finance more government services, are vague and flexible concepts.

Another supply-orientated approach explaining the growth in government expenditure is based on the fact that the productivity growth in the service industries (including government services) is less than that in other sectors of the economy.[19] Because productivity growth in the government sector is lower than that of the remainder of the economy, it follows that government expenditure will have to increase at a rate greater than that of the overall economy in order to maintain its real level relative to output.

Apart from the economic aspects, government expenditure cannot be divorced from the political and bureaucratic sphere. Unfortunately, 'the economist can do relatively little on these problems until he is assisted to a better understanding of the process of collective decision making by his colleagues in other social sciences'.[20] No such theory of government behaviour is available at the moment and whether political factors are strong, weak or nonexistent in the determination of growth in government expenditure is therefore an unresolved issue.

Some support does exist for the idea that bureaucrats can play a major role in the growth of government spending.[21] The tendency for existing programmes to increase over time, the failure to terminate old programmes and the steady increase in new programmes is found in all Western countries. The reason why this tendency is laid at the door of the bureaucracy is that a great part of its satisfaction comes from the expansion of the scope of its activities. There is also a natural reluctance to dismantle an empire, once built. A further point to be taken into account is the fact that once a programme is started, and attention is drawn to previously unmet wants, a group of civil servants is drawn into this area, and once again a tendency towards empire building is initiated.

A factor which is added in order to explain why existing programmes keep expanding relates expenditure decisions to the budgetary process. Government budgets are prepared on an incremental and disaggregated basis. This is so because it is easier and furthermore because of the inherent human inability to comprehend the magnitude and implication of all the activities of the state. Sharp increases in the face of different types of crises are, however, not precluded by this incrementalist approach.

All these viewpoints attempt to explain the steady increase in the size of the government sector. This discussion will not be complete without reference to monetarism and its implications for government expenditure. The implications of monetarism for macroeconomic policy have been discussed extensively,[22] but not the indirect implication for public expenditure. Wherever possible a preference for the replacement of existing public sector involvement by private sector activity is expressed. Explicit in the view of monetarism is the image of smoothly working competitive markets. More implicit in their approach is an unfavourable view of the political process and of the discretion of politicians and bureaucrats. In this process it drew upon other schools of thought also critical of discretionary state action, such as the free market views of Hayek and the Virginian 'public choice' school.[23] At present, free market views appear to be quite strong in South Africa, leading to demands for the limitation of the allegedly inefficient government sector in favour of the efficient private sector. Great emphasis is thus placed on the desirability of a smaller government sector. Whether the advocates of this approach are powerful enough to succeed will only be evident in the years to come.

4. DISCUSSION OF THE MODEL

Discussion of the above models shows that each tends to emphasise a different aspect to the exclusion of other approaches. In fact, the observed pattern of government expenditure behaviour results from the systematic interaction of mutually interdependent economic, social and political forces. Many researchers have tried to quantify these relations by trying to isolate the factors responsible for the size of the public sector as economic development takes place. Most of these studies are based on a single-equation multiple regression model using cross-sectional data.[24] Comparisons are made between countries or, often, in the case of local government expenditure, between localities within a specified country.[25] Usually these studies are of an aggregative type using total government expenditure as the dependent variable, and invariably the independent variables are income and demographic factors such as total population, location density and the population age distribution. Studies based on time-series data are less numerous and the hypothesis tested is also much simpler. These studies are either descriptive or consider only income as an independent variable.[26]

In a study that concentrates on the economic factors influencing government expenditure one would expect some sort of simultaneous equation approach incorporating separate demand and supply relations.[27] It is, however, difficult to devise a physical output measure as well as a price for government-produced services. It is also not clear whether a specific factor would enter the model on the supply or demand side of the market. A case in point would be population density, which may be responsible for making some services cheaper, thus influencing the supply side of the market. At the same time, population density might stimulate demand for more public services. In the face of these problems it seems reasonable to estimate the relation between expenditures and explanatory variables in a single equation, which is equivalent to estimating the reduced-form equation for the market.

In analysing government expenditure one can find some analogies with consumption theory. The basic theoretical difference between the two categories is acknowledged, since the demand for public services is not additive (public goods) and there is no market apparatus that can be assumed to be meeting these demands. It can be postulated, however, that as in the case of consumption goods[28] people get used to certain levels of public service (such as education). Individuals will thus act to maintain or reach certain desired levels of public goods. The expansion in public expenditure programmes might therefore depend on the size of the gap between desired and actual levels of services. One might assume further that this desired level of expenditure is set in some sense independently of the level that can be financed by the assumed supply constraint. A model that does not allow for these effects will not obtain true government expenditure elasticities. A single equation approach will contain elements of both the long-run expenditure elasticity, which will be based on the community's desired level of expenditure, and the short-run expenditure elasticity, describing the short-run path that expenditure follows to get to the desired levels. Such a hypothesis suggests a partial adjustment type of model.[29]

Another lesson learnt from consumption studies is that of least squares bias, suggested by Wiseman and Diamond.[30] This results from relating government expenditure to income that contains as one of its components the same government expenditure. It seems that this problem can be overcome by relating government expenditure to private expenditure only (private consumption expenditure + net exports + gross capital formation).

The incrementalist approach to the budgetary process and the influence of demographic factors were also built into the model that follows. This approach is implicitly represented by the choice of lagged government expenditures as one of the variables incorporated in the model. On a totally disaggregated basis, the use of different variables for differing expenditures would be warranted. It was felt, however, that this could not be implemented in the present study because of the essentially aggregated nature of the various functional categories.

5. EMPIRICAL ANALYSIS

Since it was felt that little could be learnt by analysing only aggregate expenditure, various functional categories as well as some other classifications were considered. Care was taken to purge the data series of exogenous shifts resulting from changes in legislation or the introduction of new programmes when the individual functional categories were analysed.

The model was:[31]

$$G_{it}^e = aQ_t^b u_t \tag{1}$$

$$G_{it}/G_{it-1} = (G_{it}^e/G_{it-1})^k (X_{jt}/X_{jt-1})^d (P_{BW_t}) fD_1 D_2 D_3 D_4 N_t \tag{2a}$$

Rewriting equation (2a) in logarithmic terms,

$$g_{it} - g_{it-1} = k(g_{it}^e - g_{it-1}) + d(x_{jt} - x_{jt-1}) + fpBW_t + D_1 + D_2 + D_3$$
$$+ D_4 + N_t \tag{2b}$$

By rewriting equation (1) in logarithms and substituting for g_{it}^e in equation (2b) the following equation is obtained:

$$g_{it} = ka + bkq_t + (1-k)g_{it-1} + d(x_{jt} - x_{jt-1}) + fpBW_t + D_1 + D_2 + D_3$$
$$+ D_4 + (kU_t + N_t) \tag{3}$$

where:

Lower case letters represent logarithms;

G_{it} current government expenditure, per capita, in the ith category in period t deflated by the implicit GDP deflator;[32]

G_{it}^e the desired level of G_{it};

Q_t private expenditure in period t (consumption + gross investment + net exports);

X_{jt} government expenditure on all other categories where $i \neq j$, $(\Sigma_{i \neq j} G_{it})$;

P_{BW_t} black/white population ratio;

D_1 to D_4 dummy variables to be explained for each category;

U_t, N_t stochastic error terms;

a, b, k, d, f are parameters.

The results obtained in Table 3 are mixed, which is perhaps a reflection of the state of hypotheses on government expenditure. On closer inspection these results seem quite reasonable, as will become clear from a discussion of the specific categories.

Table 3 INCOME ELASTICITY OF CURRENT GOVERNMENT EXPENDITURE CATEGORIES, 1948–1984[1]

Category	Constant a_k (1)	Private expenditure bk (2)	Past government expenditure $(1-k)$ (3)	Other government expenditure d (4)	D_2 (5)	D_3 (6)	D_4 (7)	Speed of response k (8)	Expenditure elasticity (Income elasticity)[2] Short run (9)	Long run (10)	R^2
Total government (excluding defence)	−1,0076	0,3381*** (1,64)	0,7533*** (5,40)	0,0713*** (1,73)	0,0729** (1,44)			0,25	0,34 (0,39)	1,36 (1,27)	0,9651
Central government (excluding defence)	−1,6619	0,4313*** (2,28)	0,7091*** (5,74)	0,8137*** (4,01)	0,1734** (2,68)			0,29	0,43 (0,48)	1,48 (1,35)	0,9687
Administration	2,6876	−0,3358 (−1,05)	0,8598*** (8,26)	0,4207 (1,31)	0,2431*** (2,57)	0,1921** (2,27)	−0,0482 (−0,78)	0,14	STATISTICALLY		0,9467
Economic	−0,4486	0,1145 (0,71)	0,8929*** (8,55)	1,2553*** (4,93)	−1,20 (−0,0668)			0,11	NON-SIGNIFICANT		0,8759
Social services	−0,2838	0,1468* (1,33)	0,7940*** (5,48)	0,5955*** (3,88)	0,0903** (1,77)			0,21	0,15 (0,18)	0,71 (0,75)	0,9404
Law and order	−1,3205	0,2799** (2,21)	0,7515*** (8,03)	0,4335*** (3,32)	0,0723* (1,34)			0,25	0,28 (0,33)	1,12 (1,09)	0,9380
Public debt	−2,4932	0,4105*** (2,01)	0,8478*** (9,12)	0,1150 (0,45)	0,0723* (1,34)			0,15	0,41 (0,46)	2,73 (2,04)	0,9426
Ethnic category	−0,8096	0,1196 (0,36)	1,0052*** (44,01)	0,7715*** (2,92)	0,1221* (1,32)	0,0442 (0,74)	−0,0746 (−0,86)	0	STATISTICALLY NON-SIG-NIFICANT		0,9959
Local government	−0,4779	0,1640* (1,37)	0,8391*** (9,25)	0,3759*** (4,25)	0,0338* (1,38)			0,16	0,16 (0,19)	1,00 (1,00)	0,9776
Provincial administration	−2,0082	0,4907** (2,91)	0,6559*** (5,97)	0,3402*** (2,81)	−0,0089 (−0,31)			0,34	0,49 (0,54)	1,44 (1,33)	0,9568

1. The t-values appear in brackets except in columns 9 and 10, where the income elasticities appear in brackets.
2. Income elasticities in this model have been calculated in a fashion similar to that of Henning and Tussing, op. cit., p. 328.
3. *** indicates the 99 per cent, ** the 95 per cent and * the 90 per cent level of significance.

Time series multiple regression models are rarely free of multicollinearity. In this case it was not considered to be serious.[33] This judgement was strengthened by the fact that experiments with the combination of variables, as specified in equation (1), included in the regression equations did not alter the critical coefficients appreciably. The variables considered critical in this case were the coefficients associated with private expenditure (income proxy) and past levels of government expenditure.

Two variables specified in equation (1) do not appear in Table 3: the dummy variable D_1 and the black/white population ratio P_{BWt}. D_1 was introduced to test whether the break in the data during 1960 as identified in section 2 was statistically significant. It was non-significant even at the 50 per cent level of significance and therefore excluded. The significance level of the population variable was of an even lower order and was also subsequently omitted from the regression equations. The omission of these two variables can also be justified on the basis of a stepwise selection procedure.[34]

The slow speed of response (k) at which actual expenditure catches up with desired levels of expenditure was surprising. This coefficient was the highest for provincial administration, where it was 0,34, with values between 0,1 and 0,25 being the most prevalent for the various categories of expenditure. The more rapid the rate of growth in income, the larger will be the gap between desired and actual expenditure and possibly also the smaller will be the value of k, because of the gradual response in the increase in the income-related demand for public services. The small value of k is therefore quite acceptable in the light of the rapid rate of growth in income in South Africa over a large part of the period concerned. This is not true for the period 1975–84, when the economy performed less satisfactorily.

In all the regressions past levels of government expenditure proved to be the most significant variable. This result can be considered as support for the incrementalist hypothesis of a gradual annual increase in expenditure through the bureaucratic process, recalling that this variable was included as being implicitly representative of such an approach. This result was perhaps to be expected, considering the relatively stable nature of socio-economic conditions (interrupted by a consistent period of unrest after 1976) in the period under review. Furthermore, it can be considered an indication that no major shifts or changes in emphasis occurred in expenditure patterns amongst localities or functional categories. This observation is further amplified by the fact that the displacement effect was not present. The other government expenditure category (X_{jt}, measured by d in Table 3) which was included in order to investigate the interdependence between expenditure categories, was mostly significant and strangely enough had a positive coefficient associated with it. All categories of expenditure therefore increased more or less simultaneously, indicating no significant displacement.[35] Not even movements in defence expenditure had a significant influence on total government expenditure.

The short-run expenditure (which corresponds to bk in the model) and income elasticities[36] are low and in all cases below unity. This is because of the slow speed of response (k) between actual and desired levels of expenditure, for which an explanation has been presented. The purpose of the partial adjustment model is, however, to get away from the postulated lag in the response between income and government expenditure. The long-run expenditure and income elasticities are therefore the relevant variables to be used when the response of government expenditure to income is considered. Although the elasticity of government expenditure with respect to total private expenditure is a useful statistic in its own right, the more familiar income elasticity will be discussed. For total government expenditure (excluding defence) the income elasticity was 1,4 and was the highest for the public debt category, namely 2,7, followed by total central government, where the income elasticity was 1,5. In the other categories, with the exception of Social Services, the income elasticities were all greater than unity.

These elasticities provide support for the Wagner hypothesis. Total government expenditures do seem to increase more than proportionally with economic growth. As to the components of government expenditure that should, according to Wagner, become dominant — such as social welfare and administration and the law and order categories — the evidence is less clear. The income elasticity is only greater than unity for the law and order category, while for administration it was not significantly different from zero and it was below unity for social services. No evidence can be found for a tendency towards decentralisation of expenditure; the income elasticity for local authorities was 1,0 versus the 1,5 for central government, which indicates a trend towards centralisation.

Any study that covers such a long period of analysis runs into the problem of structural changes in the economy which could affect the results. This is even more pronounced if public expenditure is disaggregated into functional categories. New functions come into being, executive departments are restructured, off-budget expenditure is moved to the on-budget category and vice versa.[37] Careful attention needs to be paid to the construction of time series data. Most of these could be dealt with satisfactorily or were of a minor nature. In the cases where the data could not be satisfactorily purged, use had to be made of dummy variables. Mention has already been made of dummy variable D_1 testing for a structural change in 1960, which turned out to be non-significant. D_2 was introduced to quantify the structural change that was referred to from 1976/77. The coefficients seem to indicate that the structural changes that did occur in government expenditure over the period 1976/77 were significant. One would have expected negative signs on the coefficients (indicating a downward shift in expenditure levels) but this has not been reflected in the regressions.

Structural changes in categories occurred mainly with respect to Black, Coloured and Indian Affairs and with regard to 'black education'. In the case of social services, black education was omitted from this category, leading to good results. This was not true in the case of the administrative category, where structural changes occurred in black administration, Indian Affairs and Coloured Affairs; these votes were omitted from the category. The vote for customs unions was changed in 1970 when a new agreement with neighbouring states came into being. An adjustment was made for this change in law. After these omissions and adjustments had been made certain unexplained and erratic changes did occur in the data series for the years 1953, 1954, 1955 and 1965–76. Dummy variables D_3 and D_4 were introduced in order to purge the data of these unexplained variations. The end result for this category was improved by these specifications, although the income elasticity was not statistically significant.

A final category was created for the votes omitted from the administration category, called an ethnic category. This consisted of black education, black administration, Indian Affairs and Coloured Affairs. One must have reservations about one's ability to systematise these categories, because these votes are very susceptible to exogenous forces. The black administration vote changed structurally in 1965, a new Department for Coloured Affairs came into being in 1958, and the Department of Indian Affairs in 1963. A dummy variable D_2 was introduced to take account of the structural change in black administration from 1965 to 1984 and dummy variables D_3 and D_4 were introduced to adjust for the creation of the departments of Coloured Affairs and Indian Affairs respectively. The results obtained indicated that income (or its proxy) did not figure in these expenditures and that the main determinant of the expenditure growth was once again the previous level of expenditure.

6. CONCLUSION

Government expenditure increased significantly over the years 1948–84. Whether this growth can be justified cannot be judged because of the absence of clear theoretical guidelines. So far as the positive theory of government expenditure is concerned, no universally acceptable hypothesis has been formulated. Many factors were considered relevant expenditure-determining factors but it was not always clear how relevant these factors were.

The factors considered were related to both the supply and demand for public services as well as factors reflecting the budgetary process. We assumed that desired levels of expenditure are determined by the levels of income, while actual expenditure adjusted to the desired levels with a lag. In an effort to determine whether any displacement effects were noticeable, an exclusion variable was introduced. This took the form of government expenditure on all other categories except the one analysed. Demographic factors in the form of the black/white population ratio were introduced but after testing proved to be insignificant and were subsequently dropped.

The various functional categories were then analysed with the aid of the model. It was found that the level of past expenditures as well as the income

310

variable were major determinants of the expenditure categories considered. The only category for which poorer results were obtained was the Administration category. This could be attributed to the heterogeneous nature of the components of this category. An accentuating feature was the structural changes, which were discussed in section 4.

No noticeable displacement effect occurred, as indicated by the positive coefficients attached to the displacement variable. The Wagner hypothesis, in turn, was partially confirmed by the results which showed income elasticities greater than unity. High income elasticities were found, the most important being for central government excluding defence, local authorities and total government, excluding defence. These elasticities were 1,5 and 1,0 and 1,4 respectively.

Based on the income elasticities, government expenditure can be expected to increase at a rate greater than the growth in income. The future growth pattern in the various components of total government expenditure is more uncertain. This can be changed significantly by exogenous forces. It seems probable, however, that expenditures on social services as well as those directly related to matters concerning blacks, Coloureds and Indians will increase.

It should be self-evident that government expenditure cannot continue growing indefinitely at a rate exceeding that of the economy in general without having a marked negative influence on overall growth. One can expect, therefore, policy changes leading to a reduction in the role of the government sector — in the absence, of course, of any significant exogenous shocks.

NOTES

1 See for example: Samuelson, P.A., 'The Pure Theory of Public Expenditures,' *Review of Economics and Statistics*, Vol. 36, 1954, pp. 387–389, and Lindahl, E., 'Just Taxation: A Positive Solution'. Translated from German in Musgrave, R.A. and Peacock, A.T. (eds.), *Classics in the Theory of Public Finance*. New York: St Martin's Press, 1958.

2 Arrow, K.J., *Social Choice and Individual Values*. New York: Wiley, 1951.

3 Mueller, D.C., 'Public Choice: A Survey', *Journal of Economic Literature*, Vol. 14, 1976.

4 This study is limited to current expenditures incurred by general government, consisting of central government plus local and regional government, but excludes government business enterprises.

5 Head, J.G., *Public Goods and Public Welfare*. Durham: Duke University Press, 1971.

6 See Browne, G.W.G., 'Fifty Years of Public Finance', *South African Journal of Economics*, Vol. 51, 1983, pp. 134–173.

7 Report of the Comptroller and Auditor-General on the Appropriation Accounts and Miscellaneous Accounts and the Finance Statements, printed and published by the Government Printer, Private Bag X85, Pretoria.

8 A specification of the basis on which the classification was made is available from the authors.

9 Statistical Survey in connection with the Budget Speech, printed for the Government Printer, Cape Town, 1971/72, 1972/73, 1973/74.

10 Mohr, P.J. and Rogers, C., *Macro-economics*. Johannesburg: Lexicon, 1987, p. 359.

11 This was calculated from South African Statistics 1986, printed and published by the Government Printer, Private Bag X85, Pretoria.

12 This observation must be tempered, however, by the fact that certain unaudited secret military

expenditures have been included in the Treasury vote (for example, see Part II of the *Report of the Auditor-General for the Financial Year, 1978–79*, p. 173).

13 These percentages have been calculated from the nominal, not real, data.

14 Calitz, E., Public expenditure in South Africa, unpublished paper presented at the Conference of the Economic Society of South Africa, 1987.

15 Wagner's ideas appear in many publications and have been systematised in Bird, R.M., 'Wagner's "Law" of Expanding State Activity', *Public Finance*, Vol. 26, 1971, pp. 1–26.

16 Goffman, I.J. and Mahar, D.J., 'The Growth of Public Expenditures in Selected Developing Nations: Six Caribbean Countries, 1940–1965', *Public Finance*, Vol. 26, 1971, pp. 57–74.

17 Peacock, A.T. and Wiseman, J., *The Growth of Public Expenditure in the United Kingdom*. London: George Allen & Unwin, 1967. Although it is invalid to use this continuous analysis to criticise the discrete analysis of Peacock and Wiseman, no evidence was found in the data to support any significant displacement effect. This observation must also be qualified by the available evidence which indicates no important exogenous shocks in the period under review.

18 Musgrave, R.A., *Fiscal Systems*. New Haven: Yale University Press, 1969, pp. 87–89.

19 Spann, R.M., 'The Macroeconomics of Unbalanced Growth and the Expanding Public Sector', *Journal of Public Economics*, Vol. 8, 1977, pp. 397–404.

20 Bird, R.M., *The Growth of Government Spending in Canada*. Toronto: Canadian Tax Foundation, 1970, p. 128.

21 Wildavsky, A., *The Politics of the Budgetary Process*, Boston: Little, Brown and Company, 1964.

22 Mayer, T. (ed.), *The structure of monetarism*. New York: W.W. Norton, 1978.

23 Buchanan, J.M. and Wagner, R.E., *Democracy in deficit: The political legacy of Lord Keynes*. New York: Academic Press, 1977.

24 See Kelley, A.C., 'Demographic Change and the Size of the Government Sector', *Southern Economic Journal*, Vol. 42, 1976, pp. 1056–1066.

25 Smith, D., 'The Response of State and Local Governments to Federal Grants', *National Tax Journal*, Vol. 21, 1968, pp. 349–357.

26 Mahar, D.J., and Rezende, F.A., 'The Growth and Pattern of Public Expenditure in Brazil, 1920–1969', *Public Finance Quarterly*, Vol. 3, 1975, pp. 380–399.

27 Ohls, J.C. and Wales, T.J., 'Supply and Demand for State and Local Services', *Review of Economics and Statistics*, Vol. 54, 1972, pp. 424–430.

28 Duesenberry, J.S., *Income, Saving and the Theory of Consumer Behaviour*. London: Oxford University Press, 1967, pp. 24–26.

29 Kmenta, J., *Elements of Econometrics*. London: MacMillan, 1971, p. 476.

30 Wiseman, J. and Diamond, J., 'Comment on "Longrun Growth of Non-Defence Government Expenditures in the United States"', *Public Finance Quarterly*, Vol. 3, 1975, pp. 411–414.

31 A similar type of model was used by Henning, J.A. and Tussing, A.D., 'Income Elasticity of the Demand for Public Expenditures in the United States', *Public Finance*, Vol. 29, 1974, pp. 325–341. This model also provided the initial point of departure for the study of South African data by Abedian, I. and Standish, B., 'An analysis of the source of growth in state expenditure in South Africa 1920–1982', *South African Journal of Economics*, Vol. 52, 1984, pp. 391–408.

32 The implicit GDP deflator was calculated from South African Statistics, 1986, printed and published by the Government Printer, Private Bag X85, Pretoria.

33 Correlation matrices are available from the authors.

34 Wonnacott, R.J. and Wonnacott, T.H., *Econometrics*. New York: Wiley, 1970, pp. 309–312.

35 This displacement effect does not correspond with that developed by Peacock and Wiseman. It was used in the model to test the degree of substitution that occurred between the different expenditure categories.

36 Henning, J.A. and Tussing, A.D., 'Income Elasticity of the Demand for Public Expenditures in the United States', *Public Finance*, Vol. 29, 1974, p. 328.

37 Public Debt, for example, disappeared as a separate vote item after 1976 and was included thereafter in the Treasury vote. Although an explicit item in the Treasury vote, in subsequent

years it was substantially changed by the inclusion of interest repayments on SATS issues. This, of course, has made the series inconsistent and a dummy was added in the regression analysis to account for this change.

6.5 THE MARGO COMMISSION REPORT

G.L. de Wet*

INTRODUCTION AND BACKGROUND

A commission of inquiry into the tax structure of South Africa was appointed on 20 November 1984, under the chairmanship of Judge C.S. Margo. An interim report on the taxation of fringe benefits was tabled in February 1985, followed a few days later by an appendix to it. The final report was signed and handed to the State President on 20 November 1986, and publicly released early in 1987.[1]

The appointment of a commission of inquiry became necessary as a result of widespread feelings that the tax structure had become unfair, too complicated, and was interfering with basic economic choices, thereby affecting economic growth. Piecemeal and *ad hoc* reforms over the years — and especially inflation, which complicated the measurement of income and led to bracket creep — had brought about a very unsatisfactory situation. Consequently, individuals and businesses were making decisions in which tax considerations played an unduly large role, and because the tax system was regarded as unfair, tax morality was declining. Tax avoidance and evasion were the order of the day and a lucrative, skilled tax avoidance industry had developed, eroding the tax base and diverting scarce resources and skills into unproductive activities (Report, paragraphs 3.1 and 3.4, p. 37).

THE COMMISSION'S BASIC APPROACH

The Commission's brief was to make proposals concerning the tax structure and it interpreted this as implying that a long-term perspective had to be taken. It assumed, therefore, a normal, healthy economy, accepting that short-term political and economic problems might retard implementation or even cause major short-term diversions from its recommendations (Report, paragraph 3.9, p. 38). It was clear to the Commission that tax revenue would have to increase in future, as the demand for collective or public goods and services would for various reasons continue to grow (Report, paragraph 3.22, p. 41). Against this background the Commission set out to design a system that would raise the required revenue in as neutral a way as possible (Report, paragraph 3.8, p. 37).

Continued growth in the South African economy demands continued investment and increasing savings. Yet there is only a limited potential for an increase in the personal savings ratio through adjustments in the existing tax structure. A new tax structure must therefore be introduced, based on the fol-

* Professor of Economics, University of Pretoria.

lowing principles: neutrality, equity, invisibility, simplicity and certainty. The Commission regarded it as of the utmost importance that a tax structure should be aimed at long-term growth, rather than at short-term anti-cyclical action (Report, Chapter 4).

MAJOR RECOMMENDATIONS

The Commission examined the various options which, according to its judgement, were open for tax reform. It came to the conclusion that it is not yet time to abandon income (as opposed to expenditure) as the basis for direct taxation in South Africa. *Yet the income tax base must be broadened and the marginal rates of income tax on individuals and corporations should be held as low as possible.*

In considering tax options, the Commission further expressed a preference for taxing according to the benefit principle, rather than the ability to pay. The benefit principle should be applied generally to recover user charges from those sections of the community that use public goods and services.

The Commission made a number of detailed recommendations on individual income tax. Paramount amongst these is the fact that fringe benefits — and for that matter all income — should in principle be totally taxable. There should be a slow move towards a simpler income tax structure with fewer, broader bands and lower marginal rates (Report, Chapter 6). Turning to the personal income tax unit, the Commission recommended that the individual replace the couple as the unit, after it had taken due consideration of previous South African investigations into the subject and of trends in other Western countries. The Commission attached considerable weight to the need for a situation in which taxation would be immaterial when deciding whether to marry, to work, and so forth. In addition, administrative considerations are equally important, since accurate PAYE (pay as you earn) deductions cannot be made so long as incomes of spouses must be aggregated.

Although the Commission seemed not to be unanimous on this matter, a number of technical recommendations regarding the collection of income tax were made. It was furthermore suggested that the inspection teams of Inland Revenue be expanded and even that a public relations section be introduced in the Directorate of Inland Revenue (Report, Chapters 7 and 8). When the Commission dealt with the administration of taxation an interesting proposal was submitted. This was the introduction of complete self-assessment, with only verification or auditing being carried out by the Receiver's office. This could lead to a much more cost-effective system (Report, Chapter 28).

Turning to business income, the Commission touched upon many details regarding the determination of the appropriate amount of income. As a general principle, it was taken that income should be recognised when all events have occurred which fix the right to receive it and the amount thereof can be determined with reasonable accuracy. The Commission recommended that the rates of individual and company tax be lowered substantially and that there should be neutrality between the company rate and the maximum marginal rate for individuals, so that tax considerations will not play a role in determining the form of business. The Commission concluded that the company, and not the *group*, should remain the basis for taxation (Report, Chapter 9).

Inflation makes the calculation of business income very difficult and if high inflation continues, it may become necessary to adjust the conventionally calculated business income for inflation. One possible method is the one in use in Israel, where income constitutes only part of the basis for tax. The Commission identified four taxes meriting consideration to effect this change, namely the general sales tax, a destination-based value added tax, a retail sales tax and an origin-based comprehensive business tax assessed on value added tax. Examination of the size of the bases of these taxes revealed that the imposition of more than one would have to be considered (Report, Chapter 5).

Although it was not unanimous in this respect, the Commission recommended that capital gains be not subject to taxation (Report, paragraphs 12.31 to 12.42, pp. 222–225). Another recommendation of general interest is that estate duty and donations tax should be replaced by a capital transfer tax at a flat rate of 15 per cent (Report, Chapter 20 and particularly par. 20.68, p. 322).

THE COMPREHENSIVE BUSINESS TAX (CBT)

Although many of the remaining recommendations were particularly technical — dealing, *inter alia*, with taxation of insurers, financial intermediaries, mining, agriculture and so forth, a major goal was to introduce a tax structure characterised by *low* rates and a broad and ever-increasing base. To achieve this, a major source of new revenue had to be found and for this purpose the Commission regarded the Comprehensive Business Tax (CBT) as an excellent broadly based source of revenue (Report, Chapter 22).

The Comprehensive Business Tax would be an income tax, since it would be levied on income and not products. It would, however, have many of the characteristics of an indirect tax because, being levied at a flat rate on total income, it would not take the particular circumstances of an individual taxpayer into account. The CBT would be a so-called origin-based value added tax — value added because it is based on income generated and origin-based because it would include *all* income generated. It can be calculated as a given percentage of the sum of all salaries, wages, interest, royalties, rent and profit, the latter being calculated before allowing for depreciation. In ordinary language, it is calculated on the basis of the value of *all* sales of goods and services, other than those of financial assets, less the value of *all* purchases of goods and services. The Commission was particularly attracted to this type of tax because it has a very broad base, implying that the rate could be kept very low. This would in turn discourage evasion. The broad base would furthermore ensure a minimum sensitivity to business cycle fluctuations.

In the Commission's opinion, General Sales Tax reform should represent a return towards a low rate and a clearly defined base. The appropriate base would be *retail sales*. This would eliminate double taxation, as intermediate goods and services would no longer be taxed. The Commission argued that food should be included and that direct cash subsidies in one form or another would be a more appropriate way of helping the poor, since the exclusion of food from the base for GST erodes the tax base very severely and benefits many more than just the poor (Report, paragraphs 29.7 to 29.9, p. 451).

Tax expenditures, such as investment allowances, training allowances and decentralisation allowances, erode the business income base and should be eliminated as far as possible (Report, paragraph 29.14, p. 452). The Commission was particularly in favour of regional taxes and held the opinion that the CBT lent itself excellently to that purpose (Report, paragraphs 29.24 and 29.25, p. 454).

ALTERNATIVE PACKAGE

The Commission was of the opinion that the options for reform would become very limited if, for any reason, a national Comprehensive Business Tax were rejected. This view was based on its belief that a CBT was the only means of introducing a (neutral) widely based tax which would permit various other reforms, particularly the wide reduction of tax rates and the separate taxation of husband and wife. Regional taxation, still on the basis of CBT, could, however, still be carried on with. The need for sales tax reform would remain urgent and the Commission recommended that in this case, General Sales Tax should be transformed into an invoice Value Added Tax, similar to that found in the EEC, at a single rate on a very broad base, including food. Although the Commission would eventually want to see capital goods and other inputs completely excluded from VAT, it seemed necessary to suggest the inclusion of capital goods as an intermediate measure, in order to keep the VAT rate at an acceptable level (Report, paragraphs 29.30 to 29.37, pp. 454–455).

CONCLUDING REMARKS

On the surface, the Margo Report represents a genuine attempt at tax reform in a scientifically responsible way. However, the Commission was not unanimous in all its recommendations and the diversity of opinion was even greater in the community at large.

The Comprehensive Business Tax was not accepted by the government as a result of fierce opposition from certain business quarters. Instead, the proposed introduction of a Value Added Tax was announced, intended to replace the existing Sales Tax.

It remains to be seen which of the remaining recommendations will be accepted. The only safe conclusion to be reached in the light of the recommendations of the Margo Commission and the general reaction to it, is that taxation remains a bone of grave contention.

The Commission accepted that it had not spoken the final word on tax reform in South Africa and therefore recommended a small permanent tax reform committee to continue its work (Report, paragraph 29.45, p. 456).

NOTE

1 *Report of the Commission of Inquiry into the Tax Structure of the Republic of South Africa*, RP34/ 1987, Government Printer, Pretoria, 1987, hereafter referred to as 'Report'.

7

General Reflections on Macroeconomic Policy

7.1 INTRODUCTION

It is evident from the preceding chapters that both the analysis of the South African economy and the question of appropriate macroeconomic policy prescription have spawned a good deal of debate and controversy. Given the existence of fundamental disagreements amongst economists concerned with macroeconomic theory, especially between monetarists and Keynesians, this is not at all surprising. Moreover, macroeconomic policy prescription falls within the realm of normative economics, since it seeks to assess the operation of the economy and suggest ways in which its performance can be improved. This implies at the very least implicit value judgements about the desirability of different macroeconomic policy objectives, and the costs associated with attempting to achieve these objectives. Because people hold divergent opinions regarding the optimal welfare goals of society, there will always be dispute concerning the appropriateness of both policy instruments and macroeconomic objectives.

The choice of a suitable macroeconomic policy package from a range of competing policies is thus always problematic. In essence, four separate sets of decisions must be made in deciding upon the appropriateness of macroeconomic policy. In the first place, since every policy prescription is based on a theoretical model of the macroeconomy, an assessment of the logical consistency of the model must be made. Put differently, the *validity* of the model must be examined in order to ascertain whether the policy prescriptions follow logically from the behavioural assumptions and functional relationships of the model. Given the analytically rigorous nature of modern macroeconomics, unless a particular analyst has erred in constructing or applying his model to the specific circumstances of a given country, there is usually little dispute over the question of validity.

Once the issue of validity has been settled, the usefulness of the model must be decided. The usefulness of a macroeconomic model depends largely upon the extent to which the assumptions embodied in the model approximate the conditions actually experienced in the economy under consideration. Although the very process of model building necessarily requires the invocation of simplifying assumptions, perceptions of the appropriateness of these assumptions to given economic circumstances in a particular country often differ markedly. Indeed, many of the differences between monetarists and Keynesians, and between individual members of each of these schools, stem from divergent opinions concerning the behaviour of private individuals and institutions in the modern economy. Monetarists, for instance, generally believe in the efficiency of markets — in contrast to their Keynesian colleagues, who are rather more sceptical. In South Africa, disagreement exists over the extent to which structural features of the South African economy, such as economic dualism, fragmented money and capital markets and a primary export sector, ought to be explicitly incorporated into macroeconomic models of the domestic economy. Furthermore, some South African economists believe the 'openness' of the South African economy requires special emphasis in the design of appropriate macroeconomic policies.

Having assessed the validity and usefulness of the macroeconomic model and its attendant policy prescriptions, the policy-maker must now make a third decision before adopting any proposals. Specifically, the quantitative impact of policies must be evaluated in order to gauge their likely effects on the economy. Econometric investigations of this kind require accurate estimates of certain key economic magnitudes drawn from national income accounting. Moreover, the probable rates of change of these economic magnitudes over time must be appraised, necessitating the use of economic forecasting. Given the inexactitude of economic data and the uncertainty inherent in predicting future events, it can be appreciated why disagreements can arise at this third level of decision-making.

The final decisions which require attention are those which focus on the legislative processes of decision-making in democratic societies, and the ability of state organisations and bureaucracies to efficiently and timeously implement policy proposals. It often, for example, occurs that public representatives 'water down' policy prescriptions in response to the demands of special interest groups, thus reducing their effectiveness. Moreover, the phenomenon of government failure (and its attendant problem of bureaucratic failure) implies that even when legislative approval has been bestowed on a particular set of policies, the administrative machinery is simply unable or unwilling to implement these policies in an effective manner.

The differences of opinion concerning the appropriateness of macroeconomic analysis and policy prescription for South Africa are evident in the four readings provided in this chapter. In the first article, De Kock defends the market-orientated approach followed by the authorities in South Africa since the 1970s. He contends that a process of adjustment inevitably confronted the South African economy, and that critics of the official policies mistakenly confuse the need for adjustment with the means employed to effect the adjustment. The second paper, by Lawrence McCrystal, lays the blame for the country's poor economic performance squarely at the feet of the reactive management style of the monetary and fiscal authorities. He argues that South

Africa simply cannot afford the free market philosophy as propounded, for example, by the De Kock Commission, and that economic intervention on a continuing basis is necessary if stabilisation is to be achieved. In the third paper, Black and Dollery attack official macroeconomic policy prescriptions on the grounds that the present market-orientated policies ignore fundamental structural features of the South African economy. They argue for a more selective approach to macroeconomic policy. In the final reading of this chapter, O'Dowd gives a more general perspective on the role of government in society, and identifies three important characteristics of state policy-making, namely impossibility, political failure and bureaucratic failure. Thus governments often pursue mutually exclusive objectives without either financial discipline or long-term consistency, by means of a highly imperfect and inefficient bureaucratic structure. Consequently, in the formulation of macroeconomic policy it should be noted that governments are incapable of producing ideal results.

7.2 ECONOMIC POLICY AND THE FREE MARKET SYSTEM

G.P.C. de Kock*

INTRODUCTION

It is increasingly realised that since the early seventies the South African economy has been adversely affected by a succession of unfavourable economic and socio-political developments. This has led to a lower average economic growth rate, declining real fixed investment, increasing unemployment, capital outflows, a depreciation of the exchange rate, a higher inflation rate and a decline in average real living standards on a per capita basis.

The unfavourable economic and socio-political developments are well documented and known. What is not always so clear is that these developments have made drastic and painful adjustments in the South African economy unavoidable, and created enormous challenges for economic policy.

SUCCESSFUL MONETARY AND FISCAL ADJUSTMENT POLICY NOTWITHSTANDING SHORTCOMINGS

How did the South African economy in reality fare in this adjustment process? According to all acknowledged international standards the answer is: particularly well. This achievement is especially noteworthy if the abnormal political situation which exists is taken into account. The deficit on the current account of the balance of payments has been transformed into a surplus, real salaries and wages have been adjusted downwards, much foreign debt has been repaid over the past two and a half years and the country is living well within its means.

This adjustment process obviously demanded considerable sacrifices and hardship. A tightening of the belt is never easy or painless. But there is no doubt that the economy has adjusted effectively and quickly to the hard realities. In overseas circles this has not gone unnoticed.

On occasion there were indeed serious defects of policy. One example is the way in which the 'gold bonanza' of 1978–80 was allowed to lead to excessive money creation, excessively low interest rates, excessive spending and inflation. A second example is the unsatisfactory 'mix' of fiscal and monetary policy which was applied in 1983–84, when demand inflation and balance of payments problems were facilitated by excessive increases in government spending, in

---

* Governor of the South African Reserve Bank. This paper is an extract from the address 'Market-Oriented Policy and Economic Adjustment in South Africa', delivered at the Johannesburg Sakekamer on 26 June 1986, and was first published in *The Securities Markets* No. 2, Fourth Quarter, 1986.

salaries and wages in the public sector and in the Budget deficit before borrowing.

In general, monetary and fiscal policy did succeed in promoting the adjustment of the economy and so made South Africa better equipped to resist the onslaught from outside and to lay the groundwork for sound growth in the future.

CRITICISM OF THE FREE MARKET SYSTEM — MISUNDERSTANDINGS AND FALLACIES

Notwithstanding all this there are still those who maintain that the most important single reason for South Africa's economic problems in recent years is to be found in the mistakes of economic policy and particularly in the acceptance of the so-called 'free market ideology' since the late seventies. More specifically, these critics assert that if the authorities had made more use of direct control measures instead of 'obstinately clinging to the view that the free market system is infallible', the effects of the unfavourable influences on the South African economy since the early seventies could to a large extent have been 'compensated' or 'neutralised'. Presumably we then would have experienced a higher growth rate, a lower inflation rate, a stronger rand and more stable and lower interest rates!

Although one is justified in criticising certain aspects of the official monetary and fiscal policy of recent years, the above accusations against market-oriented policy are completely unfounded and rest on either misunderstandings or fallacies.

FREE ENTERPRISE AND MARKET-ORIENTED POLICY VERSUS 'LEAVING EVERYTHING TO THE FREE MARKETS'

To begin with, the emphasis placed by the authorities in recent years on free enterprise and market-oriented economic policy in no way implies that we espouse a *laissez faire* approach of 'leaving it all to the working of the free markets'. *Market-oriented policy is still policy.* But it is a policy which recognises the existence of markets and where possible operates through the markets rather than by way of quantitative bureaucratic control measures.

For example, if the Reserve Bank wishes to curb the rate of increase in bank credit, the money supply and aggregate spending, it does not resort to imposing a direct quantitative ceiling on each bank's credit extension, with all the disruption and avoidance that goes with it. Instead, it sells government stock and other money market paper in the open market and reins in its own money creation by raising its discount rate (Bank rate). On other occasions, when the Reserve Bank deems it desirable to stimulate spending, production and income, such as at present, it supplies the banks and the money market with the necessary cash reserves by buying or discounting money market paper and by lowering its Bank rate.

Such market-oriented policy accords well with the role assigned to free enterprise and effective competition by the Constitution of the Republic of South Africa. It also fits in with declared government policy on deregulation and privatisation. *This does not mean, however, that free markets are seen as an objective per se.* In the application of a long-term economic strategy the Government will often have valid reasons for intervening in the working of the markets in order to bring about a *different* result than would have been produced by an entirely self-directed market. *But such intervention will in most cases be more effective if it takes place by way of market-oriented policy rather than direct bureaucratic control measures.* The main reason for this is that the markets and the institutions operating in them will usually soon discover quite legal means of circumventing direct controls.

In all fairness it must be said that this earlier misunderstanding as to the difference between *market-oriented policy* and 'leaving everything to the free markets' has now been largely dispelled. The advocates of market-oriented policy and their critics now do understand one another better on this point.

DISTINGUISHING BETWEEN THE ECONOMIC SITUATION AND ECONOMIC POLICY: THE FALLACY OF 'POST HOC ERGO PROPTER HOC'

The main reason why it is illogical to blame market-oriented policy for South Africa's weaker growth performance since the early seventies, lies elsewhere. It is to be found in the failure properly to distinguish between the *underlying economic situation and the economic policy applied to meet that situation.* Certain critics tend to confuse these two matters. They present statistical series to indicate that South Africa's growth performance has been substantially weaker since approximately the mid-seventies than during the sixties, that the rate of inflation increased, that the rand depreciated, etc. And they then imply that because this happened *after* the Government made more use of market-oriented policy, the events described occurred *because* this market-oriented policy stance was adopted. The further implication is that had we instead relied on direct bureaucratic control measures, these unfavourable developments would either not have taken place or not to the same extent.

Here one must guard against the classic fallacy of '*post hoc ergo propter hoc*'. Because A happened *after* B happened, therefore A must be the *result* of B! Because the drought struck us *after* mini dresses came into fashion, therefore the drought was *caused* by the mini dresses!

No, if we truly want to analyse the current serious economic situation in South Africa and apply the correct economic strategy, we must avoid this kind of reasoning. *It is important at all times to distinguish between the 'situation' and the 'adjustment policy'.* The 'situation' may be good or bad and the 'policy' to manage that situation may also be good or bad. But these are two different things.

The influence of economic policy must in any case not be overrated. Often the influence of economic policy is relatively small compared with other economic and non-economic influences which determine the course of the economy. When the going is good in economic terms, for example in South Africa during the gold boom of 1978–80, it is fallacious to describe the favourable developments as being in the main 'achievements' of economic policy. And if less good times are experienced and serious problems crop up, it is equally wrong to ascribe that state of affairs mainly to the shortcomings of economic policy.

The reasons for South Africa's weaker growth performance and other economic problems of the past decade are clearly identifiable. But market-oriented policy, even if it was at times imperfectly applied, was always part of the *solution* and never of the *problem*!

'COMPENSATING', 'NEUTRALISING' AND 'IMMUNISING' VERSUS 'ADJUSTMENT'

A further fallacy in the criticism of South Africa's market-oriented economic policy is the reasoning that the effects of unfavourable external influences (such as the socio-political developments, the drought, the fluctuations in the gold price and the weaker international growth performance), could to a large extent have been 'compensated' or 'neutralised' by applying direct control measures such as import control, exchange control, pegging of the exchange rate, quantitative credit ceilings, deposit rate control and more stringent hire purchase conditions. In this connection it has been alleged that our economic policy should have aimed at 'immunising' South Africa from the abovementioned unfavourable developments by resorting to direct control measures.

This surely cannot be right. Let us be realistic. *As a result of unfavourable exogenous economic and non-economic events since the early seventies the South African economy inevitably had to undergo a process of adjustment. Meaningful 'compensating', 'neutralising' or 'immunising' measures were impossible. What we did need was 'adjustment' and a proper 'handling' of the situation.* For South Africa the series of unfavourable exogenous developments which were analysed above necessarily implied some or other combination of slower growth, higher inflation and exchange rate depreciation, and therefore a lower average living standard per capita. We only had a choice between different methods of adjustment, and between different ways of spreading the adjustment burden. *But that we had to adjust was quite unavoidable.*

CONCLUDING REMARKS

The real debate should therefore be about the advantages and disadvantages of alternative adjustment methods which were at our disposal and not about the question whether we should have adjusted or not. And the critics owe it to us to show in detail how the direct control measures that they advocate could have

325

succeeded *better* than the policy which was applied, in making the necessary adjustment. There is always room for divergence of opinion over the way in which the authorities trim their sails to the wind, but they can hardly be blamed for the wind itself.

7.3 THE CHOICE BEFORE US: ECONOMIC STABILISATION OR THE INSTABILITY OF FREE MARKETS

Lawrence Patrick McCrystal*

It is a fact of life that after all is said and done more has been said than done. Until recently, this has unhappily been the case with South Africa's economic policy-making.

It has always been my belief that the boldest businessman in history was Noah — he floated a company when the rest of the world was in liquidation. Some may argue that it would take even greater boldness to start a new business in South Africa today. I do not share that view, given that sound economic policies are adopted.

The prevailing conventional wisdom in South Africa is that free markets are the key to economic growth and prosperity for the majority. So we should have, it is argued, free imports, freely floating foreign exchange rates, free market interest rates and generally freedom from all or most forms of government intervention in the economic affairs of the country.

If this view, which has been widely held and strongly argued in South Africa for at least the past 70 years, had been followed by our forefathers, we would today have little or no steel industry, oil from coal plants, aluminium smelting, no Industrial Development Corporation or phosphate industry and little or no textile industry. In fact, South Africa would be a predominantly mining and agricultural country with little industrialisation, secondary industry and related activities.

FREE MARKET LEGACY

The question now arises as to what the free market philosophy has done for South Africa in the six years that it has been actively promoted. Here are some of the 'blessings':

- The highest interest rates in the country's recorded economic history.
- A lower average rate of economic growth (on average only about 3 per cent per annum) than in any similar period since reasonably reliable statistics have become available.
- A wider oscillation in the growth rate than in any adequately monitored period in our history, i.e. from 7,8 per cent growth in gross domestic product in 1980 to a negative 1,2 per cent in 1982, and a negative 3,2 per cent in 1983.

* Chairman, Board of Trade and Industry, Pretoria. This paper was first published in *Indicator South Africa*, Vol. 3, No. 2. The quarterly report on social trends, Economic Monitor: pp. 13/16. Centre for Social and Development Studies, University of Natal, Durban: Spring 1985.

- A rand which has depreciated to the lowest level in our history against virtually every significant currency, including the lire and the escudo. In 1984, the rand was the ninth worst performer in the world, with only a few South American and Middle East currencies being worse.
- An excessively high rate of inflation.
- Inadequate foreign reserves to repay the country's external debts.
- High and rising unemployment.
- A high and rising rate of company liquidations, leading to an increasing degree of concentration of economic power.
- A significant deterioration in the balance sheets of the vast majority of industrial concerns in the country.
- The lowest level of savings relative to Gross National Income recorded in our economic history.
- Deteriorating returns on investment in major sectors of the economy.

With such a poor record of performance, the question is: why did the government not abandon the policies that led to this situation long ago? Part of the answer lies in the fact that the government blames our current unhappy status on the after-effects of the drought, the low gold price, and the volatile international economic environment. This certainly is true in part, but the drought has been broken over much of the country while the effects of the low gold price have been absorbed by the balance of payments long before now. Other countries which are just as exposed to the volatility of the international economy as is South Africa have succeeded in stabilising their affairs.

Government policy must unhappily bear a large part of the blame for the poor state of the economy. The fact that the free market philosophy has not been abandoned can only be explained by an apparent confusion between the concepts of 'free enterprise' and 'free markets'.

I am certainly in favour of free enterprise in the sense of freedom to start new businesses, freedom to sell one's labour in the best market, freedom to sell to whom and at what price one wishes, and so on. However, it has to be acknowledged that free markets do not necessarily tend towards an optimum position. They may in fact move even further away from it under the influence of speculation. In January 1985 this became evident when speculation drove the rand to 41 US cents. The fact is that markets do need to be disciplined from time to time in order to restore them to reasonable stability.

VOLATILITY OF A SMALL ECONOMY

South Africa's economy is inherently volatile, exceedingly dependent as it is upon an unpredictable gold price and even more erratic weather conditions. One would have thought that economic policy would have been designed to reduce this volatility rather than to increase it. Yet by pursuing a free market philosophy, the authorities have added to the volatility of the economy.

Support for this criticism is not hard to find. The violent swings in the foreign exchange rates of the rand, the wide fluctuations in the rate of economic growth in recent years, and the movements in interest rates have all been of critical importance to the decisions of businessmen. Their unpredictability in the past few years has had a major negative influence on investment by business.

The view that allowing markets freedom to find their own levels will necessarily enhance economic well-being has led the authorities into another trap. They have tended to wait for market forces to rectify the situation. Only upon finding that this is not always the way things go, have they taken action. As a consequence, they have unwittingly fallen into a reactive style of economic management. Reactive management, whether of a home, a business or an economy, is generally poor management because it implies a lack of planning and takes effect after the event. If one does not know where one is going, how can one expect to get there? It is only by adopting a pro-active management style that one can hope to influence the course of events in a sensible manner.

We have recently had some splendid examples of the poor decision-making resulting from the reactive management style adopted by the authorities. In November 1983, at a conference organised by the then Prime Minister to discuss inflation, the government was warned that consumer spending was getting out of hand and should be curbed quickly. Nothing was done until August 1984, when the spending splurge had already started to cool down. Thus our policy-makers pushed the economy down further and faster than would otherwise have been the case had they taken action sooner. Motivated by their free market philosophy, they waited for market forces to correct the situation. When this did not happen to their satisfaction, they took interventionary action but it was too late.

Another example of the negative effect of this philosophy was the speculation during January 1984 against the rand which drove it down to 41 US cents. A little bit of discipline was imposed and the exchange rate improved 25 per cent in a short space of time.

PHILOSOPHY OF THE STRONG

The kind of policies currently being followed are, in my view, exaggerating the trade cycle rather than dampening it as should be the case. This makes forward planning for businessmen almost impossible, introduces new volatility into the building and construction industry, and makes export-orientated investment almost impossible. One does not know from one hour to the next what the exchange rate is going to be, let alone being able to take a longer view.

How much further can the economy be allowed to deteriorate before it is realised that South Africa is not able to afford the free market philosophy as it is currently interpreted? Mr Edward Heath, a former Prime Minister of Britain, recently remarked: 'The truth is, as history has often shown us, that unfettered market forces lead to the rich and strong getting richer and stronger, and the poor and weak, poorer and weaker, until some conflagration in society acts to restore the balance.' Must we wait for a social conflagration to put right what the free market policies have allowed to go wrong?

The free market philosophy always has been the philosophy of the strong. South Africa's economy is neither strong enough nor diversified enough to afford a virtually freely floating currency, extraordinarily high interest rates and relatively free imports, with no incomes policy of any kind.

An unshakeable faith in the ability of free markets to rectify imbalances leads to the conclusion that whatever goes wrong is purely of a cyclical nature and, given time, will correct itself. The possibility that the ills of the economy may be caused or at least aggravated by the tendency for markets to sometimes move even further from an equilibrium position apparently does not occur to those who believe that markets always operate in the best longer-term interests of the economy.

The effects of the fall in the exchange rate are already being felt, as the cost increases it has caused filter through to the consumer level. The rate of increase in consumer prices is in danger of causing an uncontrollable inflation/depreciation spiral. Ever higher rates of increases in prices may be expected to cause further depreciation of the rand, resulting in disastrous levels of inflation.

ACCEPTABLE INTERVENTION POLICY

The effects of freer imports and high interest rates are already visible in industry, particularly in the lack of growth in investment in productive capacity, and in the concomitant deterioration of productivity levels. The lack of any form of incomes policy, even of an informal kind, is visible, in turn, in the stubbornly high level of inflation.

What is more, many manufacturers are not really being assisted by the lower exchange value of the rand, as is borne out by the recent experience of, for example, the steel and engineering industries. High local interest rates and deep-seated uncertainty about the rand's future make it unattractive to expand capacity to enter export markets. Consequently, instead of the floating exchange rate and freely-moving interest rates solving the problem, it has become necessary for special steps to be taken to assist exporters by mitigating the effects of the free market policies.

South Africa has few markets. Even those markets which are relatively free need to be re-orientated or disciplined on occasions. The August 1984 measures regarding consumer credit and the 1985 interventions in the rules governing the rand foreign exchange markets, bear this out.

The choice has to be made between those policies which accept this type of intervention as inevitable in the South African context, and those who see it as a temporary aberration in an otherwise free situation which must be returned to 'normal' as soon as possible. The former is pro-active; the latter reactive, its reaction usually coming too late, once it is clear that market forces will be unable to bring about the necessary correction — by which time interventionary action is usually too late.

THE ALTERNATIVE: CONTROLS

A change of attitude is necessary. It must be accepted that markets in South Africa's circumstances do not necessarily correct all imbalances and if left free, often aggravate the situation. It must also be accepted that the control of inflation is South Africa's highest stabilisation priority. For years, lip service accompanied by curiously little action has been paid to this. At long last it seems to have been accepted by government that some form of income policy is necessary, something for which a few economists have been pleading without being heard, for years. Since government controls such a high proportion of the total salary and wage bill in South Africa, this is obviously the place to start. The government is to be congratulated for its recent, though rather belated decision to cut back on expenditure and must be encouraged by the private sector to see it through.

The floating exchange rate policy should be limited by adopting an internal stabilisation policy and not falling into the trap of using the exchange rate as a substitute. Currency flows emanating from gold and capital movements must be separated from the flows on the current account emanating from trade. A capital stabilisation account should be created and capital movements paid into or out of this. Gold earnings, which are also frequently volatile, would go into this account as well.

Quantitative controls on credit will be necessary from time to time as part of setting targets for money supply growth. This should be accepted as an integral part of stabilisation policy. Control of government spending and fiscal policies which work in tandem with monetary policy are also essential, and the promotion of competition and reduction of interference by the state in private enterprise, as distinct from 'free markets', must be part of the package.

Let it be remembered that 'free markets' imply freedom of resources to move. If resources are not free to move across borders, particularly in a case like South Africa, where the economy is small, it hinders rather than helps matters to prescribe policies which are based on the assumption that free market prices will correct the resulting imbalances. They often will not: our present situation is evidence that these imbalances can grow steadily worse.

CLEAR CHOICE

Unhappily, if we do somehow experience a modest economic upturn in due course, the free market supporters will claim that their policies have worked. But the recession thereafter, accompanied by high inflation and a continually deteriorating rand, will probably be worse than the present one — until the inflation/depreciation spiral really does become uncontrollable. If this happens, such drastic measures will be necessary that conventional economic stabilisation policies will not be sufficient to correct the imbalance.

Sooner rather than later a clear choice is going to have to be made — economic stability with growth and a positive attitude to intervention in the economy to maintain these when necessary; or pursuit of free markets, with high volatility, greater uncertainty and lower long-term real growth.

7.4 SELECTIVE INTERVENTION AND THE SOUTH AFRICAN ECONOMY

Philip Black and Brian Dollery*

1. It is somewhat ironic that whilst policy-makers in South Africa insist on developing indigenous solutions to the country's pressing political problems, they appear quite content to rely on imported economic policy prescriptions. Indeed, several influential public figures have openly expressed an admiration for the policies followed by the governments of Mrs Thatcher and President Reagan in particular, and have stressed the need for South Africa to adopt similar policies. As Reserve Bank Governor Dr De Kock (1984: 15) recently remarked, '... the South African authorities have chosen a set of monetary and fiscal adjustment policies not dissimilar to that applied so successfully in the United States, the United Kingdom, West Germany and Switzerland'.

This paper questions the wholesale adoption of such measures by the South African authorities. It is argued that certain fundamental structural features inherent in the local economy render conventional monetary policy largely inappropriate, and require instead a more selective approach aimed at reducing unemployment *without* unduly fuelling inflation or worsening the country's balance of payments position. While the aim of this paper is broadly similar to Michal Kalecki's (1976: essay 7) analysis of the financial requirements for economic development, the approach followed here has much in common with the 'structuralist' remedies proposed by Sunkel (1958), Oliviera (1964), Cardoso (1981), Canavese (1982) and Mohr (1981; 1983).

2. The desirability of macroeconomic policies cannot be gauged by reference to their efficient application in other developed economies whose primary objectives and institutional characteristics may be entirely different from those of South Africa. The costs associated with a particular policy mix may be much higher in South Africa than in the UK or USA, whilst the corresponding returns may also compare unfavourably. Part of the reason for such differences may lie in the aggregative nature of traditional policy, which tends to discriminate between different sectors and regions in the economy. All of this indicates the need for a more selective approach to policy-making which explicitly acknowledges the structural characteristics of the South African economy as well as the urgent need to reduce unemployment.

Such a policy might operate both on the demand and the supply side of the economy. Inflation has traditionally been defined as a situation in which too much money is chasing too few goods, and its remedy is usually assumed to

* Department of Economics, University of Stellenbosch and Department of Economics, University of New England, respectively. This is a modified extract of a paper first published in *Studies in Economics and Econometrics*, No. 21, 1985.

consist of measures restricting the amount of money doing the chasing. But this ignores the fact that there is considerable excess capacity in the industrial and other sectors of many developing countries (Hughes, 1976; Schydlowsky, 1982 and Khan and Knight, 1983). Accordingly, '... in the realistic situation of many developing countries, there is scope for expansion of supply in very much the same time frame as there is scope for reduction of demand' (Schydlowsky, 1982: 125).

3. In terms of a disaggregated approach, monetary policy might include the adoption of certain direct measures designed to limit the availability of credit for *consumption* purposes. While such control measures may well prove an effective means of achieving predetermined monetary targets, they should be focused on direct instruments such as hire purchase agreements, credit cards and other such facilities[1] in order to limit consumption expenditure, rather than on interest rate adjustments. The interest elasticity of expenditure on many consumer durables is in any event low, whereas raising hire purchase deposits or shortening the length of such agreements has proved very effective (Eshag, 1983: 45). A major advantage of selective credit control is that while it can be directed at particular forms of consumption in order to alter the amount and composition of consumption expenditure, it has no pervasive influence on investment. In other words, selective credit controls may be applied whilst simultaneously maintaining relatively low interest rates to stimulate investment. Consequently, current consumption may be depressed (selectively) without inhibiting future growth.

A valid objection to the imposition of selective credit controls lies in the potentially arbitrary nature of their implementation, e.g. the question of whether all durable consumer goods or only those with a high import content should be chosen as target areas. There is, of course, no doubt that this provides fertile grounds for special interest groups to use their political leverage to avoid selection. However, it has been argued that a large increase in the rate of interest is not in itself neutral between sectors or even within sectors. The fact that a rise in the interest rate represents an indirect or 'market-orientated' method of controlling economic activity does not imply that it is non-discriminatory.

4. A disaggregated approach to economic policy in South Africa would also consider ways of alleviating the inflationary and/or recessionary consequences of an unavoidable *depreciation of the currency*. These might include various forms of credit control and such compensatory measures as multiple exchange rates, tariff reductions and selective subsidies and taxes (Balassa, 1977: 25–27; Schydlowsky, 1982). Once exchange rate equilibrium has been achieved, however, it may well be necessary to adopt a system of selective exchange control to regulate the country's external transactions.[2] The reason for such a system resides in the need to maintain imports of intermediate inputs, which make up a large proportion of South Africa's import bill, but at the same time discourage

both destabilising speculation and the importation of unnecessary luxury goods, expensive overseas holidays and the like. In terms of this policy, the relevant financial institutions would be empowered to grant foreign exchange to importers of inputs which are adjudged important in the domestic production process, whilst at the same time limiting the availability of currency intended to be used for non-essential purposes.[3] The recent increase in the surcharge on imported capital goods is a case in point. It is being done on a selective basis according to which full rebates are given on imported capital goods which are needed to increase capacity or establish a new industry not available locally, or which are required for technology advance.

If a policy of selective exchange control is pursued with sufficient vigour, it should exert a favourable influence on the rand exchange rate in two ways. On the one hand, by reducing the total demand for imports it will serve to strengthen the rand in exchange markets. This will have the positive effect of reducing imported inflation, thus restraining the rise in the level of domestic prices. On the other hand, careful management of the allocation of foreign exchange for 'non-essential' ends will enable the authorities to smooth violent fluctuations in the exchange rate. Given the relatively underdeveloped state of forward exchange markets in South Africa, this should generate a greater degree of certainty to the benefit of both importers and exporters than might otherwise be the case. However, in contrast to the more aggregative approach, which fails to distinguish between imports on the basis of their potential contribution to domestic economic activity, perhaps the major advantage of a policy of selective exchange control is the fact that it would ensure an unhindered flow of imported intermediate inputs and thus facilitate economic growth.

5. The counterpart of a disaggregated monetary and exchange rate policy is a piecemeal fiscal policy specifically designed to foster growth and the creation of employment opportunities. An important prerequisite in this regard, which is recognised by almost all commentators on the South African economy and indeed by the authorities themselves, is the urgent need to reduce government expenditure. Not only will this free resources to the private sector,[4] but it will also reduce the revenue requirements of the exchequer, thus increasing the scope for selective tax concessions. Such concessions should be directed primarily towards diversifying economic activity so as to increase the relative importance of the manufacturing sector generally, and of exported manufacturers in particular.

It is widely agreed that the possibilities offered by import substitution have largely been exhausted, and future growth will consequently depend to an important extent on the development of export-based industries as well as those importables for which the local demand is already large and rising. While the recent depreciation of the South African rand may provide a measure of support for local exporters, it could be argued that a tax cut would have been economically and socially less costly especially if it were accompanied by a relatively stable exchange rate and relatively low interest rates. Moreover, tax concessions or some alternative incentive could be made available to firms in the processing, construction, building and related industries in order to encourage a programme of 'inward industrialisation'. Such firms tend to use large quantities of unskilled labour relative to capital and imported materials, and would seem to be an appropriate target for policy in an increasingly hostile world.

Aside from selective tax concessions aimed at generating growth and employment, a reallocation of government expenditure can contribute significantly towards these goals. If less were spent on relatively unproductive government projects, this should release funds for such purposes as the provision of both formal and informal (e.g. on-the-job) training facilities, and the recruitment of skilled labour from abroad. Expenditure of this nature should assist in alleviating serious bottlenecks, thus facilitating economic growth induced by low interest rates, selective exchange controls and tax concessions.

6. In sum, a policy of selective intervention of the kind outlined above appears to be better suited to the particular structural and institutional characteristics of the South African economy than an aggregative approach. The present policy package of high interest rates and a free (i.e. falling) exchange rate is often ineffective and certainly very harmful to the community at large. Indeed, the cost in terms of increased unemployment, bankruptcies and insolvencies does not seem to justify the modest benefits that are likely to arise in the form of a relatively small decrease in the rate of inflation or a marginal improvement in the balance of payments. It is worth noting, however, that the recent introduction of selective credit and exchange control measures, coupled with the proposed shift towards indirect taxation, does seem to be a step in the right direction.

The case for selective intervention suggested here is based on an explicit value judgement about the relative importance of macroeconomic policy objectives in the South African economy. It is held that the twin policy objectives of economic growth and the expansion of job opportunities should be afforded a higher priority than that of price stability. However, the policy 'mix' outlined above does recognise the need to at least prevent further increases in the rate of inflation and imports whilst simultaneously reducing the level of unemployment. More specifically, selective credit and exchange controls together with a decrease in unproductive government expenditure should exert a restraining influence on inflation, whereas low interest rates and tax cuts ought to stimulate economic growth. Thus, it seems possible to encourage economic growth and the concomitant expansion of employment with only limited adverse effects on the rate of inflation and the balance of payments.

NOTES

1 While these are sometimes referred to as 'fixation of portfolio ceilings', supplementary policy

measures could include differential discount rates, 'import pre-deposit requirements', differential reserve requirements (Ghatak, 1981: 111–113), and bank subsidies (Tanzi and Blejer, 1982).

2 See Bhagwati (1978); Killick\and Sutton (1982, esp. pp. 64–66), and Dell and Lawrence (1980).

3 Although it may be argued that this measure could encourage the local production of imported luxuries, it seems reasonable to expect that such costly activities would be limited by the selective nature of the policy itself, together with the introduction of selective credit controls and/or tax cuts.

4 In a recent study of 24 developing countries, Blejer and Khan (1984, p. 400) concluded: 'If the policy takes the form of a cut in real public sector investment that is not related to (long term) infrastructure, then one may well observe an increase in private investment as the private sector begins to make use of physical resources, such as capital and labour, released by the government.'

REFERENCES

Balassa, B., 1977. *Policy Reform in Developing Countries*, Pergamon Press.

Bhagwati, J., 1978. *Foreign Trade Regimes and Economic Development: Anatomy and Consequences of Exchange Control Regimes*. National Bureau of Economic Research, Balinger Publishing Company.

Blejer, M.I. and Khan, M.S., 1984. 'Government Policy and Private Investment in Developing Countries', *IMF Staff Papers*, Vol. 31, No. 2.

Canavese, A.J., 1982. 'The Structural Explanation in the Theory of Inflation', *World Development*, Vol. 10.

Cardoso, E.A., 1981. 'Food Supply and Inflation', *Journal of Development Economics*, Vol. 8.

De Kock, G., 1984. 'The Economic Consequences of President Reagan and Mrs Thatcher — A South African Point of View', Address at the Barclays Bank International Seminar.

Dell, S. and Lawrence, R., 1980. *The Balance of Payments Adjustment Process in Developing Countries*, Pergamon Press.

Eshag, E., 1983. *Fiscal and Monetary Policies and Problems in Developing Countries*, Cambridge University Press.

Ghatak, S., 1981. *Monetary Economics in Developing Countries*, Macmillan Press Ltd.

Kalecki, M., 1976. *Essays on Developing Economies*, The Harvester Press.

Khan, M.S. and Knight, M.D., 1982. 'Some Theoretical and Empirical Issues Relating to Economic Stabilisation in Developing Countries', *World Development*, Vol. 10.

Killick, T. and Sutton, M., 1982. 'Disequilibrium, Financing and Adjustment in Developing Countries', in Killick, T. (ed.), *Adjustment and Financing in the Developing World*, IMF and ODI.

Mohr, P.J., 1981. 'A Possible Framework for Analyzing the Inflationary Process', in *Ninth Economic Development Programme for the RSA. 1978–1987. Revised Edition for 1981–1987*, Government Printer.

Mohr, P.J., 1983. 'Notes on Inflation', *Studies in Economics and Econometrics*, Special Edition.

Oliviera, J., 1964. 'On Structural Inflation and Latin American Structuralism', *Oxford Economic Papers*, Vol. 16.

Schydlowsky, D.M., 1982. 'Alternative Approaches to Short-term Economic Management in Developing Countries', in Killick, T. (ed.), *Adjustment and Financing in the Developing World*, IMF and ODI.

Shaw, G.K. 1977. *Macro-economic Policy*, 3rd edition, Martin Robertson.

Sunkel, O. 1958. 'Inflation in Chile: An Unorthodox Approach', *International Economic Papers*, Vol. 10.

Tanzi, V. and Blejer, M.I. 1982. 'Inflation, Interest Rate Policy, and Currency Substitutions in Developing Economics: A Discussion of Some Major Issues', *World Development*, Vol. 10.

7.5 THE PROBLEM OF 'GOVERNMENT FAILURE' IN MIXED ECONOMIES

M.C. O'Dowd*

The concept of market failure is a well-established part of orthodox mixed economy theory and presentations of this theory tend to assume that wherever a market failure is identified, government intervention is automatically called for. In recent years, however, it has become increasingly clear that however much it may be justified in theory, government intervention is not necessarily effective in practice. Just as there exist market failures there exist also government failures,[1] cases where, not as a result of individual errors of judgement or lack of expertise but for fundamental, structural or other reasons, government intervention cannot produce the results at which it is aimed. These failures may be classified into three types which might be described as inherent impossibilities, political failures and bureaucratic failures.

The first type covers the cases where a government attempts to do something which simply cannot be done; the second, where although what is attempted is theoretically possible, the political constraints under which the government operates make it impossible in practice that they should follow the necessary policies with the necessary degree of consistency and persistence to achieve their stated aim. The third type covers the cases where although the political heads of the government are capable of both forming and persisting with the genuine intention of carrying out a policy, the administrative machinery at their disposal is fundamentally incapable of implementing it in accordance with their intentions.

We must not confuse the discussion of government failure with party politics. The essence of party politics as it operates in almost all countries other than one-party dictatorships is that the opposition claims that because of its alleged superior wisdom or better intentions it would be able to do better than the government does. This may or may not be true depending on circumstances but it will never be true in the areas of government failure, unless the opposition credibly proposes fundamental structural changes and, if it does, the precise changes which it proposes must be criticised and evaluated. All too often, however, opposition parties, while criticising the growth of government and bureaucratic power, advocate policies which would require for their implementation still more government and bureaucratic power, or while criticising high taxation propose expenditures which would require still higher taxation. The most striking example in recent times of two opposing parties caught up in the same government failure is the history of incomes policy in

* Director, Anglo-American Corporation; Chairman, Anglo-American and De Beer's Chairman's Fund. This paper was first published in *The South African Journal of Economics*, Vol. 46, No. 4, 1978.

Britain which was first introduced by the labour government against strong opposition by the conservative opposition, then reintroduced by the conservative government with only trifling changes against the strenuous opposition of the labour opposition, and finally reintroduced by the labour government again with only minor changes against the still more strenuous opposition of the conservative opposition.

IMPOSSIBILITY

In the area of total impossibility we are not normally troubled by matters where the impossibility is simple and obvious; we do not say 'the market has failed to make man immortal, let the government intervene to correct this failure'. In practice, the problem normally arises in one of two situations. One case is where it is indeed possible to achieve A, but it is impossible to achieve A without also having B, which is not desired. This is the case of 'side-effects'. The other — the case of incompatible objectives — is where it is indeed possible to have A but it is impossible to have both A and B and A and B are both desired.

One of the most obvious examples of side-effects is that it is impossible to have maximum price control (unless it is ineffective and does not set prices at below the market level) without creating a shortage and therefore the necessity for rationing. Indeed the first question that should be asked of anybody who proposes any form of price control is 'what form of rationing do you propose?'

There are many examples in contemporary economics of the pursuit of incompatible objectives; for example it seems clear that 'full employment' is fundamentally incompatible with the fixing of wages at above market levels by monopoly trade union action. I would also suggest, coming nearer to home, that the objective of chasing most of one's labour force away from the centres of employment, though not impossible of achievement, is incompatible with the objective of economic growth.

The behaviour of a government actively pursuing incompatible objectives is all too familiar. It involves vacillation, slow and inconsistent decision-making, and sometimes different government agencies working against each other. It is, however, less evil than the consequences of undesired side-effects of a government policy. By far the most important example in contemporary economics is price increases as a consequence of deficit financing. It is perhaps strange to call it a side-effect since it is incontestably the main effect, but the analogy from toxic drugs, whence the term comes, justifies this use; for the desired effect of the drug, however trivial, is regarded as the main effect, and the destructive effects, however major and however inevitable, are regarded as the side-effects.

The consequence of the emergence of a major undesirable side-effect of any government policy is the phenomenon which can only be described as 'witch-hunting'. The government has to pretend that the effect is not produced by its policy, to find an 'enemy' to blame for the effect and to 'punish' this enemy. Whenever the spokesman of a government which is indulging in deficit financing attacks 'profiteers' or speculators, and blames them for price rises, he is engaged in witch-hunting and, of course, like the witch hunters of old, the modern witch hunters do not confine themselves to criticising the witches. The majority of the people put to death under the terror in the French Revolution were not accused of treason but of profiteering. They were the victims of the inflation which Robespierre was himself creating by the reckless printing of paper money.

To refer to this as witch-hunting is not a strained analogy for it is actually precisely the same activity as that engaged in by the tribal witch-doctor who smells out the witch 'responsible' for the death of the chief's cattle from rinderpest, or, in Medieval Europe, for the mildewing of the wheat. The tribal magician, under whatever guise, has claimed that he has magic powers to protect the tribe from evil. When evil occurs, he has failed, and if his own position is to survive, he must find, blame and punish an 'enemy'. The only difference between him and the government which we are discussing, which has also claimed supernatural powers which it does not possess, namely the power to create resources out of nothing, is one entirely favourable to the witch doctor. It is extremely unlikely that the witch doctor himself killed the cattle or mildewed the wheat, but the government did create the inflation.

POLITICAL FAILURE

We come now to the area of political failure, of which the most obvious example in our contemporary scene is that referred to by Buchanan and Wagner,[2] that is the political impossibility in a country with an elected government of pursuing Keynesian policies with the discipline and consistency necessary to achieve the objectives which Keynes believed could be achieved. To put it simply, according to Buchanan and Wagner, the balancing of the economy requires deficit financing in some years and fully countervailing surplus financing in others. Elected governments have proved themselves incapable of surplus financing once they have been given leave to indulge in deficit financing; hence the disastrous failure of the pseudo-Keynesian economics which have been applied in practice, as distinct from the policies actually advocated by Keynes.

It is idle in the area of political failure to bewail the irresponsibility or venality of politicians. There have been, in history, politicians who sacrificed their careers for the sake of what they believed to be right, but the system punished them in every case and even where they were spectacularly vindicated by history (as in the case of Peel and the corn laws), this did them no personal good. No system, political or otherwise, can rely for its effectiveness on being staffed with saints or heroes. Normally the system will produce the kind of behaviour which it effectively rewards and not the kind of behaviour which it effectively punishes. So where the political system effectively rewards politicians for economic irresponsibility, it will produce economic irresponsibility, and short of a total change in the political system we have a case of inescapable political failure.

There is another area of political failure which we ought not to forget. A major part of the case which Adam Smith and his contemporaries made against government involvement in the economy was the belief that any economic power possessed by the government would inevitably be used for purposes of political corruption, that is to buy or to reward political support, and in the process would both misallocate scarce resources and corrupt and undermine the political system. This belief was amply justified by the experience of Adam Smith's own time. In modern times most economists tend to assume without discussion that 'that was long ago' and 'things are different now'; but are they? We have become familiar with the disastrous economic cost which Britain incurs for the window dressing of the economy for every general election, when the government, of whatever party, sets out to bribe the entire electorate by giving them benefits before the election, the bill for which will be presented after the election. We do not suffer much in this country from this particular evil but we are very familiar with the political railway of the 20s and 30s and the political road of the present time. The use of appointments to public posts as political patronage is a massive scandal and evil in the United States and is not unknown in South Africa.

Adam Smith believed that this too was a case of incurable political failure; that governments would always abuse any patronage they possessed and that they must be consequently stripped of all patronage whatsoever — something that was nearly done in Britain in the 19th century. It may be that this objective is no longer practicable and that some of these evils have to be accepted and lived with, but that does not mean that in analysing and discussing policies we should pretend that this particular political failure does not exist.

In seeking a political solution to these two political failures we face a dilemma. It is quite clear that the economic irresponsibilities of representative governments do arise from the representative character of the government. They cannot be more responsible or far-sighted than the people they represent; but as regards the tendency to political corruption the responsiveness of the government to an electorate is the only safeguard we have, although it is not an adequate one.

In the case of a non-representative government the issue of the corrupt use of public resources for the benefit of the ruling group no longer arises because the resources are no longer public and their misuse is no longer corrupt. It is not only possible that non-representative governments will use all governmental resources for their own benefit and to strengthen their own power. It is almost inevitable that they will do so. In such a case government resources are, for practical purposes, the private property of the group which controls the government and the only restraints which there will be on their treating them as such will be their wisdom, if any, in avoiding policies which are counter-productive and their fear of revolt.

BUREAUCRATIC FAILURE

We come now to the area of bureaucratic failure.[3] In view of the large size of the government service in modern times it would be ridiculous to assume that members of government service are any other than an average cross-section of the portion of the population which has the educational qualifications required for their work. This means that they will have their statistical share of saints and heroes but no more. They will also have their statistical share of un-scrupulous and dishonest individuals and neither more nor less. The average public servant, and the great majority will, however, be none of these. They will be people of normal ability motivated by a mixture of self-interest and idealism but seeking to pursue their self-interest by conscientiously doing their work and seeking the rewards which the system offers them for doing so. They will be neither corrupt nor dishonest but by the same token they will not 'buck the system' out of considerations of conscience or idealism. What follows from all this is that the actual effect of their efforts will be crucially determined by the structure of the system in which they work.

We must also assume that the government service as a corporate entity will in a number of subtle ways and largely without anybody's conscious planning look after the corporate interests of its members and its own survival as an in-stitution and indeed that this corporate self-interest will tend to be pursued more wholeheartedly and with less scruple than most individuals would bring to bear in pursuit of their private interests. These statements do not imply any special criticism of the government service. They are equally true not only of companies in the private sector but of universities, the learned professions and even churches.

There are many areas of bureaucratic failure of which I wish to discuss only three. The first, which is very important indeed when we consider the advisa-bility of particular government interventions in the private sector, is the ratchet effect whereby it is almost impossible to dismantle an institution once it has been established in the government service. This follows from the security of tenure of public servants combined with the cumbersome machinery which makes the redeployment of public servants very difficult especially between one department and another. It is also linked with the situation which exists in any hierarchical system whereby the status and importance of the senior staff and their chances of promotion are influenced by the number and variety of functions under their control. Behind this again lies the still more fundamental fact that in the government service it is often absolutely impossible to measure objectively the value of the activities of a particular individual or agency.

Whether this analysis of causes is valid or not there is no doubt about the fact that government actions which are taken in an emergency and which are said at the time to be of a temporary nature are constantly institutionalised and made permanent; and until there is some evidence that this trend has been reversed the probability, indeed near certainty, that any intervention will be permanent must be taken into account in considering the advisability of embarking on the intervention in the first place. If a doctor knew that every time he prescribed a drug his patient would continue to take that drug for the rest of his life he would very soon alter his view on the drugs he was prepared to prescribe.

PARKINSON'S LAW

The second major area of bureaucratic failure is that related to the phenomenon known as Parkinsonism. It is perhaps unfortunate that Professor Parkinson propounded his famous law so wittily since many people have been led to believe that it is a piece of satire — a joke with a grain of truth in it. In fact, shorn of its witty presentation it is a simple statement of fact with as much serious right to be called a law as any other statement regarding human behaviour, and Parkinson's explanation of why it works is also simply true. In brief Parkinson's law states that a hierarchical organisation will tend to increase its staff entirely independent of the amount of work it has to do and the reason why this is so is that one of the most effective ways by which an individual can secure promotion in a hierarchy is by multiplying the number of his subordinates.

The operation of Parkinson's law has nothing to do with anything peculiar to the government service; it stems from the nature of a hierarchy. It obviously has no relevance to a one-man business nor indeed to any business which is under the effective control, in all matters of detail, of the owner; but as soon as any individual who has more interest in climbing the ladder of the hierarchy than increasing the profits of the organisation has any influence over staff appointments the tendency to Parkinsonism arises. It follows therefore that it exists not only in the government sector but in all private businesses other than very small ones.

The difference between the government sector and large organisations in the private sector arises from differences in the strength of the countervailing forces. In any privately owned organisation where the owners have any kind of effective control they will use this control to fight Parkinsonism since it is a deadly enemy of their profits. In those cases where the control is for practical purposes entirely in the hands of professional managers there are still two spectres which haunt them day and night, namely bankruptcy and takeover, and one or other of these is the fate of every company, large or small, in which Parkinsonism runs out of control. The crucial difference between all organisations of the government sector, whether trading or administrative, and all businesses in the private sector, however large or small, is the total security of the government sector against bankruptcy and takeover.

This is not to say that there are no countervailing forces in the government sector. The Treasury and the politicians who have to raise and justify taxes have a very real interest in opposing Parkinsonism. It must be noted in passing though that once deficit financing became fashionable this factor was considerably weakened. Pseudo-Keynesianism has 'dulled the edge of husbandry' in every corner of the government sector and the great increase in the tendency towards a cancerous growth of the government service which has been seen in many countries in recent times (notably Italy and in the local authorities in England) is not the least of the evils for which deficit financing has to answer.

PYRAMID BUILDING

Parkinsonism can take two forms. The more harmless is the one which Professor Parkinson describes whereby additional staff are taken on without their having anything particular to do so that they merely spend their time 'reading one another's minutes'. These people at least do not do much positive harm. Much more dangerous is the situation which is more likely to arise in public corporations than the government service as such, where real work is created in order to justify the expansion but the work is unconstructive. This leads us into the area of pyramid building, possibly the worst of all the evils to which the government sector is subject. This is the squandering of scarce resources on useless, unnecessary or undesirable projects for the aggrandisement of those who are in control of them.

This brings us up against another major dilemma. In seeking a solution to the political failures which we have already discussed it has been customary in modern times to give public corporations a high degree of autonomy from the government, including the Treasury. In escaping Scylla we have gone straight into the jaws of Charybdis, for governmental and Treasury controls are the only structural safeguards there are against Parkinsonism and pyramid building in public corporations.

We should note that any tendency that public corporations might have to build palaces for their Head Offices is a minor issue. The real danger is reckless over-planning for the expansion of their legitimate activities. It cannot be emphasised too strongly that monopolistic public corporations cannot be trusted to decide for themselves what the magnitude is of the future demand for their services. Of all the fallacies in classical mixed-economy theory probably the most damaging is the glib assumption that to place a monopoly in the government sector ensures that the monopoly will be conducted in the public interest. On the contrary it is an ever-present possibility that it will be used to exploit the public in order to make resources available for pyramid building. It follows that a public corporation which holds a legal monopoly needs to be subject to price control by a separate independent public body as, in South Africa, Iscor is in fact subject to price control, although this is not a good illustration of the principle since Iscor is not a full monopoly and there is no fundamental reason why it should have any kind of monopoly at all.

344

CORRUPTION

The last area of bureaucratic failure which I wish to discuss relates to the irresistible tendency to private corruption which is created by certain particular types of government activity. I should first of all make it clear that I am not talking here about the rare cases of major criminal behaviour which arise in the government service just as they do everywhere else. If a government servant perpetrates a large-scale fraud or theft this is no more a bureaucratic failure than it is a market failure when somebody does the same in the private sector. These are simply matters which the legal system attempts, with varying degrees of success, to prevent. What I am referring to is the case where the system itself creates the near inevitability of systematic bribery.

The possibility of bribery arises wherever any individual has the disposal of property which is not his own. An owner cannot be bribed to sell his property for less than it is worth since the purchase price and the bribe go to the same person and are therefore indistinguishable; but, in principle, an agent can always be bribed to sell property for less than it is worth. The buyer then shares the profit which he makes with the agent and that is the bribe.

In the field of purchasing and the awarding of tenders the problem of bribery is generally the same in the government sector and in large corporations in the private sector but the scale of the evil in this area is small. Where the buying is done in the open market and at competitive prices the favour which a buyer can confer on one supplier rather than another is small unless he buys at something other than the market price and if he does this his action is easily detected. The same is true in the awarding of tenders. If the tenders are genuinely competitive there is very little to be gained by unduly influencing those awarding the tenders and little can therefore be spent on bribery. The awarding of tenders which are not competitive is easily detected. This is why the major corruption scandals of recent times have all related to the sale of military equipment where a normal market and a normal market price do not exist.

SUB-ECONOMIC HOUSING

The real problem, however, arises when in terms of socialistic practice the government engages in the arbitrary allocation of wealth. By far the major example in the West and in South Africa is in sub-economic housing. Sub-economic housing, including that in Soweto, follows the socialistic principle that all men are equal. All the houses are alike and everybody who qualifies has an equal claim to a house. However, in the real world some men are a great deal more equal than others because some have sub-economic houses and some have no houses at all. The allocation of a sub-economic house to an individual constitutes a gift to him of a very valuable economic asset.

The author has no personal knowledge indicating that the allocation of sub-economic housing is actually corrupt in either England or South Africa but he has heard from people who are involved on the consumer side that there is a widespread belief that it is corrupt. Somebody who is on the waiting list for a council house in England said 'you never reach the top of the waiting list', the implication being that council houses are obtained only by bribery. The same belief exists, rightly or wrongly, amongst Blacks in South Africa. It seems unlikely that where there is so much smoke there is no fire at all but even if there is no fire the existence of the smoke in itself constitutes a major social evil.

It is difficult to see how this problem can ever be solved while what is substantial wealth to the individual concerned is given away as an arbitrary gift by the government. The higher in the hierarchy the decisions are removed the less the likelihood of corruption, provided that the junior officials are put in the position where they have no influence at all on the final decision, but it is difficult to see how this can be achieved and the price paid for removing decisions to a high level is to make things intolerably slow. The only other possible solution is the allocation of houses in some manner which is absolutely objective and furthermore to have machinery which operates in public in which the objectivity is ensured and can be tested, in other words some kind of court. It might well be argued that this would defeat the whole object of sub-economic housing. The fact is that corruption is the shadow of socialism and the only effective solution is reverting to the principle that wealth is not allocated but earned. Where wealth is truly earned and traded in the market the scope for corruption becomes trivial.

In conclusion I would like to emphasise once again that this discussion of government failures is not intended in any way to disparage politicians or public servants as individuals nor to belittle the legitimate and necessary role of the government in modern society. It is, however, vitally necessary if there is to be any rational debate on the boundary between the government sector and the private sector and on government intervention in the private sector that the inherent shortcomings and inadequacies of government should be as well understood and should be discussed with the same openness as the shortcomings of the market. The greatest problems lie in the area where neither the market system nor the government intervention is capable of producing an ideal result. Here the choice is between evils and if we are to choose successfully the lesser evil we must have a proper understanding of all the problems involved.

NOTES

1 The term 'government failure' in this sense is used and as far as the author knows originated in Buchanan, J. and Wagner, R., *Democracy in Deficit*, New York: Academic Press, 1977.
2 *Op. cit.* — passim.
3 In the past there has been considerable embarrassment in discussing this issue for fear of appearing to belittle or insult the members of the government service as individuals and for this reason it should be noted that nothing in this article depends on the assumption that the individual members of the government service are in any respect inferior on average to individuals engaged in the private sector. They are neither less able nor less intelligent nor less honest nor less conscientious.